Charles Carp

Theology as the Road to Holiness in Saint Bonaventure

PAULIST PRESS
New York/Mahwah, N.J.

Vidimus et approbamus ad normam Statutorum Universitatis

Romae, ex Pontificia Universitate Gregoriana
die 17 mensis aprilis anni 1997.

R.P. Prof. John Navone, S.I.
R.P. Prof. Charles A. Bernard, S.I.

Cover design by Moe Berman

ISBN: 0-8091-3861-1

Published by Paulist Press
997 Macarthur Boulevard
Mahwah, New Jersey 07430

Printed and bound in the
United States of America

This work is dedicated with gratitude to my Father Founder,
Aloysius Ellacuria, C.M.F. (1905–1981),
who taught me to know God by loving Him

PREFACE

Each fall, when sending our young missionaries off to study theology, I am posed with the usual question: How is it possible to maintain a deep spiritual life amid the intense demands of theological study? My answer is basically: Try to see God in all things—*even in theology.*

This has been going on for twenty years, and my answer still leaves something deep in me unsettled. Perhaps that is why I wrote this book. If I had found a scientific answer to their question, I may have renounced the theological challenge itself: *fides quaerens intellectum.* Most of all, had not Saint Bonaventure of Bagnorea (†1274) entered the scene—he who habitually had been submitted to the same question by his fellow friars—this book would never have been possible.

This study may be seen as an encounter with St. Bonaventure the mystagogue who, more like a mountain climber, leads us up the lofty peaks of the High Middle Ages whence we might leisurely contemplate the truth with no utilitarian end in mind. From such a vantage-point, theologians of our times may appreciate the exceptional position their own calling affords them. They have a spiritual life capable of permeating their own line of work; a spiritual life already intensely pondered and loved by the Seraphic Doctor in the tradition of St. Augustine.

Today, more and diverse kinds of people are approaching theological study. Nevertheless, works that elucidate a spiritual path for the theologian are difficult to find. After signing up in theological institutes, several questions usually arise in us: "How can I abandon myself to the rigorously scientific methods of intellectual work and continue to maintain some awareness of the interior life? What happens to prayer life when less and less time is available for it? In today's atmosphere of intellectual consumerism, how personal can I be about divine revelation?" To these and other essential questions Bonaventure provides convincing solutions for the twenty-first century. He teaches us how theology can be our spiritual path to holiness.

What Saint Paul calls the wisdom of the cross, which is madness to the world ("God's folly"– I Cor. 1:25; 2:2), emerges in St. Bonaventure as wisdom theology. The immense joy one experiences upon discovering Bonaventure undoubtedly is a share in the rejoicing Our Lord felt at the mere thought of his Father holding back from the wise and the cultured of this world what He wantonly floods into the hearts of the simplest ones (Lk.

10:21). This special kind of joy Brother Giles received when, at first trembling, he approached the great theologian Bonaventure to ask if an *idiota* can love God as much as do the scholars. The answer—that "a poor old woman can love God more than a theology professor,"—sent Brother Giles into leaps of ecstatic jubilation, shouting to the passersby: "You! Old woman! You! Poor and unlettered! Love God, and you will be greater than Brother Bonaventure!" Giles then remained in rapture three hours.

It is said that in the Middle Ages theologians elaborated theology on their knees. Indeed, St. Bonaventure defined theology as wisdom—the principal gift of the Holy Spirit—and insisted that its study has the unique purpose of making us saints (*ut boni fiamus*).

This book presents Bonaventure's teachings in such a way as to uncover one of his deepest motivations as a Doctor of the Church. Theology, he believed, is undertaken entirely for the purpose of becoming holy. Spiritual transformation is brought about when theological study is subordinated to, and integrated into, the spiritual life. Understanding this 'perspective key' to the heart of the man Bonaventure can serve as an ideal introduction to his vast literary output.

As a faithful son of St. Augustine, Bonaventure sees love of God as a *pondus* of the heart. This love, through the experiential knowledge gained by increasing union, results in the *habitus* (affective disposition) called wisdom, which Bonaventure not only equates to theology but to sanctity itself. Since the object of faith is revelation by a personal God who invites us into intimate relationship with Him, Bonaventure holds a vital message for our times. If theology is not approached with the same disposition in which we approach God, theology risks distorting the very revelation it endeavors to render intelligible.

After this book was submitted to the publishers, the Holy Father issued his encyclical, *Fides et Ratio,* which treats some of the topics of major interest to this work. The encyclical is formidable in its challenge to all those dedicated to philosophy and its relation to theology. The importance of the encyclical cannot be overstated. A few remarks made by Richard John Neuhaus may suffice to echo my own deep appreciation of the Pope's teaching: "*Fides et Ratio* is as breathtaking in its historical and intellectual reach as it is provocative in its argument. . . . This encyclical will be grist for philosophical and theological mills for a long time to come. . . . The argument of *Fides et Ratio* is breathtaking in its ambition and comprehensiveness."[1]

The encyclical is a vigorous summons to take up the task of philosophizing without fear of human weakness: "In the light of faith which recognizes in Jesus Christ this ultimate meaning, I must encourage philosophers—Christian and otherwise—to trust in the capacity of human reason and not limit themselves to aims that are too modest in their philosophizing."[2] The Pope considers all human beings by nature as philosophers insofar as we are searchers for ultimate meaning about the world, about ourselves, and about God. Nevertheless, the encyclical throughout deeply laments "the radical mistrust of reason which the most recent expositions of many philosophical studies manifest."[3] Against the "present crisis of confidence in the capacity of reason,"[4] John Paul II strongly affirms the innate power of human reason: "The most urgent commitment today is to help mankind to discover its capacity of knowing the truth."[5]

Although the Holy Father features St. Bonaventure within "the great triad" among medieval Doctors,[6] quoting his famous warning from the prologue of the *Itinerarium* about 'knowledge without devotion', and calling the Seraphic Doctor "a great master of thought and spirituality,"[7] the encyclical bestows a far more ponderous laurel upon St. Thomas Aquinas and thus becomes the strongest endorsement of Thomism to appear since Leo XIII's *Æterni Patris*.[8] Precisely because Thomas displayed much more confidence in human reason than his Augustinian counterparts, the encyclical selects him as the soundest antidote for the philosophical malaise of our times.[9] Consequently, we may ask ourselves whether St. Bonaventure and

---

1 Richard John Neuhaus, "The Public Square," *First Things* 88 (December 1998): 65; 72.

2 *Fides et Ratio*, 56.

3 Ibid., 55.

4 Ibid., 84.

5 Ibid., 102.

6 Ibid., 74.

7 Ibid., 105.

8 Ibid., 43, 57, 58, 59, 61, 78.

9 "In fact, in his reflections, the demands of reason and the power of faith have found the most elevated synthesis ever attained by human thought, for he could defend the radical originality provided by Revelation, without ever demeaning the venture proper to reason" (Ibid., 78).

Augustinianism in general, for having emphasized the limitations of human reason after the Fall, should claim our attention less, at least at this point in philosophical history, than in the past. In this respect, I believe it worthwhile to point out two ideas before the reader approaches my work and any other work within the Augustinian tradition.

First of all, it is true that Augustinianism does not place the same confidence in reason's native power that St. Thomas manifests everywhere in his works. Nevertheless, this characteristic of Augustinian thought in no wise diminishes its value. Etienne Gilson, upon the fifteenth centenary of the death of St. Augustine, when speaking of "the disagreements between Augustinianism and Thomism" recalled that "the principles [underlying both systems] are the same."[10] Gilson attributed these disagreements to "differences in temperament between the two authors of these doctrines. . . . The profound peculiarities of their interior lives have produced in St. Augustine and his followers a sort of pessimism with regard to the resources of the natural reason. This pessimism is not to be found to the same degree in St. Thomas, nor is it expressed in the same tone."[11] In an attempt to assess judiciously the contribution of St. Augustine and his followers, Gilson adds:

> [Thomists and Augustinians] do not understand in the same way the functioning of a reason which is for the Augustinians the reason of a corrupted nature, whereas in the eyes of the Thomists it has retained its essence and is for them the reason of a nature that is no more than wounded. Hence arise differences between spiritual families, to hope for whose disappearance is vain and perhaps in abstract terms the concrete and personal difference between the religious experiences that they translate into words. *Hence arises as well the even more profound unity that they reveal, since this unity is based on the identity of their principles and on their irrevocable decision to root their thought in one and the same faith* [emphasis mine].[12]

Secondly, *Fides et Ratio*, while continually urging us to lay aside all distrust of human reason, does not hesitate to remind us that "human reason is wounded and weakened by sin."[13] Inherent disadvantages persist when reason is unaided by faith: "Reason needs to fortify itself by means of faith,

---

10 Etienne Gilson, "The Idea of Philosophy in St. Augustine and in St. Thomas Aquinas," in *A Gilson Reader: Selected Writings of Etienne Gilson,* trans. and ed. Anton C. Pegis (Garden City, NY: Image Books, 1957) 79.

11 Ibid.

12 Ibid., 80.

13 *Fides et Ratio,* 51

in order to discover the horizons to which it could not arrive on its own."[14] Such ideas about reason's weakness can be found throughout the Pope's document, but they receive special emphasis in Chapter II, "Credo ut Intellegam," which forms the biblical groundwork for the main argument of this encyclical. This chapter seems to me to lend the greatest support to Bonaventure's vision, even though Bonaventure is not mentioned in this context. We should remind our readers of the great dependence St. Bonaventure manifests toward Holy Scripture. We could say that his attitudes toward human reason are the same as those found in the Bible. For example, when the encyclical, to locate the source of reason's weakness, speaks of the effects of Original Sin, we find ourselves in an atmosphere distinctly Bonaventurian:

> All men and women were caught up in this primal disobedience, which so wounded reason that from then on its path to full truth would be strewn with obstacles. From that time onward the human capacity to know the truth was impaired by an aversion to the One who is the source and origin of truth. It is again the Apostle who reveals just how far human thinking, because of sin, became "empty," and human reasoning became distorted and inclined to falsehood (cf. Rom. 1:21–22). The eyes of the mind were no longer able to see clearly: reason became more and more a prisoner to itself.[15]

In the same vein, the process St. Bonaventure calls 'hierarchization of the mind', by which supernatural faith capacitates human reason for correct thinking, is reflected in the Pope's encyclical in the various places where the reason's need of faith is pointed out.[16] For example, in extolling the Fathers of the East and of the West, His Holiness indicates that they proved how "a reason, freed from external bonds, could emerge from the blind alley of myths, to open itself up in a more adequate way to transcendence. Purified and upright, therefore, reason was capable of rising to the higher levels of reflection."[17]

Thus, although the Holy Father's principal purpose is to affirm the power of human reason against those who by their attitudes bar it from scaling the heights of metaphysics, the encyclical by no means stands as a rebuke of

---

14 Ibid., 67

15 Ibid., 22.

16 *Fides et Ratio,* 13, 16, 18, 20, 21, 22, 23, 34, 41, 42, 67, 76, 79, 104.

17 Ibid., 41.

Augustinian philosophy.[18] Rather, as always in the past centuries, we are dealing with the well-known complementarity between the two chief schools of thought in Christianity, whose very existence ultimately guarantees the delicate balance between the power of nature and the power of grace, the comprehension of which is never satisfactorily achieved. The great effort and achievement of *Fides et Ratio* are matchless among the witnesses to this age-old attempt. The delicate balance is echoed in the words: "Reason is valued but not overvalued. What reason attains can be true, but it acquires its full significance only when its contents are placed within a wider horizon, which is that of faith."[19]

Other topics in the encyclical which should hold interest for the reader who likewise will find them treated in the present work are: Christ as the ultimate source of all truth; divine revelation as interpersonal relationship with God; the creative value of sincere friendship among philosophers.

May this book in some small way further an understanding of the man Bonaventure and thereby help to harmonize theological inquiry and the spiritual life.

San José de Bácum, Sonora, Mexico
January 28, 1999
Fiesta de Santo Tomás de Aquino

---

18 Such an emphasis on reason's power is directed against today's tendency to isolate faith and religious experience as the sole path to God. Richard John Neuhaus describes it thus: "*Fides et Ratio* is a very sharp criticism of any and every form of fideism. Anything that pits faith against reason, belief against knowledge, or religious experience against critical intelligence has no place in authentically Christian thought" (Neuhaus, 73).

19 *Fides et Ratio*, 20.

ACKNOWLEDGMENTS

The present book owes is existence to several persons who, directly or indirectly, have helped me either to begin, to continue, or to persevere until it was finished. An oversight in acknowledging anyone's assistance is certainly possible on account of the large number of persons along the road who rendered some service.

First of all, Fr. Charles A. Bernard, S.J. has been a real luminary for me, both through his courses in spiritual theology and by the special attention he gave me during the composition of this book. From his deep, but concise, insights I was able to organize the divers inspirations I experienced from reading St. Bonaventure's works. I am most grateful to him and to the Gregorian's Institute of Spirituality for allowing me to have him as a guide.

Fr. Herbert Alphonso, S.J., and Fr. John Navone, S.J., of the Institute of Spirituality were ever at hand for guidance on endless aspects involved in writing a book.

Fr. Ignacio Ramírez, O.F.M., of the Franciscan community in Zapópan (Guadalajara), Mexico, specialist in St. Bonaventure, read the first full draft and gave valuable suggestions for its improvement.

To my Bishop, D. Vicente García Bernal, I owe gratitude for his generous approval of a sabbatical leave in Rome after fifteen years in the missions.

I wish to thank my religious community for allowing me to take a sabbatical leave to study spirituality in Rome and for their prayers and their sacrifices, particularly that of replacing me in my pastoral duties while I was away. I never can express adequately how much I owe them for sustaining me through their constant spiritual and material support, because without it I never would have attempted nor finished what seemed impossible.

The Pallottine Fathers in Grottaferrata warmly opened their doors to me where I could live across the road from the International Collegio S. Bonaventura, home of the Quaracchi editors and of the best Bonaventurian library in Europe.

Special thanks go to the eminent Latin poet, Prof. Arturo Carbonetto of Florence who, in spite of total blindness, helped me translate passages from Bonaventure's works which have special importance for this book and are not yet found in modern languages.

Dr. Patrick Mitchell of St. John's Seminary in Camarillo, California greatly assisted me in understanding Bernard Lonergan.

For their outstanding support of the research, I owe my deepest gratitude to Judge Alexander R. Early and his wife Mary Celeste. I am also most deeply indebted to Franklin J. Dailey, M.D. and his wife Florence. Other persons who supported me in different ways were: Mr. and Mrs. Ricardo Rivas; Mr. and Mrs. Victor Illig; Mrs. Hope Leunis; Therese Buehner; Mrs. Patricia Ann Arneson; Mrs. Betty Scully; Beatriz Marina Bours de Pineda.

Likewise, very special thanks go to Mrs. Judith Hodgins for reading the text to propose improvements in English usage, as well as to Joan Mellen who read the manuscript and assisted me in getting the finished copy ready for printing.

Alfonso and Gloria Bours provided an air-conditioned room at their home to put the final touches on the book in the torrid heat of our Sonoran desert.

Others whose role in some way had significant impact in bringing about the composition of this work were: Fr. David Sereno Bianucci; Fr. George Lannitotham, C.M.F.; Fr. Patrick Lyons, O.S.B.; Fr. Ambrogio Nguyen Van Si, O.F.M.; Msgr. Giancarlo Setti; Fr. Bogdan Fajdek, O.F.M.; Fr. Hugh McKenna, O.F.M. Cap.; Marco Arosio; Mrs. Rita Lambert; Michael Carpenter; Matthew Muñoz; Horacio Couret y Miller; José Bours Guerra; Miguel Castro Rodríguez; Norberto Figueroa Briceño; Carlos Eduardo Forte. I am especially grateful to Ernesto Becerril Arenz for the final draft.

May Our Lord reward each of these persons, as well as countless others, who contributed in some way to the eventual realization of this book, and thereby have helped to spread Bonaventure's message that theological study can be a special road to sanctity.

TABLE OF CONTENTS

Abbreviations

For periodicals, dictionaries and collections:

AF   *Analecta Franciscana*, Quaracchi, 1885–1941.

AFH   *Archivum Franciscanum Historicum*, Quaracchi, 1908–

AHDLMA *Archives d'Histoire Doctrinale et Littéraire du Moyen âge*
Paris, 1926–

AM   *Annales Minorum*, Quaracchi, 1933–1964.

Ant   *Antonianum*, Roma, 1926–

Bonav   *Bonaventuriana*, 2 Vols. Roma: Ed. Antonianum, 1988.

CC   *Corpus Christianorum*, Turnhout, 1954–

CF   *Collectanea Franciscana*, Roma, 1931–

Contributi *Contributi di spiritualità bonaventuriana*, 3 Vols. Padova,
1976.

DF   *Dizionario Francescano*, Padova, 1983.

DS   *Dictionnaire de spiritualité*, Paris, 1937–

DTC   *Dictionnaire de théologie catholique*, Paris, 1903–

DTh.P   *Divus Thomas*, Piacenza, 1880–

DtS   *Doctor Seraphicus*, Bagnoregio, 1954–

EF   *Etudes franciscaines*, Paris, 1899–

EsF   *Estudios franciscanos*, Barcelona, 1907–

ETL   *Ephemerides theologicae lovanienses*, Louvain, 1924–

FF	*Fonti Francescane*, Assisi-Padova, 1986
FrFr	*La France franciscaine*, Paris, 1912–
FS	*Franciscan Studies*, New York, 1940–
FzS	*Franziskanische Studien*, Münster-Werl, 1914–
GR	*Gregorianum*, Roma, 1920–
IncBonav	*Incontri Bonaventuriani*, 11 Vols. Montecalvo Irpinio, 1965–1974.
ItFr	*L'Italia francescana*, Roma, 1926–
LSB	*Lexique Saint Bonaventure*, Paris, 1969.
MS	*Mediaeval Studies*, New York, 1939–
MF	*Miscellanea francescana*, Foligno-Roma, 1886–
NDCS	*The New Dictionary of Catholic Spirituality*, Collegeville, Minnesota, 1993.
NRT	*Nouvelle Revue Théologique*, Louvain, 1869–
PG	*Patrologie grecque*, Migne, Paris, 1857–1866.
PL	*Patrologie latine*, Migne, Paris, 1844–1864.
RAM	*Revue d'ascétique et de mystique*, Toulouse, 1920–1971.
RFN	*Rivista di filosofia neoscolastica*, Milano, 1909–
RSPT	*Revue des sciences philosophiques et théologiques*, Paris, 1907–
RTAM	*Recherches de théologie ancienne et médiévale*, Louvain, 1929–
RTL	*Revue théologique de Louvain*, Louvain, 1970–
SB	*S. Bonaventura 1274–1974*, 5 Volumes, Grottaferrata, 1972–1974.

SBM	*San Bonaventura Maestro di Vita Francescana e di Sapienza Cristiana,* 3 Volumes published as Volume 75 (1975) of *MF* with Supplements I and II of the same year.
SFr	*Studi Francescani,* Firenze, 1914–
SRF	*Studi e Ricerche Francescane,* Napoli, 1972–
TD	*Theology Digest,* St. Mary's, Kansas, 1953–
ThPh	*Theologie und Philosophie,* Freiburg, 1926–
VM	*Vita Minorum,* Roma, 1929–
VV	*Verdad y Vida,* Madrid, 1943–
WW	*Wissenschaft und Weisheit,* Mönchengladbach, 1938–1994.
ZAM	*Zeitschrift für Aszese und Mystik.* Innsbruck, 1926–1943.

For Bonaventure's works:

Apol. paup.	*Apologia pauperum*
Brev.	*Breviloquium*
Christus mag.	*Christus unus omnium magister*
Coll. Jn.	*Collationes in Evangelium Ioannis*
Comm. Ec.	*Commentarius in librum Ecclesiastae*
Comm. Jn	*Commentarius in Evangelium Ioannis*
Comm. Lc.	*Commentarius in Evangelium S. Lucae*
Const. Narb.	*Constitutiones Generales Narbonenses*
Decem praec.	*Collationes de decem praeceptis*
De donis	*Collationes de septem donis Spiritus sancti*

De quin. fest.	*De quinque festivitatibus pueri Jesu*
De test. Trin.	*De triplici testimonio sanctissimae Trinitatis*
Ep. off.	*Epistolae officialis*
Hex.	*Collationes in hexaë meron*
Itin.	*Itinerarium mentis in Deum*
Leg. maj.	*Legenda major sancti Francisci*
Leg. min.	*Legenda minor sancti Francisci*
Lig. vit.	*Lignum vitae*
Myst. Trin.	*Quaestiones disputatae de mysterio Trinitatis*
Perf. ev.	*Quaestiones disputatae de perfectione evangelica*
Perf. vitae	*De perfectione vitae ad sorores*
Plant. par.	*Tractatus de plantatione paradisi*
Red. art.	*De reductione artium ad theologiam*
Reg. nov.	*Regula novitiorum*
Regn. Dei	*De regno Dei descripto in parabolis evangelicis*
Scien. Chr.	*Quaestiones disputatae de scientia Christi*
I, II, III, IV, Sent.	*Commentarius in I, II, III, IV, librum Sententiarium*
Serm.	*Sermones*
Solil.	*Soliloquium de quatuor mentalibus exercitiis*
Trip. via	*De triplici via*

For distinctions in individual texts:

a.	articulus
an.	annotatio
au.	articulus unicus
c.	capitulum
coll.	collatio
con.	contra
concl.	conclusio
d.	distinctio
dub.	dubium
fr.	fructus
fund.	fundamentum
n.	numerus
opp.	oppositum
p.	pars
praenot.	praenotata
prol.	prologus
prooem.	prooemium
q.	quaestio
resp.	respondeo
rub.	rubrica

...so that you too may share our life.

I Jn. 1:3

INTRODUCTION

Today's attraction to St. Bonaventure is quite evident among modern theologians as a whole.[1] Not long ago Bonaventure made a comeback, and his influence grows more relevant as time passes.[2] This should not surprise us, given the breadth of his work and the fact that, at the beginning of the twentieth century, his complete works were presented in a masterful critical edition, providing a veritable gold mine for unending research.[3] Such research has become even more intense since Vatican Council II.[4] All those who approach Bonaventure find something to satisfy their doctrinal thirst and, more particularly, their longing for spirituality. As one Bonaventurian scholar has stated: "In no other medieval Christian spiritual writer were such diverse elements present in such depth and abundance

---

1 A brief overview of Bonaventure in relation to contemporary thought can be found in Ewert H. Cousins' *Bonaventure and the Coincidence of Opposites* (Chicago: Franciscan Herald Press, 1978), 229–88. Among modern thinkers treated in these two chapters are Rahner, Tillich, Whitehead, Teilhard de Chardin, and Panikkar.

2 Speaking of Bonaventure's influence on Karl Rahner, one Rahner scholar points out: "As early as 1933 and 1934 Rahner had published two articles on St. Bonaventure... We can see the effect of Rahner's reading of Hegel and Bonaventure in his later systematic theology. From Bonaventure and Hegel Rahner learned that the Trinity is the key to a religious understanding of the universe... Both of them bolstered Rahner's own confidence in the possibilities of a metaphysics of the human spirit as a means of linking man's natural knowledge of himself and his world to the supernatural knowledge of the Trinity which comes to him through revelation and mystical experience... Thus Rahner's theological anthropology unfolds into a coherent theological synthesis around the Trinity, the Incarnation, and grace. It resembles Bonaventure's Trinitarian synthesis in the dynamic role which it assigns to the Word of God in God's self-expression in the world through creation and the Incarnation" (Gerard A. McCool, *A Rahner Reader* [New York: Seabury Press, 1975], xx–xxii).

3 Commonly referred to as 'the Quaracchi edition', this ten-volume work is called: *S. Bonaventurae opera omnia*, edita studio et cura pp. Collegii a S. Bonaventura Ad Claras Aquas, Quaracchi: 1882–1902. Unless otherwise stated, our references to St. Bonaventure's works are based on this edition. Within parentheses, Roman numerals refer to the volume and Arabic numerals to the page. Each page is divided into two columns, which we indicate by the letter *a* or *b* after the Arabic numeral.

4 J. G. Bougerol attributes Bonaventure's recent prominence to the fact that theology, reflecting the pastoral aim of Vatican II, is no longer merely speculative but sapiential: "Le retour providentiel de Vatican II, par la médiation d'une finalité pastorale, à une théologie non plus seulement spéculative, mais vitale et sapientielle, accorde à saint Bonaventure un rôle privilégié. Nous n'avons pas à en glorifier à nouveau le maître qu'il a été. La fidélité à l'inspiration qui fut la sienne nous commande d'entreprendre à notre tour l'itinéraire qu'il a suivi et de donner à notre théologie la dimension de sagesse que l'Eglise d'Orient a su lui conserver" ("Fonction du théologien," *EF* 18 [1968]: 18).

and within such an organic systematic structure. In a certain sense, Bonaventure achieved for spirituality what Thomas did for theology and Dante for medieval culture as a whole."[5]

After tapping into the rich veins of Bonaventure, my own longing has been to share with others his insights about theology as a way of approaching God, a way that makes of theological pursuits an expressed form of the spiritual life. Echoes of this aspect of Bonaventure's approach to theology are found in official Church teaching when treating of priestly formation. For example, *Pastores Dabo Vobis* cites Bonaventure's well-known advice to students:

> Let no one think that it is enough for him to read if he lacks devotion, or to engage in speculation without spiritual joy, or to be active if he has no piety, or to have knowledge without charity, or intelligence without humility, or study without God's grace, or to expect to know himself if he is lacking the infused wisdom of God.[6]

Very high ideals indeed are expressed in these words.[7] Nevertheless, after only a moment's reflection on the nature of theology as the revelation of a personal God, these words should no longer appear as ideals but as

---

5 E.H. Cousins, *Bonaventure* (New York: Paulist Press, 1978), 2.

6 This quotation is taken from Bonaventure's *Itinerarium mentis in Deum*, prol., 4 (V, 296a). The context in *Pastores Dabo Vobis* is set by the explanation that immediately precedes Bonaventure's words: "Intellectual formation in theology and formation in the spiritual life, in particular the life of prayer, meet and strengthen each other, without detracting in any way from the soundness of research or from the spiritual tenor of prayer. Saint Bonaventure reminds us: 'Let no one think . . .'" *Pastores Dabo Vobis*, 53. This same quotation also is found in a footnote to the Second Vatican Council's Decree on Priestly Formation, *Optatam Totius*, 16.

7 Even when not directly quoting Bonaventure, other statements given in the same context seem to be inspired by Bonaventure's advice. For example: "Intellectual formation is to be integrated with a spirituality marked by a personal experience of God." This sentence is taken from *Pastores Dabo Vobis*, 51. The surrounding paragraph expresses the overall line of thought: "The commitment to study, which takes up no small part of the time of those preparing for the priesthood, is not in fact an external and secondary dimension of their human, Christian, spiritual and vocational growth. In reality, through study, especially the study of theology, the future priest assents to the word of God, grows in his spiritual life and prepares himself to fulfill his pastoral ministry. This is the many-sided and unifying scope of the theological study indicated by the Council and reproposed by the Synod's *Instrumentum Laboris* [39]: 'To be pastorally effective, intellectual formation is to be integrated with a spirituality marked by a personal experience of God. In this way a purely abstract approach to knowledge is overcome in favor of that intelligence of heart which knows how «to look beyond», and then is in a position to communicate the mystery of God to the people'" (*Pastores Dabo Vobis*, 51). Another pithy statement expresses the same idea from the standpoint of living faith: "The theologian is first and foremost a believer, a man of faith." The statement then continues: "But he is a believer who asks himself questions about his own faith (*fides quaerens intellectum*), with the aim of reaching a deeper understanding of the faith itself. The two aspects (of faith and mature reflection) are intimately connected, intertwined: their intimate coordination and interpenetration

solid minimum requirements. How could theology be studied without constant sensitivity to its intimate nature?[8] We then may ask ourselves whether the spiritual life of the theologian is the main concern for Bonaventure, whereby theology must subordinate its intellectual aspirations to the devout life ('knowledge at the service of piety'); or contrariwise, if theology, from a higher perspective than spirituality, must integrate the latter into its own projects in order for theology to achieve its rational purpose — *fides quaerens intellectum*.

Yet, is this not a vain question after all? Can we not presume it already resolved by situating ourselves within a larger context—that of the superiority of grace over nature? The possibility itself of a spiritual influence intervening into, or in any way conditioning, our intellectual operations is a notion that cannot be considered unique. Even Aristotle admitted this possibility, and believed that the human mind actually could benefit more from heavenly influences that would, whenever one is moved by such forces, render human reason unnecessary.[9] But what if we are not talking about altered states of consciousness? What about the imperceptible everyday workings of grace upon nature? And if such influences, conscious or unconscious, exist, what is the responsibility of the theologian in a perspective of living faith?

For St. Bonaventure, the human mind begins to receive God's illuminating influence from the moment of conception. The power of this

---

are what makes for true theology, and as a result decide the contents, modalities and spirit according to which the sacred doctrine (*sacra doctrina*) is elaborated and studied. Moreover, since the faith, which is the point of departure and the point of arrival of theology, brings about a personal relationship between the believer and Jesus Christ in the Church, theology also has intrinsic Christological and ecclesial connotations, which the candidate to the priesthood should take up consciously, not only because of what they imply for his personal life but also inasmuch as they affect his pastoral ministry. If our faith truly welcomes the word of God, it will lead to a radical 'yes' on the part of the believer to Jesus Christ, who is the full and definitive Word of God to the world (cf. Heb. 1:1ff.). As a result, theological reflection is centered on adherence to Jesus Christ, the Wisdom of God: mature reflection has to be described as a sharing in the 'thinking' of Christ (cf. 1 Cor. 2:16) in the human form of a science (*scientia fidei*)" (*Pastores Dabo Vobis*, 53). See also: Conc. Vat. II, Decree on Priestly Formation *Optatam totius*, 16; *C.I.C.*: Can. 252, §1; and three documents from the Congregation for Catholic Education: *Orientations for the Formation of Priestly Celibacy* (April 11, 1974), 79; *Theological Formation of Future Priests* (February 22, 1976), 25; *Ratio fundamentalis institutionis sacerdotalis* (new edition, March 19, 1985), 76.

8 M. Flick and Z. Alszeghy affirm that without religious experience, we cannot "do theology": "Si se carece de experiencia religiosa, se puede aprender lo necesario para un examen de teología, se pueden explicar incluso diversos teologúmenos, pero no se puede «hacer teología», es decir, no se llega a descubrir a través de las fórmulas el significado de los misterios, en su analogía con la realidad empírica, y en su conexión entre sí y con el fin último de la vida humana" (M. Flick and Z. Alszeghy, *Cómo se hace la teología*, trad. R. Rincón, [Madrid: Ediciones Paulinas, 1982], 175).

9 *Magna Moralia*, vii, 8; cf. *Ethica*, vii, 1.

influence increases when redemption is accepted, and progressively develops in strength through commitment to a personal spiritual life. Specifically, in the case of the spiritual life of the theologian, a certain point arrives when the gifts of the Holy Spirit engage him and do far more for him and for theology than at first we may be prepared to recognize. Certain statements of Saint Bonaventure may surprise us. He declares, for example, that the gift of understanding communicates to the soul a higher knowledge than faith.[10] Or, when treating of the gift of wisdom, he confidently states that "the best way of knowing God is through an experience of sweetness."[11]

The object of my investigation is not to dissolve the mystery of such influences, but to consider them insofar as they shed light on my principle aim, which is to determine what consequences these influences imply for the spiritual life of a theology student. Saint Bonaventure had much to say about the relationship between theology and spiritual life. It would seem to me this relationship not only is extremely intimate, but these two realities practically coincide, at least in the mind of the theologian. Specifically, they unite in his "intentionality."

"Intentionality" was a favorite expression of Bernard Lonergan.[12] But, it was precisely Lonergan who, while placing great importance on the mutual influences given and received between theology and the spiritual life, did not hesitate to warn us against simply identifying theology with religion or prayer.[13] Because of Lonergan's comprehensive view of theology and the theologian's inner life, it has been to my great advantage to follow him as a modern guide in my approach to Saint Bonaventure and to help me present my exposition hopefully with some success to modern readers. Indeed, Bernard Lonergan, while not expressly referring to Saint

---

10 "Ad donum intellectus spectat contemplatio clarior et excellentior, quam sit cognitio fidei" *III Sent.* d. 35, au., q. 3, ad 4 (III, 779a).

11 "Optimus modus cognoscendi Deum est per experientiam dulcedinis" *III Sent.* d. 35, au., q. 1, ad 5 (III, 775a).

12 When speaking of intentionality in my sixth chapter, I have found valuable insights in Bernard Lonergan. If, as he states, "man achieves authenticity in self-transcendence" (*Method in Theology* [New York: Herder and Herder, 1972], 104), it is significant that the means to attain self-transcendence is nothing other than intentionality: "Self-transcendence is the achievement of conscious intentionality" (Ibid., 35). That both these concepts (self-transcendence and conscious intentionality) are his way of speaking about sanctity, should be evident from the fact that the former is the key to man's authenticity, and the latter is the key to loving God: "As the question of God is implicit in all our questioning, so being in love with God is the basic fulfillment of our conscious intentionality" (Ibid., 105).

13 "To identify theology with religion, with liturgy, with prayer, with preaching, no doubt is to revert to the earliest period of Christianity. But it is also to overlook the fact that the conditions of the earliest period have long since ceased to exist. There are real theological problems, real issues

Bonaventure, has many noteworthy and even commanding perspectives from which one might attain a better understanding of the Seraphic Doctor. All of this should enable us to make some practical applications of Bonaventure's doctrine for our times. In Bernard Lonergan's *Method in Theology* I have found many striking similarities, at the same time some illuminating contrasts, to the teaching of Saint Bonaventure. These correspondences and divergences will be pointed out in this book whenever they appear to clarify and vitalize Saint Bonaventure's doctrine for modern readers.[14]

The contribution of Bernard Lonergan to my study essentially is the role of his "transcendental method" when it is applied to theology, and what the specifically religious experience adds to this method.[15] Although Lonergan explicitly affirms that the transcendental method alone is not sufficient when it comes to theological study,[16] it certainly must play a vital role. On one hand the problem of God is already present "in all our questioning."[17] Likewise, being in love with God "is the basic fulfillment of all our conscious intentionality."[18] This would indicate that the transcendental method is never far from any intellectual discipline, theology least of all.

Now, Bernard Lonergan defines the transcendental method essentially as: "interiority in terms of intentional and conscious acts on the

---

that, if burked, threaten the very existence of Christianity. There are real problems of communication in the twentieth century, and they are not solved by preaching to ancient Antioch, Corinth, or Rome. So it is that we have been led to the conclusion of acknowledging a distinction between the Christian religion and Christian theology" (Ibid., 140).

14   The assistance from Lonergan's works generally will be limited to footnotes, so as not to interrupt the flow of our principle discussion, which is to elucidate Bonaventure's own thinking.

15   I find Lonergan's approach comparable to what some Bonaventurians call 'the existential approach' of the Franciscan Doctor. As Bonaventure is so aware of the interior life as an essential part of the intellectual search for God (typified in chapters 3 and 4 of the *Itinerarium mentis in Deum*), so also Lonergan enters into the soul as it consciously participates in the same search: "The appropriation of one's own interiority, one's subjectivity, one's operations . . . is a heightening of intentional consciousness, an attending not merely to objects but also to the intending subject and his acts. And as this heightened consciousness constitutes the evidence for one's account of knowledge, such an account by the proximity of the evidence differs from all other expression" (*Method in Theology*, 83). See: L. Veuthey, "Esistenzialismo in S. Bonaventura," in: *L'Esistenzialismo*, ed. L. Pelloux (Roma: Studium, 1943): 135–58.

16   "Transcendental method is only a part of theological method. It supplies the basic anthropological component. It does not supply the specifically religious component. Accordingly, to advance from transcendental to theological method, it is necessary to add a consideration of religion" (Lonergan, *Method in Theology,* 25).

17   Ibid., 105.

18   Ibid.

four levels of experiencing, understanding, judging, and deciding."[19] Interiority, he affirms, can give to the student "a foundation that is distinct from common sense and theory."[20] This will have importance for me when analyzing the influence of prayer life on theological study. Likewise, if the transcendental method is precisely "a heightening of consciousness that brings to light our conscious and intentional operations,"[21] and that "man achieves authenticity in self-transcendence,"[22] we may appreciate its value as a means to sanctity (i.e., living the Christian life authentically) especially when it comes to the 'authenticity' of the student in contact with divine revelation.

As for Lonergan's insistence on the separateness of theology and religion, he is quick to add that such separateness "always intends" a return to identity in unity, even if that unity is not effected until the final stage: "Such is our first instance of differentiation and dynamic unity. Religion and theology become distinct and separate. But the separateness of theology is a withdrawal that always intends and in its ultimate stage effects a return."[23]

It is my aim to show that theology and spiritual life never can be separated in the *intention* of the theologian. Indeed, neither in Saint Bonaventure nor in secondary sources have I found the clear affirmation or the expressed concept of theology *as* a spiritual life. However, I trust the

---

19 Ibid., 120. Describing this method, by which self-transcendence is achieved through conscious intentionality, Lonergan states: "There is a first step in attending to the data of sense and of consciousness. Next, inquiry and understanding yield an apprehension of a hypothetical world mediated by meaning. Thirdly, reflection and judgment reach an absolute: through them we acknowledge what really is so, what is independent of us and our thinking. Fourthly, by deliberation, evaluation, decision, action, we can know and do, not just what pleases us, but what truly is good, worth while. . . It is, finally only by reaching the sustained self-transcendence of the virtuous man that one becomes a good judge, not on this or that human act, but on the whole range of human goodness" (Ibid., 35). For similar brief descriptions of this method, see: Ibid., 53 and 133.

20 "It is only through the long and confused twilight of philosophic initiation that one can find one's way into interiority and achieve through self-appropriation a basis, a foundation, that is distinct from common sense and theory, that acknowledges their disparateness, that accounts for both and critically grounds them both" (*Method in Theology*, 85). Lonergan also states: "The withdrawal into interiority is not an end in itself. From it one returns to the realms of common sense and theory with the ability to meet the methodological exigence" (Ibid., 83). And again: "One must go behind them [common sense and theory] to the realm of interiority. For only through the realm of interiority can differentiated consciousness understand itself and so explain the nature and the complementary purposes of different patterns of cognitional activity" (Ibid., 115).

21 Ibid., 25.

22 Ibid., 104.

23 Ibid., 140.

reader will perceive, in reading this work, that Bonaventure's mind can be interpreted in this way both without embarrassment and advantageously. In addition, I calculate such an interpretation will be not only valid, but wholly enlightening for our times.

Although most people associate spiritual life with the terms 'religion' and 'prayer', it is important to note that Bernard Lonergan warns against simply identifying either of these two realities with theology, specifically rejecting such an attitude as a relapse to our remotest past.[24] Such a warning makes it especially difficult for me to manipulate the texts of a renowned modern scholar to suit my own ends. On the other hand, little can be gained by following him as a guide if that is done in a servile manner. Instead, it is evident to me that Lonergan, through his utmost care in making distinctions, is a master who has lightened significantly the burden of my study by pointing out the pitfalls to be avoided. By correcting my inherent craving to confirm my own position, he has served in the long run to purify my own perceptions of Bonaventure's thought. This is an ongoing process in which I hope to respond to his invitation to transcend my own inauthenticity.

Now, in regard to the method which I have utilized to demonstrate the consequences of St. Bonaventure's doctrine for the spiritual life of the theologian, I first should point out what others have remarked regarding the intrinsic unity of Bonaventure's system. Etienne Gilson, for example, has stated: "Paradoxical as the assertion may seem, I hold that it is the extreme unification of Bonaventure's doctrine which has made it look incomplete and unsystematized; it is easier to deny that the details form part of a system, than to grasp the system in its entirety and think out each detail in function of the whole."[25] With this unity in mind, I have attempted to interpret Bonaventure's thinking about theology as a way to God by illustrating how the major themes that constitute the pillars of his thought-system are actually the roots which account for his pastoral and spiritual convictions as he himself expresses them.

For fear of losing the overall perspective, I have preferred, throughout the book, to handle a coherent synthesis of Bonaventure's vision, rather than to dedicate excessive time to analyzing his theological preferences separately. Thus, the first difficulty in understanding St. Bonaventure's works, his 'apparent incompleteness' or 'unsystematized' approach, actually

---

24 Ibid.

25 E. Gilson, *The Philosophy of St. Bonaventure,* trad. I. Trethowen and F. Sheed (Paterson, N.J.: St. Anthony Guild Press, 1965), 436. Gilson moreover states: "In it [i.e., in the doctrine of St.

has contributed most toward the adoption of my own method, which briefly could be formulated as "interpretative-synthetic."

Two further difficulties in Bonaventure are his symbolic descriptions (found mainly in his pastoral works) and his medieval world view. Again, confronting these difficulties has only served the same purpose, that is, they encouraged me in the same direction—interpreting and synthesizing—both Bonaventure's symbolic approach and his medieval world view, then discovering the links that unite both these visions.

Each chapter of the book is dedicated to one of the topics which I have judged to form, as J.G. Bougerol states, the 'fundamental intuition' of our author. These topics closely revolve around the philosophical and anthropological presuppositions of Neoplatonic or Augustinian origin so particular to Bonaventure's entire work. Other central themes might have been studied. Nevertheless, I have chosen the topics I perceive to be most directly related to the aim of my treatise. In so doing, I have skimmed over, for example, what many rightly consider most characteristically Bonaventure's, such as the Seraphic Doctor's Christocentrism and his all-inclusive Trinitarian theology. This choice was made not because these important aspects in themselves could not form a strong buttress for the argument; in fact, in the places where I enlist their aid (particularly Christocentrism), their role should appear at least illustrative. Rather, in order for *theology as a spiritual life* to be applicable virtually in any theological context, I have emphasized more formal elements. Such elements reach elsewhere, that is, inward—into the theologian's attitude itself. This may be especially useful today since our times have seen a great increase of field specialization.[26] Basically, however, the theologian still remains he who gives us a word (λόγος) about God (θεός). Whatever material object the theologian chooses to contemplate today, formally he speaks to us about God and whatever He has revealed to us. Thus, what St. Bonaventure believes to be true for theology in general as a spiritual life,

---

Bonaventure], the totality of the system means so much that the mere notion of fragments has no meaning at all. You can either see the general economy of his doctrine in its totality, or see none of it" (Ibid.). In the same vein, J.G. Bougerol wisely has cautioned: "La pensée de Bonaventure est, en effet, tellement unifiée qu'il est impossible de vouloir isoler l'une ou l'autre notion fragmentaire sans se condamner à ne plus apercevoir l'économie générale de la pensée. Mais, d'autre part, et c'est un peu ce qui nous console, de quelque côté qu'on aborde une telle doctrine, on est ramené aux thèmes centraux qui en forment l'intuition fondamental" (*Saint Bonaventure et la sagesse chrétienne* [Paris: Editions du Seuil, 1963], 81).

26 "Contemporary theology is specialized, and so it is to be conceived, not as a single set of related operations, but as a series of interdependent sets" (Lonergan, *Method in Theology*, 125; see also: Ibid., 138, 140, and 145).

might be applicable, at least in theory, to the new forms theology may assume. If adaptations are to be made for new theological forms, I believe these adaptations will favor spiritual life wherever Bonaventure's aim is grasped.

Assuming, then, that the central themes I have chosen truly are representative of Bonaventure's thought, I hope we may find ourselves illuminated by his principle inspirations and are enabled to grasp his deeper insights about the purpose of theological study as a road to sanctity.

The sequence of chapters is arranged in such a way as to respond to two questions: 1) What makes the study of theology a spiritual life? and 2) what spiritual attitude must the theologian then assume as a consequence? The chapters substantiate Bonaventure's views by a successive study of the Seraphic Doctor's characteristic anthropology. The first chapter, "Bonaventure's Theological Spirituality," gives an overview of theology and spirituality, concentrating on their mutual relations in the works of Saint Bonaventure. By thus setting the stage, this chapter prepares us to descend to the concrete subject to be undertaken: the theologian and his experience of reality.

The second chapter deals with the soul's incompetence to know reality after the Fall and the subsequent need of "hierarchization of the soul," a process by which the soul is once more made erect. This process in itself forms the starting point and foundation of the spiritual life. From the hierarchized posture, the soul now can apprehend reality on its own terms. The third chapter takes us into Bonaventure's exemplarist teaching, which is the medieval world view that acts as a backdrop supporting all objectivity of our knowledge. This structure of reality as the object of man's knowledge corresponds to the knowing subject who, now being made erect or 'hierarchized', beholds reality as objectively as possible. Thus, the knower is not called to *create* reality by imposing principles of intelligibility upon it, but to *discover* the pattern already impressed by God upon his created design. In this sense, the process of knowing entails man's assuming a receptive role that conforms (i.e., transforms) his mind to the demands of God's reality—God is reflected in and communicated through his creatures. God's reality, even at the lowest levels, is an invitation to spiritual contact with the Creator. The closer we get to God through the hierarchized world, the greater is this contact and the greater the demands of the spirit. This is why Bonaventure can speak of three successive hierarchizations of the soul, corresponding to the transformation of the spiritual life.

In the fourth chapter, I examine St. Bonaventure's doctrine of illumination, the Augustinian theory which explains how man reaches certitude in his search for truth by being immersed in the light God gives him. Without directly beholding this divine light, man is enabled by its beams to discover truth and cooperate spiritually with the sole Teacher in his intellectual search. Light is the co-principle both of study and of spirituality.

The purpose of the fifth chapter, "*Scientia Fidei* and Christian Life," is to pause in our study of the effect of grace upon the human mind and to question its compatibility with reason's freedom. Reason grew in self-confidence in the Middle Ages, and its gradual 'separation' from the authority of faith at first seemed to favor man's intellectual autonomy. But accompanying this liberation came a double danger: that of rationalism and then the reaction to it by those who feared the risk of the new autonomy. Is the spiritual life in some way an antirational element that could undermine the legitimate demands of intellectual rigor? With the help of M.D. Chenu's analysis of the two complementary forces at work in that age, we behold how the historical circumstances led our Seraphic Doctor to produce a well-balanced synthesis. In the same chapter I have given an example of Bonaventure's rational procedure, precisely in the case of the proofs of God's existence, to show to what degree his theology is based on his spirituality.

This investigation into reason's rights necessarily is preliminary to the even more extensive study that follows—the gifts of the Holy Spirit—in the sixth and final chapter. The logic here is that once we have clarified the difficulties attendant on reason's rightful claims, we more confidently can accept the powerful influence from above as represented by the doctrine on the gifts of the Holy Spirit. In general, this influence produces the kind of spiritual life that is an effect of faith upon the intellect and the free will, and concretely, the role of the gifts of understanding and of wisdom. Stated simply, this amounts to the role our love of God plays in the learning process.

Hopefully the chapter order that I have chosen will manifest how the student of theology gains a "feel" for theology, or perhaps a concrete participation in *sensus fidelium*. The theologian, undertaking theology as a spiritual life, embarks upon the discernment process of the matter studied. This attitude implies both progressing in new horizons of theology and at the same time thinking with the Church. The theologian's prayer life becomes integrated with his intellectual formation as two facets of the same process.

The theologian's prayer life is the perspective from which he is best capacitated to do theology because the object of his study is the person, Christ, who invites the theologian toward personal union with him. This is what meditation on the Incarnate Word brings with it: "In this consideration is the perfect illumination of the mind."[27] Through prayer, in Bonaventure's sense, the theologian "is given understanding of the Scriptures."[28] The result of this approach to theology is a more perfect integration of the life of prayer and the life of study. These two aspects are benefited both powerfully and mutually.

The purpose of this book, then, is to call on St. Bonaventure's teaching to demonstrate why theology should be undertaken solely for the purpose of spiritual progress. This means that theology, unless it informs and, more importantly, is informed by the spiritual life, cannot be undertaken without serious detriment to its nature as subordinate to and dependent upon Revelation. By respecting the nature of theology, as the study of a living God who personally appeals to us in Revelation, theology undertaken with the intention of being a spiritual way to God directly empowers the theologian to know God on God's own terms—through experience. Contrarily, to know God solely on our own terms, that is, outside an interpersonal relationship with Him, inherently distorts the object of theological study, to say nothing of the harm it may cause to the human spirit. It is my hope that this modest contribution to spiritual theology may help us in some small way not only to avoid the personal harm involved in treating the sacred sciences with insensitivity, but principally to undertake the same as a sure way to personal holiness by knowing God through love.

---

27 "In hac consideratione est perfecta illuminatio mentis" *Itin.* 6, 7 (V, 312a).

28 "In oratione datur homini intelligentia Scripturarum" *Comm. Lc.* 9, 55 (VII, 234b). This is reminiscent of St. Augustine's expression: "Orent ut intellegant!" (*De doctr. christ.,* III, 56 [*PL* 34, 38]).

Sólo quien ama a Dios
posee la verdadera ciencia de Dios.

I Cor. 8:3, *L.H.*

God is love and he is knowable to those who love him.

Clement of Alexandria, *Stromata*

I.

BONAVENTURE'S THEOLOGICAL SPIRITUALITY[1]

    Students of Saint Bonaventure often point out that his works bear a common mark which distinguishes him from other theologians in the past. What they have found to be his outstanding trait amounts to a profound orientation toward mystical union with God.[2] For the same reason, it is presumed that a motivation both more personal and pastoral on the part of the author must account for this common characteristic. Bonaventure is seen as expressing his spiritual yearnings and, as the mystagogue, sharing with others the treasures he has found in theology as a means of achieving holiness.[3]

---

1 This expression is from J.G. Bougerol: "Knowledge is only a stage in the journey of our return to God. This basic belief explains why Bonaventurian theology is so spiritual and Bonaventurian spirituality is so theological" (*Introduction to the Works of Bonaventure*, trans. José de Vinck [Paterson, N.J.: St. Anthony Guild Press, 1964], 153).

2 Many authors have seen Bonaventure this way, and the following statements appear typical: J.G. Bougerol states: "[Bonaventure's] purpose is union with God through love" (Ibid., 168); E. Gilson: "St. Bonaventure is essentially a mystic" (*Philosophy of St. Bonaventure*, 441); "St. Bonaventure's doctrine marks for us the culminating point of Christian mysticism and constitutes the completest synthesis it has ever achieved" (Ibid., 448); F. Copleston: "[Bonaventure was] principally interested in the soul's advance to God" (*A History of Philosophy*, 3 vols. [New York: Image Doubleday, 1993], 2: 243); ". . . a thinker who was chiefly concerned with the soul's approach to God" (Ibid., 2: 248); ". . . a man whose whole interest centered round the soul's ascent to God" (Ibid., 2: 249). T.J. Tekippe: "Indeed, this mystical tendency makes Bonaventure a very unusual thinker in the Western tradition as a whole" ("An Investigation of the Balance between Conceptual and Primordial Knowing in Major Figures of the Western Philosophical Tradition," Ph.D. diss., [New Orleans: Tulane University, 1980], 244).

3 "Bonaventure intends to be a theologian for no other reason than to form saints" (Bougerol, *Introduction to Bonaventure*, 108). Pope Leo XIII called St. Bonaventure "the prince par excellence who leads us by the hand to God": "Quemadmodum PP. Dominicani Angelicum Doctorem, S. Thomam, sibi vindicant, ita vos, Franciscales, Doctorem Seraphicum, S. Bonaventuram, vobis iure quidem optimo vindicatis. Is postquam maxime arduas speculationis summitates conscendit, de

Given such a tendency in Saint Bonaventure, it should not surprise anyone that when defining theology he has holiness uppermost in mind. In fact, theology for him is the royal road to God,[4] the queen of all the sciences,[5] and is undertaken precisely for the purpose of becoming holy.[6] If theology is a way to God, can we go so far as to say that the study of theology, for our Seraphic Doctor, is not simply subordinated to the spiritual life as a means to an end, but *is* itself a spiritual life? Saint Bonaventure all but affirms this to be so.

At the beginning of his *Commentary on the Sentences*, we find Saint Bonaventure defining theology as a *«habitus affectivus»* [a subjective disposition] which is "midway between the speculative and the practical, and embracing both"; having as its end both "contemplation and personal progress, but principally personal progress (*ut boni fiamus*)" [....] "and this *habitus* is called wisdom, which means at the same time both knowledge and love."[7]

Here we see Saint Bonaventure, at the outset of the most speculative of all his works, stating that the purpose for studying theology is that of becoming good, in the sense of attaining personal holiness. Now, if the end pretended in studying theology is personal holiness, a question may be posed, and it is whether sanctity, understood either as a grace or at least as the effort involved on the part of the student who leads a spiritual life, brings

---

mystica Theologia tanta perfectione disseruit, ut in ea, communi hominum peritissimorum suffragio, habeatur facile princeps. Frequens libensque Nos Doctorem hunc legimus; ex qua lectione incredibili animi voluptate percellimur et fere in aëra levamur: ipse enim manuducit ad Deum" (Allocutio of 11 November, 1890, recorded in *Acta Ordinis Minorum*, Anno IX, 177–78, as well as by the Quaracchi editors [X, 34b]).

4 "Quia cum sacra Scriptura sive theologia sit scientia dans sufficientem notitiam de primo principio secundum statum viae, secundum quod est necessarium ad salutem" *Brev.* 1, 1, 2 (V, 210a); see also remainder of chapter 1 (V, 210a–b).

5 "Omnes cognitiones famulantur theologiae" *Red. art.* 26 (V, 325b). To place theology at the top is nothing unusual for Bonaventure's time, but his particular way of relating theology to the other sciences is of special interest. Bernard Lonergan has observed that "theology is accounted traditionally *regina scientiarum*, and the relation of theology to other sciences is a matter of more than apologetic interest" (Bernard Lonergan, *Insight, A Study of Human Understanding*, [London: Longmans, Green and Co., 1958], 743).

6 The final cause of theology, as we shall see presently, is spiritual progress. Commenting on this tendency, Bougerol states: "Bonaventure considers theology as a stage in the soul's ascent toward wisdom: the last step before the vision of heaven" (*Introduction to Bonaventure*, 90).

7 "Si autem medio modo consideretur ut natus extendi ad affectum, sic perficitur ab habitu medio inter pure speculativum et practicum, qui complectitur utrumque; et hic habitus dicitur sapientia, quae simul dicit cognitionem et affectum. . . . Unde hic est contemplationis gratia, et ut boni fiamus, principaliter tamen ut boni fiamus" *I Sent.* prooem., q. 3, concl. (I, 13a–b).

any advantages to theology? From this standpoint, a whole series of related questions arise. But our first question, in order to clarify the field into which we are treading, could be: How do these two realities, theology and spiritual life, resemble each other? Secondly, how do they distinguish themselves from each other? Afterwards, we may ask ourselves if the end pretended by the theologian—sanctity—in its turn, exerts an influence upon the theologian himself who undertakes theology with this precise Bonaventurian aim of becoming a saint? And if so, what does this new influence consist of? In other words, does the spiritual life, as Bonaventure understands it, add anything to theology, or even inform theology, thereby making it possible to affirm that theology is a spiritual life? In order to answer this question, which is the ultimate purpose of the present contribution to Bonaventurian studies, first of all we must examine briefly Bonaventure's concept of theology. Our second step will be to behold in a comprehensive glance his understanding of the spiritual life. In this way we hope to determine where these two realities may be seen to coincide, and what lessons can be drawn from the influences they might exert on each other from mutual contact. After comparing and contrasting these two realities, presumably we shall be in a better position to begin our study of the key concepts of Bonaventure's doctrine which underlie and confirm his vision of theology as a spiritual life.

Of the key concepts, I have chosen three which I consider among the most characteristic, dedicating to each a chapter: hierarchization, exemplarism, and illumination. Hopefully, through an investigation of these concepts we shall discover how knowledge and love are the means by which man and God approach each other, through any science, but especially through the privileged science of theology. Afterwards we attempt to formulate a response to the possible apprehension about antirationalism in a system which limits the power of reason and yields to the 'captivity' of the mind by grace. Finally, we shall dedicate the end of our study to the gifts of the Holy Spirit, determining how each of the cognitive gifts among them acts upon the soul, producing the precious fruit of sapiential theology. It is my belief that the theologian who leads the life of this habit called wisdom, as Bonaventure defined theology, is both leading the life of a theologian and a holy life.[8]

---

8 By "a holy life" I mean the life of aiming at goodness, or the process of becoming good (*ut boni fiamus*). As we shall see later on, the theologian is called to participate in the good aim he pursues, as a pilgrim somehow lives by the destination he is constantly yearning for.

1. Theology for Saint Bonaventure

What concept did Saint Bonaventure have of theology that would allow him to make the statement that its aim is to make us holy? In this chapter we shall consider the three places in Bonaventure's works where he defines theology so as to clarify the intention he assigns to the theologian. The three places and their immediate contexts are: a) the Prooemium to the first book of the *Commentary on the Sentences,* in which Bonaventure studies the four causes of theology; b) the Prologue to the *Breviloquium,* where he treats of the relationship between theology and Sacred Scripture; c) and in chapter IV of *Collationes de septem donis Spiritus sancti,* where he outlines theology as a science.

a) *The four causes of theology (**Prooemium of I Sent.**):*

Actually, the statement that the aim of theology is "to become good" is found within Bonaventure's fourfold definition of theology following the classical philosophical division into four causes.[9] The ultimate aim of theology is its *final cause,* and this is precisely the one I have exhibited above, as taken from the *Prooemium* of Bonaventure's *Commentary on the Sentences.* The other three definitions, specified by Bonaventure in the same treatise, continue the same philosophical arrangement as follows:

— *Material cause:* The object of faith (whatever is revealed by God, in creation and redemption) as this is rendered intelligible with the help of human reason.[10]

—*Formal cause:* Theology explains revealed truth in such a way as to fortify the faith of others. Thus, theology's mode of procedure is inquisitive or argumentative. This mode of procedure by itself is the formal cause.[11]

---

9 Ibid., Quaestiones Prooemii (I, 6a–15b).

10 Ibid., prooem., q. 1, fundª. 1–3 (I, 6a–b). It is important to notice that for Saint Bonaventure, the object *of theology* is distinguished from the object *of faith* as such (i.e., the *credibile*). Theology's object also is the *credibile,* but insofar as the *credibile* is submitted to human reason to conform it to our legitimate thirst for intelligibility: "Et sic est credibile, prout transit in rationem intelligibilis, et hoc per additionem rationis" (Ibid., concl. [I, 7b]).

11 Ibid., q. 2, con. 1–4 (I, 10a–b).

— *Efficient cause*: The theologian, as the author of a particular work which explains revelation, is the efficient cause. However, God must be considered as the principal efficient cause, since He is the origin of the *habitus* making it possible for the theologian to work. Thus, the theologian is the instrumental (or secondary) efficient cause.[12]

Of the four definitions given to theology the *final cause* holds the most important place for Saint Bonaventure. It is the principal end of theology—to make us better as Christians.[13] Theology does not come to its full realization simply by understanding revelation (material cause), nor even by converting and strengthening the faith of others (formal cause) but in making us holy (final cause). Even though beatitude is the ultimate, total end of Sacred Scripture (to which theology is subordinated), our sanctification is the proximate end of theology as a science, ordered to our final beatitude in heaven.[14]

Nevertheless, we may ask ourselves whether Saint Bonaventure offers any other definition of theology that may differ from or complement the above. In effect, he explains the function of theology in two other places: in the Prologue of the *Breviloquium* and in the *Collationes de septem donis Spiritus sancti*. In each place, although his approach is different, the same conclusion is reached. Let us first turn to the *Breviloquium*.

b) *Theology and Sacred Scripture (**Breviloquium**):*

In the *Breviloquium* the Seraphic Doctor sees theology as a parallel science to Sacred Scripture, but subordinated to it, having a similar origin, development and end as Sacred Scripture.[15] Because of their similarity, it is not unusual for Bonaventure to equate Sacred Scripture and theology

---

12 Ibid., q. 4, concl. (I, 14b–15b).

13 Ibid., q. 3, fund. 3 (I, 12a–b).

14 "Doctrina particularis convenit cum totali in fine; sed finis totalis Scripturae sacrae non est tantum ut fiamus boni, sed etiam ut fiamus beati; et beatitudo est optimum: ergo finis istius scientiae est ut boni fiamus" (Ibid.).

15 *Brev.* prol. ". . .et intelligentiarum." (V, 201a–202b). For a brief explanation of Bonaventure's approach to Sacred Scripture in the *Breviloquium*'s Prologue, see A. Blasucci, "S. Scrittura e teologia nel Prologo del Breviloquio," in: *Incontri Bonaventuriani* (hereafter *IncBonav*), 11 vols. (Montecalvo Irpino, 1965–1974), 7: 93–119.

(*'sacrae Scripturae, quae theologia dicitur'*) as was the custom among the early Scholastics before him.[16]

Now, the purpose of Scripture is virtually the same as that of theology: "The purpose of Scriptural doctrine is that we become virtuous and attain salvation."[17] We also may notice how Bonaventure, as he did when defining the final cause of theology, here again makes the connection between the end of theology and the gift of wisdom: "Scripture takes on the very diversity of created things, to teach us through them that wisdom which leads to eternal life."[18]

c) *Theology as a science* (*Chapter 4 of De donis*)

The third place where Saint Bonaventure describes the nature of theology is in his *Collationes de septem donis Spiritus sancti* where he shows how theology's purpose, both for those who study it and those who govern the Church, is to promote the good of the Christian life.[19] Again, the same comparison is made between Sacred Scripture and theology, and this comparison is what substantiates their having a similar purpose. Unfortunately, he does not go deeper, but is content to mention that theology

---

16 Ibid., prol., fund. 1 (V, 201a); "Ut merito ista scientia appareat una esse et ordinata et theologia non immerito nuncupata" (Ibid., prol. 6 [V, 208b]). "Le cours magistral demeurera, jusqu'en plein XIIIe siècle, la *lectio* scripturaire: la Bible est le texte de base de l'enseignement, et les Sommes ne seront que des oeuvres personnelles, hors la discipline scolaire publique" (M.D. Chenu, *La théologie au douzième siècle*, [Paris: J. Vrin, 1957], 337). See: B. Smalley, *The Study of the Bible in the Middle Ages* (Oxford: Blackwell, 1983ᵃ); H.J. Klauck, "Theorie der Exegese bei Bonaventura," in: *S. Bonaventura 1274–1974* [hereafter *SB*] 5 vols. (Grottaferrata: Collegio S. Bonaventura, 1974), 4: 71–128.

17 "Haec doctrina est, ut boni fiamus et salvemur" *Brev.* prol. 5 (V, 206b); "Status vero sive fructus sacrae Scripturae non est quicumque, sed plenitudo aeternae felicitatis. . . . Hoc igitur fine, hac intentione sacra Scriptura perscrutanda est et docenda et etiam audienda" (Ibid., prol. [V, 202a]); "Scriptura sacra est notitia movens ad bonum" (Ibid., prol. 1 [V, 203a]). J. Pedersen remarks that "pour Bonaventure, l'Ecriture n'a pas d'autre objet que n'a le livre du Lombard" ("L'intellectus fidei et la notion de théologie chez saint Bonaventure," in: *Studia Theologica* 5 [1951]: 27).

18 "Competit nihilominus ipsi fini, quia Scriptura data est, ut per ipsam dirigatur homo in cognoscendis et agendis, ut tandem perveniat ad optanda. Et quia omnes creaturae ad hoc factae sunt, ut serviant homini tendenti ad supernam patriam, ideo Scriptura assumit ipsarum creaturarum species diversas, ut sic per illas doceat nos sapientiam dirigentem nos ad aeterna" *Brev.* prol. 4 (V, 206a–b). In another work, he states that wisdom results from many mysteries of the Scripture: "Haec sapientia resultat ex multis mysteriis Scripturae, sicut ex multis speculis fiunt multiplicationes radiorum et ignium" *Hex.* 2, 19 (V, 339b); and that one of the four reasons why Scripture is given to us is "to manifest wisdom, which is only found in it": ". . . tertio ad reserandam sapientiam, quae sola est in ista" *Hex.* 14, 7 (V, 394b).

19 *De donis* 4, 13–18 (V, 476a–477b).

is a "pious knowledge of the truth as believable."[20]   Perhaps his purpose in treating theology in the fourth chapter, that is, under the gift of knowledge and not under the gift of wisdom, is to ground its scientific character, and thereby free himself for higher approaches to this topic. I will interpret this choice further on in my study. But for now, let us observe how he emphasizes the usefulness of theology as a science for the correct government of the Church, but warns that he who does theology without putting it into practice will do more harm than good.[21]   Thus, although he admits that theology is to be numbered among the sciences, he recognizes its limitations *as a science*. He adds that because such harm is possible, we stand in need of light from another science, *scientia gratuita*, which he defines as "a holy knowledge of the truth as lovable."[22]   At the end of the same chapter, he states that the highest knowledge, *scientia gloriosa*, "begins in contemplatives" but finds its completion after this life.[23]

Thus, we find St. Bonaventure in *De septem donis* only touching upon the topic of theology which he places within the gift of knowledge as one of the sciences. He appears to use this opportunity to emphasize that theology, far from being an infused science, needs to be the object of rigorous work on the part of those in charge of governing the faithful.[24]

Evidently, neither the *Breviloquium* nor *De septem donis* add anything essentially different to his earlier treatments of the same question when it comes to the nature and purpose of theology. They are simply different approaches by which the same concept of theology is described.

We may be tempted at this point to suppose that Saint Bonaventure definitely took the purpose of Sacred Scripture, as explained in the *Breviloquium*, and attributed this same purpose to theology. He may have felt justified in doing so for two reasons: (a) theologians before him were

---

20   "Scientia theologica est veritatis ut credibilis notitia pia" (Ibid.,4, 5 [V, 474b]); cf. Ibid.,4, 13 (V, 476a).

21   "Item, repellitur scientia, quando homo scit scientiam et non vult secundum scientiam vivere nec eam implere. . . Ex scientia culpa augetur etiam et poena. . . . Ista scientia, si non adsit operis impletio, non est utilis, sed damnosa" (Ibid., 4, 18 [V, 477b]).

22   "Ista scientia est veritatis ut credibilis et diligibilis notitia sancta" (Ibid., 4, 19 [V, 477b]).

23   "Ista scientia initiatur in contemplativis, perpetuatur in dormientibus et consummatur in resurgentibus" (Ibid., 4, 25 [V, 479b]).   Both names, 'scientia gratuita' and 'scientia gloriosa', are interchangeable.

24   "Si fundamenta Ecclesiae consistunt in scientia sacrae Scripturae, ideo qui sacram Scripturam nescit repellendus est ab officio et dignitate ecclesiastica. Si caecus vellet alium ducere, maxima fatuitas esset. . . . Et sciendum, quod scientia repellitur, quando homo non curat eam addiscere" (Ibid., 4, 18 [V, 477a]).

accustomed, as we have seen, to identify the Bible and theology; (b) and even though theology was becoming "more and more surrounded with *quaestiones*,"[25] as it became more influenced by speculation, it still remained strongly dependent on Sacred Scripture.[26] From this close connection between Scripture and theology, it would have been easy for Saint Bonaventure to declare that theology has the same purpose as Scripture, that of leading us to sanctity. Such a statement would seem based exclusively on authority, even though this authority is none other than the Bible itself. This authority is known by faith to have the highest guarantee of certitude, as it "exceeds every certitude of reason."[27] And, when it comes to faith, should we not feel comfortable with authority? To this effect, Bonaventure often quotes Saint Augustine's axiom: "What we believe, we owe to authority, and what we understand, we owe to reason."[28] Thus it would seem to end all need for further inquiry. By submitting our reason to God's infallible word, we are bound to accept this statement about theology's purpose. God wants us to be holy (Mt. 5: 48; I Thess. 4:3; Eph. 1:4; I Pet 1:16). Does St. Augustine's saying, alluded to by St. Bonaventure, imply that no further investigation into other sources of knowledge can help us whenever the argument from authority is invoked?

d) *The authority of faith*

If such be the case, that the purpose of theology—to make us good— is deduced from Sacred Scripture and received by our intellect on divine authority, it may appear as something outside man's own capacity for discovery, not appearing as a conclusion he might reach through human reasoning, and therefore belonging uniquely to the realm of mystery. Is

---

25 M.D. Chenu, *Nature, Man, and Society in the Twelfth Century* (hereafter *Twelfth Century*), selected, edited and translated by J. Taylor and L.K. Little, (Chicago: University Press, 1968), 146.

26 "Dans une théologie qui, non seulement par ses bases, mais par ses visées et ses techniques, est encore une méditation de la *pagina sacra*. . . . En plein XIIIe siècle, la Bible servit encore de base textuelle à l'enseignement de la théologie, la *lectio* était en fait de plus en plus cernée par les *quaestiones*" (Chenu, *Théologie au douxième siècle,* 210).

27 "Cum Magistro deficit certitudo rationis, recurrit ad auctoritatis certitudinem sacrae Scripturae, quae excedit omnem certitudinem rationis" *I Sent.* prooem., q. 2, ad 4 (I, 11b).

28 "Quod credimus debemus auctoritati, et quod intelligimus, rationi" (St. Augustine, *De utilit. cred.* XI, 25 [*PL* 42, 83; *CSEL* 25, 32]). This saying is quoted by Bonaventure in: *I Sent.* prooem., q. 2, ad 4 (I, 11b); Ibid., d. 37, p. 1, dub. 4 (I, 650b); *II Sent.* d. 23, a. 2, q. 3, concl. (II, 545a); *III Sent.* d. 23, a. 2, q. 2, con. 2 (III, 490b); Ibid., d. 24, a. 2, q. 2, fund. 3 (III, 520a); Ibid., d. 24, dub. 3, concl. (III, 530b); *IV Sent.* d. 10, p. 2, a. 2, q. 1, ad 2 (IV, 234b); *Christus mag.* 2 (V, 568a); *Brev.* 1, 1, 4 (V, 210b); *Coll. Jn.* prooem., q. 2, resp. (VI, 243b).

there any other way of discovering this truth besides the authority of faith and the efforts of human reason? Does the actual experience of attaining personal holiness through theology afford a knowledge of this truth?[29]

Before entering upon the possibility of personal experience as a source of our knowledge about spiritual things, it must be pointed out that the maxim of St. Augustine does not separate totally the realm of faith and the realm of reason. His statement does not mean that whatever is believed cannot be understood, nor that what is understood can no longer be in some way the object of faith. What it means is that whatever we believe, insofar as it is an object of faith, receives its ultimate certitude from authority. Whereas what we understand, insofar as it is an object of rational argument, receives its certitude from human reason. In theology, however, human reason, elevated by faith and aided by the gifts of the Holy Spirit, is rendered capable of a better understanding of the object of faith, but its certitude is based principally on divine authority and only secondarily on human reason.[30]

From the above it becomes clear that although reason has a role in making the object of faith intelligible, it must be subordinated to the life of faith. For Bonaventure, the merit of faith is lost when our assent to divine truth depends more on reason than on the authority of faith. When this happens it is usually "because the violence of reason dominates in the soul of a man."[31]

e) *Faith and reason*

In this brief overview of Bonaventure's definitions of theology, we are faced immediately with the unavoidable conclusion that in theology, reason never works in isolation. Not only is reason subordinated to the truths of Sacred Scripture, but whether it is aware of it or not, grace, in the form of a *habitus*, is needed in order to adequately understand those truths.

---

29 That experience is a source for theology has been the object of numerous studies in the last forty years. See: J. Mouroux, *L'expérience chrétienne: Introduction à une théologie* (Paris: Aubier, 1954); J.A. Paredes, "Teología y experiencia," *V V* 155 (1981): 173–89.

30 "Et quod obiicitur, quod credibile est supra rationem; verum est, supra rationem quantum ad scientiam acquisitam, sed non supra rationem elevatam per fidem et per donum scientiae et intellectus. Fides enim elevat ad assentiendum; scientia et intellectus elevant ad ea quae credita sunt intelligendum" *I Sent.* prooem., q. 2, ad 5 (I, 11b).

31 "Quod obiicitur, quod non convenit fini, quia evacuat meritum; dicendum, quod, quando assentitur propter se rationi, tunc aufertur locus fidei, quia in anima hominis dominatur violentia rationis. Sed quando fides non assentit propter rationem, sed propter amorem eius cui assentit, desiderat habere rationes: tunc non evacuat ratio humana meritum, sed auget solatium" (Ibid., ad 6 [I, 11b]).

For some, this prospect may seem to take us immediately outside the realm of theology, into the realm of mystery, and therefore be territory prohibited to human reason.[32] We are touching here the very concept of theology, which for many people is principally speculative. Some would have us believe that by leaving the realm of the purely rational, theology becomes no longer possible.[33] For Bonaventure, however, theology's proper object is God and all that originates from Him.[34] Nothing, therefore, is foreign to theology, and at the same time mystery permeates all its subject matter, since theology establishes a connection, or a 'ladder', between heavenly and earthly realities.[35] In fact, it would seem for Bonaventure, that theology not only is at home in the realm of mystery, but without mystery as its object theology has no utility above philosophy.[36] "The light of philosophy is great to the eyes of the world; yet it is small compared with the light of Christian knowledge."[37]

At the outset, we must observe that for Saint Bonaventure the truth about God "is infinitely greater than any created truth, and brighter than the light of our intellect" and therefore "one must believe not only what is

---

32 "Haec sapientia abscondita est in mysterio. Sed quomodo? Si in cor hominis non ascendit, quomodo comprehendetur, cum sit nulliformis? —Nota, quod hic est status sapientiae christianae, unde cum Dionysius . . ." *Hex.* 2, 29 (V, 341a).

33 Chenu deals with the encroaching speculative trends in theology in the latter part of the thirteenth century, holding to the belief that theology is a wisdom, not a science. The mystery of theology must not be subjected "to an irresponsible scientism, preserving a free and close relationship with faith even while pursuing the most rigorous investigations" (Chenu, *Twelfth Century*, 237).

34 "Nam subiectum, ad quod omnia reducuntur ut ad principium, est ipse Deus. . . . Subiectum quoque, ad quod omnia reducuntur sicut ad totum universale. . . . Possumus et unico vocabulo nominare; et sic est credibile, prout tamen credibile transit in rationem intelligibilis, et hoc per additionem rationes" *I Sent.* prooem., q. 1, concl. (I, 7b).

35 "Sed theologia, tanquam scientia supra fidem fundata et per Spiritum sanctum revelata, agit et de eis quae spectant ad gratiam et gloriam et etiam ad Sapientiam aeternam. Unde ipsa, substernens sibi philosophicam cognitionem et assumens de naturis rerum, quantum sibi opus est ad fabricandum speculum, per quod fiat repraesentatio divinorum, quasi scalam erigit, quae in sui infimo tangit terram, sed in suo cacumine tangit caelum" *Brev.* prol., 3 (V, 205a); cf. *Itin.* 4, 2 (V, 306a–b) and ibid., 7, 1 (V, 312a–b).

36 Theology is beyond philosophy precisely because it participates in a light that is inaccessible to us, since we are human and have eyes like bats: "Ultra scientiam philosophicam dedit nobis Deus scientiam theologicam, quae est veritatis credibilis notitia pia: quia lux eterna, scilicet Deus, est lux inaccessibilis nobis, quamdiu sumus mortales et habemus oculos vespertilionis" *De donis* 4, 13 (V, 476a).

37 "Claritas scientiae philosophicae est magna secundum opinionem hominum mundialium, parva tamen est in comparatione ad claritatem scientiae christianae" (Ibid., 4, 3 [V, 474a]); cf. Ibid., 4, 12 (V, 475b).

accessible to reason, but even what exceeds reason and contradicts sense experience."[38]

This does not mean reason lacks a role in theology. Bonaventure emphasizes reason's important role in theology, precisely when explaining its definition according to the formal cause.[39] But this role is subordinated to the authority of faith. Thus, although theology is similar to Sacred Scripture, theology is subordinated to Scripture as reason is to the authority of faith.[40] Reason *alone* is incapable of making the object of belief understandable. But, again, reason elevated by faith and the gifts of the Holy Spirit is rendered apt to undertake such a task.[41] And that task is simply *fides quaerens intellectum*, to use the expression of Saint Anselm.[42]

As Saint Bonaventure gives the definitions of theology, particularly at the beginning of his more speculative works, we are made aware immediately that theology inextricably is bound up with the life of grace and the gifts of the Holy Spirit, particularly the gift of wisdom. Although at first sight this might appear to some as an unfair introduction of elements

---

38 "Veritas primi principii in infinitum maior est omni veritate creata et luminosior omni lumine intellectus nostri. . . . Ac per hoc, quod non solum credat quae sunt secundum rationem, verum etiam quae sunt supra rationem et contra sensuum experientiam" *Brev.* 5, 7, 4 (V, 260b).

39 "Modus perscrutatorius convenit huic doctrinae. . . . Modus enim ratiocinativus sive inquisitivus valet ad fidei promotionem" *I Sent.* prooem., q. 2, concl. (I, 10b).

40 St. Bonaventure's subordination of theology to Scripture has gratified modern scholars who, especially since Vatican Council II, have restored to Scripture and the literal sense their primary place. W. Hellmann points out the place the literal sense has in Bonaventure's works: "Modern Scripture studies through the development of hermeneutics stress the objective literal sense. As indicated above, the literal sense is also seen by Bonaventure to be important. Unless one works to the fullest of his capacity in understanding the literal sense, 'quid dicitur per nomen', he can never come to the understanding of the spiritual sense. Thus to arrive at a spiritual understanding man must use his capacity, but this is not in itself sufficient. In the last analysis it is the Spirit who leads us to the internal spiritual sense: '. . . quia Spiritus sanctus non dat spiritualem . . . intelligentiae' (*Hex.* 19, 8 [V, 421b])" ("Scripture: the dawn of contemplation as found in the Collationes in Hexaëmeron" in: *San Bonaventura Maestro di vita francescana e di sapienza cristiana* [hereafter *SBM*] Atti del Congresso Int. per il VII Centenario di S. Bonaventura, ed. A. Pompei, 3 vols., [Roma: Pont.Fac.Teol. "San Bonaventura", 1976]: 569).

41 "Ad illud quod obiicitur, quod omne, quod creditur, aut creditur ex ratione, aut praeter rationem; dicendum, quod credere aliquid ex ratione est dupliciter: vel ex ratione mera, vel ex ratione adiuta. Quamvis ergo Deum esse trinum non sit credibile ex ratione mera, est tamen credibile ex ratione adiuta per gratiam et lucem desuper infusam. Et quod sic est credibile non irrationabiliter creditur, quia gratia et lux desuper infusa potius rationem dirigit, quam pervertat" *Myst. Trin.* q. 1, a. 2, ad 3 (V, 57a).

42 "For Bonaventure, the *fides quaerens intellectum* has an absolute value. He is philosophizing, but within the domain of faith. His thoughts, like Anselm's, are those of a believer: faith stands at the head of his search" (Bougerol, *Introduction to Bonaventure*, 37); "Historians admit that the acceptance of Anselm was due to Alexander of Hales, for whom *fides quaerens intellectum* is the definition and foundation of scholastic theology" (Ibid., 35).

quite uncontrollable and foreign to human reason—grace and the spiritual gifts—it is quite consistent with Bonaventure's overall view of human reality. Except through sin, human reality as it is lived concretely does not shield our reason from the influence of grace. Saint Bonaventure always considers man in the concrete circumstances, that is, as redeemed by Christ, and thus under the constant influence of the supernatural order of grace. Grace has become so much a part of man's reality, that it serves little or no purpose after the Incarnation to consider man in the abstract, if by "abstract" we mean isolated from any influence flowing from the dynamic principle of divine life in his soul. In the case of *homo theologicus*, the specific influence of grace is that exercised through the «habitus» of wisdom.

Therefore, we must return to the definition of theology given by Bonaventure and, by focusing as closely as possible upon the role of wisdom, try to determine what this gift of the Holy Spirit brings to the study of theology.

f) *Sapiential theology*

Returning to the definition of theology classified as its final cause, we see how Bonaventure investigates in Question 3 of the preface to his *Commentary* to determine whether theology is "a grace of contemplation or a rule of action."[43] If it is the former, he observes, it is a speculative science; if the latter, it is a practical science. Bonaventure then steers a middle course by saying that theology is neither entirely speculative nor entirely practical, but embraces both these aspects and requires another habit that is midway between the speculative and the practical. This new habit is wisdom and in some way pertains to the will, to the affective part of man (*natus extendi ad affectum*). The result is that theology includes both aims, contemplation and becoming holy, but principally that of becoming holy (*principaliter tamen ut boni fiamus*). He points out that this wisdom is "both knowledge and love at the same time" (*sapientia, quae simul dicit cognitionem et affectum*).[44]

In support of this definition Bonaventure immediately points out that the knowledge most specific to theology, that Christ died for our sins,

---

43 "Si consideremus intellectum in se, sic est proprie speculativus et perficitur ab habitu, qui est contemplationis gratia, qui dicitur scientia speculativa. Si autem consideremus ipsum ut natum extendi ad opus, sic perficitur ab habitu, qui est ut boni fiamus; et hic est scientia practica sive moralis" *I Sent.* prooem., q. 3, concl. (I, 13a).

44 "Si autem medio modo consideretur ut natus extendi ad affectum, sic perficitur ab habitu medio inter pure speculativum et practicum, qui complectitur utrumque; et hic habitus dicitur sapientia,

would move anyone to love, unless he or she is a hardened sinner. Therefore, the kind of knowledge specific to theology, whose formal cause is to help our faith, cannot be something purely conceptual. Although faith resides in the intellect (*fides sic est in intellectu*), its purpose is to move us to love (*nata sit movere affectum*). This power upon the will is according to the very nature of the knowledge of faith (*quantum est de sui ratione*).[45]

Already we can see here a certain preference for the will, which is typical of Franciscan theology.[46] This is not to be taken as a rejection of the intellect, but rather as a choice about where the emphasis is to be placed. "Haec doctrina," Bonaventure affirms at the beginning of the *Breviloquium*, "est, ut boni fiamus et salvemur; et hoc non fit per nudam considerationem sed potius per inclinationem voluntatis."[47] What interests me at this point is not the preference of will over intellect, but the pervading influence of grace, in the form of an affective habit, wisdom. If theology is a habit, and this habit is received from God as a gift, as something above and beyond our own capacities, we need to turn eventually to an explanation of Bonaventure's concept of grace as a transforming element introduced into human nature. This is necessary because Bonaventure's definition of theology seems to presuppose, or at least foreshadow, some knowledge on our part about the *habitus* of wisdom. And although Bonaventure does not state openly in the particular passages cited above that he is speaking of wisdom as identical to the gift of the Holy Spirit, he does leave some hint of this in the only scriptural citation he uses, following the example of Alexander of Hales, to back up the choice of the word "wisdom" as applied

---

quae simul dicit cognitionem et affectum. . . . Unde hic est contemplationis gratia, et ut boni fiamus, principaliter tamen ut boni fiamus" (Ibid., [I, 13a–b]).

45 "Nam cognitio haec iuvat fidem, et fides sic est in intellectu, ut, quantum est de sui ratione, nata sit movere affectum. Et hoc patet. Nam haec cognitio: quod Christus pro nobis mortuus est, et consimiles, nisi sit homo peccator et durus, movet ad amorem" (Ibid., [I, 13b]).

46 "La spiritualité franciscaine, par suite de ses rapports avec la philosophie volontariste de l'École Séraphique, exalte beaucoup l'activité de l'âme, sa coopération aux motions surnaturelles de la grâce" (E. Longpré, "La théologie mystique de S. Bonaventure" *AFH* 14 [1921]: 54). Works dealing with this aspect of the Franciscan School are: E. Bettoni, *Visione francesanca della vita* (Brescia: Morcelliana, 1948) chap. I: "Il Volontarismo Francescano"; F. Sirovic, *Der Begriff «Affectus» und die Willenslehre beim hl. Bonaventura: Eine analytisch synthetische Untersuchung* (Mödling bei Wein: Druckerei St. Gabriel, 1965); C. O'Donnel, "Voluntarism in Franciscan Philosophy" *FS* 2 (1942): 397–410; E. Rivera de Ventosa, "El voluntarismo psicológico de San Buenaventura," *EsF* 52 (1951): 289–315; L. Veuthey, "Il Volontarismo di San Bonaventura," *IncBonav* 7 (1972): 81–92.

47 *Brev.* prol., 5, 2 (V, 206b). After Bonaventure, Duns Scotus will take this preference a little further. For him, we do not love a thing because we know it; rather, we know it because we first love it (*Reportata Parisiensa* IV, d. 49, q. 2, n. 11–12).

to this habit.[48] We only find by examining further into his works, particularly in the same *Commentary to the Sentences* (Book III) and in other works in which wisdom is specially treated, that this wisdom is, in fact, none other than the gift of the Holy Spirit.[49]

Such being the case, we are already in a realm proper to the spiritual life which is the suitable context for speaking of the gifts of the Holy Spirit. Since for Saint Bonaventure spiritual theology and speculative theology were not watertight areas of study as they appear today, he was comfortable dealing with the spiritual life, both within his more speculative works as well as in works of a more pastoral nature. While he recognized the threefold division of theology (symbolic, speculative, and mystical), which he received from the tradition flowing from Dionysius the Areopagite, he looked upon them more as different modes of approaching the same truth, not as separate disciplines.[50] Thus, the very fact of seeing theology, not only under the influence of divine illumination, but as an affective habit, a gift of the Holy Spirit, did not constitute an invasion on the part of spiritual theology into alien territory. Is it possible for us to see speculative theology as unconnected, prohibited terrain, to spirituality?[51]

In order for us to understand more adequately why Bonaventure defined theology as a *habitus* of wisdom, we are obliged at this point to enter into the realm of spirituality as he saw it. Not to do so might condemn our study to the abstract level wherein definitions have value only to the degree of their close dependence on a priori premises. Furthermore, the insertion of the term "wisdom" in the definitions we have just studied does not seem to arrive as a strictly logical conclusion. The statement that

---

48 "*Sapientia enim doctrinae est secundum nomen eius,* Ecclesiastici 6, 23" *I Sent.* prooem., q. 3, concl. (I, 13b). This is the same scriptural reference he uses when defining wisdom as the gift of the Holy Spirit: *III Sent.* d. 35, au., q. 1, concl. (III, 774b). Cf. Alex. Hales, *Summa Theologica*, Liber Primus, Tract. Introd., q. 1, c. 1, solutio (t. I, p. 2).

49 *III Sent.* d. 35, au., q. 1, (III, 772–75); *Brev.* 5, 5 (V, 257a–258a); *Hex.* passim.

50 "Scientiam veritatis edocuit [Verbum incarnatum] secundum triplicem modum theologiae, scilicet symbolicae, propriae et mysticae, ut per symbolicam recte utamur sensibilibus, per propriam recte utamur intelligibilibus, per mysticam rapiamur ad supermentales excessus" *Itin.* 1, 7 (V, 298a); cf. *Hex.* 20, 21 (V, 429a). See C. Bernard, "Les formes de la théologie chez Denys l'Aréopagite," *GR* 59 (1978): 39–69. In our times, some encouraging signs have appeared. Commenting on Karl Rahner, G.A. McCool states: "For Rahner, like Bonaventure and the great medievals, pastoral and spiritual theology are not something *added on to* a systematic theology with which they have little or no connection. Spiritual and pastoral theology are moments of the same *unified theological activity* from which systematic theology arises" ("Introduction," *A Rahner Reader*, ed. *Idem*, [New York: The Seabury Press, 1975], xxv).

51 The medieval origins of the split between theology and mysticism are dealt with by F. Vandenbroucke, "Le divorce entre théologie et mystique: Ses origines," *NRT* 82 (1950): 372–89.

theology is a habit that is called wisdom, evidently can reach full comprehension only through an inquiry into Bonaventure's teachings about the habits in general, and specifically about the habit of wisdom. Such an inquiry would take us fully into the area of Bonaventure's teachings on the spiritual life. And even though these teachings are not compartmentalized in his works, but form a harmonious and integrated whole in his very unified system, we need to glean from his works some concept of the spiritual organism in order to clarify those statements made at the outset of his more speculative works which seem to connect theology and spirituality.

2. The spiritual life for Saint Bonaventure

a) *Wisdom and holiness*

Saint Bonaventure makes it clear that no one can have wisdom without first becoming holy. "There is no sure passage from science to wisdom; a medium must be provided, namely holiness."[52] "Holiness is the immediate disposition for wisdom."[53] "Without holiness a man is not wise."[54] The whole aim of the spiritual life for Saint Bonaventure, then, is the quest for wisdom, because it is the highest good: "If [wisdom] is the highest good, it must be loved in the highest way; if it is all good, it must be loved universally and above all things."[55]

Paradoxically, wisdom is not only the aim of the spiritual life but is as well a condition for salvation: "Salvation only comes through wisdom,"[56] and a means toward union with God: "We are made perfect by our union with the sovereign good, which is the supreme being: this union is operated by the gift of wisdom."[57]

One possible way to reconcile these two statements is that salvation and sanctity ultimately be understood as the same thing. As we shall see, when studying the gifts of the Holy Spirit, there are difficulties involved

---

52 "Non est ergo securus transitus a scientia ad sapientiam; oportet ergo medium ponere, scilicet sanctitatem" *Hex.* 19, 3 (V, 420b).

53 "Sanctitas immediata dispositio est ad sapientiam" (Ibid., 2, 6 [V, 337a]).

54 "Sine sanctitate non est homo sapiens" (Ibid., [V, 337a]).

55 "Si enim summum bonum est, summe amanda est; si autem omne bonum est, universaliter appetenda est et super omnia" (Ibid., [V, 337b]).

56 "Salus enim non est nisi per sapientiam" (Ibid., 14, 7 [V, 394b]).

57 "Perfici autem habemus per accessum ad summum, quod consistit in uno, et hoc per donum sapientiae" *Brev.* 5, 5, 8 (V, 258a).

in this interpretation.[58]   For now, it appears that wisdom is not only an end, but a means placed at our disposal by God, in order to reach salvation\sanctity.   And by implication all persons are called to attain holiness.

b) *Universal call to holiness*

Knowing the aim of the spiritual life makes it easier to understand its various demands as well as the forms which divine assistance will assume along the journey toward holiness. We observe that the itinerarium toward and into God eventually reaches the 'transitus' which is passed either in this life through mystical death with the Crucified seraph, or by death in the strict sense of the word. All eventually must pass through this transformation, either mystically or materially. Thus, although all Christians are called to this union with God, the fact that only few reach it in this life, does not contradict Bonaventure's open invitation to all: *"Qui igitur vult in Deum ascendere..."*[59] Bonaventure recognizes that not many arrive at true wisdom in this life, and he attributes this to their unwillingness to travel on the road of wisdom.[60] Strangely enough, then, although sanctity depends on God, it is there for anyone who would have it.[61]

All are called to sanctity. However, this kind of sanctity is not simply being a good Christian. As is evident from the terminus reached in the *Itinerarium mentis in Deum*, the *excessus mentales* are a normal passageway to the state of perfection. A mystical elevation is necessary for us to reach the final goal.

At this point, not a few persons may object that this high expectation clearly appears to be elitist. Bonaventure's system might seem to apply only to the great Saints, and have very little or no utility for the common run. In order to remove possible misgivings at the outset, let us listen to him preaching to a group of persons whom we may sense as being made up of "the man on the street":

---

58   See Chapter VI, subdivisions: 1. "The supernatural habits" and 2. "A gift is freely given."

59   *Itin.* 1, 8 (V, 298a).

60   "Per istam autem viam sapientiae pauci vadunt, et ideo pauci perveniunt ad veram sapientiam" *Hex.* 2, 3 (V, 337a). "Si homo non velit ad istam perfectionem pervenire, magnum tamen est quod lex christiana habet tales" *De Sabbato sancto, Sermo I* (IX, 269b).

61   "Hanc autem rectitudinem non habet quis nolens, sed volens" *III Sent.* d. 23, a. 1, q. 1, concl. (III, 471a).

Now, you ought not despair, simple folk, when you have heard these things, because the simple person cannot have these things. But you will be able to have them later on. The only thing we do is talking, but when a holy soul has these six [degrees], it is then disposed to see glory. This is the repose that we should seek. . . If you wish to be a tabernacle of wisdom, you should strive to have these dispositions. And if a person does not wish to arrive at this perfection, it is nevertheless a great matter that the Christian dispensation includes such persons. All others, apart from Christians, are dry of this grace.[62]

All are called, but only few become truly holy. The spiritual life is a road open for everyone to travel, but not everyone wishes to walk by this road. Thus, the so-called dizzying heights of spirituality are an ordinary grace, a normal development of the grace of baptism, even though historically speaking we find it uncommon for souls to desire and to persevere in this ordinary way to union with God. We are faced with the conclusion that what is *ordinary* and *normal* is not always, nor necessarily, *common*. But at least a distinction between these two concepts, which very often are confused, will prevent us from seeing Bonaventure's spirituality as anything more demanding than what the Gospel expects from all Christians.[63]

c) *Continuity of the spiritual life*

The universal call to holiness is a consequence of faith as the radical beginning of all spiritual life. The theological virtue of faith received through the grace of baptism is the foundation for the entire spiritual edifice (*totius spiritualis aedificii fundamentum*).[64] Everything after faith is simply the development and growth of this seed like a tree producing branches, leaves and finally fruit.[65] Thus, faith continues to be, during all the spiritual

---

62 "Modo, non debetis desperare, vos simplices, quando audistis ista, quia simplex non potest ista habere, sed poteritis postea habere. Nos non facimus nisi dicere, sed quando anima sancta habet ista sex, tunc disponitur ad videndum gloriam. Haec est requies quam quaerere debemus. . . . Si vis esse tabernaculum sapientiae, studeas istas dispositiones habere; et si homo non velit ad istam perfectionem pervenire, magnum tamen est quod lex christiana habet tales. Omnes alii a christianis sunt sicci ab ista gratia" *De Sabbato Sancto, Sermo 1* (IX, 269b).

63 Mt. 5:20; 7:13–14; 19:22; 21:31; 22:14.

64 *II Sent.* d. 43, a. 2, q. 1, ad 5 (II, 988b); cf. *III Sent.* d. 23, a. 1, q. 1 (III, 470–472); *IV Sent.* d. 3, p. 1, a. 1, q. 3 (IV, 68a–70b); *Hex.* 1, 33 (V, 334b); Ibid., 2, 14 (V, 338b); Ibid., 23, 16 (V, 447b); *In Purific. B.V. Mariae, Sermo II* (IX, 642b–643a); *De S. Dominico, Sermo* (IX, 563b).

65 "Primum est, qualiter gratia una ramificatur in habitus virtutum; secundum est, qualiter ramificatur in habitus donorum; tertium est, qualiter ramificatur in habitus beatitudinum" *Brev.* 5, 4, 1 (V, 256a); "Licet una sit gratia vivificans, ramificari tamen necessario habet in varios habitus propter varias operationes" (Ibid., 5, 4, 3 [V, 256a]).

life as well as in the highest mystical degrees, a dynamic principle: "For faith, that has hope and charity with good works, heals the soul, and once it has been healed, cleanses and lifts it up and makes it into the likeness of God."[66] Thus faith is not only the starting point of the spiritual life, but all virtue ultimately is based on faith, and Saint Bonaventure does not hesitate to attribute the heights of wisdom as proportionate to the degree of faith:[67]

> For while we are exiled from the Lord, faith is, as regards every supernatural illumination, the foundation that supports us, the lamp that guides us, and the door that leads us in. It is by faith, moreover, that the wisdom given us by God must be measured.[68]

The unbroken continuity of the spiritual life from its humble beginnings to its fullest development indicates that there is an intrinsic unity among any number of stages in which one may wish to divide the spiritual life. This accounts for the fact that Saint Bonaventure resists seeing such stages as chronologically successive. He speaks of three «ways» to God: purgative, illuminative, unitive.[69] However, in some fashion, each of the three is present alongside and within the other two ways. We always are being purified, enlightened, and united more intensely with God. A point does not arrive at which the baptismal grace stops providing for further perfection.[70]

Bonaventure's outlook prevents us from seeing the spiritual life, even in its highest expressions, as leaving the realm of what is ordinary in

---

66 "Fides enim, habens spem et caritatem cum operibus, sanat animam et ipsam sanatam purificat, elevat et deiformat" *Hex.* 7, 13 (V, 367b). Josef Ratzinger also perceives this in Bonaventure: "The stages of faith are also the stages of mysticism" (*The Theology of History in St. Bonaventure,* trans. Zachary Hayes [Chicago: Franciscan Herald Press, 1971], 68).

67 "Fundamentum autem virtutis fides est" (Ibid., 1, 33 [V, 334b]).

68 "Est enim ipsa fides omnium supernaturalium illuminationum, quamdiu peregrinamur a Domino, et fundamentum stabiliens et lucerna dirigens et ianua introducens; secundum cuius etiam mensuram necesse est mensurari sapientiam nobis divinitus datam" *Brev.* prol. (V, 201b).

69 *Trip. via* (VIII, 12a).

70 Nevertheless, ". . . necesse est gratiam et virtutes gratuitas differre per essentiam" *II Sent.* d. 27, a. 1, q. 2, con. 6 (II, 657a); "Concedendum est igitur, sicut rationes plures ostendunt, quod habitus gratiae gratum facientis et virtutum habitus sunt diversi" (Ibid., concl. [II, 658a]). This is why J.F. Bonnefoy, who recognizes the utility of the "branch" theory, also warns against pushing it too far, since that would eventually distort an important nuance in Bonaventure's thinking. Even though the Seraphic Doctor uses this image, especially in the *Breviloquium* (5, 4), it is nonetheless true that he maintains the difference between grace acting directly upon the substance of the soul and that acting upon the natural powers of the soul: "La comparaison du tronc et des rameaux a néanmoins ses avantages. Elle montre fort bien comment toute gratuité dérive d'une seule et même grâce. C'est la même sève en effet qui circule dans le tronc de l'arbre et dans ses branches. Mais, à vouloir pousser

the development of grace. For the highest degree of sanctity no extraordinary graces are needed. This clearly is evident when Bonaventure defines the four ways of knowing God (i.e., by faith, contemplation, apparition, and vision).[71] Knowing God by means of contemplation is the proper work of wisdom.[72] Contemplation is called an "excellent" grace, whereas knowing Him through apparition is called a "special" grace.[73] Again, this statement about contemplation does not contradict Bonaventure's teaching that wisdom is the "highest good" and thus should "be desired above all things."[74] Nowhere do we find Saint Bonaventure teaching that wisdom is reserved for a select few nor even implying that such a grace is to be classified apart, for example, with charismatic graces such as visions or rapture. The latter graces are "extras" and do not belong to a normal development of the life of baptismal grace. As such, these special graces, when God so desires, are added on to the spiritual life, but as something extraneous to its internal dynamism. Therefore, the extraordinary graces do not effect directly the work of personal sanctification which is the proper role of sanctifying grace. Saint Bonaventure, far from connecting sanctity with extraordinary gifts (e.g., prophecy, miraculous healing, and other charismatic privileges), sees sanctity as meant for everyone. This is why it is to be longed for with ardent desires.

Sanctifying grace received at baptism branches out through its normal growth. This growth takes place only through the cooperation of the free will, giving rise to the virtues, the gifts, and the beatitudes. Growth is the result of the combined work of grace's action upon the natural faculties and the will's response.[75] Saint Bonaventure links up this three-level

---

plus loin le parallélisme, on tomberait dans l'erreur" (J.F. Bonnefoy, *Le Saint Esprit et ses dons selon S. Bonaventure* [Paris: J. Vrin, 1929], 77). The error would be in direct opposition to Bonaventure's statement: "Virtutes enim non dicuntur esse virtutes ipsius gratiae, per quas ipsa gratia operetur, sicut anima operatur per suas potentias" *III Sent.* d. 23, a. 2, q. 5, ad 6 (III, 500a).

71 "Nota quod quadruplex est modus cognoscendi Deum, scilicet per fidem, per contemplationem, per apparitionem et per apertam visionem. Et primum est gratiae communis, secundum est gratiae excellentis, tertium gratiae specialis et quartum gratiae consummantis" *II Sent.* d. 23, a. 2, q. 3 (II, 545a); ibid., ad 6 (II, 546a).

72 "Qui igitur vult in Deum ascendere necesse est, ut . . .naturales potentias supradictas exerceat. . .ad sapientiam perficientem et hoc in contemplatione" *Itin.* 1, 8 (V, 298a).

73 *II Sent.* d. 23, a. 2, q. 3 concl. (II, 545a); ibid., ad 6 (II, 546a).

74 *Hex.* 2, 6 (V, 337b).

75 *Brev.* 5, 4–6 (V, 256a–260a); "Secundum quod ad actus diversarum virtutum liberum arbitrium secundum plus et minus cooperatur, secundum hoc plus et minus facilitatur, licet etiam habitus virtutum quantum est de se, adaequentur" *III Sent.* d. 36, au., q. 5, ad 6 (III, 804b).

ramification with the purgative, illuminative and perfective or unitive ways.[76] The virtues characterize the purgative way, the gifts the illuminative way, and the beatitudes the unitive way. Nevertheless, one does not progress along these ways by passing from one level to the next, nor by superseding or even integrating a former way in order to establish oneself in a more advanced stage. Although the work of the virtues is more intense in the purgative way, this does not imply that the gifts and the beatitudes do not exist and exert their influence at the same time.[77] Although the gifts are more prevalent in the illuminative way, these gifts of the Holy Spirit are operative, although less perfectly, in the purgative way; in the unitive way they do not cease to operate, rather, their operation is at its consummate best.[78]

3. Spiritual life and theology

a) *Contemplation and theology*

The spiritual life, for Bonaventure, reaches its normal fulfillment in mystical union achieved through the operation of the gift of wisdom, the most excellent of the seven gifts of the Holy Spirit.[79] The gift of wisdom achieves this goal of uniting the soul with Christ first by producing and then perfecting infused contemplation in the soul.[80] Mystical union normally comes as the flowering of the grace of contemplation.[81] From what has been said above about the intrinsic unity between the levels of spiritual progress, it becomes evident that contemplation is a normal unfolding of

---

76 "Et quoniam in primis actibus potentiae rectificantur, in secundis expediuntur et in tertiis et ultimis perficiuntur, hinc est quod habitus virtutum sunt ad agendum recte, habitus donorum ad agendum expedite, habitus beatitudinum ad agendum sive patiendum perfecte" *III Sent.* d. 34, p. 1, a. 1, q. 1, concl. (III, 737a); cf. Ibid., ad 5 (III, 738b–739b); cf. *Brev.* 5, 4, 3 (V, 256a–b).

77 Jordan Aumann has explained it thus: "Saint Bonaventure canonized the classification of the spiritual life into the three ways and uses the same terminology as pseudo-Dionysius: purgative, illuminative and unitive or perfect. He does not see them as progressive and separate stages, however, although at a given time one or another will predominate" (*Christian Spirituality in the Catholic Tradition* [London: Sheed & Ward, 1985], 140).

78 This is why Bonaventure defends the existence of the gifts even in glory (*III Sent.* d. 34, p. 1, a. 2, q. 3 [III, 749a–751b]).

79 *III Sent.* d. 34, p. 1, a. 2, q. 2 (III, 739a–741b).

80 "Ad sapientiam perficientem et hoc in contemplatione" *Itin.* 1, 8 (V, 298a).

81 "In cuius consideratione statim visum est mihi, quod visio illa praetenderet ipsius patris suspensionem in contemplando et viam, per quam pervenitur ad eam" (Ibid., prol. 2 [V, 295b]).

sanctifying grace.[82] Likewise, it is correct to say that all Christians, since they receive the gift of wisdom from the first moment of sanctifying grace, are eligible to receive contemplation.[83] This means that the experience of contemplation, produced by the gift of wisdom, is a normal Christian experience and consonant with the universal call to the heights of holiness.[84] "All rational beings, however little they may partake of the light, are intended to grasp God through knowledge and love."[85]

The fact that Saint Bonaventure considers infused contemplation to be produced by the gift of wisdom already may suggest to us what kind of influence the spiritual life has on theology. This influence would be a contemplative movement exerted on the soul of the theologian, giving him a spiritual outlook unaccountable to pure reason.

As we proceed, it already must be noticeable how mystical union, contemplation and wisdom, are connected to each other as effects originating from causes. Mystical union proceeds from contemplation, and contemplation in its turn is effected by the gift of wisdom.

My purpose in emphasizing such spiritual activity as normal to the life of Christian holiness will become more crucial when I try to clarify the relationship between the spiritual life and theology. In our search to determine what this relationship concretely implies, the question invariably arises

---

82 "Sicut Deus sex diebus perfecit universum mundum et in septimo requievit, sic minor mundus sex gradibus illuminationum sibi succedentium ad quietem contemplationis ordinatissime perducatur" (Ibid., 1, 5 [V, 297b]).

83 "Cum autem anima deiformis facta est, statim intrat in eam Sapientia" *Hex.* 2, 6 (V, 337a).

84 Contemplation would seem to be the *only* way to reach mystical union with God. For example: "Quasi dicat, quod per contemplationem ingredi non potest Ierusalem supernam, nisi per sanguinem Agni intret tanquam per portam. Non enim dispositus est aliquo modo ad contemplationes divinas, quae ad mentales ducunt excessus, nisi cum Daniele sit *vir desideriorum"* (*Itin.* prol. 3 [V, 296a]). But even though this is the Seraphic Doctor's teaching, the notion itself of contemplation is not univocal. He speaks of perfect and imperfect contemplation. Imperfect contemplation, through the gift of understanding and the beatitude of purity of heart, is one of the ways to attain perfect contemplation. He also teaches that fervor and happiness are two other ways of obtaining perfect contemplation. How many ways are there of living the contemplative life? How often nowadays we hear the expression 'contemplative in action'. On the other hand, spiritual writers, Bonaventure included, often speak in a parenetic style of ways to reach holiness. We are reminded of St. Teresa of Avila who, after many years of exhorting souls to follow the path of contemplative prayer, was surprised to meet a gentleman who for fifteen years had never had a free moment to practice such methods of prayer and yet of whom she firmly believed he had arrived at the same liberty of spirit possessed by the perfect. She adds that she has actually met many others like him. This led to her famous utterance that God also walks "entre los pucheros" (*Libro de las Fundaciones*, 5, 7–8 [Madrid: B.A.C., 1967], 528).

85 "Omnis intellectus, quantumcumque parum habens de lumine, natus est per cognitionem et amorem capere Deum" *Brev.* 2, 12, 2 (V, 230a).

as to whether or not our purpose is to speak about theology as written by perfect souls, that is, by 'mystics' only.[86]

b) *Who are the theologians?*

In order to forestall the impression that I am limiting theology to the saints, two things must be kept in mind: (1) that the spiritual life is not lived only by souls in the unitive or perfective way, (2) nor is the gift of wisdom operative only in the elaboration of theology. The gifts of the Holy Spirit accompany us in the spiritual life from its beginning to end, and in no way are the exclusive domain of certain vocations or occupations (e.g., monastic life, theological study, contemplative prayer). Likewise, their operation becomes typical of, but by no means exclusive to, the illuminative way. The gifts of the Holy Spirit are habits received from the first moment of sanctifying grace.[87] These habits are received together with the habits of the infused virtues, and at no time do they replace the habits of the virtues. Rather, their purpose is to perfect the activity of the virtues.[88] The gifts are an integral part of the spiritual life, and their operation becomes more and more prevalent as one progresses along the illuminative way. Therefore, we are speaking of souls who are dedicated seriously to the spiritual life, but who need not be among the perfect, and even may be still quite distant from Christian perfection. We might say that these souls, consciously or

---

86   In this sense, the statement by F.-M. Léthel—"seuls les saints sont théologiens"—could be misunderstood (*Connaître l'amour du Christ* [Venasque: Ed. du Carmel, 1989], 3). Nevertheless, if the aim of the theologian is union with God, the statement is full of meaning. In this regard, we may recall an incident in the life of Saint Bonaventure, in which he declared that a poor old woman could love God more than a teacher of theology: "Semel frater Aegidius dixit Generali fratri Bonaventurae: 'Pater mi, multas gratias fecit vobis Deus. Nos insipientes et idiotae, qui nullam sufficientiam accepimus, quid poterimus facere, ut salvemur?' Respondit Generalis: 'Si Deus nullam gratiam daret homini, nisi quod posset eum diligere, sufficeret.' Et frater Aegidius ait: 'Potest idiota Deum tantum diligere sicut litteratos?' Respondit Generalis: 'Potest una vetula plus etiam quam magister in theologia.' Tunc frater Aegidius in fervore spiritus surrexit, vadens in hortum versus partem, quae respicit civitatem, et clamavit: 'Vetula paupercula, simplex et idiota, diligas Dominum Deum et poteris esse maior quam frater Bonaventura.' Et sic fuit raptus, immobilis per tres horas" (*Chronica XXIV Generalium*, in: *AF*, vol. III, 101; cf. A. Gemelli, *San Francesco e la sua gente poverella* [Milano: Vita e Pensiero, 1950], 192).

87   "Sicut principium productivum sua summa perfectione in dando vitam naturae non tantum dat vivere quantum ad actum primum, verum etiam quantum ad actum secundum, qui est operari; sic necesse est, quod principium reparativum vitam tribuat spiritui in esse gratuito et in quantum ad esse et quantum ad operari" *Brev.* 5, 4, 3 (V, 256a).

88   "Propter expedienda septem virtutum officia, septem debent esse Spiritus sancti dona" *Brev.* 5, 5, 5 (V, 257b); J. Bonnefoy, seeing how this statement from the *Breviloquium* has given rise to misunderstandings, emphasizes another important nuance in Bonaventure's teaching. The gifts of the Holy Spirit do not perfect the *virtues* as such, but the *natural faculties* in which the virtues act.

unconsciously, are doing their best to live the teaching of the *Itinerarium mentis in Deum.*[89] They may find themselves in any of the three ways described in this journey manual, and thus under the more or less constant influence of the gifts of the Holy Spirit.

The only persons who exclude themselves from this influence of the infused gifts of the Holy Spirit either are those who have rejected deliberately divine life through sin, or those who consciously refuse to take up the road to holiness. The first class of persons freely cuts itself off from this influence, whereas the latter class remains at least indecisive about discipleship. The only necessary condition calling for the activity of the gifts is that the soul be *advancing* in the spiritual life. This is clear from the teaching of Saint Bonaventure that affirms the gifts are needed, over and above the virtues, to succeed in rising upward to greater perfection.[90] Since the gifts do not suppose perfection but help us reach it, it is unjustifiable to attribute the influence of the gifts only to perfect souls. This is why Saint Bonaventure is found in his works to concentrate the operation of the gifts on those who are progressing in the illuminative way.

In order to understand the teaching of Saint Bonaventure about the influence spiritual life can have upon theology, I cannot insist enough on the operation of the gifts as a normal development in the spiritual life. Although to some it may appear I am belaboring my point, unless this element is made sufficiently clear at the outset we run the risk of creating a

---

Bonaventure has said: "Propria ratio sumendi sufficientiam donorum non est penes expeditionem virtutum, sed magis penes expeditionem ipsarum potentiarum in suis actibus" *III Sent.* d. 34, p. 1, a. 2, q. 1, ad 4 (III, 746b); "Isti habitus [i.e., dona] reddunt potentiam facilem et expeditam... Potentias facilitant et ad actus excellentes expediunt" *III Sent.* d. 36, au., q. 2, concl. (III, 795b); cf. *III Sent.* d. 34, p. 1, a. 1, q. 3, concl. (III, 742a–743b). "Cette erreur d'interprétation est d'autant plus grave que nous sommes ici à un point cardinal de la doctrine des dons. . . Mais notre Docteur, très conséquent avec lui-même, affirmera toujours ce qu'ils a dit dès le début, à savoir que les dons sont ordonnés à faciliter l'exercice de nos facultés" (Bonnefoy, 100).

89 "It is not difficult to place the *Itinerarium* within the system of mysticism that we find developed in *De Triplici Via.* Where would be, then, the proper place of the *Itinerarium*? It has been said that its proper place is in the perfective way, but we believe that it belongs rather to the illuminative way, reaching at the end the contemplation of the unitive way and merging with it. For throughout the six chapters of the *Itinerarium* we are concerned with six *illuminationum suspensiones* (uplifting illuminations)" (P. Boehner, "Introduction" to Vol. II of *Works of Saint Bonaventure: ItinerariumMentis in Deum* [St. Bonaventure, N.Y.: Franciscan Institute, 1990²], 22)

90 "Ad illud quod obicitur, quod habitus virtutum sufficienter ordinant animam ad Deum secundum omnem eius comparationem, dicendum quod, licet ordinent sufficienter quantum ad ea quae sunt rectitudinis et necessitatis, utpote quantum ad illos actus primos, in quibus primaria rectitudo consistit, tamen ultra hoc liberalitas benignitatis divinae providit homini et contulit habitus, per quos expediretur, non solum ad opera necessaria rectitudinis, sed etiam perfectionis et supererogationis" *III Sent.* 34, p. 1, a. 1, q. 1, ad 5 (III, 738b)

mistaken impression. This impression, to which I have already alluded, is that theology under the influence of the spiritual life becomes necessarily and exclusively the domain of a select group of persons who have reached an accomplished degree of holiness, and who perhaps constitute another kind of "parallel magisterium."

All of these reasons signal the inner cohesion existing between the various ascetic means to sanctity taken up at the beginning of the spiritual life and the mystical graces God normally grants to produce the end result, which is human transformation. Such transformation is the normal consequence of God's action and our cooperation. How many ways are there of cooperating with grace? Although theology, at least arguably, is the best way, Bonaventure would exclude no one from tasting the goodness of the Lord, which is the nectar characteristic of the wisdom needed for salvation.

c) *Grace, the root of holiness*

The next step in our inquiry is to confront a more fundamental question about Bonaventure's view of the spiritual life. If the spiritual life, as a result of the normal flowering of the seed of sanctifying grace, eventually leads to holiness, then before I fully answer the question about what influence holiness may have upon theology, we must face a more radical problem. This problem can be formulated thus: What influence does grace itself have on human nature?

Although it is true in Saint Bonaventure, as I stated above, that human nature is never studied for its own sake in the abstract, that is, as separated from its grace dimension, nevertheless, once we receive grace, we must ask what this new supernatural reality brings to our nature. I pose this question because to speak of the spiritual life without first examining the more radical subject of grace itself, is similar to studying the fruits of a tree without first considering the root, trunk and branches, from which the fruit is simply the final outcome.[91] Saint Bonaventure assigns a massive task to grace: "It is the duty of grace to re-create, to reform, to fill up with life, to illuminate, to assimilate, to unite, to lay the groundwork, to make acceptable and to raise up the human soul to God."[92] The following chapter of my study will

---

91 ". . . quod totum fit per gratuitam et condescensivam infusionem doni gratuiti" *Brev.* 5, 3, 3 (V, 255a).

92 "Gratiae est recreare, gratiae est reformare, vivificare, illuminare, assimilare, unire, stabilire, acceptum facere, sursum levare" *II Sent.* d. 26, au., q. 2, concl. (II, 635a).

be dedicated to the overall effects sanctifying grace has on the human person, whether or not this person, in the concrete, accepts the invitation to holiness.

Conclusion

In this rather lengthy overview of my inquiry into theology as spiritual life, I recognize that my search eventually must determine what influence the spiritual life may have on theology. Although the latter aim has never been absent, I have attempted first to define theology as Saint Bonaventure sees it. Second, I have given a summary view of his notion of the spiritual life. My third attempt, to determine the influence of spiritual life on theology, has led me to recognize that to proceed further such a question must be approached upon a more general footing—what influence does grace have on human nature? Chapter Two deals with this matter, the "hierarchization of the soul," a name by which Bonaventure describes the operation of grace which effects a complete restructuring of the mind. The object of my inquiry remains the same. That is, if Saint Bonaventure defines theology as the habit wisdom, and wisdom is the goal of the spiritual life, what does the spiritual life, and wisdom concretely, bring to theology which would thereby justify our calling theology a spiritual life? An explanation of the general effect of sanctifying grace on the soul will provide for us a firmer basis for entering into the more specialized question about wisdom's particular effect on theology.

Miser factus sum,
et curvatus sum usque in finem.

Ps. 37:7, Vg.

II.

THE FALL OF THE MIND AND ITS REMEDY BY HIERARCHIZATION

Approaching theology as a spiritual life is made necessary first of all by the concrete, historical conditions of human nature, and particularly the human mind, after the Fall.[1] Even while holding before the spiritual man the attractive ideals of the intellectual life, Bonaventure is unwilling to set any realism aside. Instead, the Seraphic Doctor approaches the topic of study with courage, frankly and humbly recognizing the wounds in our human intellect left through the sin of our first parents. The sight of such grave intellectual weaknesses and deep-rooted maladies does not discourage Bonaventure but rather incites him to find and apply the remedy most apt to heal the mind and insure our victorious search for truth.

For an understanding of the sickness of the human intellect and its remedy, St. Bonaventure has tapped into the vein of traditions coming before him. To describe the intellectual sickness he principally has followed St. Augustine's teaching on the effects of original sin. For the remedy, he has found Dionysius Areopagite's teaching on the hierarchical nature of creation to be a model of the way in which grace achieves a complete healing and restructuring of the mind.

1. The effects of original sin on the mind

The fallen state of humanity is not simply a given in Bonaventure's point of departure. St. Bonaventure, in the tradition of St. Augustine, is unwilling to look upon man without first taking fallen nature into account, not only globally but also particularly as it affects our thinking processes.[2]

---

1 For studies on the doctrine of sin in Bonaventure, see: M. De Wachter, *Le péché actuel selon saint Bonaventure*, (Paris: Editions Franciscaines, 1967), 25–70; M. da Caggio Montano, *Dottrina bonaventuriana sul peccato originale* (Bologna: Tip. S. Giuseppe, 1943); E. Catazzo, *De Iustitia et peccato originali iuxta S. Bonaventuram* (Vicenza: Convento S. Lucia, 1942); O. Lottin, "Les théories sur le péché originel de saint Anselme à saint Thomas d'Aquin" in *Psychologie et morale aux XIIe et XIIIe siècles,* vol. IV (Gembloux: Duculot, 1954), 220–29.

2 "This primary stage in St. Bonaventure's argument both explains the general suspicion which he seems to have thrown upon all the achievements of human reason. . . . On its way from St. Augustine

St. Augustine's teaching was conditioned by the historical context of the Pelagian controversy, leading him to go so far as to say that human nature is "wounded, hurt, damaged, destroyed" by sin's disobedience.[3] Nevertheless, when isolated statements of his are seen within the immense corpus of his works we are unjustified in taking those extreme views typical of the Jansenist and Lutheran positions.[4] It remains obvious that St. Augustine's intention was to defend the primacy of grace, and with his position the Council of Trent was able to defend itself against erroneous attitudes that attempted to find support in the same Doctor of Grace. The point Augustine emphasizes is the necessity of healing so that the will might accomplish the good it is incapable of fulfilling through obedience to the law when unaccompanied by grace.[5]

Modern theologians often tend to neglect the fact of our wounded nature or, when they recognize it, quickly pass over its important consequences in practice. St. Bonaventure however will not proceed to speak about human activities without situating his topic in the perspective of our disadvantageous historical condition.

Bonaventure speaks of a fourfold negative effect of original sin on our dispositions:

> The disease is a depravation of the affective powers. Now this is fourfold, for through its union with the body, the soul contracts weakness, ignorance, malice, and concupiscence. By means of them are infected the soul's powers to understand, to love, and to act: and so the whole soul is infected.[6]

---

to Pascal, the Christian theme of man's misery without God runs through St. Bonaventure's philosophy, and it is here developed as a critique of our faculty of knowledge, as it is developed elsewhere as a critique of our faculty of will or of action: *nam quod omnia judicia nostra sint directa, imperia tranquillata, desideria consummata, impossible est dum sumus in hac vita* [*Sermo II de reb. theol.* IV (V, 540b)]" (Gilson, *Philosophy of Bonaventure,* 349).

3 *De natura et gratia* 53, 62 (*PL* 44, 277).

4 Bonaventure himself recognized this danger: "Hoc credendum est sensisse beatum Augustinum, licet verba eius exterius propter detestationem erroris Pelagianorum, qui aliqualem felicitatem eis concedebant, aliud sonare videantur. Ut enim eos reduceret ad medium, abundantius declinavit ad extremum" *Brev.* 3, 5, 6 (V, 235a).

5 *Epistola 145*, 3–4 (*PL* 33, 593–94).

6 "Morbus autem est depravatio affectus. Haec autem est quadruplex, quia contrahit ex unione ad corpus anima infirmitatem, ignorantiam, malitiam, concupiscentiam; ex quibus inficitur intellectiva, amativa, potestativa; et tunc infecta est tota anima" *Hex.* 7, 8 (V, 366b). "Traditur Scriptura ad commendandam gratiam Spiritus sancti. Gratia autem Spiritus sancti non est nisi in homine grato; gratus autem esse non potest, nisi agnoscat suam indigentiam. Indigentia autem triplex est: virtutis cognoscitivae, potestativae, amativae, quia caeci sumus, infirmi, maligni. Oportuit ergo, ut homo prius agnosceret suam caecitatem, infirmitatem, malignitatem." (Ibid., 14, 8 [V, 394b]). Cf. *II Sent.* d. 22, dub. 2 (II, 528a).

To approach theology ignoring this vital aspect of our condition as fallen creatures exposes us to innumerable errors that inevitably crop up in study: "No one is healed unless he knows his disease, its cause, a physician, and the proper medicine."[7] These errors may concern the subject matter studied, for example, our interpretation of Divine Revelation, caused from our remaining on the conceptual level. Bonaventure sees this mistake in persons who follow "the speculative way, as do those who engage in examination of Scripture, which is understood only by clean minds."[8] Sacred Scripture was made necessary from the fact that man after the Fall became incapable of seeing God's vestiges in nature.[9] The root cause of this blindness, however, which must account for the intellect's inability to grasp properly the subject matter itself, is a defect on the level of the will.[10] St. Bonaventure, again following St. Augustine, saw the will as going before the intellect, like a weight drawing it.[11]

The greatest punishment of the first sin was loss of intimacy with God (Gen. 3:23) for the simple reason that "all rational beings, however little they may partake of light, are intended to grasp God through knowledge and love."[12] Thus, there remained in the will a defective or obfuscated

---

7 "Non sanatur autem aliquis, nisi cognoscat morbum et causam, medicum et medicinam." *Hex.* 7, 8 (V, 366b).

8 ". . . per modum speculatorium vel speculativum, ut illi qui vacant speculationi Scripturae, quae non intelligitur nisi ab animis mundis" (Ibid., 22, 21 [V, 440b]).

9 "Et ideo in statu innocentiae, cum imago non erat vitiata sed deiformis effecta per gratiam, sufficiebat liber creaturae, in quo se ipsum exerceret homo ad contuendum lumen divinae sapientiae" *Brev.* 2, 12, 4 (V, 230b). "Et tamen nos non invenimus eam, sicut laicus nesciens litteras et tenens librum non curat de eo; sic nos; unde haec scriptura facta est nobis Graeca, barbara et Hebraea et penitus ignota in suo fonte" *Hex.* 2, 20 (V, 340a). "Qui igitur tantis rerum creatarum splendoribus non illustratur, caecus est; qui tantis clamoribus non evigilat, surdus est; qui ex omnibus his effectibus Deum non laudat, mutus est; qui ex tantis indiciis primum principium non advertit, stultus est" *Itin.* 1, 15 (V, 299b).

10 "Peccatum omne, in quantum huiusmodi, et est a voluntate sicut a prima origine et est in voluntate sicut in proprio subiecto" *Brev.* 3, 1, 4 (V, 231b). In the following paragraph (Ibid.), Bonaventure quotes Augustine (*De vera religione*, 14, 27 [*PL* 34, 133]): "Adeo voluntarium, quod, si non est voluntarium, iam non est peccatum."

11 "Amor est pondus mentis et origo omnis affectionis mentalis" *Brev.* 5, 8, 4 (V, 262a). Cf. St. Augustine: "Pondus meum, amor meus" (*Confessiones* 13, 9, 10 [*PL* 32, 848–49; *CSEL* 33, 351]). Lonergan may help us to understand this: "There are in full consciousness feelings so deep and strong, especially when deliberately reinforced, that they channel attention, shape one's horizon, direct one's life. Here the supreme illustration is loving. A man or woman that falls in love is engaged in loving not only when attending to the beloved but at all times. Besides particular acts of loving, there is the prior state of being in love, and that prior state is, as it were, the fount of all one's actions" (Lonergan, *Method in Theology*, 32–33).

12 "Omnis intellectus, quantumcumque parum habens de lumine, natus est per cognitionem et amorem capere Deum" *Brev.* 2, 12, 2 (V, 230a).

relationship with the One who "teaches interiorly" and "is intimate to every soul."[13] Speaking within the Augustinian tradition, Bonaventure calls sin an aversion against God.[14] Thus, the medicine of the will is that "intimate" knowledge proffered as an invitation to renew friendship with God through conversion.[15] On account of the deformed relationship to God, we may summarize Bonaventure's view of man after the Fall as *homo incurvatus* or *recurvus*.[16] Man no longer is standing up straight in his intermediate position between heaven and earth.[17] Previous to the Fall his posture was erect and he was capable of looking upward, that is, of conversing familiarly with God, and of looking downward upon the earth to cultivate it.[18] After the Fall, man is bent over, entirely absorbed in earthly matters as well as centered

---

13 "Christus est doctor interius, nec scitur aliqua veritas nisi per eum, non loquendo, sicut nos, sed interius illustrando. . . . Ipse enim intimus est omni animae" *Hex.* 12, 5 (V, 385a).

14 "In peccato namque est aversio" *II Sent.* prooem. (II, 5b); ". . .quod quidem facit voluntas, quando sua defectibilitate, mutabilitate et vertibilitate, spreto bono indeficiente et incommutabili, bono commutabili inhaerescit" *Brev.* 3, 1, 4 (V, 231b), which is the same teaching found in Augustine, *De libero arbitrio* II, c. 19, n. 53 (*PL* 32:1269; *CSEL* 74:86). Cf. *II Sent.* d. 35, dub. 6 (II, 838a–839b) and Ibid., d. 42, a. 2, q. 1 (II, 964a–966b) where, in both places, Bonaventure follows Augustine's *De natura boni*, 34 and 36 (*PL* 42, 562; *CSEL* 25, 872).

15 *II Sent.* d. 42, a. 3, q. 1, ad 1 (II, 972a). In Bonaventure's famous sermon *Christus unus omnium magister,* he envisions theology as subordinate to the teaching of the sole Theologian. Thus theologians are to aspire to love, thereby conforming themselves to their only Teacher (*Sermo IV* [V, 567a–574b]). Cf. *I Sent.* d.3, p. 1, q.1, ad 5 (I, 70a): "God is present in the soul and in each intelligence with the truth, in such a way that conceptual abstractions are not needed to know him. Nevertheless, the reason that succeeds in knowing him, obtains his notion (*notitia*), which is like a copy that is not abstract but impress (*impressa*)."

16 "Avertens se a vero lumine ad commutabile bonum, incurvatus est ipse per culpam propriam, et totum genus suum per originale peccatum" *Itin.* 1, 7 (V, 297b–298a); "Affectus enim hominis recurvus est et mercenarius, quantum est de se; unde si quid facit, intendendo proprium commodum facit. . ." *II Sent.* d. 26, au., q. 2, concl. (II, 636a); "Cum ergo spiritus rationalis, hoc ipso quod de nihilo, sit in se defectivus; hoc ipso quod natura limitata et egena, sit in se recurvus, amans proprium bonum. . . . Quia recurvus, per se non assurgit ad rectitudinem perfectae iustitiae. . . . Quod ad hoc ut se praeparet ad donum supernae gratiae, cum sit recurvus, indiget dono alterius gratiae gratis datae, maxime post naturam lapsam, per quam habilis efficiatur ad bona moralia" *Brev.* 5, 2, 3 (V, 253b–254a); cf. *Red. art.* 25 (V, 325b). The source for this image of fallen man as "incurvatus" is Saint Bernard: *Sermones in Cantica canticorum*, sermo 80, 3–4 (*PL* 183, 1167–1168). St. Bonaventure, when commenting on the woman in Luke's Gospel who is bent over, utilizes Psalm 37:7, Vg ("Miser factus sum et curvatus usque in finem") in the same fashion as St. Bernard. See: *Comm. Lc.* 13, 23 (VII, 342b).

17 "Homo enim in medio constitutus, dum factus est ad Deum conversus et subiectus, cetera sunt ei subiecta" *II Sent.* prooem. (II, 5a).

18 "Fecit igitur Deus hominem rectum, dum ipsum fecit ad se conversum. In conversione enim hominis ad Deum non tantum rectificabatur ad id quod sursum, sed etiam ad id quod deorsum. Homo enim in medio constitutus, dum factus est ad Deum conversus et subiectus, cetera sunt ei subiecta, ita quod Deus omnem veritatem creatam subiecerat eius intellectui ad diiudicandum, omnem bonitatem eius affectui ad utendum, omnem virtutem eius potestati ad gubernandum" (Ibid.).

upon himself, all but forgetful of his former relationship to God and, by his aversion to Him through sin, made virtually incapable of such a relationship.

In Bonaventure's crowning work, *Collationes in Hexaëmeron,* an unfinished series of twenty-three lectures given at the University of Paris and which illuminate the task of the theologian, our author underscores the ignorance and degradation of the human mind after the Fall of our first parents:

> It is certain that as long as man stood up, he had the knowledge of created things and through their image, was carried up to God, to praise, worship, and love Him. This is what creatures are for, and this is how they are led back to God. But when man had fallen, since he had lost knowledge, there was no longer anyone to lead creatures back to God.[19]

The perception of man after the Fall (*recurvus*) is similar to the beasts of burden who walk with their gaze fixed upon the earth, and without grace they cannot help being occupied only with earthly things: "A man who lacks it [grace] is beastlike, with his face bent down to the earth (*habens faciem inclinatam ad terram*), like an animal."[20] Such a condition makes it impossible for him to consider higher things. Even if the philosophers of old, in their quest for ultimate reasons, sought to rise above this downward inclination, they were doomed to become entangled in their own deformed patterns of thinking: "Yet, they were wrong, for these weaknesses are in the mind, and not only in the senses: the powers to understand, love, and act are infected to the marrow."[21] So, the great philosophers of classical times, for as much as they would have liked to soar from the earth, remained even in their greatness like ostriches whose wings are simply ornamental: "These philosophers had the wings of ostriches, for their affective powers were not cleansed or ordained or straightened: for this can be obtained only through faith."[22]

---

19 "Certum est, quod homo stans habebat cognitionem rerum creatarum et per illarum repraesentationem ferebatur in Deum ad ipsum laudandum, venerandum, amandum; et ad hoc sunt creaturae et sic reducuntur in Deum. Cadente autem homine, cum amisisset cognitionem, non erat qui reduceret eas in Deum"*Hex.* 13, 12 (V, 390a).

20 "Bestialis est homo carens his et habens faciem inclinatam ad terram sicut animal" *Hex.* 20, 2 (V, 425a–b).

21 "Et tamen decepti fuerunt, quia hae infirmitates in parte intellectuali sunt, non solum in parte sensitiva: intellectiva, amativa, potestativa infectae sunt usque ad medullam" (Ibid., 7, 8 [V, 366b–367a]).

22 "Isti philosophi habuerunt pennas struthionum, quia affectus non erant sanati nec ordinati nec rectificati; quod non fit nisi per fidem" (Ibid., 7, 12 [V, 367a]).

Thus, if the study of theology is to be a way of perfection, a major obstacle with which we must contend, as a first step before study is undertaken, is our condition itself as fallen creatures.[23] A conversion has to take place which thus situates the theologian on a footing in some way proportionate to and worthy of the object of his study.[24] Baptism, although it removes original sin, does not remove its evil effects which may coexist with healing grace.[25]

Baptism's principal operation is to remove guilt.[26] But the existential effects (*concupiscentia et languor membrorum*) last for life.[27] These negative psychological factors condition human experience in all its dramatic manifestations and remain poised against every worthwhile human enterprise and stand concretely against the search for truth. What other alternative can we substitute for facing them with realism? These existential effects may be grouped under ignorance and concupiscence. Ignorance because we no longer are easily receptive to divine illumination. Concupiscence because in the search for truth, when not motivated by curiosity,[28] we constantly are exposed to the subtle risk of substituting self-seeking for higher ends: "Through knowledge, temptation easily leads to ruin. *You*

---

23 "Oportuit ergo, ut homo prius agnosceret suam caecitatem, infirmitatem, malignitatem" (Ibid., 14, 8 [V, 394b]); "Qui quidem oculus contemplationis actum suum non habet perfectum nisi per gloriam, quam amittit per culpam, recuperat autem per gratiam et fidem et Scripturarum intelligentiam, quibus mens humana purgatur, illuminatur et perficitur ad caelestia contemplanda; ad quae lapsus homo pervenire non potest, nisi prius defectus et tenebras proprias recognoscat; quod non facit, nisi consideret et attendat ruinam humanae naturae" *Brev.* 2, 12, 5 (V, 230b).

24 "Exerce igitur te, homo Dei, prius ad stimulum conscientiae remordentem, antequam oculos eleves ad radios sapientiae in eius speculis relucentes, ne forte ex ipsa radiorum speculatione in graviorem incidas foveam tenebrarum" *Itin.* prol. 4 (V, 296b).

25 "Et ideo, sicut poenalitas et corruptio per gratiam non aufertur a carne, sic sequela illa sive concupiscentia et languor membrorum simul stare potest cum gratia curativa"*Brev.* 3, 7, 5 (V, 236b). In another place, Bonaventure distinguishes that Christ has come to cure the *person* and not the *nature*: "Deus sic venit . . . ut curaret personam, non ut curaret ipsam naturam" *III Sent.* d. 12, a. 3, q. 2, concl., ad 2 (III, 273a). Commenting on this sentence, Antonio Blasucci explains: "Il battesimo rigenera l'uomo, ma non distrugge la ribellione della carne allo spirito. Rimane perciò uno stato di guerra spirituale, che esige nell'uomo abnegazione e mortificazione come armi di difesa o di attacco" (A. Blasucci, "La spiritualità di San Bonaventura," *SB* 4: 602).

26 "Ideo transit originale per baptismum quantum ad reatum" (Ibid., 3, 7, 4 [V, 236a]).

27 "Sic tollitur originalis peccati macula, quod remanet sequela, cum qua oportet pugnare, quamdiu vivimus in hac vita, quia in nullo prorsus exstinguitur concupiscentia per gratiam communem" (Ibid., 3, 7, 1 [V, 236a]).

28 "Unde intelligentia, avertendo se a summa veritate ignara effecta, infinitis quaestionibus se immiscuit per curiositatem" *II Sent.* prooem. (II, 5b).

will be like Gods, knowing good and evil."[29]   In describing Eve's motivation, Bonaventure states: "In her craving for superior knowledge, she rose to pride."[30]

2. The remedy: hierarchization of the soul

Against the deformed condition of the soul, St. Bonaventure affords a remedy that is characteristic of his spiritual anthropology. He calls it the hierarchization of the soul, using the concept and terminology of Dionysius Areopagite.[31]

Dionysius defines hierarchy as follows:

> "In my opinion, hierarchy is a sacred order (τάξις ἱερά), a state of understanding (καὶ ἐπιστήμη) and an activity (καὶ ἐνέργεια) approximating as closely as possible to the divine.   And it is uplifted to the imitation of God in proportion to the enlightenments divinely given to it."[32]

The soul has to be reordered according to a process of hierarchization that restructures the soul according to its place in God's design and to its true image, that is, both among other creatures above and below it, and within itself.[33]   Just as human nature is not responsible for its own creation, once fallen it cannot repair the damage incurred by its own fault without

---

29 "Per scientiam enim est tentatio facilis ad ruinam. Unde: *Eritis sicut dii, scientes bonum et malum" Hex.* 19, 4 (V, 420b).

30 "Appetendo igitur excellentem scientiam, erecta est in superbiam" *Brev.* 3, 3, 2 (V, 232b–233a).

31 "The concept of 'hierarchy' was the keystone of the system of pseudo-Dionysius; it dominated and supported everything else within that system and accounted for its spirit. *Ordo sacer* (sacred order) —this Latin rendering of the term conveyed very little of the metaphysical and religious richness of the original concept, which, despite this weakening and despite the loss of fundamental features, was to exercise an astonishing attraction" (Chenu, *Twelfth Century*, 80–81). See: R. Roques, "La notion de hiérarchie selon le Pseudo-Denys," AHLDMA 17 (1949): 183–222; 18 (1950–51): 5–54; R. Guardini, *Systembildende Elemente in der Theologie Bonaventuras* (Leiden: W. Dettloff, 1964), passim; J. Ratzinger, *Die Geschichtstheologie des heiligen Bonaventura* (Munich & Zurich: Snell & Steiner, 1959), 89–96: in English, *The Theology of History in St. Bonaventure*, trans. Z. Hayes (Chicago: Franciscan Herald Press, 1971), 86–94; P. Kuntz, "The Hierarchical Vision of St. Bonaventure," *SBM*, 1: 233–48.

32 *The Celestial Hierarchy*, chap. 3 (164 D). The translation given here is by Colm Luibheid in *Pseudo-Dionysius. The Complete Works* (New York: Paulist Press, 1987), 153.

33 "Rursus, quoniam rectitudo animae perfecta requirit, quod ipsa rectificetur secundum duplicem faciem, scilicet superiorem et inferiorem" *Brev.* 5, 4, 4 (V, 256b). Strictly speaking, the words "hierarchization" and the verb "to hierarchize" when applied to the human soul are an extended use made by Bonaventure of the Dionysian concept of hierarchy as ecclesiastical and celestial order. One bonaventurian lexicon states: "Respecto al alma humana, en sí misma considerada, no se le

going through a veritable "re-creation" which is properly the work of infused grace.[34]

For the Areopagite, all of created reality conforms to a most orderly structure. Spiritual and corporal intelligences occupy the level that corresponds to their proximity to God who is the source of all order, knowledge, and activity. On a descending scale, those intelligences that are further from God receive their light from Him as from the same source, but mediated through the levels just above them. In its turn, each level communicates light to the level beneath it. The only level that receives this light directly from God is the first level; the only level which does not communicate light to any other level is the last one.[35]

Now, for man bent over (*recurvus*) from original sin, the impossible comes about only through grace.[36] "What was deformed through the evil of sin, [God] recreates by reforming it through the habits of grace and righteousness."[37] With the hierarchization of grace, begun by faith, the soul undergoes a change "because [faith] heals, straightens and ordains: in

---

aplica la palabra jerarquía, pero sí conceptos incluídos en ella, tales como el de la jerarquización, el de grados o actos jerárquicos, el de jerarquizarse, etc. Y esta jerarquización se explica no sólo por las iluminaciones graduales que los seres espirituales reciben, sino también por la expresión progresiva con que se asemejan a Dios en sus hábitos y en sus actos" ("Lexicon Bonaventuriano," in: *Obras de San Buenaventura*, Vol. III: *Camino de la Sabiduría* [Madrid: B.A.C., 1972], 766–67. The lexicon is also found at the end of the other volumes in this set of Bonaventure's works, but the expanded definition of "Jerarquía" is given only in vols. III–VI).

34 "Et quoniam, ubi quis ceciderit, necesse habet ibidem recumbere, nisi apponat quis et adiiciat, ut resurgat, non potuit anima nostra perfecte ab his sensibilibus relevari ad contuitum sui et aeternae Veritatis in se ipsa, nisi Veritas, assumta forma humana in Christo, fieret sibi scala reparans priorem scalam, quae fracta fuerat in Adam" *Itin.* 4, 2 (V, 306a). For an example of Bonaventure's use of the term *recreatio* (which he has taken from Hugh of St. Victor), see *Brev.* 5, 4, 4 (V, 256b). The action of infused grace which effects a reformation of the soul is treated in *II Sent.* d. 26, au., qq. 3–6 (II, 637a–646b).

35 "Communication of divinity along a descending scale, along an emanation of the multiple forms of being, rank on rank, all participating directly but differently in God, whose fulness was thus manifested through them (the provision for direct participation avoided the emanationism of Proclus but not the peril of a theory of intermediaries): such was the grand vision which intoxicated pseudo-Dionysius and provided the master plan within which the universe and man, God and Christ, the sacraments and contemplation, body and soul, light and shadows, symbols and negations all found a sublime explanation" (Chenu, *Twelfth Century*, 81–82).

36 "Impossibile est, quod homo resurgat a culpa, nisi recreetur in vita gratuita" *Brev.* 5, 3, 2 (V, 255a).

37 "Quia vero recreat, deformatum per vitium culpae reformando per habitum gratiae et iustitiae" (Ibid., 5, 3, 3 [V, 255a]). See *III Sent.*, d. 33, au., q. 1 (III, 711a–712b): "Dicendum, quod generalis necessitas virtutis est ad rectificandum potentias animae contra obliquitatem" (Ibid., [III, 712a]).

this manner the soul may be changed, straightened and ordained."[38]

In a hierarchized scale, the human person is located beneath angelic spirits and above other bodily, nonhuman creatures.[39] In this perspective, creation is viewed in a descending scale from what is closer to God down through the lower ranges of created beings. Lower ranges are subjected to the influence of the higher ones, whence order, knowledge and operation ultimately originate.[40] This movement 'from above' reflects Bonaventure's well known statement that the whole of his metaphysics can be summed up in "emanation, exemplarity, and consummation."[41] We are part of a dynamic movement much larger than what falls beneath our eyes, and what is above us constitutes so many channels through which this emanation reaches us.[42] Its purpose is to unite us to God, through the threefold activity of purifying, illuminating, and perfecting.[43]

Not only in our relation to the rest of the universe but likewise within ourselves (a microcosm),[44] a process of hierarchization must restructure the manner in which the mind proceeds.[45] Bonaventure envisions the

38 "Sanat ergo, rectificat et ordinat; hoc modo anima potest modificari, rectificari et ordinari" *Hex.* 7, 13 (V, 367b).

39 Dionysius, *De coelesti hierarchia,* III, 2; VII, 3; IX, 2, et X. Cf. St. Bonaventure, *Itin.* 4, 4 (V, 307a); *Brev.* 5, 1, 3 (V, 252b); *Hex.* 21, 17 (V, 434a).

40 "Hierarchia dicit potentiam, scientiam, actionem" *Hex.* 21, 17 (V, 434a).

41 "Haec est tota nostra metaphysica: de emanatione, de exemplaritate, de consummatione" (Ibid., 1, 17 [V, 332b]).

42 "Inspired by the Father, each procession of the Light spreads itself generously toward us, and, in its power to unify, it stirs us by lifting us up. It returns us back to the oneness and deifying simplicity of the Father who gathers us in" (Dionysius, *Celestial Hierarchy* 120 B [Luibheid, 145]).

43 "The goal of a hierarchy, then, is to enable beings to be as like as possible to God and to be at one with him" (Ibid., 165A [Luibheid, 154]); "Indeed for every member of the hierarchy, perfection consists in this, that it is uplifted to imitate God as far as possible. . . . Therefore when the hierarchic order lays it on some to be purified and on others to do the purifying, on some to receive illumination and on others to cause illumination, on some to be perfected and on others to bring about perfection, each will actually imitate God in the way suitable to whatever role it has" (Ibid., 165B–C [Luibheid, 154]).

44 "Grandis res est anima: in anima potest describi totus orbis" *Hex.* 22, 24 (V, 441a). Cf. J. Mc Evoy, "Microcosm and Macrocosm in the Writings of St. Bonaventure," in: *SB* 2: 309–43. "According to the almost unanimous opinion of believers and unbelievers alike, all things on earth should be related to man as their center and crown" (Vatican II, *Gaudium et Spes,* no. 12).

45 "Each intelligent being, heavenly or human, has his own set of primary, middle, and lower orders and powers, and in accordance with his capacities these indicate the aforementioned upliftings, directly relative to the hierarchic enlightenment available to every being. It is in accordance with this arrangement that each intelligent entity—as far as he properly can and to the extent he may— participates in that purification beyond purity, that superabundant light, that perfection preceding all perfection" (Dionysius, *Celestial Hierarchy,* 273C [Luibheid, 174]).

restructured soul as the heavenly Jerusalem.[46] "Our spirit, inasmuch as it is in conformity with the heavenly Jerusalem, is made hierarchic in order to mount upward."[47] This interior hierarchization is fulfilled by the purification, illumination and perfection that the soul continually must realize. "[Grace] comes down into our heart when, by the reformation of the image, the theological virtues, the delights of the spiritual senses, and uplifting transports, our spirit becomes hierarchic, that is, purified, enlightened, and perfected."[48] This triple activity of hierarchization is not conceived by St. Bonaventure as different levels ascending toward higher union with God, but rather as concomitant efforts that the soul constantly must put forth no matter at what stage of the spiritual life the soul finds himself.[49] Thus the hierarchization process never can be considered over and done with, while at the same time the beginning of this process is a prior condition for the acquisition of truth through study.[50] Why? Because through hierarchization, the creature "rises toward the lights conferred upon it—going up through influence."[51]

Again, the utility of hierarchization, which Gilson translates as "a total reorganization of the soul,"[52] necessarily is based upon the deformed condition of human nature following the Fall. The attitude of St. Bonaventure may be labeled too hastily by some as another instance of what they choose to call Augustinian pessimism. Nevertheless, given the doctrine of grace that permeates his works, in the same Augustinian tradition, Bonaventure's attitude is actually a source of realistic optimism about what

---

46 "Necesse est enim, ut anima, quae est hierarchizata, habeat gradus correspondentes supernae Ierusalem. Grandis res est anima: in anima potest describi totus orbis. *Pulchra* dicitur *sicut Ierusalem*, quia assimilatur Ierusalem per dispositionem graduum hierarchicorum. Disponuntur autem in anima tripliciter: secundum ascensum, secundum descensum et secundum regressum in divina" *Hex.* 22, 24 (V, 441a).

47 "Efficitur spiritus noster hierarchicus ad conscendendum sursum secundum conformitatem ad illam Ierusalem supernam" *Itin.* 4, 4 (V, 307a).

48 "Tunc autem in cor descendit, quando per reformationem imaginis, per virtutes theologicas et per oblectationes spiritualium sensuum et suspensiones excessuum efficitur spiritus noster hierarchicus, scilicet purgatus, illuminatus et perfectus" (Ibid.).

49 "La triple activité hiérarchique, purification, illumination et perfection désigne, chez saint Bonaventure, non des périodes dans l'ascension, mais trois efforts qui s'imposent constamment à l'âme à toutes les étapes" (*Lexique saint Bonaventure*, s.v. "Hierarchia," by J.G. Bougerol).

50 That hierarchization of the soul is progressive accounts for Bonaventure's speaking of further hierarchizations. See *Hex.* 22, 27 (V, 441b), where he speaks of a "third hierarchization" in which the soul "receives divine illuminations and speculates above itself on what has been granted to it."

51 "Et ideo ascendit ad inditas ei illuminationes, ascendens per influentiam" *Hex.* 21, 17 (V, 434a).

52 Gilson, *Philosophy of Bonaventure*, 402.

we are capable of attaining with God's help.[53] He can joyfully exclaim: "Holiness is an immediate disposition toward wisdom,"[54] because "grace is the foundation of righteousness of the will, and of penetrating enlightenment of reason."[55] The human person is not left abandoned to his own efforts, but is preceded by grace along an itinerarium already laid out for him by Christ, the Truth that transcends and explains all other truths.

At bottom is the idea that the study of theology, as well as the study of any human discipline, cannot be undertaken without preparation on the part of the one who approaches this study. All would agree that we carry dispositions or attitudes which form our "mental baggage" and influence our perspective from beginning to end. In an effort to be as objective as possible in any search for truth, the student must take his own condition into consideration. It is not enough to take the objectivity of the content of our study into consideration, no matter how rigorously scientific we claim to be. With some amount of disdain for our own opinions we must face our own reality as members of a fallen race. Even those who are least solipsistic of all must submit themselves to this cautious self-examination. How is it that so many philosophers and theologians have disagreed on fundamental positions unless their perspectives initially were hindered by unsuspected self-seeking, subliminal blindnesses, and cultural and social prejudices commonly accepted in their historical context? Even Socrates, according to Bonaventure, realized he needed to purify his soul in order to arrive at understanding.[56]

The theologian approaching the sources of Revelation with humility readily will understand the necessity of purifying his own eyesight before pretending admittance to the highest of all forms of knowledge.[57] Afterwards, he will realize that he cannot continue to study theology without submitting constantly his own perspective to the wider perspective of grace that elevates his fallen nature which, when left alone, ever tends toward

---

53 "Die Unmöglichkeit der Bewaltigung ist für Bonaventura nicht Anlaß der Verzweiflung oder einer Erfahrung angstvollen Scheiterns, sie ist restlose Seligkeit angesichts der Unerschöpflichkeit Gottes" (H. von Balthasar, *Herrlichkeit,* zweiter Band *Fächer der Stile,* Part One: *Klerikale Stile,* 1. Der Seraph und die Stigmata [Einsiedeln: Johannes Verlag, 1961], 274).

54 "Sanctitas immediata dispositio est ad sapientiam" *Hex.* 2, 6 (V, 337a).

55 "Gratia fundamentum est rectitudinis voluntatis et illustrationis perspicuae rationis" *Itin.* 1, 8 (V, 298a).

56 "Hoc fecit, quia videbat, quod ad illum intellectum non potest pervenini, nisi anima sit purgata" *Hex.* 5, 33 (V, 359b).

57 "Ammirevole, però, in S. Bonaventura, è la concezione non tanto della teologia, quanto del teologo: vicina agli antichi, da un lato; modernissima dall'altro, anche se ignara dei 'nuovi metodi di fare teologia'. Egli non concepisce un teologo che sia privo di una certa abissale umiltà. . ." (A. Luciani, "San Bonaventura ai cristiani del secolo XX," *SBM*: 46–47).

moral and intellectual error.[58] Working as a member of the Church he will consider himself as only one of an immense communion wherein his views must tend toward greater bonds of charity and doctrinal harmony.[59] What all of this implies is a spiritual life undertaken by the theologian as a means of enabling himself to approach God on God's terms, never forgetting the full enormity of one's own misery inherited through original sin.

The myriad effects of original sin in us imply a constant hierarchization of our human nature, that is, the ongoing process of restructurization of our human powers by grace. Thus these human faculties become ever more capable of approaching Revelation with a mind that, in virtue of the illumination received by the study of theology itself, is willing to purify itself and conform itself to the demands of what will ever remain superior to his own capacities, "because nothing satisfies the soul except what goes beyond its capacity of understanding."[60]

> There is no sure step from knowledge to wisdom; a means is needed, and that is holiness. And this step is made through discipline: a discipline leading from the concern for knowledge to the application to holiness and from the concern for holiness to the application to wisdom... The man who chooses knowledge over holiness will never prosper.[61]

Such a preference for knowledge over holiness ever endangers the theologian, and Bonaventure warns us of the need to rectify our intention: "The hunger for knowledge must be changed: wisdom and holiness must be preferred to it."[62]

---

58 "Intellectus semper est rectus . . . secundum quod respicit leges aeternas et ab ipsis recipit et in eis speculatur, non autem qualitercumque ex se movetur, immo frequenter est obliquus et erroneus" *III Sent.* d. 33, au., q. 3, ad 5 (III, 718b); "Ratio non solum infirmatur per ignorantiam sed etiam per hebetudinem et praecipitationem" *III Sent.*, d. 34, p. 1, a. 2, q. 1, ad 2 (III, 746b); cf. *II Sent.* d. 24, p. 2, a. 1, q. 1, ad 2 (II, 575a–b).

59 "Et quoniam omnes doctores christianae legis finaliter debent tendere ad vinculum caritatis, ideo debent concordare in suis sententiis" *Christus mag.* 26 (V, 573b). Elsewhere, speaking of the concordance of the divine praise elevated by rational men, Bonaventure hints at the strong dependence between doctrinal orthodoxy and ordered unity within the Church (*Hex.* 1, 5+8 [V, 330a+b]).

60 "Quia nihil sufficit animae, nisi eius capacitatem excedat" *Scien. Chr.* q. 6, concl. (V, 35a).

61 "Non est ergo securus transitus a scientia ad sapientiam; oportet ergo medium ponere, scilicet sanctitatem. Transitus autem est exercitium; exercitatio a studio scientiae ad studium sanctitatis, et a studio sanctitatis ad studium sapientiae. . . . Qui enim praefert scientiam sanctitati nunquam prosperabitur" *Hex.* 19, 3 (V, 420b).

62 "Appetitus scientiae modificandus est, et praeferenda est ei sapientia et sanctitas" (Ibid., 19, 4 [V, 420b]).

If the tendency of a theologian is to forget his condition as fallen there will soon be little or no concern for the "changing, straightening and ordaining" of his soul.[63] The more intelligent the theologian is, the more confidence he may have in his own powers of mastering his science. Thus the greater danger to such persons exists in the neglecting of their spiritual obligations which never should be divorced from their intellectual pursuits.[64] It is the whole person who approaches the study of theology, not simply the intellect.[65] In a day and age when theological errors abound, and when they are obstinately and repeatedly asserted by their proponents in spite of the pondered reactions of the Church, might we suspect the proponents of divorcing the spiritual life from theology? Since when has any person enough contact with God, even through the hierachization of his own soul, to rise up against the faith of millions with so much assuredness of his own lights?[66] The more lights one has, the more cautious he becomes, because such light brings with it a knowledge of his own ignorance.[67] Even among the pagan philosophers it was true that the more intelligent was the more convinced of his ignorance and thus the more cautious about what he affirmed.[68]

---

63 Ibid., 7, 13 (V, 367b).

64 "Nec mirum, quia de alto cadit. Cadit enim per errorem et per praesumptionem. Videt enim se illuminatum et praesumit, et fit luciferianus et cadit a luce in tenebras horribiles" (Ibid., 22, 42 [V, 444a–b]).

65 Thus the theologian's task is delicate, according to R. Moretti, and "richiede una perenne vigilanza da parte del teologo—sia egli dogmatico, moralista o spirituale—il quale è sempre esposto al rischio di una sopravvalutazione dell'attività e soprattutto della luce della ragione quando questa va cercando 'l'intelligenza della fede'" (R. Moretti, "Natura e compito della teologia spirituale," in: *Spiritualità: fisionomia e compiti*, Atti del I Congresso nazionale dell'Associazione Italiana Spiritualità, Roma, 30 sett. – 3 ottobre 1980, eds. B. Calati, B. Secondin e T.P. Zecca, [Roma: Libreria Ateneo Salesiano, 1981], 18).

66 "Cadit similiter per errorem aestimationis, quae oritur ex praesumptione, quando credit se omnia habere per revelationem" *Hex.* 22, 42 (V, 444b).

67 "'Recognosce te ipsum'; sine hoc impossibile est venire ad sapientiam. Unde quanto sapiens plus proficit, tanto plus se despicit" (Ibid., 19, 24 [V, 424a]).

68 "Chaerephon, a devoted friend of Socrates, asked the Oracle if there was any man living who was wiser than Socrates, and received the answer 'No'. This set Socrates thinking, and he came to the conclusion that the god meant that he was the wisest man because he recognised his own ignorance . . . . However strange the story of the Oracle may appear, it most probably really happened, since it is unlikely that Plato would have put a mere invention into the mouth of Socrates in a dialogue which obviously purports to give an historical account of the trial of the philosopher, especially as the *Apology* is of early date, and many who knew the facts were still living" (Copleston, *History of Philosophy*, 1: 98). Cf. I Cor 8:2: "Anyone who claims to know something does not yet have the necessary knowledge."

3. Hierarchization and modern theology

The process by which the soul is restructured and the influence this has on theology can still be a valid approach to understanding what conversion brings to the study of theology. Bernard Lonergan has given this special emphasis in his works, and sees it as the effect of grace.[69] What Bonaventure calls hierarchization, Lonergan refers to as conversion: "Foundational reality, as distinct from its expression, is conversion: religious, moral, and intellectual. Normally it is intellectual conversion as the fruit of both religious and moral conversion; it is moral conversion as the fruit of religious conversion; and it is religious conversion as the fruit of God's gift of his grace."[70] When speaking of the effect such a conversion can have on theology, Lonergan does not doubt in asserting, but at the same time qualifying, its importance:

> Such conversion is operative, not only in the functional specialty, foundations, but also in the phase of mediating theology, in research, interpretation, history, and dialectic. However, in this earlier phase conversion is not a prerequisite; anyone can do research, interpret, write history, line up opposed positions. Again, when conversion is present and operative, its operation is implicit: it can have its occasion in interpretation, in doing history, in the confrontation of dialectic; but it does not constitute an explicit, established, universally recognized criterion of proper procedure in these specialties. Finally, while dialectic does reveal the polymorphism of human consciousness—the deep and unreconcilable oppositions on religious, moral, and intellectual issues—still it does no more: it does not take sides. It is the person that takes sides, and the side that he takes will depend on the fact that he has or has not been converted.[71]

When speaking of the threefold conversion (intellectual, moral, and religious), Lonergan affirms that it is "not a set of propositions that a theologian utters, but a fundamental and momentous change in the human reality that a theologian is."[72] We may ask ourselves how this can influence theology. Again, "neither the converted nor the unconverted are to be excluded from research, interpretation, history, or dialectic."[73] What

---

69   "Because we acknowledge interiority as a distinct realm of meaning, we can begin with a description of religious experience, acknowledge a dynamic state of being in love without restrictions, and later identify this state with the state of sanctifying grace" (Lonergan, *Method in Theology*, 120).

70   Ibid., 267–68.

71   Ibid., 268.

72   Ibid., 270.

73   Ibid., 271.

changes is the interpretation the theologian gives to what he is learning. And this is so because "the converted have a self to understand that is quite different from the self that the unconverted have to understand."[74] The effect is a much better capacity to discover and assent to the truth.[75] Thus, it would seem the idea itself—that the soul's condition after the reception of grace influences the way we think and do theology—is still valid, and may be explained in a way different from Bonaventure's hierarchization of the soul. The difference between Bonaventure and Lonergan, seems to remain in the concept of a hierarchized spiritual world that Bonaventure saw as somehow corresponding to the hierarchized soul and its desires to know. This world view was based on Dionysius' writings. How are we to regard this view in the twenty-first century?

It is objected that Dionysius' authority is no longer as important as it was in medieval times, when he still was identified as Paul's convert in Athens. For the same reason the "alexandrine vision of the world" upon which he built his entire system may seem to be of dubious validity in a day and age when theology "from below" is increasingly growing in interest.[76]

By returning to the definition of hierarchy which Dionysius attempts to provide us, we see that he amply allows for the subjective element in the search for truth.[77] He qualifies his definition three times: first, by clarifying he is giving his own opinion; second, by stating that the three aspects of hierarchy approximate similarity to the divine form "as closely as possible," thus recognizing the impossibility of exact duplication; and third by recognizing that these three aspects approach the imitation of God "in proportion to the enlightenments divinely given," thereby not attributing to

---

74 Ibid.

75 "If one desires foundations for an ongoing, developing process, one has to move out of the static, deductivist style—which admits no conclusions that are not implicit in premises—and into the methodical style—which aims at decreasing darkness and increasing the light and keeps adding discovery to discovery. Then, what is paramount is control of the process. It must be ensured that positions are accepted and counterpositions are rejected. But that can be ensured only if investigators have attained intellectual conversion to renounce the myriad of false philosophies, moral conversion to keep themselves free of individual, group, and general bias, and religious conversion so that in fact each loves the Lord his God with his whole heart and his whole soul and all his mind and all his strength" (Ibid., 270).

76 R. Roques identifies the hierarchized vision of the world with the alexandrine vision of the world: "La vision alexandrine du monde. . . consiste essentiellement dans une représentation graduelle des divers ordres de réalité à partir du premier principe dont ils procèdent tous, soit directement, s'il s'agit du premier, soit, pour tous les autres, par la médiation des ordres plus élevés. C'est dans cette tradition de pensée qu'il convient de situer la notion dionysienne de hiérarchie" (R. Roques, "La notion de hiérarchie selon le Pseudo-Denys," *AHLDMA* 17 [1949]: 183).

77 *The Celestial Hierarchy*, ch. 3 (164 D).

them an unlimited power.

The value of the Dionysian system is not so much to be sought in the content itself of the alexandrian vision of the world. What is important to recognize is Dionysius' belief that reality conforms to a divine plan. This is the essential place it has in Bonaventure's system, where symbols are the vehicles of more transcendent realities. Symbols may change according to the sensibilities of succeeding ages. What matters is the truth which such symbols convey, more or less successfully, depending often on the culture utilizing these symbols.[78]

In our study of Dionysius' influence on Bonaventure, what concerns us principally is the fact that Bonaventure recognizes that God's reality, the reality of Himself and His creation, constitutes the object of an ascending search by man: "Not indeed by a bodily ascent, but by an ascent of the heart. But we cannot rise above ourselves unless a superior power raise us."[79] This reality, which is prior to man's intellectual power to discover it, is there to be *found* by us, not *invented* by us.[80] Because this reality supposes an absolute objectivity, that is, a total independence of our capacity to find it, it behooves us to know the route by which to ascend to this truth, even if, and perhaps more so, we are doing theology "from below," as long as it proceeds from what Bernard Lonergan calls "authentic subjectivity."[81]

Dionysius' own hesitations to affirm categorically the validity of the hierarchized vision of the world should remind us of his views about man's limits in knowing God. Not all of Dionysius' theology is apophatic, because he has written other works beside *Mystical Theology* which represent

---

78 Symbols belong to the notion of mediation. As Lonergan explains: "Operations are said to be immediate when their objects are present. So seeing is immediate to what is being seen, hearing to what is being heard, touch to what is being touched. But by imagination, language, symbols, we operate in a compound manner; immediately with respect to the image, word, symbol; mediately with respect to what is represented or signified. In this fashion we come to operate not only with respect to the present and actual but also with respect to the absent, the past, the future, the merely possible or ideal or normative or fantastic. . . This distinction between immediate and mediate operations has quite a broad relevance. It sets off the world of immediacy of the infant against the vastly larger world mediated by meaning" (Lonergan, *Method in Theology*, 28).

79 "Non ascensu corporali, sed cordiali. Sed supra nos levari non possumus nisi per virtutem superiorem nos elevantem" *Itin.* 1, 1 (V, 296b).

80 Our lights come from above, not from below: "Origo luminum est a supremis ad infima, non e converso" *Hex.* 22, 29 (V, 442a); *Hex.* 20, 1 (V, 425).

81 "Genuine objectivity is the fruit of authentic subjectivity. It is to be attained only by attaining authentic subjectivity. To seek and employ some alternative prop or crutch invariably leads to some measure of reductionism" (Lonergan, *Method in Theology*, 292). We find a similar insight in Saint Bonaventure, for whom revelation is not fully received until we go much deeper than the objective expression of it in Sacred Scripture. This could be misunderstood today by those who undermine the objective origin of supernatural revelation. To obviate this possibility, Ratzinger explains: "In

his affirmative theology, both symbolic and conceptual. We still must remember that, for him, it is impossible to know God adequately in our accustomed, human way of knowing.[82] We can know God in this life in a direct way, but this knowledge is a "ray of darkness" to our rational powers, although forcefully experienced by our affective powers.[83] Was not the image of Christ crucified a kind of knowledge that spurred an emotional response (*nata sit movere affectum*)?[84] In this sense, symbolism can be more adequate than concepts to convey this experiential knowledge to us.[85]

Thus, instead of denying the possibility of objective knowledge of God in this life, which certainly could lead us into a discouraged state of agnosticism, the vision proposed by Dionysius, with no small amount of caution on his part, is principally an affirmation of an order of reality existing outside the mind. The way to God through the hierarchized levels of reality may not be the only way to God, but it certainly finds its validity in what it

---

the light of this, it should be obvious enough what a difference lies between Bonaventure's view and any actualistic misinterpretation of it. We can express this difference as follows. The understanding which elevates the Scripture to the status of 'revelation' is not to be taken as an affair of the individual reader; but is realized only in the living understanding of Scripture in the Church. In this way the objectivity of the claim of faith is affirmed without any doubt. If we keep this in mind, we can say that without detriment to the objectivity of the faith, the true meaning of Scripture will be found only by reaching behind the letters. Consequently, the true understanding of revelation demands of each individual reader an attitude which goes beyond the merely 'objective' recognition of what is written. In the deepest sense, this understanding can be called mystical to distinguish it from all natural knowledge. In other words, such an understanding demands the attitude of faith by which man gains entrance into the living understanding of Scripture in the Church. It is in this way that man truly receives 'revelation'" (*Theology of History in St. Bonaventure*, 67–68).

82 "Since the way of negation appears to be more suitable to the realm of the divine and since positive affirmations are always unfitting to the hiddenness of the inexpressible, a manifestation through dissimilar shapes is more correctly to be applied to the invisible" (Dionysius, *Celestial Hierarchy* 141A [Luibheid, 150]). "Iste autem ascensus fit per affirmationem et ablationem, per affirmationem, a summo usque ad infimum; per ablationem, ab infimo usque ad summum; et iste modus est conveniens magis, ut: non est hoc, non est illud" *Hex.* 2, 33 (V, 342b).

83 "Ablationem sequitur amor semper. . . . Sic notitia divinitatis per ablationem reliquit in nobis nobilissimam dispositionem" (Ibid.).

84 *I Sent*. prooem. q. 3, concl. (I, 13b); cf. *Hex*. 18, 4 (V, 415b): "Sicut ergo intellectus ordinatur ad affectum. . ."

85 "A manifestation through dissimilar shapes is more correctly to be applied to the invisible" (Dionysius, *Celestial Hierarchy* 141A [Luibheid, 150]). "C'est de Denys que nos médiévaux tiennent la loi première du symbolisme: le ressort essentiel de sa dialectique, de sa *demonstratio*, semble bien être l'épreuve du hiatus apparemment infranchissable que notre esprit perçoit entre deux réalités par ailleurs apparentées; les joindre alors, par le jeu du symbole, c'est établir en nous, non sans un sursaut d'exaltation intérieure, en tout cas dans une décharge affective qui provoquera la création poétique, une relation secrète avec la réalité transcendante. Loi de l'intelligence, nous l'avons vu ailleurs, aux prises avec une participation où transcendance et immanence jouent simultanément" (Chenu, *Théologie au douzième siècle*, 180).

basically affirms—that reality has an order (τάξις), is knowable (ἐπιστήμη), and is an activity (ἐνέργεια).

Such a prospect of finding truth, not only in physical realities but also in spiritual realms above us, fits well into Bonaventure's system of exemplarism. Exemplarism as a system recognizes both the reality of the transcendent and the validity of the symbolism which represents it for us. In some way, exemplarism is a 'theology from below', because it is willing to read the signs around us. New symbols may be found for different ages of theological research. But such symbols hold their validity based on their fidelity to the truth one attempts to convey. This truth ultimately is confirmed through Revelation and the experience of the saints. Whether the 'hierarchized' soul should be compared to the heavenly Jerusalem or to another symbol is conditioned by various factors, both cultural and religious. But the power of grace to transform, restructure and reorganize the soul according to God's purpose of salvation is a reality so rich in content as to challenge our imaginations. Whatever images we may find for recasting the theological truth about grace's dynamism in us will ever serve to enrich this concept. Hopefully it even will communicate something of the reality itself (divine life) that is signified by theological concepts.[86]

Conclusion

The gift of faith is a knowledge that transforms the human mind. Saint Bonaventure has shown how faith brings with it a power that draws the human spirit toward a pre-existing reality. The human mind is conformed to this reality—it is made hierarchic—that is, conformed to the heavenly Jerusalem in order, knowledge and activity.

The study of theology is made possible by a discovery of this pre-existing reality, not by a creation of it.[87] It is a discovery of a path (itinerarium) to be followed upward. This path not only indicates where the mind must travel, but also empowers and perfects in the mind the very faculties that mirror reality.[88] Thus whatever one knows in theology, one also experiences as a living reality.

---

86 God's purpose in communicating divine truth (I Jn 1: 3).

87 ". . . ad illam Ierusalem supernam, in quam nemo intrat, nisi prius per gratiam ipsa in cor descendat" *Itin.* 4, 4 (V, 307a).

88 *Hex.* 12, 16 (V, 386a–b); Ibid., 20, 8 (V, 426b); Ibid., 5, 25 (V, 358a). As we shall see later on, one of the specific traits of Bonaventure's doctrine on the gifts of the Holy Spirit is that they perfect the faculties.

J.G. Bougerol describes this vital aspect of theology which makes the content of the theologian's faith "not only an object of knowledge, but at the same time a principle of total conversion to the Gospel."[89] This mysterious reality not only is discovered by the mind but also reaches out toward the mind by its own activity, bidding its participation, and acting continually upon the mind.[90] This is the dynamic aspect of theology which transforms the mind far above the power of conceptual truth (*scientia*) thus meriting for it the name of wisdom (*sapientia*).[91]

How is it possible for reality, not only material but spiritual reality (including knowledge), to serve as a point of departure for reaching God? Such a possibility rests on Bonaventure's basic tenet about exemplarism. All created reality exemplifies, that is, manifests, points to, and carries us toward God, through Christ, the divine exemplar who is the icon from which all things receive their being. In this sense, Christ is the "supreme hierarch."[92]

---

89 For the same reason, Bougerol sees the theologian, unlike any other scientific researcher, to be essentially '*un chrétien engagé*': "En réalité, le théologien n'est pas un chercheur à la manière dont on peut définir le chercheur scientifique. L'objet de sa recherche l'engage en tant qu'homme puisqu'il est cróyant et que, soumettant son esprit au Christ, il lui soumet aussi sa vie. Adhérant au Christ par la foi, il doit pouvoir témoigner dans sa vie que le contenu de sa foi n'est pas seulement pour lui objet de connaissance, mais en même temps principe de sa conversion totale à l'Evangile. Comme Paul, le théologien est apôtre par vocation et serviteur du Christ-Jésus pour prêcher à l'honneur de son nom, l'obéissance de la foi; il doit même accepter d'aller jusqu'au martyre plutôt que de renier celui dont il cherche à mieux entendre le message. Il s'engage à tout cela, à titre de chrétien comme à titre de théologien. Le théologien est essentiellement un chrétien engagé" (Bougerol, "Fonction du théologien," *EF* 18 [1968]: 17).

90 "Uberrima est sacra Scriptura, per hoc quod Deus visitat eam sua influentia, producens pullulationes uberrimas. . . . Non enim est sicut ceterae scientiae, sed eam Deus visitat. . . . Iste ros est influentia gratiae Spiritus sancti, qui visitat Scripturam, et in qua invenitur suaviter" *Hex.* 14, 3 (V, 393a–b).

91 "Sapientia est *lux descendens a Patre luminum* in animam et radians in eam facit animam deiformem et domum Dei" (Ibid., 2, 1 [V, 336a]).

92 "Qui etiam summus hierarcha est" *Itin.* 4, 5 (V, 307b).

The invisible existence of God and his everlasting
power have been clearly seen by the mind's
understanding of created things.

Rm. 1:20

III.

BONAVENTURE'S DOCTRINE OF EXEMPLARISM

As I pointed out at the end of the last chapter, ideas may be means by which we reach God and conversely, by which God reaches us. In theology, we may ask what the ideas studied represent and how closely they approach the reality to which they refer. In this regard, we must first listen to Saint Bonaventure:

> The exemplary likeness expresses the thing more perfectly than the caused thing itself expresses itself. On account of this, God knows things more perfectly through their likenesses than he would know them through their essences; and angels know things more perfectly in the Word than in their own reality.[1]

Before speaking of the influence of Bonaventure's doctrine of exemplarism on the spiritual life of the theologian, it would be good to point out the importance a key concept, of a philosophical nature, has on theology in general, and particularly on St. Bonaventure's entire system of thought.[2]

---

1 "Illa enim similitudo exemplaris perfectius exprimit rem, quam ipsa res causata exprimat se ipsam. Et propter hoc Deus perfectius cognoscit res per similitudines illas, quam cognosceret per suas essentias; et Angeli perfectius cognoscunt in Verbo quam in proprio genere" *Scien. Chr.* q. 2, ad 9 (V, 10a).

2 Tina Manferdini, speaking of exemplarism in Saint Bonaventure, states that it is precisely here that the question of the distinction between philosophy and theology arises: "Tale problema si acuisce in rapporto all'esemplarismo, trattandosi della dottrina in cui la compenetrazione dei due ordini di consapevolezza è particolarmente intima" ("L'esemplarismo di San Bonaventura," *IncBonav* 7 [1972]: 49). For an in-depth study on Bonaventurian exemplarism, see: J.M. Bissen, *L'exemplarisme divin selon S. Bonaventure* (Paris: J. Vrin, 1929). For other studies on Bonaventurian exemplarism see: E. Gilson, *The Philosophy of Saint Bonaventure*, chap. 7: "Universal Analogy"; E. Saurer, *Die religiöse Wertung der Welt in Bonaventuras Itinerarium mentis in Deum* (Werl/Westf: Franz. Druck., 1937); L. Berg, "Die Analogielehre des hl. Bonaventura," *Studium Generale* 8 (1955): 662–70; M. Oromí, "Filosofía ejemplarista de S. Buenaventura," in: *Obras de S. Buenaventura*, Vol. 3 (Madrid: B.A.C., 1972), 3–134.

1. Where philosophy ends

In every Christian thinker we may attempt to find some type of philosophical underpinning, more or less consciously expressed, even though a point may arrive beyond which the philosopher in us must surrender the reins to the theologian.[3] When we approach Bonaventure in this frame of mind, our attempt quickly will uncover a use of philosophical terminology and concepts that situate the Seraphic Doctor within the Augustinian tradition. By the time this tradition had reached Bonaventure, it had undergone over the centuries some Neoplatonic and even Aristotelian influences which reshaped it without, however, distorting it, at least in the form Bonaventure knew it.[4] Although Bonaventure recognizes his principal teacher to be Augustine, he does not hesitate to harmonize Augustine's concepts with the teachings of Dionysius Areopagite and the Victorine school. By aligning Bonaventure with Augustine, one thereby reconfirms the customary tendency to place Western thinkers in one of the two alternative currents originating in Platonism or Aristotelianism. Of course, what is done for the sake of clarity must not mean sacrificing any effort at nuancing the various influences in the history of philosophy. Concerning Bonaventure, such efforts again became quite intense during the heated debate over the "Bonaventurian question" thirty to forty years ago.[5] Nevertheless, it is sufficient to see the general path of Bonaventure's thought to discover immediately where he laid the emphasis in elaborating his theology.[6] J.G. Bougerol does not hesitate to state that "Bonaventure

---

3 "Ipsa [i.e., theologia] etiam sola est sapientia perfecta, quae incipit a causa summa, ut est principium causatorum, ubi terminatur cognitio philosophica" *Brev.* 1, 1, 3 (V, 210a–b).

4 "Bonaventura da Bagnoregio definisce se stesso come uomo della tradizione. . . Da Agostino in poi, sino a tutto il secolo XII e i primi decenni del XIII, questa tradizione aveva cercato di riconsiderare, alla luce dell'esperienza della fede cristiana, il patrimonio dottrinale antico, e particolarmente la dottrina platonica nelle varie rielaborazioni metafisiche dei neoplatonici e particolarmente di Plotino. . . Bonaventura, aderendo a questa tradizione, ne raduna enciclopedicamente i vari elementi, diventando uno dei più grandi maestri del cristocentrismo metafisico-teologico del medioevo" (A. Pompei, "La centralità di Cristo," in: *Lettura critica di San Bonaventura*, [Firenze: Città di Vita, 1974], 51). For Bonaventure's use of the sources, see Bougerol, *Introduction to Bonaventure,* 23–49: «Saint Bonaventure's Library»

5 The debate is well presented by J.F. Quinn, *The Historical Constitution of St. Bonaventure's Philosophy* (Toronto: Pontifical Institute of Medieval Studies, 1973), especially in the Introduction (pp. 17–99) and the General Conclusion (pp. 841–96). Camille Bérubé reduces "le problème bonaventurien par excellence" to "celui de la nature de la philosophie de Saint Bonaventure" ("De la philosophie à la sagesse dans l'itinéraire bonaventurien" *CF* 38 [1968]: 264).

6 In regard to Augustine's influence on the Seraphic Doctor, Bougerol has stated that "Bonaventure quoted Augustine over 3,000 times" and "Bonaventure represented the fulfillment of Augustinianism"

accepted Augustine's central themes on knowledge and exemplarism."[7] Since exemplarism finds its remotest origins in Plato, it usually is found in some form in all Neoplatonic systems. We find it, for example, in Dionysius.[8] Bonaventure bemoans the fact that it was rejected by Aristotle, thus vitiating Aristotle's entire system. Following exemplarist teaching, Augustine had taught that the 'eternal reasons' of all created things abide in an unchangeable manner in God.[9] The eternal reasons, or divine ideas, are "certain archetypal forms or stable and unchangeable reasons of things, which were not themselves formed but are contained in the divine mind eternally and are always the same. They neither arise nor pass away, but whatever arises and passes away is formed according to them."[10] Although influenced by Neoplatonic teaching, which considered the Platonic exemplary ideas as abiding in the *Nous* (a subordinate hypostasis emanating from God), Augustine, like Bonaventure who followed him, believed the ideas to exist in the Word, who is of the same nature as the Father, being the second Person of the Trinity.[11]

Now, it has been affirmed, without provoking contentions, that exemplarism lies at the very heart of Bonaventure's entire system.[12] In one of Bonaventure's well-known statements we discover him attempting to synthesize the whole thrust of his philosophical leaning: "This is the sum total of our metaphysics: emanation, exemplarity, and consummation, that

---

(*Introduction to Bonaventure,* 33). Nevertheless Bougerol, relying on Chenu, qualifies the influence of Augustine in Bonaventure's day as "strongly marked by Platonism" (Ibid., 32; cf. Chenu, *La théologie au XIIe siècle,* chap. V: "Les platonismes au XIIe siècle," pp. 108–41). In regard to determining exact sources, one can only attempt to avoid extremes: "The history of theology has a long way to go before it can shed true light on the sources of medieval thought" (Bougerol, *Introduction to Bonaventure,* 25).

7 Ibid., 33.

8 "All this holds all the more truly with respect to the Cause which produced the sun and which produced everything else. The exemplars of everything preexist as a transcendent unity within it. It brings forth being as a tide of being. We give the name of 'exemplar' to those principles which preexist as a unity in God and which produce the essences of things. Theology calls them predefining, divine and good acts of will which determine and create things and in accordance with which the Transcendent One predefined and brought into being everything that is" *Divine Names* 8, 5 (*PG* 824C; Luibheid, 102).

9 *Confessiones* I, 6, 9 (*PL* 32, 664).

10 "Sunt namque ideae principales formae quaedam, vel rationes rerum stabiles atque incommutabiles, quae ipsae formatae non sunt, ac per hoc aeternae ac semper eodem modo sese habentes, quae in divina intelligentia continentur. Et cum ipsae neque oriantur, neque intereant; secundum eas tamen formari dicitur omne quod oriri et interire potest" *De Ideis* 2 (*PL* 40, 30).

11 *De Trinitate* 4, 1, 3 (*PL* 42, 888).

12 "Exemplarism is at the very core of Bonaventure's thought" (Bougerol, *Introduction to Bonaventure,* 9). Zachary Hayes states that "for Bonaventure the most properly metaphysical question

is, to be illuminated through spiritual radiations and return to the Supreme Being. And in this you will be a true metaphysician."[13]

It was chiefly on account of Aristotle's rejection of Plato's exemplarism that Bonaventure in turn refused to accept Aristotle as a true metaphysician.[14] Although Bonaventure respected Aristotle as one of mankind's greatest thinkers, he could not consider Aristotle to be more than a natural philosopher. Bonaventure utilizes Aristotle's valid philosophical conclusions and his physics whenever some scientific explanation is needed. But again, for Bonaventure, Aristotle was doomed inherently to fall into certain very serious errors since he did not have any recourse to a reality transcending what meets our senses. He did not have access to a reality that might correspond to the actual truth for which the senses only provide so many symbols.[15]

2. Symbolism: a bridge to the transcendent world

As we read Bonaventure's pastoral and mystical works, we are struck by a rich symbolism based on our author's attentive eye to all of God's works, both in nature and in history. Such a symbolism, by gradually becoming Bonaventure's most comfortable way of expressing even the most elevated concepts, almost is inseparable from the ideas he wishes to inspire in his hearers.[16] Of course such a symbolism is also a direct connection to

---

is that of exemplarity. . . . Exemplarity has a critical role to play in Bonaventure's thought both at the philosophical and at the theological levels" (Z. Hayes, *The Hidden Center: Spirituality and Speculative Christology in St. Bonaventure* [St. Bonaventure, N.Y.: The Franciscan Institute, 1992], 13–14). Tina Manferdini writes: "L'esemplarismo è uno dei più importanti punti di convergenza al quale confluiscono le diverse linee di sviluppo e i vari piani del pensiero bonaventuriano. Si può affermare che s. Bonaventura, traendo ispirazione dalla patristica, soprattutto da Agostino, e inserendosi con ciò nella linea del platonismo cristiano, fa dell'esemplarismo la chiave di volta del suo pensiero teologico-filosofico, in quanto lo connette strettamente con la dottrina della trinità e della creazione e proprio per questo ne coglie le implicazioni cristologiche più profondamente ed esplicitamente di quanto non avesse fatto lo stesso Agostino" (Manferdini, 41).

13 "Haec est tota nostra metaphysica: de emanatione, de exemplaritate, de consummatione, scilicet illuminari per radios spirituales et reduci ad summum. Et sic eris verus metaphysicus" *Hex.* 1, 17 (V, 332b). "St. Bonaventure identifies exemplarism with metaphysics" (Gilson, *Philosophy of Bonaventure,* 144).

14 *Hex.* 6, 2–5 (V, 360b–361b).

15 The principle errors of Aristotle, at least in the form his philosophy reached Bonaventure under the influence of Averroes, were three: the denial of Platonic exemplarism, the belief the world had never begun, and the unity of the active intellect. "Even granting a dialectical tension between the power of creation to manifest God and its complete inferiority to God, symbolism revealed nothing less than God's transcendence" (Chenu, *Twelfth Century,* 128).

16 "Far from being an accident or an adventitious element, St. Bonaventure's symbolism has its roots deep in the very heart of his doctrine; it finds its whole rational justification in his fundamental

his hierarchized concept of reality, and for this very reason we find Bonaventure again strongly influenced by Dionysius.[17] M.-D. Chenu has described the Dionysian influence in respect to the symbolist mentality on medieval thought:

> It was from pseudo-Dionysius that medieval men enunciated the primary law of symbolism. The essential appeal of his dialectic, his "demonstration," seems to have been that it bridged the apparently nontraversible gap that the mind perceived between two realities otherwise akin; to join these two realities within a single symbol was to put the mind into secret contact with transcendent reality, not without a sense of inward exaltation, and certainly with an affective response that inspired poetic creativity. Here was a law that pertained to men's search for understanding, as we have seen; the understanding confronted transcendence and immanence held in simultaneous tension.[18]

For Dionysius, symbols had a much more powerful reach than the "sign" for Saint Augustine.[19] Symbolism in Bonaventure is likewise a consequence of his own exemplarist vision of a world created to manifest

---

metaphysical principles, and it is itself rigorously demanded by them as the only means of applying them to the real" (Gilson, *Philosophy of Bonaventure,* 186). "Pour saint Bonaventure, idée signifie similitude ou, mieux, expression, puisqu'il s'agit d'une similitude engendrée par la vérité" (Bissen, *L'exemplarisme,* 30).

17 "In realist symbolism . . . including that of pseudo-Dionysius, symbolic action is a normal part of the dynamism of a cosmos reaching upward toward God in hierarchical stages" (Chenu, *Twelfth Century,* 135). "According to this theory, the situation of man in the universe, in the 'hierarchy' of the universe, governed the knowledge of which man was capable, especially his knowledge of God. Connatural with matter, a man's intelligence had to work through matter to attain a grasp of transcendent realities, unknowable in themselves. Paradoxically, man's intelligence, in its operation, must heartily accept matter and yet must austerely pass beyond it. The movement between the two aspects of this operation was not a matter of simple psychological transference or of aesthetic interpretation; it derived from the very nature of things, which, given their sacred emanation, comprised graded representations of the inaccessible One, the Godhead. This *anagoge*, this upwards reference of things, was constituted precisely by their natural dynamism as symbols. The image of the transcendent was not some pleasant addition to their natures; rather, rooted in the 'dissimilar similitudes' of the hierarchical ladder, it was their very reality and reason for being. The symbol was the means by which one could approach mystery; it was homogeneous with mystery and not a simple epistemological sign more or less conventional in character" (Ibid., 123).

18 Ibid., 131.

19 About St. Augustine's concept of "sign," Chenu comments: "It is important to take stock of the difference between the Augustinian 'sign' and the pseudo-Dionysian 'symbol'. . . . Augustine's 'sign' belonged on the level of his psychology of knowledge and was developed with materials drawn from that psychology. . . . It was consequently the knower himself who was the principle and rule of the 'sign'; it was he who gave the sign its value, over and above any objective basis in the nature of things, always extrinsic to the soul. . . . This concept could doubtless account for the potential representationalism of nature, but it denied any mystical content to nature and any native sacredness concealed within it" (Ibid., 124–27). In contrast, Chenu speaks of Dionysius' concept: "For pseudo-Dionysius, it was not the believer who gave signs their meaning; it was objective

God.[20] God as creator has left his mark on everything surrounding us, as the writing of a book which speaks of Him.[21] All we have to do is open our eyes to see this,[22] "for creatures of this visible world signify the invisible things of God."[23] In this sense, Bonaventure was a faithful disciple of Francis who saluted all of nature as making God present in so many different ways.[24] Many have liked to see Bonaventure as the one who raised Francis' mystical life to the level of conceptual thought.[25] In one sense it is erroneous for us to say he "raised" it, because for Bonaventure, St. Francis' experience certainly was closer to the divine wellsprings than the theological explanation of such experiences. The transforming of this experience into a metaphysical system is actually a descent from primordial knowledge to conceptual knowledge.[26] Even though St. Francis' mysticism had no use for books, principally ascending to God through the material universe, St. Bonaventure praised the intellectual life as a most valid way to ascend to God.

---

elements themselves which, before anything else and by their very nature, were so many representations, so many 'analogies'. The symbol was the true and proper expression of reality; nay more, it was through such symbolization that reality fulfilled itself. . . . In pseudo-Dionysian symbolism, wholly taken up with mystagogy, such conceptualization [of the scholastic matter-form axiom for sacraments as signs] did not come into play. The symbol was the starting point of knowledge, of 'initiation', and it was no more reducible to analysis than the mystery it made present" (Ibid., 126–27).

20 "Creation was a theophany, a manifestation of God, and symbolism was the means appropriate to that manifestation" (Ibid., 128).

21 "Totus mundus est umbra, via, vestigium et est *liber scriptus forinsecus*. In qualibet enim creatura est refulgentia divini exemplaris" *Hex.* 12, 14 (V, 386b). "Creatura mundi est quasi quidam liber in quo relucet, repraesentatur et legitur Trinitas fabricatrix" *Brev.* 2, 12, 1 (V, 230a).

22 "Qui igitur tantis rerum creaturarum splendoribus non illustratur caecus est" *Itin.* 1, 15 (V, 299b).

23 "Significant autem huiusmodi creaturae huius mundi sensibilis invisibilia Dei" (Ibid., 2, 12 [V, 302b]).

24 How very different the world may appear to those who, even if they have faith, do not share the faith of a St. Francis. Søren Kierkegaard, for example, laments: "The whole order of things fills me with a sense of anguish, from the gnat to the mysteries of incarnation; all is entirely unintelligible to me, and particularly my own person. Great is my sorrow, without limits. None knows of it, except God in Heaven, and He cannot have pity" (Søren Kierkegaard, *Journal*, for May 12th, 1839).

25 "What St. Francis had simply felt and lived, St. Bonaventure was to *think*" (Gilson, *Philosophy of Bonaventure,* 60). See A. Pegis, "St. Bonaventure, St. Francis and Philosophy," *MedStud* 15 (1953): 1–13; B. McGinn, "The Influence of St. Francis on Theology of the High Middle Ages: The Testimony of St. Bonaventure" in: *Bonaventuriana* (hereafter *Bonav*), ed. F. Chavero Blanco, 2 vols. (Roma: Edizioni Antonianum, 1988), 1:97–118; Bernardino de Armellada, "San Buenaventura ¿Un San Francisco metido a filósofo? La filosofía de San Buenaventura según Camillo Bérubé," *CF* 60 (1990): 429–57.

26 "The prizing of primordial knowing shows itself in his [i.e., Bonaventure's] evaluative epistemology, his placing at the peak of human knowing an intuitive contemplation" (Tekippe, "Conceptual and Primordial Knowing," 281).

Exemplarism remained for him the key word to this intellectual search for God and is for us a key word to our understanding of Bonaventure's vision.

Unmistakably, therefore, in Bonaventure's system exemplarism forms the basis of his invitation to see God in all things, because they lead us to Him.[27] "In everything which is perceived or known God Himself lies hidden within."[28] There is no form of pantheism here. We see God in all things because God created all things. Just as an artist is seen through his works, created things are *vestigia*, or traces, of God, which express the presence of the first Artist.[29] In addition, this presence of God applies not only to material things, but also to ideas.[30] It is precisely here that we find Bonaventure elongating Francis' vision, not parting from it.

For Bonaventure, there are three states in which existence can be considered: in our minds (*in mente*), in the thing itself (*in proprio genere*), and in the mind of God (*in arte aeterna*). In the first and the third cases, we are speaking of a kind of knowledge. Now knowledge requires a likeness of the thing known, to manifest that very thing, either in our mind or in God's mind. In our minds, such a likeness is a *likeness of imitation*, which is a knowledge that is caused by things (*notitia causata a rebus*). The likeness existing in God's mind is an *exemplary likeness*, and this is a knowledge that causes things to be (*notitia causans res*).[31] Only in the mind of God can the ideas of things be considered exemplars, and these are

---

27 "Colligere possumus, quod omnes creaturae istius sensibilis mundi animum contemplantis et sapientis ducunt in Deum aeternum" *Itin.* 2, 11 (V, 302b). In this regard, Robert Javelet's comment is more than justified: "Saint Bonaventure présente ainsi *une vision du monde—qui est, en même temps, une spiritualité*" (R. Javelet, "L'exemplarisme bonaventurien," *SB* 4: 353).

28 ". . . in omni re, quae sentitur sive quae cognoscitur, interius lateat ipse Deus" *Red. art.* 26 (V, 325b).

29 Alexander Gerken points out that for Bonaventure the 'divine Art' is at the origin of all created nature and is a notion proximate to the 'divine Ideas' by which God created the world (see *LSB*, s.v. «Ars»). Realism in art undoubtedly is based on the innate capacity of everyday reality to hint at the transcendent world. This is why the realist Dostoyevsky proclaimed that for him *nothing could be more fantastic than reality itself:* "I have my own particular opinions about the real. . . A record of everyday events is for me far from realism, rather it is the opposite. . . These stories are the deep and living reality, because they are the facts. They happen every day, every moment; they are in no way exceptional" (quoted by Geir Kjetsaa in *Fyodor Dostoyevsky: A Writer's Life* [New York: Viking Penguin Inc., 1987], 137–38). For similar reasons, G.K. Chesterton appreciated the ordinary more than the extraordinary: "Ordinary things are more valuable than extraordinary things; nay, they are more extraordinary" (*Orthodoxy* [Garden City, N.Y.: Doubleday Image Books, 1959], 46).

30 "Et sic patet, quomodo multiformis sapientia Dei, quae lucide traditur in sacra Scriptura, occultatur in omni cognitione et in omni natura" *Red. art.* 26 (V, 325b).

31 This difference is well explained by Bonaventure: "Alio modo dicitur similitudo, quia unum est similitudo alterius; et hoc est dupliciter: quaedam est similitudo imitativa, et sic creatura est similitudo Creatoris; quaedam autem est similitudo exemplativa, et sic in Creatore ratio exemplaris est similitudo creaturae. . . . Et haec est similitudo, quae requiritur ad rerum notitiam habendam.

the eternal ideas that are not distinct from His essence.[32] While an idea in our own minds "involves some degree of imperfection, [in the divine mind] it implies neither composition nor any imperfection, but only absolute perfection."[33] Thus, as to the idea's capacity of representing the truth, no question arises in Bonaventure about which of the likenesses is superior: "It is found particularly and in the supreme degree in that likeness which is the exemplar of creation."[34] This reminds us of Gregory the Great's statement: "What do they not see, who see Him who sees all things?"[35]

Once the exemplarist foundations supporting this symbolic vision of reality are known, we find no difficulty understanding Bonaventure's invitation to cross the bridge of symbolism to the transcendent world: "Omnis creatura magis ducat in Deum quam in aliquod aliud."[36]

When we move to the area of the sciences, and especially that of theology, Bonaventure's basic presuppositions about reality do not change. In fact, it is precisely because of the exemplarism at the root of Bonaventure's teaching that we are able to classify the different areas of knowledge, culminating in theology which holds the privileged place because of its immediate reference to God. Inferior knowledge, in each of its areas, refers to created realities which in turn mirror the Creator. But in the case of theology, we are given the means to interpret the ultimate meanings which

---

Sed notitia quaedam est causans res, quaedam est causata a rebus. Ad notitiam causatam a rebus requiritur similitudo imitativa. . . . Ad notitiam autem causantem res requiritur similitudo exemplativa" *Scien. Chr.* q. 2, concl. (V, 9a). From the context, it is obvious that Bonaventure, when affirming here that this likeness is required for knowledge, is referring to both imitatory and exemplary likenesses, as against a likeness "per convenientiam duorum in tertio" (Ibid., [V, 8b–9a]), which he elsewhere calls "similitudo univocationis" *I Sent.* d. 35, q. 1, resp. (I, 601a).

32 "Divinus intellectus, sua summa veritate omnia aeternaliter exprimens, habet aeternaliter omnium rerum similitudines exemplares, quae non sunt aliud ab ipso, sed sunt quod est essentialiter" *Scien. Chr.* q. 2, concl. (V, 9a) .

33 Ibid. (English translation of text is taken from: *Works of Saint Bonaventure:* Vol. IV: *Disputed Questions on the Knowledge of Christ* [hereafter *Knowledge of Christ*], trans. Zachary Hayes, [St. Bonaventure, N.Y.: The Franciscan Institute, 1992], 90.)

34 "Sed veritas illa, quae est ratio cognoscendi proxima et immediata, illa magis salvatur in similitudine, quae est apud intellectum, maxime et potissime in illa similitudine, quae est exemplativa rerum" *Scien. Chr.* q. 2, ad 9 (V, 10a); (Hayes, *Knowledge of Christ*, 93).

35 "Quid est quod non videant, qui videntem omnia vident?" *Dialogue* IV, 33 (quoted by Bonaventure in: *II Sent.* d. 11, dub. 2 [II, 289b]). In the same treatise Bonaventure quotes Gregory again from *Dialogue* IV, 33: "Quid est, quod ibi nesciant, ubi scientem omnia sciunt?" (*II Sent.* d. 11, c. 2 [II, 275b]), and to the same effect in *II Sent.* d. 46, dub. 9 (IV, 953b). Gregory the Great, in another work, states: "Quid enim de his quae scienda sunt, nesciunt qui scientem omnia sciunt?" II *Moralia in Job,* c. 3, n. 3.

36 *I Sent.* d. 3, au., q. 2, concl. (I, 72a).

nature on its own cannot supply. Nature does indeed point to God, but *vestigia* alone are the weakest and haziest of the similitudes at our disposal. Now, although all creatures share the rank of vestigia, only human beings are the *imago Dei*. As the image of God, human beings are endowed with a closer and more specialized resemblance to God because they have spiritual powers which both reflect God's inner life and enable us to become ever more conformed to God.[37] The mystery of the Trinity is reflected in the three powers—intellect, will, and memory. This means that (and speaking only by analogy) just as God is one in nature and yet three Persons related to each other in the divinity, so also are we equipped with three faculties that interrelate inside us similar to the way the Three Persons relate to each other.[38] Bonaventure does not use this image as a proof of the Trinity in one God. Rather, being faithful to the exemplarist approach, he finds within himself a reflection of the intertrinitarian life.[39] Knowing the mystery of the Trinity first by Revelation, he finds it quite natural to see reflections of the same divine artisan not only in nature outside us, but also equally and more so inside us, because the image of God is a stronger resemblance than the vestige.[40] The authority of Scripture and of experience are sufficient to defend the relatively exalted state of man at the moment of creation, when he manifested the divine image—God's idea of man.[41] When compared with the other creatures of the Genesis account, and with our present concrete existence, we perceive the extent of obfuscation resulting in the image as we find it. All philosophical proofs, as well as those of natural science and psychology, simply are supporting arguments for those who may have

---

37 "La doctrine de l'exemplarisme situe les êtres à leur vraie place vis-à-vis de la Trinité créatrice, et nous invite à retrouver Dieu en gravissant les échelons qui vont de l'ombre de la divinité que l'on peut saisir en toute créature, jusqu'à l'image des trois personnes que l'être intelligent doit contempler en lui-même; jusqu'à la similitude même de la Trinité à laquelle est configurée l'âme rachetée" (L. Mathieu, *La Trinité creatrice d'après saint Bonaventure* [Paris: Editions Franciscaines, 1992], 101–2).

38 "Considera igitur harum trium potentiarum operationes et habitudines, et videre poteris Deum per te tanquam per imaginem, quod est videre per speculum in aenigmate" *Itin.* 3, 1 (V, 303b).

39 "Dum igitur mens se ipsam considerat, per se tanquam per speculum consurgit ad speculandam Trinitatem beatam" *Itin.* 3, 5 (V, 305b).

40 "Quoniam autem duo gradus praedicti, ducendo nos in Deum per vestigia sua, per quae in cunctis creaturis relucet, manuduxerunt nos usque ad hoc, ut ad nos reintraremus, in mentem scilicet nostram, in qua divina relucet imago; hinc est, quod iam tertio loco, ad nosmetipsos intrantes et quasi atrium forinsecus relinquentes, in sanctis, scilicet anteriori parte tabernaculi, conari debemus per speculum videre Deum" (Ibid., 3, 1 [V, 303a]).

41 After stating that Bonaventure is the last theologian of the thirteenth century to consider the theme of the image as at the center of theology, J. Bougerol adds: "Il n'est pas sans interêt de constater que le fondement même de la Constitution pastorale sur l'Eglise dans le monde de ce temps, *Gaudium et Spes*, est précisément la théologie de l'image" (Bougerol, "Fonction du Théologien," *EF* 18 [1968]: 18, n. 46).

difficulty accepting or understanding Scripture, or their own inner experience.[42]

3. Christ, the exemplar

Beyond the idea that God created our surrounding world, which includes man and the celestial beings, is another truth, known only through Revelation—that Christ, the Word expressed by God, is the one through whom all things were made. Christ is the exemplary cause of all things, the Divine Exemplar, and He came into our world because the book of nature had become illegible to fallen human nature.[43] Thus whatever theology, as well as philosophy and all natural sciences, choose to make the object of study (*exemplata*), the same objects have Christ as their ultimate model (*exemplar*) and medium.[44] Christ is the center through whom all knowable realities proceed, as through a pattern. This forms the basis of what Bonaventure asserts in his short work *De reductione artium ad theologiam*.[45] What theology is directly concerned with, the study of God, is not to be considered as something existing isolated from the rest of reality. All other created realities, to which the various disciplines apply adequate methods of research, are "ordained" to theology.[46] This does not mean they amount to the same thing as theology, having no right to citizenship within their own scientific fields. Rather, it means they only attain their ultimate meaning when we «return» them to theology as the queen of all sciences for the final answers to the questions these sciences eventually stimulate within us

---

42   Growth in our understanding of Scripture depends to a large extent on living interiorly the realities communicated therein: "Crescit enim tam rerum quam verborum traditorum perceptio, tum ex contemplatione et studio credentium, qui ea conferunt in corde suo (cfr. Lc. 2, 19 et 51), tum ex intima spiritualium rerum quam experiuntur intelligentia" (Vatican II, *Dei Verbum*, n. 8).

43   *Hex.* 1, 10 (V, 330b–331a); 1, 13 (V, 331b); 3, 4 (V, 343b–344a); cf. 13, 12 (V, 390a); cf. *Regn. Dei* 12 (V, 542).

44   "Propositum igitur nostrum est ostendere, quod in Christo *sunt omnes thesauri sapientiae et scientiae Dei absconditi*, et ipse est medium omnium scientiarum" *Hex.* 1, 11 (V, 331a). For the same reason, Gilson was comfortable in stating: "St. Bonaventure makes no specific distinction between our theological knowledge of the Word and our philosophical knowledge of the ideas" (Gilson, *Philosophy of Bonaventure,* 144).

45   "Per hunc modum intellige, quod a summo Opifice nulla creatura processit nisi per Verbum aeternum, 'in quo omnia disposuit', et per quod produxit non solum creaturas habentes rationem vestigii, sed etiam imaginis, ut eidem assimilari possint per cognitionem et amorem" *Red. art.* 12 (V, 323a).

46   "Et sicut omnes illae ab una luce habebant originem, sic omnes istae cognitiones ad cognitionem sacrae Scripturae ordinantur, in ea clauduntur et in illa perficiuntur, et mediante illa ad aeternam illuminationem ordinantur. Unde omnis nostra cognitio in cognitione sacrae Scripturae debet habere statum" *Red. art.* 7 (V, 322a).

concerning their nature.[47] Bonaventure was looking for a unified and harmonized arrangement of all human disciplines under theology which, just as the sun illuminates the world below it, would clarify for our naked eye the ultimate nature of those realities around us. This includes human sciences and philosophical ideas, which we study and utilize for human development.[48] This arrangement reflects the ordered, hierarchized, inner and outer unity we saw in our first chapter treating of man in a hierarchized universe. Not to respect this unity produces a division between God and his creation, and Bonaventure steered a middle course between positing an independent world on the one hand (as taught by Averroistic Aristotelianism) and pantheism on the other. To avoid likewise an inner splitting of man's purpose every time he studies different created realities, Bonaventure felt the necessity of unifying human sciences. This unity was not envisioned as a form of reductionism. Rather, everything was seen as ordered, each thing at its proper level, toward God as the final end, since He is their supreme origin.[49]

In Bonaventure's theology, the center is always Christ because, as Scripture tells us, and as Bonaventure is fond of repeating, all that has been created, has been created through him (Jn. 1:3). Thus, that the divine Word

---

47 B. Hinwood explains that the ordering of the sciences under theology substantiates the orientation of human reason to a truth beyond itself: "The reduction of the arts to theology in no way destroys that proper limited autonomy which belongs to them, and is presupposed in the reduction as being logically, and most likely temporally, prior to their relation to their deeper significance. . . Thus St. Bonaventure does not fail to recognize the legitimate existence of the order and activity of reason, but he denies its self-sufficiency because it is inherently oriented to something beyond itself. It is a path to other forms of knowledge, but he who tarries on the path ends up in the dark" ("The Principles Underlying Saint Bonventure's Division of Human Knowledge," *SB* 3:501–2).

48 This sun-image of the *reductio* is well expressed in *Itinerarium mentis in Deum*: "Omnes autem hae scientiae habent regulas certas et infallibiles tanquam lumina et radios decendentes a lege aeterna in mentem nostram. Et ideo mens nostra tantis splendoribus irradiata et superfusa, nisi sit caeca, manuduci potest per semetipsam ad contemplandam illam lucem aeternam" *Itin.* 3, 7 (V, 305; *ed. min.* 5, 199). Elsewhere the sun is called Christ, e.g. *Red. art.* 21 (V, 324b). Unfortunately St. Bonaventure's meaning has not always been interpreted correctly, perhaps because the word "reductio" in modern languages reminds us of "reductionism." Against any misunderstanding, it is well to keep in mind that Bonaventure classifies each of the "arts" on its own level, and even more, that Bonaventure sees faith as a safeguard to reason when it comes to finding ultimate explanations (*pace* Gilson's remarks in his *The Unity of Philosophical Experience,* [London: Sheed & Ward, 1938], 37–60). In Bonaventure's treatise, however, the word might better be translated according to its Latin etymology from the verb "reducere," and thus, as a leading back, or an ordination of the arts and philosophy to theology. See definition given in *Lexicon latinitatis medii aevi,* ed. Albert Blaise (Turnholt: Brepols, 1975), 778, where the same use is exemplified in the words of St. Thomas Aquinas.

49 A. Rigobello sees the *reductio* as the very essence of research for Bonaventure, so befitting an exemplaristic or symbolic cosmology: "Che cosa è la ricerca per Bonaventura se non *reductio artium ad theologiam?* Ma la complicata argomentazione della *reductio* non fa che applicare e

70

is the exemplary cause of creation can be known by Scripture; but without Scripture, it would be impossible to deduce this. Instead of referring to the Platonic Ideas as the ultimate beyond which we cannot ascend, Bonaventure sees these ideas within Christ. Christ, being the most perfect expression of the Father's own thought of himself, contains within himself all that exists and all that might possibly come into existence.[50] He is the great pattern for all that exists and thus, to understand what exists, the surest road is Christ.[51] "Christ himself is the source of all sound knowledge... He is even the master of rational knowledge."[52] He who knows Christ, and in the measure in which he knows Christ, knows all things.[53]

In the hands of the theologian this principle is the key to understanding all points studied by theology and without which nothing in theology can be understood.[54] All of Scripture speaks either in an overt or veiled way about Christ.[55] Thus, the center of all Bonaventure's theology is Christ.[56] It already is commonplace among theologians today to recognize that the ultimate and integrating truth Scripture pretends to teach us is the mystery of Christ, and that all of it must be understood in subordination to

---

explicitare la natura simbolica ed allusiva que caratterizza la cosmologia bonaventuriana. Il compimento della ricerca, la compiuta *reductio*, è un procedimento discorsivo reso possibile da un'intuizione dell'autentico valore ontologico, ossia del ruolo simbolico delle cose stesse. Ma questa intuizione, che è la condizione formale della ricerca, è allo stesso tempo una qualche conoscenza di Dio, condizione formale della preghiera" (A. Rigobello, "Teologia e preghiera in san Bonaventura: confronto fra due esperienze," *SBM*, 2: 42).

50 "Pater enim ab aeterno genuit Filium similem sibi et dixit se et similitudinem suam similem sibi et cum hoc totum posse suum; dixit quae posset facere, et maxime quae voluit facere, et omnia in eo expressit, scilicet in Filio seu in isto medio tanquam in sua arte. Unde illud medium veritas est" *Hex.* 1, 13 (V, 331b).

51 J. Châtillon has pointed out that Bonaventure, far from considering studies unnecessary, frequently proclaims their necessity, but that Christ is the key for arriving at truth: "Bonaventure en effet ne veut pas nous détourner du savoir, de la recherche théologique ou de la philosophie. Il en proclame au contraire fréquemment la nécessité. Mais ce qu'il ne cesse de nous répétir, c'est qu'il n'y a pas et qu'il ne peut y avoir d'accès à la Vérité que par le Christ, qui est le Verbe de Dieu" ("Saint Bonaventure et la philosophie," *SBM* 445).

52 *Christus mag.* 1 (V, 567a); Ibid., 6 (V, 568b).

53 "Si igitur intelligis Verbum, intelligis omnia scibilia" *Hex.* 3, 4 (V, 344a).

54 "Horum ostium est intellectus Verbi increati, qui est radix intelligentiae omnium; unde qui non habet hoc ostium, intrare non potest" *Hex.* 3, 4 (V, 343b); "Nec aliquo modo aliqua veritas sciri potest nisi per illam veritatem" *Hex.* 1, 13 (V, 331b); "Nec scitur aliqua veritas nisi per eum" *Hex.* 12, 5 (V, 385a).

55 "In omnibus Scripturae mysteriis explicatur Christus" *Hex.* 14, 17 (V, 396a).

56 "From early in his academic career, Bonaventure had been fascinated with the universal dimensions of Christology and with the central place held by Christ in all of reality" (Hayes, *The Hidden Center*, 192).

the mystery of Christ. But, as Ratzinger points out, if we wish to speak of such a vision which places Christ as the radical center of all things, it seems to come "entirely from Bonaventure's own world of thought and can be traced to no outside influence."[57]

It is only from this Christological perspective that the full import of Bonaventure's exemplarism becomes clear. When the student considers everything "in the light of that principle which is the exemplary of all things," only then does he deserve to be called by Bonaventure a true metaphysician.[58] This teaching only becomes clearer in *De reductione artium ad theologiam* in which Bonaventure expressly gives the full overview of the place of theology in the realm of all knowledge.[59] Christ is seen as the sun illuminating the soul.[60] This leads eventually to Bonaventure's exclaiming how through finding God in all things, the fruit of seeing all sciences as handmaids of theology, "faith may be strengthened, God may be honored, the moral man may be formed, and consolation may be derived."[61] Thus, Christ is both the intelligibility of things and the intelligible light of the mind.[62]

4. The theologian's itinerarium

The sense of gradation in nature acquires the highest importance in the *Itinerarium mentis in Deum*, which actually is structured on these lines as a road for the theologian to ascend toward God.[63] Urged by the need of providing his brothers in religion with a method for approaching study without betraying the will of the Founder, it was while on retreat on Mount La Verna that St. Bonaventure analyzed the six-winged seraph of the stigmata of Francis, as a perfect six-step approach to study that would be a most

---

57 *Theology of History in St. Bonaventure*, 109–10.

58 "Sed ut considerat illud esse in ratione omnia exemplantis, cum nullo communicat et verus est metaphysicus" *Hex.* 1, 13 (V, 331b).

59 *Red. art.* 26 (V, 325b).

60 "Per hunc etiam modum anima non potest opera viva facere, nisi suscipiat a sole, id est a Christo, gratuiti luminis beneficium" *Red. art.* 21 (V, 324b).

61 "Et hic est fructus omnium scientiarum, ut in omnibus aedificatur fides, honorificetur Deus, componantur mores, hauriantur consolationes" *Red. art.* 26 (V, 325b).

62 "Multiformis sapientia Dei . . . occultatur in omni cognitione et in omni natura." . . . "Patet etiam . . . quomodo in omni re, quae sentitur sive quae cognoscitur, interius lateat ipse Deus" (Ibid.).

63 "[Bonaventure] accentuated the spiritual orientation of theological studies, that they would be an apprenticeship for his religious in the contemplative life exemplified by St. Francis" (J.F. Quinn, *Historical Constitution,* 77).

privileged spiritual way to God.[64] Not only was study not a hindrance to spiritual elevation, but now was seen to be the surest way for us to reach God.[65] This is the theologian's way, *par excellence*. Both in the light of the *De reductione* and with the exhortations found in the *Hexaëmeron* to rise from science to wisdom, for any student, this way is the golden road.

What the *Itinerarium mentis in Deum* does is simply apply the doctrine of exemplarism to progress in study. If one is faithful to the doctrine of exemplarism, he sees God in every level of human knowledge. On the lowest level, we first discover that things around us are God's effects—we see God through them (*per creaturas*) as though they were mirrors. Next, by speculating upon them in faith, we discover that God is present within them (*in creaturas*). The third step is going within oneself and beholding our interior nature with its faculties as an image of God. The fourth step is beholding the same interior nature elevated by grace which perfects, through the virtues and gifts, the image of a God who now lives in us. The fifth step is contemplating God above us as Being itself, a notion we already possess in the idea we form of every being. The sixth step leads us to contemplate God as the Good, as *diffusivum sui,* leading us to the contemplation of the Blessed Trinity. It is impossible for the intellect to go any further. What lies ahead is the luminous darkness of mystical experience, the *apex affectus* which outstrips the mind, because love goes further than the intellect (*"Ubi deficit intellectus, ibi proficit affectus"*).[66]

The culmination of the six steps, then, is this going beyond oneself through love, which is called *ecstasy*. Ecstasy, in its Greek significance, is a going out of oneself.[67] The theologian, through death to self by conformity with Christ crucified, eventually is called to leave his own intellectual convictions, much as St. Thomas Aquinas is seen to have done at the end of his life by saying that everything he had written was straw. This conviction, that all our ideas are as straw, only can arise from the reception of superior

---

64 *Itin.* 1, 5 (V, 297b).

65 This is what led Copleston to exclaim: "Indeed for him [i.e., for Bonaventure] the intellectual life and the spiritual life cannot properly be separated" (Copleston, *History of Philosophy,* 2: 287).

66 *II Sent.*, d. 23, a.2, q. 3, ad 4 (II, 545b); *III Sent.* d. 31, a. 3, q. 1, concl. (III, 689a). This statement is evidently inspired by William of St.-Thierry's "Amor plus se extendit quam visio" (see S. Bonav., *Op. omnia* II, 545, n. 11).

67 This is the sense Dionysius Areopagite gives to the term: "The human mind has a capacity to think, through which it looks on conceptual things, and a unity which transcends the nature of the mind, through which it is joined to things beyond itself. And this transcending characteristic must be given to the words we use about God. They must not be given the human sense. We should *be taken wholly out of ourselves* and become wholly of God, since it is better to belong to God rather than to ourselves" *Divine Names* 7, 1 (*PG* III, 865D–868A; Luibheid, 106). The same idea is

light. The light from above is so profound that by looking at it directly, we are blinded. This blindness causes an awareness of the disproportion between our human concepts about God and what God really is in Himself. This is why Bonaventure's theological journey only ends in the next life, in the vision of God in glory. Only love can attain unity with Him on earth, but this unity is without vision, that is, without adequate comprehension.

It is evident from the culminating experience in the *Itinerarium mentis in Deum* that Bonaventure places more importance on love than on intelligence in our search for God.[68] We shall see later what this implies when we speak expressly of sapiential theology in Bonaventure and what kind of knowledge results from union with God. For now, let us point out that Bonaventure's most important teacher, Alexander of Hales, does not allow reason *alone* any rights of citizenship within theology, but prefers to see theology perfecting the soul in the affective order to move it toward the good. This it does through reverential fear and love, since theology "properly and principally is wisdom."[69] This teaching is maintained by Bonaventure and as we proceed we shall have to face once again the important issues regarding reason's relationship to theology. This issue is one of the most fascinating within Bonaventure's system and at the same time has caused not a few misunderstandings that erroneously would place Bonaventure among the fideists.[70] We will address these objections when dealing with illumination in Bonaventure.

For Bonaventure, reason has to be guided by faith in order to safeguard reason from falling into error. Faith, by its very nature, already ushers us into a spiritual domain. For this reason, Bonaventure's system

---

expressed in his *Mystical Theology* 1: "By an undivided and absolute abandonment of yourself and everything, shedding all and freed from all, you will be uplifted to the ray of the divine shadow which is above everything that is" (*PG* III, 1000A; Luibheid, 135). Ecstasy is dependent upon love: "This divine yearning brings ecstasy so that the lover belongs not to self but to the beloved" *Divine Names* 3, 13 (*PG* III, 712A; Luibheid, 82).

68 "In hoc autem transitu, si sit perfectus, oportet quod relinquantur omnes intellectuales operationes, et apex affectus totus transferatur et transformetur in Deum" *Itin.* 7, 4 (V, 312b).

69 "Theologia igitur, quae perficit animam secundum affectionem, movendo ad bonum per principia timoris et amoris, proprie et principaliter est sapientia. . . Unde secundum hoc dicendum quod doctrina Theologiae est sapientia ut sapientia" (Alex. Hales, *Summa Theologica*, Liber Primus, Tract. Introd., q. 1, c. 1, solutio [Quaracchi: Coll. S. Bonaventurae, 1926], t. I, p. 2).

70 Gilson, to his own statement: "Into Bonaventure's system one can enter only by an act of faith" (*Philosophy of St. Bonaventure.*, 438), adds in a footnote: "Need we say that there is here no question of fideism? Fideism substitutes faith for reason and denies the efficacy of reason, whereas Augustinianism requires the help of faith for the right use of reason as reason" (Ibid., p. 495, n. 12). Gilson then defends this affirmation by referring the reader to: Vacant, *È tudes sur les constitutions du Concile du Vatican*, p. 286 and Document VII, p. 609.

has been seen widely as a mystical approach and methodology. I do not disagree about classifying Bonaventure as a mystical theologian. Nevertheless, I consider it unjustifiable to consider his theology as weakened by this fact. Nor do I feel that his theology is less faithful to the truth because it is less "objective," if objectivity means remaining purely on the level of conceptual theology.

In a system in which faith plays such a dominant role, the place of exemplarism is subordinate to, and at the service of, revealed truth. Thus, in proceeding according to exemplarism, that is, by viewing all of created reality as symbolic of higher truth, and finally of God himself, the thinker will understand the book of nature precisely because he is supplied with the key to understanding it. It is not initially the creature which illuminates, in a symbolic way, the mind of the beholder. The creature remains mute, or better, the beholder remains deaf, unless the beholder is equipped with the supernatural light of faith. Again, we are speaking of nature's symbolic meaning, which for Bonaventure is nature's true and ultimate meaning. The prima facie or direct representation to our senses is what forms for Bonaventure the object of the lower reason or inferior *aspectus*. The lower reason is not a separate mind within human nature, but the same mind insofar as it looks only to reality beneath it without any reference to what is above it. The same reason, when directed to the highest meaning of things is called the superior reason.[71] He who remains fascinated by creation without reference to this superior perspective, is obeying the downward tendency (*recurvatus*) in fallen human nature. Such is the situation of the natural sciences, natural philosophy included, when working without the light of faith.[72] But should not the same be said, and with greater reason, when

---

71 *Brev.* 2, 9, 7 (V, 227b); *II Sent.* d. 24, p. 1, a. 2, q. 2, concl. (II, 564a–b). This is another doctrine received from Augustine: *De Trinitate* 12, 4, 4 (*PL* 42, 1000). The division into three *aspectus* comes from Hugh of St. Victor, *De Sacramentis* 10, 2: human reason considering what is above it, what is inside it and what is below it. Again, it is not the object itself of reason that determines the aspectus. Rather, it is the level of awareness upon which the cognitive activity is taking place. Thus, one may behold the inner truth of the soul without, however, rising from *scientia* to *sapientia*. In order for knowledge to be called wisdom our mind must behold the truth in relation to its ultimate source. This is achieved, according to St. Augustine, through a *diligens inquisitio*, that is, through assiduous mental activity in which the mind considers the truth it beholds, submitting it to meditation and contemplation, and thereby rising to the source of all knowledge, God, or the divine ideas: "Ad sapientiam pertineat aeternarum rerum cognitio intellectualis, ad scientiam vero temporalium rerum cognitio rationalis" *De Trinitate* 12, 14 (*PL* 42, 1012); "Sapientia mihi videtur esse rerum humanarum divinarumque, non scientia solum, sed etiam diligens inquisitio" *Contra Academicos* 1, 8 (32, 917).

72 "Sapientia autem est supra tanquam nobilis; sed scientia infra, at videtur homini pulchra, et ideo vult sibi coniungi, et inclinatur anima ad scibilia et sensibilia et vult ea cognoscere et cognita experiri et per consequens eis uniri. Et ita enervatur, ut Salomon, qui voluit omnia scire . . . et oblitus est principalis, et ideo est factus vanus" *Hex.* 19, 3 (V, 420b).

studying theology?

If the light of faith supplies for us what is lacking to behold the true nature of material reality, (and if we take this principle alone, before entering fully into the question of the relation between reason, faith, and theology), we see at least how study for the theologian, even more than for the natural scientist or philosopher, must presuppose faith as a point of departure in virtue of the very concept of Revelation.[73] In order to study what God has revealed (i.e. Himself and His plan), the approach of faith is the only warranted avenue since faith (in the Person revealing) supplies the student with the light necessary to uncover the meaning of what is studied (His will for us). To study without faith would deprive us of the key to understanding the deeper meaning of Scripture as *veritas ad nostram salutis causam*.[74] Any other truth sought in Revelation is not pertinent directly to the only truth God wished to reveal under images (words and deeds) which form His own symbolism.[75]

Thus, the doctrine of exemplarism, although primarily a metaphysical principle in Bonaventure's system, is actually a characteristic mark of the theological methodology found in all his works. This accounts for his extensive use of symbolism, especially in his pastoral and mystical works. It may be argued that such an approach begins with a bias because it presupposes faith. Nevertheless, it also may be asserted that all great thinkers had personal desires inextricably mixed within their systems of thought, even those who claimed the greatest amount of objectivity. We might grant to St. Bonaventure the same right we grant to other thinkers. Thus, when F. Copleston situates Bonaventure's thought in historical overview, he is not ashamed to note that "it is largely a question of approach and method."[76]

---

73 Renato Tononi finds the openness to God's revelation, which ends in man's encounter with God, at the origin of Bonaventure's sapiential pursuit: "La teologia bonaventuriana [è] una continua ricerca della «sapienza», dove il sapere è impregnato di sapore e di amore, perché aperto continuamente al rivelarsi di Dio e finalizzato all'incontro con lui" (*Attesa umana e salvezza di Cristo* [Brescia: Morcelliana, 1983], 28).

74 Vatican II (*Dei Verbum*, no. 11). Commenting on *Dei Verbum*, Robert Moretti has this to say: "Quel che appare in primo piano dalla dottrina conciliare è la immensa ricchezza vitale racchiusa sia nella rivelazione che nella fede. La fonte della rivelazione è il grande amore di Dio; lo scopo o termine è di ammettere l'uomo nella intima comunione con Dio; il tramite è il Verbo fatto carne e insieme l'azione dello Spirito Santo; l'indole della rivelazione è un tratto amichevole; il contenuto è costituito da eventi e parole intrinsecamente connessi e integrati; l'attuazione assume la forma di una storia di salvezza" (Moretti, "Natura e compito della teologia spirituale," 25).

75 God's approach to us through symbolism inspired Bonaventure to utilize a similar approach. A thorough study on the symbolic aspect of Bonaventure's theology can be found in: C. Del Zotto, *La Teologia dell'immagine in San Bonaventura* (Vicenza: L.I.E.F., 1977).

76 Copleston, 2: 243.

Likewise Copleston, commenting on Bonaventure's exalted view of the purpose and value of study, says this view was "determined as much by his own inclinations and spiritual tendency as by his intellectual training."[77]

To Bonaventure, it always would imply less fidelity to the demands of any truth to seek it without faith. Faith adds to our natural capacities a new power that, instead of distorting our power of understanding reality, actually enhances and fortifies its abilities. The anthropological vision implied here is that nature and grace work together (*gratia supponit perficitque naturam*)[78] and no splitting occurs between our supernatural and natural life. The whole person, redeemed and elevated by grace, strives to learn more about God. This very process of learning about God through his creatures, and even more so, through his revealed word, is a spiritual way to God, so typical of Augustinianism and of its Neoplatonic followers. Theological study, for St. Bonaventure, would amount to an unrelenting search for God.[79]

The theologian, equipped with the key of exemplarism in his attitude toward his study, will be disposed to search for the hidden, more spiritual meanings of Scripture and Tradition. Scripture is the "other book" seen by Bonaventure to interpret and clarify the book of nature. Without neglecting the literal meaning of Scripture, just as one does not neglect what the senses tell us in the book of nature, the theologian does not stop there.[80] He is equipped with a living faith and reads the Scripture with the help of the same spirit by which it was inspired.

Conclusion

At the beginning of this chapter we asked how closely our ideas in theology approach the reality they signify. What we have found is something virtually at the opposite extreme of nominalism.

In fact, if we return at this point to Bonaventure's opening statements about the purpose of theology, we are struck by an image that may not have had as much significance as it now assumes. In the midst of his speculative

---

77 Ibid., 242.

78 *Myst. Trin.* q. 1, a. 2, concl. ad 5.6 (V, 57b)

79 "If the spirit of Augustinianism, born of the writings of the Fathers, was that of *fides quaerens intellectum,* it might also be called a spirit of *homo quaerens Deum.* This aspect of Augustinianism is especially marked in St. Bonaventure, whose thought was steeped so deeply in the affective spirituality of Franciscanism" (Copleston, 2: 554).

80 "Qui litteram sacrae Scripturae spernit ad spirituales eius intelligentias nunquam assurget" *Brev.* Prol., 6, 1 (V, 207b).

explications about the nature of theology, Bonaventure suddenly introduces an image, seeming to have found words too limited to signify the kind of knowledge theology deals with. The image is none other than Christ on the Cross, and "others like it":

> Talis est cognitio tradita in hoc libro. Nam cognitio haec iuvat fidem, et fides sic est in intellectu, ut, quantum est de sui ratione, nata sit movere affectum. Et hoc patet. Nam haec cognitio: quod Christus pro nobis mortuus est, et consimiles, nisi sit homo peccator et durus, movet ad amorem; non sic ista: quod diameter est asymeter costae. Concedendum ergo, quod est, ut boni fiamus.[81]

The same image is supplied at the end of the *Itinerarium*: "Ad quod propitiatorium qui aspicit plena conversione vultus, aspiciendo eum in cruce suspensum"[82]; "Transeamus cum Christo crucifixo ex hoc mundo ad Patrem."[83]

This is an echo of Saint Paul's ". . . only knowledge, that of Christ crucified."[84]

The very object of our theological study is an image that moves us to love, by its very nature (*nata sit movere affectum*). Evidently the purpose of theology (*ut boni fiamus*) is attained by this loving approach of the theologian to Christ, the center of all theology, and the symbol which carries us to God. If theological study is a spiritual life, such a spirituality is christocentric.

---

81 *I Sent.* prooem., q. 3, resp. (I, 13b).

82 *Itin.* 7, 2 (V, 312b).

83 Ibid., 7, 6 (V, 313b). In this regard, it is interesting to recall Bonaventure's reply to Saint Thomas Aquinas' query: "'What book did you find that in, Brother Bonaventure?' 'In that one,' said Bonaventure, raising his eyes to the crucifix on the whitewashed wall" (M. Quinn, *To God Alone the Glory: A Life of St. Bonaventure* [Westminster, Maryland: The Newman Press, 1962], 53). P. Evangéliste de Saint-Béat called Bonaventure "le Docteur de la Passion; le vêtement de sa pensée a été trempé, rougi dans le sang du Rédempteur; sur chaque mot de ses écrits perle une goutte de ce liquide précieux qui a purifié et sauvé le monde" (*Etudes franciscaines* 4 [1900]: 111), quoted by J. Bonnefoy, *Le Saint Esprit et ses dons selon S. Bonventure*, 151.

84 I Cor 2: 2; cf. *Perf. vitae* 7, 2: "Statim recurre ad memoriam Crucifixi, ut cum Apostolo nihil scias inter homines *nisi solum Iesum et hunc crucifixum*" (VIII, 483b).

He put his own light in their hearts to show them
the magnificence of his works.

Si. 17:8

IV.

THE THEOLOGIAN APPROACHES THE LIGHT

The theme of illumination in Saint Bonaventure is inextricably
wound up with his metaphysics of exemplarism and is simply a consequence
of it. Since the world is filled with innumerable signs that point to God,
only he who is illuminated, and in the degree to which he is illuminated,
grasps their true meaning. Specifically, just as Christ is the *exemplar* in
which all of the *exemplata* acquire for us their significance, Christ is the
only Light by which our world is seen for what it truly is: "As the shining
sun determines the variety and multitude of colors, so the variety of things
is determined by the Word. Whence there is no intellection except through
the Word."[1]

The image of light was used widely in the Middle Ages as something
which formed an essential part of the metaphysical and religious worldview.[2]
Thus Bonaventure's free use of light in his works is not something that sets
him apart from other thinkers, although for modern man this theory may
appear outdated.[3] Actually we find no essential difference between

---

1 *Hex.* 3, 9 (V, 344b–345a).

2 "The image of light was far more than a literary figure; it was the consistent effect of the
metaphysics of emanation, which saw not only intelligences but nature itself as filled with the light
of the supreme and motionless One and as becoming assimilated to the One through conscious or
unconscious contemplation of it. Whether in St. Augustine or pseudo-Dionysius, in Alexandrian
theology or the liturgy, one of the best established commonplaces of Christian thought is the connection
seen between such 'light' and Biblical uses of the image, all the way from religious exaltation of the
sun in the Old Testament to the concept of the Logos, light of men. The entire stock of such
commonplaces was common during the Middle Ages" (Chenu, *Twelfth Century*, p. 52, n. 2). For St.
Bonaventure, following the Augustinian teaching as developed by Robert Grosseteste, corporeal
light is the noblest of all substantial forms (*II Sent.* d. 13, a. 2, q. 2, fund. 2 [II, 319a]). Robert
Grosseteste's teaching on light can found in his *De luce seu de inchoatione formarum*, pp. 51–59 of:
Die philosophischen Werke des Robert Grosseteste, Bischof von Lincoln, (München: L. Baur, 1912);
see also: J. McEvoy, *The Philosophy of Robert Grosseteste*, (Oxford: Clarendon Press, 1982).

3 "Queste teorie ci appaiono forse sorpassate; esse ci complicano, anche, la lettura delle opere
scolastiche e, persino, ce ne allontanano. Se tuttavia accostiamo (e non senza fondamento) il termine bonaventuriano *lux* al termine «*energia*» dei fisici moderni, fuori di ogni facile concordismo,
riusciamo a sintonizzarci con il pensiero di Bonaventura" (A. Pompei, "Il 'De reductione artium ad

Augustine's and Bonaventure's theories of illumination. What is special to the Seraphic Doctor is the particular interpretation he gives to Augustine's theory of illumination,[4] as well as the extended meaning he assigns to illumination in his more spiritual works, applying it to grace and the gifts.[5] Bonaventure's doctrine of illumination, following the teaching of St. Augustine, is concerned initially only with the human mind unaided by grace.[6] But when further developing his doctrine, particularly in pastoral and mystical works, he does not hesitate to move toward higher kinds of illumination depending on grace in the form of the virtues and gifts, making it often difficult to discern the difference between the natural and supernatural illuminations.[7] Even though a basic difference between the natural and supernatural lights is posited,[8] ultimately, almost every type of influence coming from God upon our minds can be called light.[9] But to clarify the nature of the ulterior illuminations, we need to start by explaining what

theologiam': Espressione di posizioni caratteristiche di Bonaventura da Bagnoregio," in: *Bonaventura da Bagnoregio. Il pensare francescano*, [Roma: Miscellanea Francescana, 1993], 163).

4 The particular interpretation is the manner in which Bonaventure describes our contact with the eternal ideas without directly beholding them. "It seems to us that the whole of Augustinianism is a conscious effort to explain how man reaches certitude without containing the sufficient reason for them" (Gilson, *Philosophy of Bonaventure*, p. 481, n. 2). See: E. Bettoni, "La dottrina bonaventuriana dell'illuminazione intellettuale" *RivFilNeoscol* 36 (1944): 139–58.

5 "Anima continue debet recipere illuminationes a gratia Spiritus sancti" *Hex.* 13, 30 (V, 392b); cf. *Coll. Jn.* 1, 12 (VI, 249a); *De donis* 4, 2 (V, 474a). Bonaventure often cites and explains the words from the Letter of St. James: "Omne datum optimum et omne donum perfectum desursum est, descendens a Patre luminum" (1:17); see: *Red. art.* 1 and 5 (V, 319a & 321b); *Brev.* prol. 2 (V, 201a); *Itin.* prol. 1 (V, 295a).

6 St. Augustine, *De libero arbitrio,* II, cc. 9–15, nn. 25–39 (*PL* 32, 1253–1262); *De vera religione*, c. 30, nn. 54–59 (*PL* 34, 145–149); *De magistro*, c. 11, nn. 36–38, (*PL* 32, 1215–1216); *De musica*, VI, c, 12, nn. 35–36 (*PL* 32, 1182–1183); *De Trinitate*, VIII, c. 3, n. 4; c. 6, n. 9 (*PL* 42, 949–950; 42, 953–956).

7 "The mystic treatises of St. Bonaventure, especially those expounding his theory of illumination, present many difficulties to our feeble minds, and we must admit that in many passages we are at a loss to know whether the Saint is referring to the natural light of the understanding or to the supernatural light which illumines beyond reason" (E. Healy, "Commentary on the Four Lights" in: *Works of Saint Bonaventure*, 5 vols., eds. P. Boehner and M.F. Laughlin [St. Bonaventure, N.Y.: The Franciscan Institute, 1955], 1:97).

8 "Donum scientiae duo antecedunt: unum est sicut lumen innatum, et aliud est sicut lumen infusum. Lumen innatum est naturalis iudicatorii sive rationis; lumen superinfusum est lumen fidei" *De donis* 4, 2 (V, 474a).

9 "In conclusion, let us state that St. Bonaventure places no bounds to the influence of the light coming down from above. It extends to natural knowledge acquired by the powers of the mind and to supernatural knowledge which requires a revelation from above" (Healy, 98). "Hic notandum est, quod est claritas scientiae philosophicae, scientiae theologicae, scientiae gratuitae, et claritas scientiae gloriosae" *De donis* 4, 3 (V, 474a).

illumination means at its lowest level because, as we shall see, the higher illuminations work in an analogous way to these lower illuminations.

1. St. Augustine and the basis of certitude

The purpose of St. Augustine's teaching on illumination was to afford certitude to our ideas. Just as our eye alone is not sufficient, but needs a corporeal light, to behold material objects, in like manner our mind needs another kind of light, this time incorporeal, to grasp what is intelligible: "[The mind] when directed to intelligible things in the natural order, according to the disposition of the Creator, sees them in a certain incorporeal light which is *sui generis*, just as the corporeal eye sees adjacent objects in the corporeal light."[10] Augustine, convinced of the instability or changeableness on the part of created things and of the weakness or fallibility on the part of the human mind, considers truth as something necessarily "superior and more excellent" than our nature.[11] Since experience confirms we actually attain such certitude, he concludes there must be contact with a transcendent, immutable truth somewhere in our processes of knowing.[12] Thus, in some way we must participate in eternal Truth in order to accomplish the awesome feat which the attainment of certitude implies, "for no creature, howsoever rational and intellectual, is lighted of itself, but is lighted by participation of eternal Truth."[13] Nothing less than God himself, therefore, can be responsible for our knowing any truth in its changelessness and

---

10 "Credendum est mentis intellectualis ita conditam esse naturam, ut rebus intelligibilibus naturali ordine, disponente Conditore, subjuncta sic ista videat in quadam luce sui generis incorporea, quemadmodum oculus carnis videt quae in hac corporea luce circumadjacent" *De Trinitate* XII, 15, 24 (*PL* 42, 1011); "Nam et terra visibilis, et lux; sed terra, nisi luce illustrata, videri non potest. Ergo et illa quae in disciplinis traduntur, quae quisquis intelligit, verissima esse nulla dubitatione concedit, credendum est ea non posse intelligi, nisi ab alio quasi suo sole illustrentur" *Soliloquia* 1, 8, 15 (*PL* 32, 877); "Deus intelligibilis lux, in quo et a quo et per quem intelligibiliter lucent, quae intelligibiliter lucent omnia" (Ibid., 1, 1, 3 [*PL* 32, 870]).

11 *De libero arbitrio* II, cc. 12–13, nn. 34–35 (*PL* 32, 1259–1260).

12 "It is the part of the higher reason to judge of corporeal things according to incorporeal and eternal considerations, which, if they were not above the human mind, would certainly not be immutable. And yet, unless something of our own were subjoined to them, we should not be able to employ them as standards by which to judge of corporeal things. . . But that faculty of our own which is thus concerned with the treatment of corporeal and temporal things, is indeed rational, in that it is not common to us and the beasts, but is drawn, as it were, out of the rational substance of our mind, by which we depend upon and adhere to the intelligible and immutable truth and which is deputed to handle and direct the inferior things" *De Trinitate*, XII, c. 2, n. 2 (*PL* 42, 999).

13 "Nulla quippe creatura, quamvis rationalis et intellectualis, a seipsa illuminatur, sed participatione sempiternae veritatis accenditur" *In Psalmum 118,* sermo 23, 1 (*PL* 37, 1567).

eternity. "God created man's mind rational and intellectual, whereby he may take in His light . . . and He so enlightens it of Himself, that not only those things which are displayed by the truth, but even truth itself may be perceived by the mind's eye."[14]

In St. Bonaventure we find a total acceptance of Augustine's theory of illumination. The only differences are simply on the level of explicitations or further applications which do not imply any modification of the theory itself. For example, while Augustine does not offer a genesis of ideas, Bonaventure admits the validity of Aristotle's theory of knowledge but considers it insufficient when it comes to the point of abstraction. For abstraction, or *diiudicatio*, illumination becomes necessary.[15] Likewise, the concrete applications Bonaventure makes, for example in the *Itinerarium*, belong to his mystical theology with its peculiar characteristics.

What, then, is the theory of illumination as Augustine and Bonaventure understood it? As we stated above, when it concerns the basic kind of illumination, which is strictly rational, we are in a realm where the pursuit of knowledge fails unless some light, other than the sole powers of reason, intervenes to give stability and infallibility to our knowledge. Bonaventure repeats the same ideas he learned in Augustine's teaching. "The human intellect," he affirms, "cannot be sufficiently illuminated without the assistance of a superior and higher light."[16] In *De Scientia Christi*, which is the essential source of Bonaventure's teaching on illumination, in order for us to attain to the truth, immutability is necessary on the part of the object, and infallibility on the part of the mind.[17] This affirmation does not mean we know nothing without illumination. We are

---

14 "Deus autem et hominis mentem rationalem atque intellectualem fecit, qua posset capere lumen ejus . . . et eam sic illuminat de seipso, ut non solum illa quae a veritate monstrantur, sed ipsam quoque proficiendo perspiciat veritatem" *In Psalmum 118,* sermo 18, 4 (*PL* 37, 1553).

15 J. Bougerol defines *diiudicatio* as an "Augustinian term equivalent to Aristotelian abstraction." Nevertheless, he adds that Bonaventure assigns to *diiudicatio* a different role than it has in Aristotelian and Thomist abstraction: "Nous sommes capables de saisir, dans l'appréhension sensible concrète, quelque chose qui la transcende, c'est l'universel ou contenu abstrait de l'appréhension; nous sommes ainsi capables de former une idée de la chose appréhendée. La fonction de la *diiudicatio* est donc de purifier l'espèce sensible de toutes ses imperfections contingentes, et de la concevoir dans sa pure forme spirituelle ou idéale" (*LSB*, s.v. «Diiudicatio»). See also: J. Rohmer, "La théorie de l'abstraction dans l'école franciscaine d'Alexandre de Halès à Jean Peckam," *AHDLMA* 2 (1928): 158; Ph. Boehner, p. 118, n. 8; Bissen, *L'exemplarisme,* 235; Gilson, *Philosophy of Bonaventure,* 361.

16 "Nec potest iste intellectus sufficienter illuminari sine adminiculo superioris et altioris lucis" *De donis* 8, 20 (V, 498b); cf. *I Sent.* d. 3, p. 1, au., q. 1, fund. 2 (I, 68a); *II Sent.* d. 28, a. 2, q. 3, concl. (II, 690a). Theodore Crowley's article, "Illumination and Certitude" (*SB*, 3:431–48), provides a clear overview on Bonaventure's teaching on the mind's need of illumination.

17 "Nobilitas, inquam, cognitionis, quia cognitia certitudinalis esse non potest, nisi sit ex parte scibilis immutabilitas, et infallibilitas ex parte scientis" *Scien. Chr.* 4, resp. (V, 23b).

able to know in an imperfect manner, but a perfect judgment about the nature of things is withheld from us without superior light: "To have real knowledge means to know that a thing cannot possibly be otherwise."[18]

Bonaventure does not situate divine illumination within the order of nature but somewhere between the order of nature and that of grace.[19] This means that illumination is neither part of the ordinary assistance God gives to all creatures, nor is it a special help in the form of grace. If it were the former, it would be no more extraordinary than rain is for the tillage, but we would not be respecting Bonaventure's three grades of resemblance to God found in creatures according to the degree of their participation in His being. If it were the latter, we would be speaking of infused graces, thus robbing the thought processes of their autonomous potential to acquire knowledge as well as the possibility of some innate knowledge.[20] An indirect contact would be insufficient to guarantee certitude, and thus would call for some sort of fideism for our adherence. In some form, the human mind must attain direct contact with the eternal ideas, without directly beholding these ideas since they are identified with God's essence.[21] Again this contact is demanded in order that knowledge might attain certitude, not as a source of new intellectual content. Therefore, although contact with the eternal ideas cannot be through direct vision (intuition), these same ideas act directly upon our mind. Our awareness of their presence and their activity come about in us through what Bonaventure calls contuition, a term characteristic of his teaching. *Contuitio* refers to that conviction arising in us from the evidence supplied by the effects whose presence can only be accounted for by divine intervention.

Instead of dedicating my attention to the two pitfalls (ontologism and fideism) which Bonaventure successfully avoids,[22] my interest in this

---

18 "Si enim scire est cognoscere, rem aliter impossibile se habere. . ." *Hex.* 12, 5 (V, 385b).

19 "Quodam modo medio inter utrumque" *Christus mag.* 16 (V, 571b).

20 "Illa lucis influentia aut est generalis, quantum Deus influit in omnibus creaturis, aut est specialis, sicut Deus influit per gratiam. Si est generalis: ergo Deus non magis debet dici dator sapientiae quam fecundator terrae, nec magis ab eo diceretur esse scientia quam pecunia; si specialis, cuiusmodi est in gratia: ergo secundum hoc omnis cognitio est infusa, et nulla est acquisita, vel innata; quae omnia sunt absurda" *Scien. Chr.* 4, resp. (V, 23a–b).

21 "Ergo impossibile est, quod intellectus noster certitudinaliter cognoscat aliquod verum, quin attingat aliquo modo summam veritatem" (Ibid., fund. 29 [V, 20a]); "Divinus intellectus, sua summa veritate omnia aeternaliter exprimens, habet aeternaliter omnium rerum similitudines exemplares, quae non sunt aliud ab ipso, sed sunt quod est essentialiter" (Ibid., 2, concl. [V, 9a]).

22 "Et ideo est tertius modus intelligendi, quasi medium tenens inter utramque viam, scilicet quod ad certitudinalem cognitionem necessario requiritur ratio aeterna ut regulans et ratio motiva, non quidem ut sola et in sua omnimoda claritate, sed cum ratione creata, et ut ex parte a nobis contuita secundum statum viae" *Scien. Chr.* 4, concl. (V, 23b).

chapter is to ascertain to what degree the human mind needs divine assistance and what dangers lie in wait for those who place too much confidence in the native powers of the intellect. After dealing with the power of human reason in this perspective as collaborator with the divine mind, I will consider in my following chapter the specific question of whether a higher form of illumination does not violate rational autonomy and thus invite a form of antirationalism.

2. Light, a co-principle for study

Before the theologian undertakes the study of revealed truth, it is merely prudence which moves him to take stock of his own powers so as not to be like the man who wanted to build a tower without sufficient materials (Lk. 14:28). Bonaventure fully recognizes the importance of human reason,[23] and grants ample rights to the theologian as efficient cause of theology.[24] But the theologian, upon approaching his study, must know first of all of what his own role consists in the matter of study. The doctrine of illumination attempts in some way to manifest for us the capacities and the limitations of the human mind. It does so by establishing the human mind as a co-principle in the search for truth, the other principle being God.[25] If our success or failure in attaining truth depends not only upon our natural talents but furthermore upon the amount of light we receive from God, the approach only can be one of greater humility added to a desire to be rid of one's own darkness: "By His most clear ideas He shines upon the dark ideas of our minds."[26] For the man without these lights is

---

23 "Modus perscrutatorius convenit huic doctrinae" *I Sent.* prooem., q. 2, resp. (I, 10b). Many studies are dedicated to the rational method and its relationship to wisdom. An example is M. Arosio's article "«Credibile ut intelligibile». Sapienza e ruolo del «modus ratiocinativus sive inquisitivus» nell'epistemologia teologica del Commento alle Sentenze di Bonaventura da Bagnoregio," *DtS* 41 (1994): 175–236.

24 *I Sent.* prooem., q. 4 (I, 14a–15b).

25 Quoting St. Augustine ("Nullus potest addiscere nisi Deus doceat"), Bonaventure explains: "Hoc enim non dicitur quia omnis cognitio sit infusa, sed quia lumen creatum non potest efficere operationem suam absque cooperatione luminis increati per quod illuminatur omnis homo. . . . Haec enim dicta sunt non quia Deus sit tota causa, sed quia sine ipso non potest agere aliqua virtus creata" *II Sent.* d. 28, a. 2, q. 3, concl. (II, 690a). "La nostra conoscenza non è, nè tutta opera di Dio, nè tutta opera nostra, ma frutto di una cooperazione metafisica e necessaria della luce increata con la creata, propria dell'intellecto umano. La soluzione giusta quindi non è nè quella platonica, nè quella aristotelica, ma quella di S. Agostino. La 'ratio aeterna' agirà direttamente nel nostro atto intellettivo, ma nè 'tota' nè 'sola'; cioè nè con tutta la sua perfezione ed efficacia, nè esclusivamente, ma in collaborazione con le cose create" (E. Bettoni, "La dottrina bonaventuriana dell'illuminazione intellettuale," *RivFilNeoscol* 36 [1944]: 147).

26 *Hex.* 12, 5 (V, 385a).

like an animal, just as the man full of these lights is wholly angelical.[27]

Some have wished to see Bonaventure's recourse to illumination as simply stemming from the reverence he shared with his contemporaries for this Augustinian theory, or from a kind of religious duty permitting him to exalt the authority of God while emphasizing the poverty of the human mind.[28] Although there is much truth to this view, the expressed purpose of the theory is reduced solely to that of obtaining certitude.[29] And Bonaventure's recourse, besides St. Augustine, is his own experience: we have the experience of arriving at certitude and we have the experience of the changeableness of the objects of knowledge as well as the unreliability of the human mind.[30]

For Bonaventure truth is the *adaequatio rei et intellectus*.[31] Again, for something to be known with certainty, two conditions must be met, each of which refers to one of the two poles that come together to form the truth: the thing to be known must be stable or unchanging and the mind that judges it must be infallible.[32] But we see that things around us are ever

---

27 "Bestialis est homo carens his; sed plenus luminibus est totus angelicus" (Ibid., 20, 2 [V, 425a–b]).

28 St. Augustine, in fact, had stated: "Si ergo natura nostra esset a nobis, profecto et nostram nos genuissemus sapientiam . . . nunc vero quia natura nostra, ut esset, Deum habet auctorem, procul dubio ut vera sapiamus, ipsum debemus habere doctorem" (*De Civitate Dei*, Lib. XI, chap. 25 fin [*CChr* 48:345]). "The theory of illumination and of knowledge in the eternal principles appeared to the followers of the Augustinian tradition, such as John Peckham and Matthew of Acquasparta, as a sacred repository which religious sentiment was passionately concerned to protect. Just as the doctrine of the seminal principles is superior to the efficacy of the creature, so the doctrine of the eternal principles is more religious, in the affective sense of the term, than that which allows to the human intellect the faculty of engendering concepts by mere contact with the sensible" (Gilson, *Philosophy of Bonaventure*, 351). "Bonaventure had recourse to the Augustinian theory of illumination, which commended itself to him, not only because St. Augustine had held it but also because it emphasized both the dependence of the human intellect on God and the interior activity of God in the human soul. For him it was both an epistemological truth and a religious truth, something that could be established as a necessary conclusion from a study of the nature and requirements of certainty and also something upon which one could profitably meditate in the religious sense" (Copleston, 2:287).

29 "Illumination is Bonaventure's solution to the problem of certitude" (M. Hurley, "Illumination according to S. Bonaventure," *GR* 32 [1951]: 389).

30 "Hoc patet per explierientiam, si quis recurrat ad suae mentis arcana" *Myst. Trin.* q. 1, a. 2, concl. (V, 56b); "Et de experientia cognitionis humanae; dicendum, quod hoc ponit, ad nostram intelligentiam concurrere lumen et rationem veritatis creatae" *Scien. Chr.* concl. ad 7.8.9. (V, 25a); "Intelligentia autem fertur in hanc lucem tripliciter: ratiocinando, experiendo, intelligendo; rationaliter, experimentaliter, intelligentialiter" *Hex.* 5, 29 (V, 359a).

31 *I Sent.*, d. 40, a. 2, q. 1, ad 1, 2, 3 (I, 707b); cf. *Brev.* 6, 8, 2 (V, 273a).

32 *Scien. Chr.* 4, Resp. (V, 23b).

changing; nothing is permanent in the created world. Likewise a created mind cannot be endowed with infallibility on its own account, since only God can have a perfect knowledge of anything. But we have the experience of knowing some things, that is, unchanging principles, with certainty.[33] Since this certainty cannot come from ourselves, nor from any other created object, recourse must be had to a light from God who is the only one who cannot err. In order for human beings not to be doomed to uncertainty, Bonaventure sees no better alternative than the Augustinian theory of illumination.

In what way does Bonaventure see this illumination take place? Bonaventure is not an ontologist and expressly distances himself from such a theory of knowledge.[34] He teaches that we never see this light directly. We are similar to one who can see by the light of the sun but will be blinded if he looks directly at the source of light.[35] We only will behold directly this light in the state of glory. Such direct vision is called "intuition." But here on earth, the light that illuminates our minds is a light that is invisible to us.[36] By virtue of this light we have an indirect awareness of truth and such a perception is what Bonaventure calls *contuitio*.[37] In some sense this is like our coming to realize a thing after all the clues have been given to us. Something becomes evident by implication without, however, being directly revealed.[38] The fullest clarity of the object itself is not attained, but the mind is summoned to attain ultimate truth with certainty, albeit through

---

33 "Necessario intelligentia experitur in se, quod habeat aliquod lumen" *Hex.* 5, 30 (V, 359a).

34 "Unde si quae auctoritates id dicere inveniantur quod Deus in praesenti ab homine videtur et cernitur, non sunt intelligendae quod videtur in sua essentia, sed quod in aliquo effectu interiori cognoscitur." *II Sent.* d. 23, a. 2, q. 3, Resp. (II, 544b).

35 Like bats, we are blind to this light: "Et Philosophus dicit: 'Sicut se habet oculus vespertilionis ad lucem solis, sic se habet intellectus noster ad manifestissima naturae'" *De donis* 8, 20 (V, 498b); *Itin.* 5, 4 (V, 309a). Another Bonaventurian comparison refers to the eye of the owl: we do not see the light itself unless it is reflected upon creatures (*Assisi Manuscript 186,* 41ra; this manuscript of an unpublished notebook of St. Bonaventure was discovered in Assisi's municipal library. For reasons supporting its authenticity, see: F. Henquinet, O.F.M., "Un brouillon autographie de S. Bonaventure sur le commentaire des Sentences," *EF* 44 [1932]: 633–55; 45 [1933]: 59–81).

36 "Haec lux est inaccessibilis, et tamen proxima animae etiam plus quam ipsa sibi. Est etiam inalligabilis et tamen summe intima" *Hex.* 12, 11 (V, 386a). The obvious sense given to light is metaphorical. What is signified by the metaphor of light is the direct influence of the eternal reasons.

37 "Spectacula nobis ad contuendum Deum proposita" *Itin.* 2, 11 (V, 302b). "Dum haec igitur percipit et consurgit ad divinum contuitum" *Hex.* 5, 33 (V, 359b). "Cette atteinte obscure est proprement une contuition, mot propre au vocabulaire bonaventurien et que l'on pourrait rendre par connaissance implicite et virtuelle" (Bérubé, "De la philosophie à la sagesse dans l'Itinéraire bonaventurien," 41).

38 *Scien. Chr.* 15 (V, 25b); Ibid., 18 (V, 26a).

shadowy signs embedded in a reality waiting to be deciphered.[39]

For Bonaventure this illumination is likewise not a form of revelation by means of infused knowledge.[40] Nowhere in Bonaventure is sense perception denied as necessary in the thought process for acquiring knowledge about the material world. Here Bonaventure would agree with Aristotle in positing the mind as a *tabula rasa,* and we find Bonaventure utilizing Aristotle's theory of knowledge in everything except its final stages. We cannot number Bonaventure among those who believe in the existence of innate ideas.

In Bonaventure's theory of knowledge there are basically three steps: *apprehensio, oblectatio* and *diiudicatio.* It is only the third step, abstraction,[41] that falls under illumination and this is discovered to occur when and if the mind attains certainty. Evidently, *diiudicatio,* since it already supposes the influence of illumination, is much more than simple abstraction in the Aristotelian sense. This three-step process is detailed in the *Itinerarium mentis in Deum,* which I shall describe briefly.[42] The exterior sense receives the likeness through contact with sensible objects and judges each object in such a way that it recognizes simply what it is (*apprehensio*). Next the interior sense judges its utility or aesthetic value (*oblectatio*), seeing it as pleasurable or unpleasurable. Finally, the intellect, through a kind of secondary reflection, decides why it believes such a judgment to be true. When such a judgment (*diiudicatio*) is experienced as true and certain it is because of its direct reference to the eternal reasons (*rationes aeternae*). Otherwise, against what backdrop could we possibly hold up our ideas so as to guarantee their objectivity, their inherent validity? Bonaventure finds no other way except by this logical conclusion of recourse to a source of certainty that is neither subject to change itself nor submitted directly to the gaze of fallible human minds.[43]

---

39   Ibid., 4, Concl. (V, 23b); cf. Ibid. ad «*Quoniam igitur*» (V, 24a–b); *II Sent.* d. 23, a. 2, q. 3, Concl., ad «*Et ideo est quartus modus*» (II, 544b–545a); *Hex.* 2, 9–10 (V, 337b–338a); *De donis* 8, 15 ad «*Sed unde est. . .*»(V, 496b–497b); *Itin.* 2, 9 (V, 301b–302a); Ibid., 3, 2 (V, 303b–304a).

40   "Cadit similiter per errorem estimationis, quae oritur ex praesumptione, quando credit se omnia habere per revelationem" *Hex.* 22, 42 (V, 444b).

41   I have retained the word "abstraction" here only as a parallel, or point of reference, to help us appreciate the deeper import of *diiudicatio.* Furthermore, there may be no word in English that properly designates this particular type of abstraction.

42   "Diiudicatio igitur est actio quae speciem sensibilem, sensibiliter per sensus acceptam, introire facit depurando et abstrahendo in potentiam intellectivam" *Itin.* 2, 6 (V, 301a).

43   The eternal reasons remind me of Bernard Lonergan's transcendental precepts: "All special methods consist in making specific the transcendental precepts, Be attentive, Be intelligent, Be reasonable, Be responsible. But before they are ever formulated in concepts and expressed in words,

Even though this light is invisible (*inaccessibilis*) and we are incapable of looking at it directly, its influence upon us certainly is direct. That is to say, this illumination actually reaches our minds directly, and is not simply an influence that operates by means of a *habitus mentis* in us which would belong to our own mental capacity.[44] But in order for its influence to be direct and at the same time invisible to us, Bonaventure states that its direct action upon us is *ut regulans et motiva*: "The eternal reason (*ratio aeterna*), as a regulating and stimulating reason, is a necessary requirement for certitude in knowledge."[45] He avoids stating that reason has no part to play, which would thereby invite fideism, by immediately adding: "This knowledge however does not come to us alone and in direct clarity, but uses created reason and our collaboration by the intellect grasping (*contuitio*) according to our human condition (*secundum statum viae*)."[46]

From what has been stated so far, by way of explaining Bonaventure's theory of illumination, it becomes clear that the theory of illumination does not belong properly within the limits of the origin of ideas, as in a theory of knowledge, such as Aristotle's. Rather, illumination lies at the basis of man's capacity to discover the deeper meaning in things, as creatures of God.[47] What exemplarism brings to the objects of our knowledge to provide their stability with a metaphysical foundation, illumination brings to the mind itself to provide infallibility in knowing the divine exemplars.

those precepts have a prior existence and reality in the spontaneous, structured dynamism of human consciousness" (Lonergan, *Method in Theology*, 20). Such transcendental notions also make it possible to form judgments about what is true: "On questions for intelligence follow questions for reflection. We move beyond imagination and guesswork, idea and hypothesis, theory and system, to ask whether or not this really is so or that really could be. Now self-transcendence takes on a new meaning. Not only does it go beyond the subject but also it seeks what is independent of the subject. For a judgment that this or that is so reports, not what appears to me, not what I imagine, not what I think, not what I wish, not what I would be inclined to say, not what seems to me, but what is so" (Ibid., 104). Perhaps self-transcendence is to Lonergan what illumination is to Augustine and Bonaventure, at least judging by the fruit of certainty.

44 "Alio modo, ut intelligatur, quod ad cognitionem certitudinalem necessario concurrit ratio aeterna quantum ad suam influentiam, ita quod cognoscens in cognoscendo non ipsam rationem aeternam attingit, sed influentiam eius solum. Et hic quidem modus dicendi est insufficiens secundum verba beati Augustini, qui verbis expressis et rationibus ostendit, quod mens in certitudinali cognitione per incommutabiles et aeternas regulas habeat regulari, non tanquam per habitum suae mentis, sed tanquam per eas quae sunt supra se in veritate aeterna" *Scien. Chr.* 4, resp. (V, 23a).

45 "Ad certitudinalem cognitionem necessario requiritur ratio aeterna ut regulans et ratio motiva" (Ibid., [V, 23b]).

46 "Non quidem ut sola et in sua omnimoda claritate, sed cum ratione creata, et ut ex parte a nobis contuita secundum statum viae" (Ibid., [V, 23b]).

47 "La dottrina dell'illuminazione del nostro intellecto da parte di Dio non si riferisce propriamente al problema filosofico delle facoltà conoscitive dell'uomo che si dedica alla conoscenza scientifica dei fenomeni dell'esperienza sensibile. In questo campo, Bonaventura segue Aristotele e la sua dottrina della struttura, delle operazioni e delle funzioni dell'intelletto umano che si applica alle

3. The theologian participates in the light from God

In speaking of illumination, we have not touched yet upon the effect of the gifts of the Holy Spirit on the human mind. We have been speaking here about light upon the mind that all thinkers need in order to reach certitude. Nevertheless, this light is ultimately identified with Christ so that Bonaventure does not doubt in exclaiming: "Nothing can make things perfectly knowable unless in the presence of Christ, the Son of God and the Master."[48] We saw in a previous chapter St. Augustine substituting the Neoplatonic *Nous* with the Divine Word as the abode of the eternal ideas. Similarly, behind Bonaventure's metaphysics stands Christ, the Exemplar of all created reality. At the basis of all that is knowable lies the mind of God who first thought, and then patterned every created being through the divine model in which every possible being finds its archetype.[49] Together with exemplarism, which has to do primarily with the order of being, we see Bonaventure bringing to bear the Augustinian theory of illumination upon the order of knowledge as a tool whereby he reveals for us the close relationship between knowing and participating in God's life.

The consequences of the theory of illumination are expressed well in the *Itinerarium mentis in Deum*. The title itself alludes to this—the mind, in virtue of its proper intellectual activity (contuition), is on a journey into God.[50] All the author need do is explain to the reader what happens in the thought processes by their very nature. The rest is simply an encouragement to travel this road in fidelity to the light that accompanies us along each of its six stages. Even before grace comes into play by means

---

conoscenze scientifiche. Ma l'uomo, in quanto essere spirituale, è anche aperto verso l'alto. Questa sua apertura verticale pone nell'intelletto una funzione conoscitiva superiore a quella scientifica. Questa conoscenza superiore percepisce, anche se non sa ben definirla, l'esistenza di un senso profondo insito nelle cose in quanto creature del Dio di amore" (A. Pompei, 'La centralità di Cristo," in: Antonio Blasucci et al., *Lettura critica di San Bonaventura* [Firenze: Città di Vita, 1974], 58–59).

48 "Nihil potest facere res perfecte scibiles, nisi adsit Christus, Dei Filius et magister" *Christus mag.* 7 (V, 569a).

49 "Illa lux aeterna generat ex se similitudinem seu splendorem coaequalem . . . qui ubique est per primam sui generationem, sicut obiectum in toto medio generat similitudinem" *Itin.* 2, 7 (V, 301b).

50 "Sicché la realtà ci è stata data per 'cointuire' Dio, l'Esemplare eterno, ossia per riconoscerla nel suo valore allusivo al Verbo eterno di Dio, che è Dio stesso. Ed è proprio in questo atto con cui riconosce e riferisce ('cointuisce'), che l'uomo realizza il proprio *ascensus*" (Pompei, "Il 'De Reductione artium ad theologiam': Espressione di posizioni caratteristiche di Bonaventura da Bagnoregio," 38).

of the virtues and the gifts, the human mind has Christ as its teacher.[51] This is so whether or not one is conscious of it, as man is essentially in dependence and in relationship to God from the beginning.[52] However, when conscious of this continual interaction between us and Christ, who "is intimately present to every soul. . . enlightening us interiorly," we become impelled by another title to cooperate with this light.[53]

It might be objected at this point: Why talk about the illumination of human reason, considered apart from faith and Revelation, when our chief interest is the theologian under the influence of grace as a supernatural illumination? For two reasons primarily: [a] The theologian never is excused from using his human reason, because his task is to make faith intelligible; he may be tempted to believe that, at least when depending more on human reason than on faith, he is laboring independently; [b] As I stated above, supernatural illumination, although different from the natural illumination given to all human minds, has many features in common with it and can be understood analogously.[54] Pagan philosophers were not aware of the ultimate source of their certitude. What matters for Bonaventure is that for anyone "to have real knowledge," that is, "to know that a thing cannot possibly be otherwise, it is necessary that He alone should cause us to know,

---

51 "Scit igitur in illa luce, *quae illuminat omnem hominem venientem in hunc mundum*, quae est, *lux vera* et *Verbum in principio apud Deum" Itin.* 3, 3 (V, 304b).

52 "Imago est essentialis dependencia et relatio" *Hex.* 10, 7 (V, 378a); "Relatio creaturae ad Creatorem non est accidentalis, sed essentialis" *Hex.* 4, 8 (V, 350a). Commenting on this teaching, Bougerol has stated that "[Bonaventure] est le dernier théologien du XIIIe siècle à considerer que le thème de l'image est au centre de la théologie, parce qu'il considère ce thème comme le seul fondement possible d'une théologie de la relation" ("Fonction du théologien," in: *EF* 18 [1968]: 18). On his part, Xavier Zubiri emphasized how St. Bonaventure "hacía consistir toda persona, aun la finita, en una relación, y caracterizaba dicha relación como un *principium originale*. La persona envuelve en sí misma una relación de origen para San Buenaventura. La religación no es una propiedad ni una necesidad; es algo distinto y superior: una dimensión formal der *ser* personal humano" (*Historia, naturaleza y Dios*, 4th edic., [Madrid: Alianza, 1959], 320).

53 "Secundum sententiam omnium doctorum Christus est doctor interius, nec scitur aliqua veritas nisi per eum, non loquendo, sicut nos, sed interius illustrando. . . . Ipse enim intimus est omni animae et suis speciebus clarissimis refulget super species intellectus nostri tenebrosas" *Hex.* 12, 5 (V, 385a). What alternative remains for receiving God's truth? Commenting on the ambiguous acceptance of truth, Anthony Padovano writes: "The mind may not only resist the truth but may even accept it and keep it at a personal distance. Logical convictions are not necessarily existential imperatives" ("Aesthetic Experience and Redemptive Grace," in: *Aesthetic Dimensions of Religious Education*, eds. Gloria Durka and Joanmarie Smith [Ramsey, N.J.: Paulist Press, 1979], 6).

54 Although natural illumination, as explained above, is not produced by ordinary assistance in the order of nature, nevertheless, no confusion should arise in calling this illumination 'natural', as Saint Bonaventure himself is wont to do [e.g. *Myst. Trin.* q. 1, a. 2, concl. (V, 55b–56b)]. The *Lexique saint Bonaventure* does not hesitate to call 'natural' all lights that are inferior to the light of faith: "Au-dessus et en-dessous de toutes les lumières naturelles, le chrétien est illuminé par la lumière de la foi" (s.v. «Illuminatio,» by T. Crowley).

who knows the truth and has the truth in Himself."[55] What is implied here is no less than our attaining the idea of what we know, not as it exists in things, nor in our minds, but in the mind of God.[56] This already implies contact, if not union, with God.[57]

Thus, for the theologian there comes the realization that God is participating with him on every level of human knowledge, helping him, not only regarding the meaning of revealed truths, but also regarding the very functioning of our human operations of thought. At no point is the assistance of God taken for granted. Nor is the human mind, at any point in the work of theology, discredited or put aside as useless, unless of course we refer to the final stage in the itinerarium into which reason cannot intrude.[58] But at that point we are no longer doing theology, at least in the accustomed way, because reason will have another manner of knowing and understanding the truth that surpasses conceptual knowledge. The truth will be communicated to us in a new way, in a direct contact, not as we behold the Truth face to face, but in darkness. Before that point we count on the normal functioning of our human reason. No matter what approach we take in theology, we need to apply a tireless and unflagging human reason even when, nay more so, it has to do with the study of the more elevated truths under the influence of the virtues and the gifts, because of the principle *"Gratia supponit perficitque naturam."* At no point in the formulation of Bonaventure's system do we find him prescinding of the role of human reason in theology, even though its customary activity eventually will be superseded.[59] Beyond a doubt, for Bonaventure, grace

---

55 *Hex.* 12, 5 (V, 385b).

56 "Unde cum res habeant esse in mente et in proprio genere et in aeterna arte, non sufficit ipsi animae ad certitudinalem scientiam veritas rerum, secundum quod esse habent in se, vel secundum quod esse habent in proprio genere, quia utrobique sunt mutabiles, nisi aliquo modo attingat eas, in quantum sunt in arte aeterna" *Scien. Chr.* 4, concl. (V, 23b–24a); cf. *Itin.* 3, 3 (V, 304a–b).

57 "Ex quo manifeste apparet, quod coniunctus sit intellectus noster ipsi aeternae veritati" *Itin.* 3, 3 (V, 304b).

58 "Si autem quaeras, quomodo haec fiant, interroga gratiam, non doctrinam; desiderium, non intellectum; gemitum orationis, non studium lectionis; sponsum non magistrum; Deum, non hominem; caliginem, non claritatem" (Ibid., 7, 6 [V, 313b]). M. Schlosser dedicates her thesis to negative theology in St. Bonaventure. For extract, see "«Lux inaccessibilis»: Zur negativen Theologie bei Bonaventura," *FzS* 68 [1986]: 1–140).

59 "Il misticismo non significa abbandono della ragione. Il misticismo cristiano non è un annientamento dell'essere sotto la forma reale, perchè tra la creatura e il creatore infinita è la distanza, infinita è la diversità della natura. Questa forma di annientamento panteistico è ignorata dai nostri mistici. Il loro è, se mai, un annientamento dell'essere sotto la forma morale, un atto di amore e di umiltà, un tentativo di squarciare i nostri limiti e di estendere la nostra finitezza infinitamente quanto infinito è il desiderio del nostro cuore. Ma il loro è un amore razionale, una conoscenza, un vivo

has much more importance than nature. Nevertheless, this is simply a matter of recognizing what is immeasurably more valuable between two co-principles. It is never a denial to reason of any positive value. So also, there is an analogy of proportion between grace and nature on one hand, and between the illumination from above and the abstraction process of our human judgments (even theological), on the other. As grace is to nature, so illumination is to abstraction, even when the said illumination is not yet the supernatural illumination introduced by grace.[60]

Thus the theologian realizes that Christ never is missing at any point, nor under any title, in his intellectual labors. He is present not only when one feels particularly inspired by grace—some few, unforgettable but isolated, moments to be cherished along the often lonely path toward truth, but also at all points in our challenging search for truth. His influence upon us is not a unilateral force, but an agent that cannot function without our collaboration, put forth through effort.[61] The gifts of the Holy Spirit, specifically those of knowledge and understanding, suppose the diligent, and even arduous, collaboration of the theologian with grace. In the intellectual life we are working together with this light and thus the intellectual life necessarily becomes, for those who live it in fullness, a virtuous life. In the virtuous life, one lives the realities he knows through union with them, otherwise he renounces true knowledge of them. This is why even the natural philosophers, who lacked the infused habits coming with grace, eventually perceived they only could advance intellectually in the measure they practiced virtue: "When they discovered it was impossible to attain such a high summit except through the virtues, they turned to the teaching of these same virtues, as did Socrates."[62]

---

sperimentale possesso di Dio, una conoscenza sotto forma di amore" (G. Bonafede, "Il problema dell'illuminazione in S. Bonaventura," *Sophia* 4 [1936]: 79).

60 "The light of philosophy is great to the eyes of the world; yet it is small compared with the light of Christian knowledge" *De donis* 4, 3 (V, 474a).

61 "Gratia non solum operatur cum libero arbitrio, sed etiam operatur in liberum arbitrium et liberum arbitrium movet" *II Sent.* d. 26, au., q. 6, concl. (II, 646a); "[Voluntas] movetur a Deo quod movetur etiam a se ipsa; et ideo omne opus meritorium attribuitur gratiae et libero arbitrio" (Ibid., ad 1 [II, 646b]).

62 "Quando viderunt, quod tam alte non posset perveniri nisi per virtutes, converterunt se ad docendum illas, ut fecit Socrates" *Hex.* 5, 33 (V, 359b).

Conclusion

As the theologian progressively advances in the way of light, his own activities become proportionately reduced to give way to the ever increasing power of God's light. This reduction in his own activities is relative. That is, he does not become less active in his performance as a student, but becomes less independent of God's activity upon him. God illuminates the theologian as he progresses in sanctity, since greater sanctity means greater dependence on God, particularly in the cognitive powers, until full union is achieved. The spiritual life becomes ever more primary as a motivating force and as a source of inspiration. Precisely at this point in our study of theology, the motivations of the spiritual life become so intertwined with the aims of study, that we may become suspect of disrespecting, or even of violating, the autonomy universally accorded for reason to attain "objectivity" in its search for truth. Thus, before advancing in my investigation of the influence of grace on the study of theology, I shall consider Bonaventure's apparent anti-intellectualism, while giving due regard to the historical circumstances which induced him to resort to prophetic denunciation.

I am going to destroy the wisdom of the wise
and bring to nothing the understanding
of any who understand.

Is. 29:14

V.

SCIENTIA FIDEI AND CHRISTIAN LIFE

When speaking of theology as a spiritual life, I should remind my readers that it is not my intention to impose the speculative models of theology upon the spiritual life, even when that particular spiritual life is one lived by the theologian. The spiritual life has its own laws to which all other interests, even theological methods, must remain secondary.[1] Thus, even when undertaken as a spiritual life, theology does not thereby acquire the status of a master who would subordinate, or integrate, the spiritual life to conform it to the scientific procedures necessarily inherent in any theology worthy of the name.

Truly, theology's scientific character must be maintained in order for theology to be faithful to its mission of making our faith comprehensible in the clearest and most objective way possible. In the words of St. Augustine, "fides, si non cogitatur, nulla est."[2] At least in theory, almost any method, provided it be neither at odds with common sense nor closed to the possibility of divine intervention, may serve as an instrument in the theologian's task. The difficulty arises when we realize that faith itself necessarily implies some degree of nonrationality. If the spiritual life, in essence, is simply a life of faith, or "faith in action," whereby we live according to principles that are not always "reasonable" to human prudence, but involve the acceptance of mystery, some voluntary acceptance of nonrational influences upon our behavior is expected of us in order for the "obedience" of faith to have supernatural merit.[3]

---

1 Theology can be considered as a derivative of spirituality, if we understand spirituality as Christian life. Lonergan notes that "Christian theology has been conceived as *die Wendung zur Idee*, the shift towards system, occurring within Christianity. It makes thematic what already is a part of Christian living" (Lonergan, *Method in Theology*, 144). This idea inspired my title to this chapter.

2 St. Augustine, *De praedestinatione sanctorum*, 5 (*PL* 44).

3 B. Lonergan notes that "initially the Christian religion and Christian theology were not distinguished" (*Method in Theology*, 138). But he points out that their gradual separation was necessary for apostolic or apologetic ends, even during the first ecumenical Councils: "Painfully it [the main tradition] learnt from Nicea the necessity of going beyond scriptural language to formulate what was considered scriptural truth. Painfully it learnt from Chalcedon the necessity of employing

Furthermore, does the nonrational aspect of the Christian life increase in the measure of the intensity with which the spiritual life, the vitalization of faith, is lived? If so, what are the prospects for the scholarly life when submitted authentically to the demands of the Christian life? If the theologian undertakes his study as a form of spiritual life, he necessarily submits his scientific way of life to higher considerations coming from his love of God and his desire for union with Him. While the rational life and the spiritual life must not be conceived of as mutually antagonistic by some inherent incompatibility, nevertheless, any attempt to make them mutually dependent, or worse, to identify one with the other, risks mutilating their specific natures and their rights to autonomous operation. What would be the consequences of a confusion of these two realities?

On one hand, the spiritual life, if it were considered as a theological pursuit, could become an academic enterprise where rational principles almost exclusively dominate our interior and exterior life. What does the spiritual life have to gain from theology as a science? Does not the very process of conceptualization represent a threat to devotion which, admittedly, is a primary condition for spirituality? After all, as we have seen, for the theologian the greatest temptation militating against the spiritual life is undue dependence on the powers of the intellect. When scientific knowledge is sought for its own sake, above wisdom and sanctity, we easily fall into pride of mind, the chief vice of which is *curiositas*.[4] On the other hand, if theology were considered only as one form of spiritual life among others, should the theologian risk his scientific rigor by enlisting it into serving an inherently subjective role—that of conceptualizing his own religious experiences? If so, feelings would have a large part to play, perhaps dangerously so, in the search for truth. What would become of the scientific nature of theology? For the theologian to look upon theology as a spiritual life, must he lower or relativize the standards of theology as a science? So, at least in some way, the unity between theology and the spiritual life would seem to bring with it a set of disadvantages, most evident among which are those that undermine the scientific rigor of theology.

---

terms in senses unknown both to scripture and to the earlier patristic tradition. But it is in reflection on such developments, as in Byzantine Scholasticism, and in the extension of such reflective consideration to the whole of Christian thought, as in medieval Scholasticism, that theology became an academic subject, at once intimately connected with the Christian religion and manifestly distinct from it. The validity of this first differentiation is, of course, questioned today. Is not such academic theology merely a cultural superstructure, divorced from real life, and thereby inimical to it? A distinction, I feel, must be made" (Ibid., 138–39).

4 "Beatus Bernardus dicit de gradibus superbiae, quod primum vitium est curiositas, per quod lucifer cecidit; per hoc etiam Adam cecidit. Appetitus scientiae modificandus est, et praeferenda est ei sapientia

1. Further implications of illumination

Having studied Bonaventure's teaching on illumination, our purpose has not been primarily to discover how man reaches certitude in his abstractions. Likewise, since the origin of ideas is not what interests the Seraphic Doctor, it would be of slight advantage to speak of a Bonaventurian gnoseology.[5] Bonaventure set the limits for a mind that would dare to operate independently, denying to it any secure road to truth. What really mattered was to emphasize man's dependence on God. But once this point is made, we may ask ourselves what are the implications arising afterwards, beyond natural knowledge? Since illumination, even on the lowest level, is a direct intervention by God into rational thought processes, what must illumination be when its meaning is extended to include a supernatural energy that uplifts and enriches our capacity to do theology? This is where the Augustinian opposition between scientific knowledge and sapiential knowledge takes on importance.[6] Even though the eternal reasons are reached by all men, both by the scientists and by the truly wise, we discover Bonaventure discussing the difference between the kind of attainment implied in each case:[7]

> It must be said that for knowledge through the eternal reasons, it is not necessary for the mind to be focused on them except in the case of sapiential knowledge. The person of wisdom attains to the reasons in one way and the person of knowledge in another. The person of science attains to them as to the principles that move the mind. The person of wisdom attains to them as to that in which

---

et sanctitas" *Hex.* 19, 4 (V, 420b).

5 "Processus, qui S. Bonaventurae, suo tempore, videbatur esse sufficienter et satisfacienter criticus, nobis hodiernis non iam sufficit, nec hodiernis criteriis undequaque respondet: quia nimia praesupponit et nimia probat" (N. Picard, "Gnoseologia bonaventuriana?" *Ant* 18 [1943]: 244).

6 "Cette opposition entre la connaissance scientifique et la connaissance sapientielle est essentielle à l'appréciation de la valeur philosophique ou théologique de la doctrine bonaventurienne de l'illumination. Aussi juge-t-il opportun d'y insister pour dire que c'est une doctrine qui relève non de la science mais de la sagesse, et que c'est la foi qui fait accéder à cette sagesse" (Bérubé, "De la philosophie à la sagesse dans l'Itinéraire bonaventurien," 300). We already have quoted St. Augustine's statement: "Ad sapientiam pertineat aeternarum rerum cognitio intellectualis, ad scientiam vero temporalium rerum cognitio rationalis" *De Trinitate* 12, 14 (*PL* 42, 1012). Cf. also: "Et in hominibus quidem haec ita discerni probabiliter solent, ut sapientia pertineat ad intellectum aeternorum, scientia vero ad ea quae sensibus corporis experimur" *De diversis quaestionibus ad Simplicianum* 2, 2 (*PL* 40, 140).

7 "Concedendum est igitur, sicut rationes ostendunt et Augustini auctoritates expresse asserunt, quod in omni certitudinali cognitione rationes illae cognoscendi a cognoscente attinguntur, licet aliter a viatore

the human spirit finds rest. And no one arrives at this wisdom "except those who are first purified by the justice of faith."[8]

This statement takes on the greatest interest for us since theology is "a habit that is called wisdom."[9] But before discussing theology as wisdom, it is profitable to re-examine the question of human reason and its limits. This becomes more urgent as we find we are dealing with a God who not only has participated in our thought processes all along our life journey, but increasingly participates in them in the measure of our advancement in sanctity and even seems to overpower them completely:

> That which moves us principally is the illumination which begins in the natural light and finds its consummation in the infused light, for this leads us to think of God not only in a lofty manner but also in a reverent manner, because this illumination proceeds from the eternal light itself which takes our intellect into obedient captivity; in capturing the mind, it subjects it to God in worship and veneration and renders it ready to believe whatever pertains to the divine honor and veneration, even though such things be beyond our reason.[10]

Such a prospect—of reason being taken into captivity by a superior light—may arouse some amount of apprehension, and perhaps even distress, in those who defend man's necessary autonomy for developing rational activity. Thus, the question of reason acting in virtue of its own "lights" (if not "rights") must briefly be treated before approaching the question of reason completely invaded by the divine spirit.[11] To bypass this juncture in our study may invite the charge of anti-intellectualism or expose

---

et aliter a comprehendente, aliter a sciente et aliter a sapiente" *Scien. Chr.* 4 concl. (V, 24b).

8 "Dicendum, quod ad hoc, quod cognoscat per aeternas rationes, non oportet, quod in illis figatur, nisi in quantum cognoscit sapientialiter. Aliter enim attingit illas rationes sapiens, et aliter sciens: sciens attingit illas ut moventes, sapiens vero ut quietantes; et ad hanc sapientiam nemo pervenit, 'nisi primo per fidei iustitiam emundetur'" (Ibid., ad 2 [V, 24b; Hayes, *Knowledge of Christ*, 137]).

9 *I Sent.* prooem., q. 3 (I, 13b).

10 "Dicendum, quod principaliter movens ad hoc est ipsa illuminatio, quae inchoatur in lumine indito et consummatur in lumine infuso, quae quidem facit, nos non solum alte, verum etiam pie sentire de Deo; et hoc, quia illuminatio procedit ab ipso lumine aeterno, in cuius obsequium nostrum captivat intellectum, et captivando, dum ipsum subiicit Deo, colit et veneratur et reddit habilem ad credendum quaecumque ad divinum honorem et cultum spectant, etsi sint supra rationem nostram" *Myst. Trin.* q. 1, a. 2, concl. (V, 56b). Eng. trans.: Z. Hayes, *Disputed Questions on the Mystery of the Trinity* [hereafter *Mystery of the Trinity*] in: *Works of Saint Bonaventure*, vol. 3 (St. Bonaventure, N.Y.: Franciscan Institute, 1979), 132.

11 Lonergan observes the province of reason, once it was distinguished from faith, increasing during the period we are studying: "Still a distinction between reason and faith is a distinction within theology. It pertains to the theologian's delimitation of his own field and to the elaboration of his own methodology.

Bonaventure's teaching to other unjustifiable interpretations (e.g. of confusing philosophy, theology and mysticism).[12] If one judges Bonaventure's works only on the philosophical level[13] or "fails to recognize the basic concern of Bonaventure's concept of wisdom,"[14] he loses the key that opens the door to his whole system. This is what led Gilson to warn us: "You can either see the general economy of his doctrine in its totality, or see none of it."[15]

Perhaps one of the best approaches to grasping Bonaventure's "basic concern" is by considering the historical context within which his works were born and toward which they are addressed, often in a prophetic, and at times polemical nature. Just as "the philosopher cannot be separated from the man,"[16] we cannot know the man without knowing the circumstances he faced.

There are two historical circumstances that often are examined in order to facilitate an understanding of Bonaventure's central philosophical positions. One is the change in theological perspective that originated in the twelfth century and the other is the thirteenth century Franciscan crisis. Since the latter only concerns the necessity or uselessness of study and culture for Franciscan life, and in some way simply mirrors the larger conflict, for our

---

But it possesses implications outside the theological domain. Its meaning is not confined to the erection of distinct and subordinate departments of philosophy and science within theological schools and for the furtherance of theological purposes. For once reason is acknowledged to be distinct from faith, there is issued an invitation to reason to grow in consciousness of its native power, to claim its proper field of inquiry, to work out its departments of investigation, to determine its own methods, to operate on the basis of its own principles and precepts. Such was the underlying significance of the discovery of Aristotle by the medieval age of faith" (Lonergan, *Insight*, 527).

12 "Esa mezcla de filosofía, teología y mística que se encuentra en las obras bonaventurianas ha sido la causa de que se acuse a su autor de confusión. Se le critica de abordar diversos géneros literarios y de ser indiferente a la distinción de los objetos formales. De hecho, el Doctor Seráfico descarta y condena toda *filosofía separada*. No obstante, él sabe muy bien que un argumento filosófico pertenece a otra especie muy distinta del argumento teológico" (J.M. Merino, *Historia de la Filosofía Franciscana*, [Madrid: B.A.C., 1993], 33).

13 Apparently Etienne Gilson did not completely escape such a danger, perhaps because he wished to look upon Bonaventure's teaching too exclusively as a philosophy: "If piety is not theology, still less is it philosophy. Yet it cannot be denied that, as a philosopher, St. Bonaventure sometimes allowed himself to be carried away by his religious feelings" (Gilson, *Unity of Philosophical Experience*, 53).

14 Ratzinger, *Theology of History*, 133.

15 Gilson, *Philosophy of Bonaventure*, 436. As I quoted him in my Introduction: "Paradoxical as the assertion may seem, I hold that it is the extreme unification of Bonaventure's doctrine which has made it look incomplete and unsystematized; it is easier to deny that the details form part of a system, than to grasp the system in its entirety and think out each detail in function of the whole" (Ibid.).

16 Ibid., 36.

purposes, it is more than sufficient to treat the first of these circumstances.[17] Afterwards we shall dedicate some time to Bonaventure's attempts to synthesize two differing attitudes toward theology that survived from the twelfth century.[18]

Finally, an example of Bonaventure's approach—his proofs for the existence of God—is set forth as a model of his procedure in theology.

2. A theological shift: from monastic «lectio» to speculative «quaestio»

Much has been written about the history of thought in the twelfth century and about the many sociological changes that took place causing a kind of revolution in the theological schools. Since the consequences of these changes became fully apparent in the thirteenth century, powerfully

---

17 Regarding the Franciscan crisis, history's opinion of Bonaventure's term as Minister General has undergone significant change in our times. Today we are warned that Bonaventure's influence on the Franciscan Order should neither be looked upon as that of an innovator, nor as a 'second founder' as it was previously popular to regard him: "Se ha exagerado al dar a san Buenaventura el calificativo de 'segundo fundador'... Hemos visto que la evolución estaba ya completa. Buenaventura no corrigió ni reformó nada. Conservador por temperamento, aceptó las cosas tal como las halló; pero se percató de los peligros reales externos e internos y se propuso conjurarlos con prudencia y energía" (Lázaro Iriarte, *Historia franciscana* [Valencia: Editorial Asís, 1979], 81). Gratien de Paris (against the attitudes popularized by Paul Sabatier in the early part of this century) already had expressed the same opinion fifty years earlier: "Saint Bonaventure interprète la Règle plus largement que les contemporains de saint François, car il est obligé de tenir compte de l'évolution qui a amené l'Ordre au point où il l'a trouvé" (Gratien de Paris, *Histoire des frères mineurs* [Gembloux, Belgium: J. Duculot, 1929], 267–68). This likewise is clear in regard to study, which is the point that interests us: "Bonaventure n'ignore pas et ne songe pas à nier le changement qui s'est opéré depuis l'époque encore assez rapprochée des origines: à peine un demi-siècle. Il ne s'en scandalise pas; il l'admire... L'état des choses qu'il trouve à son entrée dans l'Ordre, reçoit donc sa plus vive approbation et il n'imagine pas qu'il en puisse être désormais autrement: la science est pour lui un élément essentiel de l'activité franciscaine. Si différent que cela soit de la volonté de saint François et du caractère primitif de sa congregation, Bonaventure n'éprouve aucune gêne à démontrer que l'étude est en parfaite conformité avec le texte de la Règle" (Ibid., 269–70). Shorter treatments on St. Bonaventure's role as major superior of the Franciscans can be found in Rosalind Brooke's "St. Bonaventure as Minister General," *S. Bonaventura francescano*, Convegni del Centro di Studi sulla spiritualità medievale 14 (Todi, 1974), 77–105; Raoul Manselli, "St. Bonaventure and the Clericalization of the Friars Minor," *Greyfriars Review* 4 (1990): 83–98.

18 Bernard Lonergan believes that the theological problem (which he terms as the distinction between reason and faith) originating in the twelfth century, and technically formulated in the thirteenth, has only grown in importance over the centuries: "The demand for method in metaphysics rose out of medieval theology. The twelfth century was oppressed with an apparently insoluble problem, with the necessity of distinguishing between divine grace and human freedom and, at the same time, an inability to conceive either term without implying the other. In the first third of the thirteenth century, there gradually was evolved the notion of two entitative orders so that grace stood above nature, faith above reason, and charity above natural human excellence. With increasing thoroughness this distinction between a natural order and a supervening gratuitous order was carried through by successive theologians to receive

affecting the following centuries, it is important to realize, as Chenu points out, that the environment plays a significant role in determining what kind of theology appears in any age.[19]

He finds this especially true for the twelfth century.[20]   What most concerns us can be summarized as the shift from the monastic approach to theology, typified by the Victorines, to a speculative approach to theology, typified by the canons' schools, such as Chartres. Such a shift was responsible to a large extent for the crisis that inevitably left its mark on all theological undertakings from the late twelfth century onward.   Chenu speaks of a veritable '*choc de deux mentalités*':

> The disagreement was basic. It was by no means a quibble between exegetes over a verse in the Bible; it was a clash between two mentalities, on the one hand the naturalist idealism of Chartres instinctively picking up the outlook of the *Timaeus*, on the other hand [représenté par] Hugh of Saint-Victor with his practical sense of a historical order in which divine and human liberties were at play, over and above any natural determinisms.[21]

Thus the school of Chartres represented a new 'scientific' tendency. Such an outlook was naturalistic or physicistic in the sense that it allowed for the more or less complete autonomy of the forces of nature.[22]   Nature enclosed within itself a broad and entirely self-sufficient basis for scientific

---

after the middle of the century its complete formulation and its full theological application in the writings of St. Thomas Aquinas. Finally, despite the condemnations of Aquinas at Paris and Oxford, despite the aridity of fourteenth-century nominalism and the sterility of its scepticism, despite the worldly contempt of the Renaissance for the Schoolmen and the pious contempt of the Reformation for carnal knowledge, despite the semirationalism of a Hermes, a Gunther, a Frohschammer, and the agnosticism of modernists, the technically formulated distinction between reason and faith has only grown in importance in the Catholic Church since its basic formulation in the thirteenth century. Within his own terms of reference, Aquinas did his work well" (Lonergan, *Insight*, 527).

19 For the historical background of this period, I have depended chiefly on the excellent study done by M.D. Chenu, *La théologie au douzième siècle*. English translations are taken from: idem: *Nature, Man, and Society in the Twelfth Century*. Complementary studies can be found in: J. de Ghellinck, *Le mouvement théologique du XII siècle*, (Bruges: Editions "De Tempel," 1948²); F. Van Steenberghen, *La philosophie au XIIIe siècle* (Paris: Béatrice Nauwelaerts, 1966).

20 "The economy of salvation is not defined exclusively in the reflective and cautiously reasoned understanding of a few licensed thinkers, but also in the concrete decisions, in the states of life embraced, in the ideals of sanctity, in the evangelical work which the church, in its head and members, approves, sets up, promotes—in short, defines. This sociological approach to ideas is illuminating for any period. But it seems especially appropriate for the twelfth century" (Chenu, *Twelfth Century*, 202–3).

21 Ibid., 9–10.

22 "Naturalism was the crime of the masters, according to William of Saint-Thierry and William of Saint-Jacques" (Ibid., 303).

investigation, with reason being the key to unlocking its meaning. Reason in many ways had come of age.

The Victorines, on the other hand, appear 'voluntarist' in the sense that both nature and history are not seen as scientifically determined, but rather as symbolic of the free intervention of divine creativity, which calls for a free response on the part of man. The latter outlook can be seen as the recipient, and continuator, of the traditions of monastic theology.[23] The monastic approach to theological study owed much to the environment itself in which theology customarily had been nurtured:

> The monk led an other-worldly life in this world. This pervasive theme colored his way of thought as well as his behavior, his understanding of scripture as of the universe . . . In such a perspective, theological projects developed under the inspiration and in the climate of spiritual quietude (*otium*), a term much loved and characteristically used, but best seen as the expression of an interior law. Not that they failed to appreciate the stringent demands of the exercises of *lectio-meditatio*, but they insisted that these were free of external involvements. . . It was purely contemplative theology, at leisure to turn towards God (*vacare Deo*) in a mystical sabbath where the labors of the week were all over. The activity of reason, too, gave priority to the tranquillity of the soul. In such activity, as in others, the monk imitated the heavenly life on earth. His theology was an anticipation of paradise where all dialectic would be ludicrous, where wisdom would absorb all science, even sacred science.[24]

In general, the world at that time had reached a crossroads in some ways similar to the Age of Reason in later centuries.[25] A process of rationalization took place in the doctrinal movement in the twelfth century that had irreversible effects in the following century. By the middle of the thirteenth century when St. Bonaventure had matured in his theological positions, as faithful disciple of Alexander of Hales,[26] an intellectual controversy was in full force.[27]

---

23 "The term 'monastic theology' has been justly employed to describe its peculiar manner and method of defining the essential components of the Christian economy of salvation" (Ibid., 204).

24 Ibid., 306.

25 Chenu has called the twelfth century "a century universally acknowledged to be the turning point of the Middle Ages in the West" (Ibid., xv). Nevertheless, he adds that its merit has been undervalued since our concept of it is distorted: "Our understanding of the twelfth century has been distorted by the rationalist prejudices of Enlightenment philosophy" (Ibid., xix).

26 ". . . et fratris Alexandri de Hales, patris et magistri nostri" *II Sent.* d. 23, a. 2, q. 3 (II, 547b); ". . . et potissime magistri et patris nostri bonae memoriae fratis Alexandri." *II Sent.* praelocutio (II, 1a).

27 Lonergan refers to it as "a raucous knock-down controversy" that still is not over: "The methodological problems surfaced towards the end of the thirteenth century in a raucous knock-down controversy between Augustinians and Aristotelians. That controversy, so far from being settled, simply shifted into a permanent opposition between the Thomist and the Scotist schools, as did later the

Etienne Gilson tends to oversimplify this problem throughout his masterful study on Saint Bonaventure:

> While the Aristotelians saw the evil effect upon Christian truth of a definite metaphysical error and accepted battle upon the ground of pure philosophy, the Augustinians chose to remain upon the field of Christian wisdom and block the advance of Averroism by denying the principle of a pure philosophy—a philosophy independent of revelation.[28]

Although we shall not enter into what eventually was called the *Bonaventurian problem*, wherein various authors in our century have debated over how precisely to define Bonaventure's attitude toward philosophy as a separate science (or conversely, as this problem regards our own times, the possibility of a "Christian philosophy"), suffice it to give J.F. Quinn's conclusive statement which both sums up and explains the controversial tone of Bonaventure's later works:

> Toward the end of St. Bonaventure's life, some Christian masters in Paris were not guided or directed by their faith in their philosophical thinking. In St. Bonaventure's judgment, they deliberately chose to ignore their faith while teaching as true according to philosophy what they knew to be false according to divine revelation. They clung to the errors of non-Christian philosophers, particularly Averroes, rather than correct them in view of the teaching of Christ. Thus, adhering to a mundane wisdom, those Christian masters falsified the truth of philosophy and distorted the truth of Scripture, which they tried to explain by natural reason.[29]

---

controversies between Catholics and Protestants, between Jesuits and Dominicans, and between the followers of different Protestant leaders. The needed solution to such ongoing differences is a theological method radical enough to meet head on the basic issues in philosophy. What is one doing when one is knowing? Why is [*sic*] doing that knowing? What does one know when one does it?" (Lonergan, *Method in Theology*, 297). But Lonergan himself immediately adds to this solution: "Though necessary, it is not enough. One must also ask what one is doing when one is doing theology" (Ibid.). We shall see if Bonaventure gives us some clues about how to solve this ongoing controversy.

28 Gilson, *Philosophy of Bonaventure,* 25; Ibid., pp. 3–5, 7–8, 26, 30, 169. In judging Gilson as 'oversimplifying', I refer my reader to the excellent overview of differing opinions of Gilson's contemporaries, given by J.F. Quinn, *Historical Constitution of St. Bonaventure's Philosophy*, especially in the Introduction: "Historical Views of Thirteenth-Century Philosophy" (pp. 17–99) and in the General Conclusion: "The Historians and Bonaventurean Philosophy" (pp. 841–96). Warning of this danger, Chenu, for his part, states: "Aristotelianism did not destroy Platonic 'spiritualism'. . . . Nor did Aristotelianism diminish in any way the nobility and the truth of twelfth-century Neoplatonism—a fact that rules out any simplistic contrast between 'the Aristotelianism of the scholastics' and 'the Platonism of the fathers', a distinction which represents a historical error and a misunderstanding of theology" (Chenu, *Twelfth Century*, 98). In the same spirit, Ratzinger states: "We cannot, therefore, agree with Gilson who interprets the entire work of Bonaventure as anti-Aristotelian on the basis of certain texts in the *Hexaemeron* and the late sermons" (Ratzinger, *Theology of History*, 161).

29 J.F. Quinn, *Historical Constitution,* 838–39.

Thus, the role of reason, although always necessary in theological study, became more predominant, ultimately to the detriment of faith, since reason attempted to impose its own structures upon revealed truth.[30] The word of God then became treated, as Fr. Chenu observes, as an 'object'.[31] "The religion of Christ was not based on logic but on a series of facts arranged in a history, a history that one must read—in the technical sense of the medieval *lectio*—according to an appropriate method, not according to the dialectical pattern of some system of thought."[32] Thus, the development of an ever more speculative theology also was accompanied by a gradual distancing from Holy Scripture.[33] "Although in the mid-thirteenth century the Bible was still to serve as the textual basis for the teaching of theology, scriptural *lectio* (reading and commentary by the master) had by then become more and more surrounded with *quaestiones*, so that direct apprehension of the Bible became lost in the systematization of theological arguments."[34] Reason yearned for greater independence, not only from Sacred Scripture, but also from all texts that would impose the traditional limits.[35]

Of course we can observe historical antecedents to the late medieval preference shown for speculation at the cost of time-honored doctrines. As far back as the sixth century, Boethius, often called "the last Roman and the first Scholastic," is the example Fr. Chenu selects as "an extreme instance

---

30 "But in the second half of the twelfth century, reason and its various disciplines no longer furnished simply the tools for studying the sacred text (*sacra pagina*). Reason, by introducing 'well ordered arrangement' (*artificioso successu*), somehow entered into the structuring of the faith itself, as Alain de Lille suggested in his *Ars fidei*" (Chenu, *Twelfth Century*, 280).

31 "The word of God was treated as an 'object', given, to be certain, within the context of the faith, but apart from one's own fervor and experience... Scholastic objectivity robbed the traditional *meditatio* of its ends and of its dynamism . . . Within this objectivity there were widely divergent intellectual trends. The masters of the twelfth century, employing Neoplatonic metaphysics based on Augustine or on pseudo-Dionysius, maintained a more spontaneously religious orientation than their successors, who were equipped with Aristotle as their guide to reason and eventually also their guide to an understanding of nature and of man himself. The intervention of this new guide caused great tension, this time within scholasticism. The causes of this tension and its effects on the history of Christian thought are well known" (Ibid., 302).

32 Ibid., 165–66.

33 Fr. Chenu speaks of a gradual abandonment of Scripture parallel to the growth of the new speculative method, resulting eventually in "the encroachment of speculation on theology in the thirteenth century, when the *quaestiones* (and their products, the *summae*) were divorced from the historical *lectio* of sacred texts. Scholasticism detached itself from sacred history" (Ibid., 168).

34 Ibid., 146.

35 "This independence from texts was an external sign of the independence of a new doctrinal style and scientific curiosity. Problems and their solutions were no longer immediately associated with some text. The age of the *summa* had arrived" (Ibid., 295).

of theological reliance upon reason."[36] Coming closer to our period of study we have the well-known model for all later rationalists, Peter Abelard (1079–1142). Abelard's intention was to apply "the analogies of human reason to the fundamentals of the faith."[37] This he accomplished, notes Chenu, "with an audaciously rational clarity which threatened to weaken all taste for mystery."[38] Of course, Abelard's fate, that of straying from orthodoxy, became less unusual as time progressed and as the power of reason drew more theologians away from pastoral concerns and personal sanctification:

> The place of the masters in the church became increasingly difficult to deter-
> mine as they organized theology into a science with its own rules, constructed
> within the faith and its premises to be sure, but according to criteria stemming
> from the intelligible nature of the subjects they were examining, and not according
> to the needs and opportunities of pastoral responsibility or of subjective, pious
> intentions. There would now necessarily be "theological" errors, whereas hitherto
> the term heresy simply denoted any lapses from orthodox faith. In the second
> half of the twelfth century there was a long list of masters who came under
> suspicion of heresy, rightly or not, privately or publicly.[39]

Eventually, by the beginning of the thirteenth century, we find William of Auxerre establishing the way henceforth followed by the *summae*. The speculative approach to theology had thrown deep its roots.[40] Thus, by the time of St. Bonaventure's activity, the victory of speculative theology almost was complete. This does not mean that the traditional, or monastic, appreciation for theology had vanished. In a sense, the triumph of the more scientific approach became the very stimulus for revitalizing a more traditional approach. Let us hear Fr. Chenu give a summary and a judgment

---

36 "The *Consolation*, deliberately constructed upon a purely rational foundation, is an extreme instance of theological reliance upon reason. It was not at all a 'profane', a 'pagan' work; no medieval writer, not even the most anti-intellectual among them, would ever have taken it for that. From this point of view and on this ground, Boethius was the first of the scholastics—a title one would not think of bestowing upon Augustine. He succeeded in using the logic of Aristotle in a domain of inquiry to which it could claim no special right of entry—the domain of the First Being and of pure spirits" (Ibid., 77).

37 ". . . ad ipsum fidei nostrae fundamentum humanae rationis similitudinibus disserendum" (Abelard, *Historia calamitatem* 9 [*PL*, 178, 140–1]), cited by Chenu (Ibid., 290).

38 Ibid.

39 Ibid. In regard to 'pastoral responsibility', the impact pastoral life had on Bonaventure's own theology is formidable. Because he was elected Minister General (1257) he had to leave his chair at the University of Paris and immediately was thrown into various pastoral concerns of no little importance. Although his literary output decreased in volume, it only increased in vitality.

40 "From William of Auxerre, at the time of the Fourth Lateran Council, we have a prototype of the classic *summa* of the thirteenth century where every element in the legacy of revelation was brought

of the climate facing St. Bonaventure as he began his career:

> Still valid, despite their passionate rhetoric, were the diatribes of St. Bernard against the pretentious and too clever dialectic of Abelard who neglected the mysterious *via negativa* of all theology. Still valid was the appeal of the conservatives at the Fourth Lateran Council—those who had challenged the evangelical enterprises and the new religious orders—who declared, "There is less of a similarity between creatures and the Creator than of a dissimilarity," and that consequently the mystery of God was impermeable to reason. Theology was thus a kind of wisdom more truly than it was a science, and the theologian could never be more than a professor, i.e., one who professes. Herein lay both the triumph and the defeat of theology. A scientific approach must be used to build the spiritual and temporal framework of Christendom in any age—and such an approach triumphed in the thirteenth century. But it could continue triumphant only if it continued evangelical, always carrying the word of God as a message, returning always to the ancient testimonies, resisting the subjection of mystery to an irresponsible scientism, preserving a free and close relationship with faith even while pursuing the most rigorous investigations.[41]

3. Bonaventure attempts a synthesis

Simply by commenting upon them, Peter Lombard's *Sentences* were a well accepted place to start doing theology . Written in the middle of the twelfth century, the *Sentences* cannot escape reflecting the shift of theology's center, as a simple remark of Fr. Chenu testifies: "Peter Lombard, insensitive to Neoplatonism, ignored pseudo-Dionysius and impoverished Augustine."[42]

Alexander of Hales was the first to produce a commentary on the *Sentences*. Even though his spiritual son, St. Bonaventure, defends the *Sentences* as being subordinated to Scripture, the Seraphic Doctor views reason in some way as pulling theology away from its proper object of study, which is holy Scripture.[43] Thus we perceive an attempt by Bonaventure to harmonize two different approaches to theology, the

into question and dealt with by various rational methods in order to extract certain internal connections and convincing subtleties of the objects of the faith. Thus conceived, theology would more and more assume the forms and procedures of the Aristotelian science (*scientia*)" (Ibid., 291).

41 Ibid., 237–38.

42 Ibid., 95.

43 "Liber iste [of Lombard] ad sacram scripturam reducitur per modum cujusdam subalternationis, non partis principalis; similiter et libri doctorum qui sunt ad fidei defensionem. Quod patet sic: quia non quaelibet determinatio trahens in partem facit subalternationem scientiae, sed determinatio quodam modo *distrahens*. Nam scientia de linea recta non dicitur subalternari geometriae, sed scientia de linea visuali, quoniam haec determinatio quodam modo trahit ad alia principia. Quoniam igitur sacra scriptura est de credibili ut credibili, hic est de credibili ut facto intelligibili, et haec determinatio *distrahit*—"nam

rationalistic and the monastic. How does he proceed?

Not by condemning reason, but simply by recognizing the risks of its magnetic force, which tends to draw us away from the authority of faith,[44] Bonaventure resorts to the notion of 'subalternation': reason must be *subalternated* to Scripture. In this way, as already we have seen Bonaventure point out, the intellect believes

> . . . not only what is accessible to reason, but even what exceeds reason and contradicts sense experience; otherwise, it would fail to show due reverence to supreme Truth, preferring its own judgment to the teaching of eternal light— which necessarily implies the puffing up of pride and of blameworthy conceit.[45]

Fr. Chenu, commenting on Bonaventure's recourse to the term 'subalternation', states:

> Until then it was said, and Bonaventure objected, that the scriptural method was symbolic and narrative; consequently theological knowledge born of Scripture must necessarily conform to this method, leaving no space for rational inquisition. No, Bonaventure says. In Scripture, which is the word of God, we deal with the *credibile ut credibile*; in theology, under the aegis of Lombard, we deal with the *credibile ut intelligibile*. We find here, Bonaventure explains, a determination which in some way pulls the object studied away from its original axis (*determinatio distrahens*), and under which determination it is no longer treated as forming part of its original body, but is submitted to other principles of explanation. Bonaventure names this with a technical term: subalternation. . . . The object of faith, without losing anything of its nature and quality, falls beneath another order, in which the *modus ratiocinativus* reigns. The book of Lombard, which is a work of this type, finds its source in Scripture, but does not form part of it, since it has reference to Scripture only through subalternation, that is, by an epistemological determination which is centered around other principles. Thus, one will be the method of the exegete, another will be that of the theologian.[46]

---

quod credimus debemus auctoritati, et quod intelligimus, rationi"— hinc est quod sicut alius modus certitudinis est in scientia superiori et inferiori, ita alius modus certitudinis est in sacra scriptura et alius in hoc libro; et ideo alius modus procedendi. . ." *I Sent.* prooem., q. 2, ad 4 (I, 11a–b); cf. *Brev.* 1, 1, 4 (V, 210b).

44 "Non debemus auctoritates Sanctorum trahere ad nostram rationem, sed magis e converso rationem nostram auctoritatibus subiicere, ubi non continent expressam absurditatem" *I Sent.* d. 15, p. 1, au., q. 4 (I, 265a).

45 *Brev.* 5, 7, 4 (V, 260b; de Vinck, 208).

46 "On disait jusqu'alors, et Bonaventure s'objecte, que la méthode scripturaire est symbolique et narrative, que par conséquent la connaissance théologique qu'implique l'É criture doit se conformer à cette méthode, sans inquisition rationnelle. Non, dit Bonaventure; dans l'É criture, parole de Dieu, il s'agit du *credibile ut credibile*; en théologie, sous l'égide du Lombard, il s'agit du *credibile ut intelligibile*. C'est là, explique Bonaventure, une détermination qui tire en quelque sorte hors de son axe primitif (*determinatio distrahens*) l'objet étudié, et sous laquelle il n'est plus traité comme une partie de son donné primitif, mais soumis à d'autres principes d'explication. Bonaventure appelle cela

What makes it possible to subordinate theology to Sacred Scripture is faith in the word of God. Faith, likewise, is what makes it possible for us to link up all the sciences in a hierarchized order below theology, with theology below Scripture.[47] Subalternation provides the necessary context in which to understand fully both theology and the sciences subordinated to it.[48]

In this sense, faith can be seen as the connecting tissue between the multiple beings which form the complex data of our knowledge:

> The link between these intelligibilities is established by the 'faith' whereby the sciences are subordinated one to another— that is, the 'subalternation of the sciences', to use the more technical Latin term. . . It is faith which ensures a continuity between the 'Science of God' (subalternating) and theological science (subalternated). There follows not only the delivery of a datum, of a set of propositions accepted authoritatively by a legitimate intellectual 'obedience' to a self-revealing God, but an organic, psychological and religious continuity wherein the light of faith— an emanation of the divine light in the mind of man— constitutes the indispensable *milieu* for the knowledge of what has been revealed. Consequently the mystic . . . finds justification in this law

---

d'un mot technique: une subalternation. . . . L'objet de foi, sans rien perdre de ses nature et qualité, passe sous un autre régime, où règne le *modus ratiocinativus*; le livre du Lombard, oeuvre de ce genre, se ramène à l'É criture, mais n'en fait pas partie, car il ne se réfère à elle que par subalternation, de par une détermination épistémologique qui l'axe sur d'autres principes. Autre sera donc la méthode du croyant, autre celle de l'exégète, autre celle du théologien" (M.D. Chenu, *La théologie comme science au XIIIe siècle* [Paris: J. Vrin, 1957³], 57).

47 Perhaps a parallel activity can be found in Lonergan's method of sublation, ". . . where each successive level [of the four levels of conscious and intentional operations] sublates previous levels by going beyond them, by setting up a higher principle, by introducing new operations, and by preserving the integrity of previous levels, while extending enormously their range and their significance" (Lonergan, *Method in Theology*, 340).

48 Bonaventure's vision in *De reductione artium ad theologiam* finds an echo in Bernard Lonergan's ideas about the unity of human sciences. Lonergan states: "Transcendental method is a constituent part of the special method proper to theology, just as it is a constituent part in the special methods proper to the natural and to the human sciences. . . In unity with all fields, however disparate, is again the human mind that operates in all fields and in radically the same fashion in each. Through the self-knowledge, the self-appropriation, the self-possession that result from making explicit the basic normative pattern of the recurrent and related operations of human cognitional process, it becomes possible to envisage a future in which all workers in all fields can find in transcendental method common norms, foundations, systematics, and common critical, dialectical, and heuristic procedures" (Ibid., 23–24); "Self-appropriation of itself is a grasp of transcendental method, and that grasp provides one with the tools not only for an analysis of commonsense procedures but also for the differentiation of the sciences and the construction of their methods" (Ibid., 83). Even though Lonergan admits that the "transcendental method is only a part of theological method" because "it is necessary to add a consideration of religion," (Ibid., 25), he affirms that the heightened state of consciousness coming from withdrawal into interiority is what provides us "with the ability to meet the methodical exigence" to establish "the differentiation of the sciences and the construction of their methods" (Ibid., 83).

of the subalternation of the sciences, for it insists that 'continuity' within the hierarchy of mental disciplines is the essential condition of their validity and vitality.[49]

We bring reasons to support our faith, but they would be useless unless we first had faith. *Nisi credideritis, non intelligetis.*[50] The reasons do not "take away the merit of faith, but simply increase our consolation."[51] Nowhere do we find in Bonaventure an actual rejection of reason, but rather a balanced appreciation of its value. He recognizes that reason sometimes may precede faith, and other times follow it, and that both reason and faith can be ordered to the same truth.[52] He affirms reason's powers of understanding many things with its natural lights.[53] The formal cause of theology absolutely demands the use of reason, even for the man who already has reached the state of perfection.[54] What chiefly concerns Bonaventure, in regard to reason, are two things: (a) that the certitude of reason must be held as inferior to that of Sacred Scripture,[55] and (b) that reason, elevated by faith and the gifts, is made fit for the work of theology:

> As a man's judgment surpasses that of a boy, so does the judgment of a Christian surpass the judgment of a philosopher, and the judgment of a mind turned upward that of a mind sunken down toward lower things. . . because [the Christian] believes in things that, to the animal man, seem irrational: whereas they are rational to the spiritual man.[56]

---

49 M.D. Chenu, *Is Theology a Science?* (London: Burns & Oates, 1959), 90–91.

50 Isaias 7:9 (*Vet. Lat.*), cited in: *III Sent.* d. 24, dub. 3 (III, 530a).

51 "Quando fides non assentit propter rationem, sed propter amorem eius cui assentit, desiderat habere rationes: tunc non evacuat ratio humana meritum, sed auget solatium" *I Sent.* prooem., q. 2, ad 6 (I, 11b).

52 "Patet quod intelligere aliquando praecedit fidem, aliquando sequitur"; "Fides et intellectus circa idem possunt se compati et . . . circa idem . . . ordinari" *III Sent.* d. 24, dub. 3, resp. (III, 530b).

53 "Ipse enim intellectus intra se habet lumen sufficiens ex propria conditione, per quod posset dubitationem istam longius propulsare et se ab insipientia eripere" *Myst. Trin.* q. 1, a. 1, ad 1.2.3. (V, 50a).

54 "Tertio valet ad delectandum perfectos. Miro enim modo anima delectatur in intelligendo quod perfecta fide credit. Unde Bernardus: 'Nihil libentius intelligimus, quam quod iam fide credimus'" *I Sent.* prooem., q. 2, concl. (I, 11a).

55 "Cum Magistro deficit certitudo rationis, recurrit ad auctoritatis certitudinem sacrae Scripturae, quae excedit omnem certitudinem rationis" *I Sent.* prooem., q. 2, ad 4 (I, 11b).

56 "Et quantum praecellit iudicium viri iudicium pueri, tantum praecellit iudicium viri christiani iudicium unius philosophi et iudicium rationis sursum conversae iudicium rationis ad inferiora depressae. . . quia credit aliqua quae videntur esse irrationabilia homini animali: sunt enim rationabilia homini spirituali" *III Sent.* d. 23, a. 1, q. 1, ad 4 (III, 472b).

The object of belief is above reason. . . as acquired knowledge, but not above reason elevated by faith and by the gifts of knowledge and understanding. For faith elevates to assent; knowledge and understanding elevate to understanding what is believed.[57]

Bonaventure plainly sees the influence from above as the basis of reason's excelling power: "Grace is the foundation of penetrating enlightenment of reason."[58]

The very existence of the speculative method in theology, therefore, was not to provoke in Bonaventure anything comparable to the violent opposition on the part of Stephen of Tournai toward some of the first attempts made at writing the *summae*.[59] In a pithy phrase we may compress Bonaventure's thought on the role of reason: for more rational activity, more dependence on divine illumination is needed. His appreciation of speculative activity is made all too manifest by the use he made of it in his own speculative works. It would be a most unhappy and deceptive oversimplification to believe Bonaventure did not value the *quaestio disputata* and all it implied for the progress of theology.[60] Moreover, had he not esteemed it, he would not have assumed, during the Franciscan crisis, the lead role in favor of studies. As for the "rights" of human reason, J.F. Quinn, speaking of the historical backdrop of thirteenth-century thought, warns about reason's risk of exaggerated independence from grace: "When *autonomy* was taken in the sense of *self-sufficiency* . . . there resulted a rationalism denying the supernatural order and the involvement in it of nature."[61]

---

57 "Credibile est supra rationem . . . quantum ad scientiam acquisitam, sed non supra rationem elevatam per fidem et per donum scientiae et intellectus. Fides enim elevat ad assentiendum; scientia et intellectus elevant ad ea quae credita sunt intelligendum" *I Sent.* prooem., q. 2, ad 5 (I, 11b).

58 "Sicut igitur gratia fundamentum est rectitudinis voluntatis et illustrationis perspicuae rationis" *Itin.* 1, 8 (V, 298a).

59 Stephen of Tournai speaks of young masters who, from a spirit of ambition, would write 'little *summae*' in which they ignored the time-honored rules and works of the authorities: ". . . ut comatuli adolescentes eorum magisteria impudenter usurpent, et in cathedra seniorum sedeant imperbes; et qui nondum norunt esse discipuli, laborant ut nominentur magistri. Conscribunt et ipsi summulas suas pluribus salivis effluentes et madidas philosophorum sale nec conditas. Omissis regulis artium abjectisque libris authenticis, artificum muscas inanium verborum sophismatibus suis, tanquam aranearum tendiculis includunt" (Stephen of Tournai, *Epp.* 251 [PL, 211, 516]).

60 "In the thirteenth century this [i.e., the *quaestio disputata*] was the characteristic and singularly effective activity of the university masters: the *disputatio magistralis*. But we must insist on its great intellectual force, especially in the speculative disciplines where it furnishes an instrument superbly suited to the mental processes, at least to certain processes and to certain modes of thought" (Chenu, *Twelfth Century*, 295).

61 J.F. Quinn, *Historical Constitution,* 87. Quinn is actually reporting the opinion of H. Van der Laan, who states in English: "Autonomy may not be understood in the sense of self-sufficiency.

Already faithful to the Augustinian tradition, Bonaventure was in possession of a system of thought that tended to depend more on God than on man's resources for every aspect of human existence, including the intellectual sphere.[62] He only tended to emphasize this dependence more and more as the effects of Latin Averroism increasingly became felt at the University of Paris.[63] This explains the polemical nature of his later works in contrast to the more positive attitude toward Aristotle in his earlier works.[64]

Therefore, a balanced judgment of Bonaventure's teaching only can be made against the historical backdrop of controversy in which we see the Franciscan Doctor gradually taking an ever more active role, culminating only in his death at fifty-six years of age. Thus, the *Hexaëmeron*, the most polemical of all his works, in many ways is a masterpiece and, even when read apart from the *Opera Omnia*, can stand alone as one of the greatest ecclesiastical works.[65] Nevertheless, although "in perfectly clear language, manifesting thought in full possession of its means of expression," as Bougerol describes this work,[66] it is not well received always in our times, perhaps, again, because the key to interpretation is lost by isolating it from the historical context.[67] Again, we must keep Bonaventure's main intention before our eyes. Theological study is undertaken for the purpose of becoming holy, and this end is attained through the habit that is called wisdom. Bonaventure in his polemical works is not bent on demeaning human reason, but rather, by pointing out its limitations, is intent on clearing the way for

There is a dialectic of nature and grace dominated by grace and the directedness of philosophy to the supernatural" (H. Van der Laan, *De wijsgerige grondslag van Bonaventura's theologie*, [Amsterdam: Buijten & Schipperheijn, 1968], 210).

62 "Creatura essentialiter et totaliter a Creatore dependet" *II Sent.* d. 1, p. 1, a. 3, q. 2, concl. (II, 35a).

63 "Nor is it difficult to explain why St. Bonaventure preferred St. Augustine and Christian Neo-Platonism to the new Aristotelian philosophy. The method of Platonic-Augustinian thought . . . tends to place in relief the dependence of things on God" (E. Bettoni, *St. Bonaventure*, trans. A. Gambatese, [Notre Dame, Indiana: University Press, 1964], 19).

64 Ratzinger gives an in-depth and carefully nuanced view of Bonaventure's progressively manifested "anti-Aristotelianism," examining the various and sometimes opposing scholarly opinions on this subject, but striking a delicate balance (Ratzinger, *Theology of History,* chap. IV: "Aristotelianism and the Theology of History" [pp. 119–63]).

65 "El *Hexaëmeron* es una obra sumamente rica de contenido, de penetración y de intuiciones geniales. De este libro se ha escrito que es 'la obra más original, más rica y quizá la más vigorosa de la literatura eclesiástica', e incluso que es 'una de las más sorprendentes obras del genio cristiano'" (Merino, *Historia de la Filosofía Franciscana*, p. 56, n. 29).

66 Bougerol, *Introduction to Bonaventure,* 131.

67 As this historical context of theology applies to Bonaventure's roots in religious experience, Z. Hayes clarifies Bonaventure's purpose: "Scholastic theology at this time did not know the sort of chasm

that wisdom which comes from above our human capacities. His statements inimical to human reason simply point out the temptation and the dangers stemming from that admittedly best among our talents—our capacity to think. The power of reason captivates us when, rather, it should be God's light that captivates us along with our reason. Led by *curiositas*, the chief expression of our pride, we are left "empty of praise and devotion although filled with the splendors of knowledge."[68] If these words embarrass us, Gregory IX's solemn warning to Bonaventure's contemporaries, the "reigning masters in theology," may be even more painful to our ears. Pope Gregory says that since these masters had become "content, as professors, to be theorists about God instead of active theologians," he orders them "not to profane their sacred wisdom in vain ostentation, 'transposing by profane innovations the terms defined by the fathers'."[69]

St. Bonaventure speaks of two kinds of discipline necessary to attain wisdom, one by hearing alone, which he calls 'scholastic', and the other by living what one learns, which he calls 'monastic'. Although both are needed, he stresses the importance of the latter: "Discipline is of two kinds: scholastic and monastic or of customs; and in order to possess wisdom it is not enough to have scholastic discipline without the monastic kind, because not by hearing alone, but by observing does man become wise."[70] This is simply another way of saying what we have already seen Bonaventure insisting upon: holiness is the only sure passage to wisdom.[71] The science of faith must presuppose and proceed from a faithful Christian life.[72]

When elaborating theology, St. Bonaventure proceeds as a man of faith and presumes that his readers, theologians themselves, are equipped with a 'sense' for the revealed truths they endeavor to understand. Let us

---

between the speculative and the practical as we have experienced it more recently to the detriment of speculative theology and of spirituality. Above all, for Bonaventure there is no speculation in isolation from the concerns of religious experience.... Hence, such works as sermons, collations, and spiritual tracts are clearly sources for the theological views of Bonaventure" (Hayes, *The Hidden Center*, 8).

68 *Hex.* 1, 8 (V, 330b).

69 "... quidam apud vos spiritu vanitatis ut uter distenti positos a patribus terminos prophana transferre satagunt novitate ..." (Gregory IX, Paris, July 7, 1228, in: *CUP*, I, 114–15 [#59]). The rest of the citation given in English is the paraphrased version provided by M.D. Chenu, *Twelfth Century*, 309.

70 "Disciplina autem duplex est: scholastica et monastica sive morum; et non sufficit ad habendam sapientiam scholastica sine monastica; quia non audiendo solum, sed observando fit homo sapiens" *Hex.* 2, 3 (V, 337a).

71 "Non est ergo securus transitus a scientia ad sapientiam; oportet ergo medium ponere, scilicet sanctitatem" *Hex.* 19, 3 (V, 420b).

72 When it does, the science of faith (i.e. the knowledge that springs from a living faith) is justifiably called wisdom: "Haec sapientia datur secundum mensuram fidei" *Hex.* 2, 19 (V, 339b);

now study an example of Bonaventure's theological procedure, to appreciate how faith and Christian life inevitably presuppose one another.

4. An example of Bonaventure's procedure: the proofs of God's existence

In practice, how did St. Bonaventure proceed when elaborating his theological expositions? Among various possible articles of faith treated by Bonaventure, I have chosen his proofs of the existence of God as the easiest way to display his particular mental pattern in bringing faith to the highest possible degree of understanding.[73] Truly the proofs occupy a privileged place on account of their simplicity but, primarily, because God is the point of reference of all theological development in St. Bonaventure: "The theme of theology is, indeed, God and the first Principle. Rather, being the highest knowledge and the highest teaching, it resolves everything in God as the first and supreme Principle."[74] Therefore, I trust that Bonaventure's approach to the proofs, notably in the spirit in which they are presented, to be quite characteristic of Bonaventure's procedure throughout all his works.[75]

When it comes to the proofs of God's existence, probably we think first of St. Thomas Aquinas' five ways.[76] The five ways depend on sense data, and since they have become popular as "proofs," we may be inclined to regard other proofs, outside those depending on sense data, as somehow

---

"Sapientia autem non reseratur nec habetur nisi per fidem" *Hex.* 14, 7 (V, 394b). Wisdom's chief characteristic is a felt experience (*affectio*) or 'savoring' of what is known (See: *III Sent.* d. 27, a. 2, q. 5, concl. [III, 612a).

73 The question of God's existence is treated chiefly in: *I Sent.* d. 3, p. 1, au., qq. 1–4 et dubia (I, 67–80); d. 8, p. 1, a. 1, q. 2 (I, 153–156); *Myst. Trin.* q. 1, a. 1 (V, 45–51); *Itin.* (V, 295–316).

74 "Quia vero theologia sermo est de Deo et de primo principio, utpote quia ipsa tanquam scientia et doctrina altissima omnia resolvit in Deum tanquam in principium primum et summum" *Brev.* prol. 6 (V, 208b). Lonergan points out the God-centeredness of traditional theology as contrasting with modern field specialization in theology: "Theology in the past has been defined as the science of God and of all things in their relations to God, conducted under the light of revelation and faith. On the other hand, field specialization is dominant in contemporary thought concerned with biblical theology, patristic theology, medieval theology, renaissance theology, modern theology" (Lonergan, *Method in Theology*, 145).

75 For a comprehensive study on Bonaventure's approach to the existence of God, see: Thomas R. Mathias, "Bonaventurian Ways to God through Reason," *FS* 36 (1976): 192–232; *FS* 37 (1977): 153–206.

76 "Although the Five Ways of Thomas Aquinas have in the ensuing centuries been the subject of voluminous analyses and commentaries, setting forth radically different approaches to and interpretations of the Five Ways, only minimal attention comparatively has been accorded to the Bonaventurian

less secure. Commenting on the differences between St. Thomas' and St. Bonaventure's proofs, Gilson himself seems to qualify, in a restrictive sense, the rational value of Bonaventure's proofs:

> The very idea of a proof of God's existence does not refer to the same intellectual operation in the two systems. For St. Thomas, a proof remains what it is, no matter at what moment the intellect considers it: anyone who can understand the terms and the chain of propositions of which the proof from the First Mover is composed can understand and prove in his turn that God exists. For St. Bonaventure, by reason of the mystical turn of his mind, each kind of proof corresponds to a definite state of the soul's return to God by ecstasy, and their order of succession depends upon the degree to which the human soul is penetrated by grace... They reveal their true meaning only to the soul already at the summit of the interior life and about to make contact with God by love.[77]

Nevertheless, since the study of theology presupposes faith, a faith seeking understanding (more or less avidly), another remark of Gilson would rather justify Bonaventure's approach for theologians specifically: "[Bonaventure] tended to make the existence of God appear evident rather than to demonstrate it... He is less concerned with establishing the existence of God than of showing his eminent 'knowableness'."[78]

In Saint Bonaventure's *Disputed Questions on the Mystery of the Trinity*, the Seraphic Doctor sets forth three ways of knowing God's existence. The first is psychological: since man is made in the image of God, to know man's soul is to know God in some way.[79] The second is composed of metaphysical proofs based on the sensible world: to know creatures is to know God.[80] The third is the so-called ontological argument: St. Anselm's proof.[81] This tripartite focus may remind us of the plan of the

---

approaches to God. Although that in itself affords a distinct motive for entering upon this study, there are additional reasons for such an undertaking" (Mathias, *FS* 36 [1976]: 192–93).

77 Gilson, *Philosophy of Bonaventure*, 125–26.

78 Etienne Gilson, *The Christian Philosophy of St. Thomas Aquinas*, trans. L. K. Shook, C.S.B. (New York: Random House, 1956), 53.

79 "Est enim certum ipsi comprehendenti, quia cognitio huius veri innata est menti rationali, in quantum tenet rationem imaginis" *Myst. Trin.* q. 1, a. 1, concl. (V, 49a). See also: Ibid., q. 1, a. 1, 4 (V, 45b), where Bonaventure relies on St. Augustine.

80 "Omne verum, quod clamat omnis creatura, est verum indubitabile; sed Deum esse clamat omnis creatura: ergo [Deum esse est verum indubitabile]" *Myst. Trin.* q. 1, a. 1 (V, 46b).

81 *Myst. Trin.* q. 1, a.1, 21–24 (V, 47b). St. Anselm's argument is given also in: *I Sent.* d. 8, p. 1, a. 1, q. 2, concl. (I, 155a); and in *Itin.* 5, 6 (V, 309b). "The Bonaventurian adaptation of the Anselmian argument briefly comes to this: if all thought is grounded on being, First Being must somehow be

Itinerarium mentis in Deum, with the exception of the order followed.[82]

In all three ways, what do we find in common? Both the first and the second ways fundamentally find their origin in exemplarism. Whether inside ourselves (*imago*) or in the material universe (*vestigia*), God is reflected in the mirror of his creatures. But these reflections imply in man some knowledge, no matter how vague it may be, of what is above himself, making it possible for man to give creatures meaning by transcending them. This third kind of knowledge constitutes the basis of the third way and is a knowledge prior to, or at least simultaneous with, man's knowledge of creatures. Such prior knowledge brings Bonaventure to declare with St. Augustine: "No truth can be seen except through the first truth."[83] So, the second way (metaphysical proofs from observing the sensible world), as we have seen, is evaluated differently in St. Bonaventure than in the Aristotelian tradition.[84] This is so because for Bonaventure the proofs based on our knowledge of created reality simply reflect and confirm our innate knowledge of God's existence.[85] There are ten of these proofs (or "self-evident postulates"), proclaimed by creatures.[86] But the approaches that do not depend on the senses occupy a privileged position, not simply because

present in every act of predication" (Mathias, *FS* 37 [1977]: 182).

82 In the *Itinerarium* the order is: (1) the created world; (2) man's soul; (3) God: "Quoniam autem contingit contemplari Deum non solum *extra nos* et *intra nos*, verum etiam *supra nos*: *extra* per vestigium, *intra* per imaginem et *supra* per lumen, quod est signatum supra mentem nostram, quod est lumen Veritatis aetaernae, cum 'ipsa mens nostra immediate ab ipsa Veritate formetur'" *Itin.* 5, 1 (V, 308a).

83 "Nulla veritas videri potest nisi per primam veritatem" *Myst. Trin.* q. 1, a. 1, 25 (V, 47); cf. St. Augustine's *Soliloquies*, Book I, chap. 8, no. 15.

84 Copleston, in discussing St. Thomas's preference for proofs from the sensible world above the 'innate' knowledge of God, states: "It may appear that St. Thomas's attitude in regard to 'innate' knowledge of God does not differ substantially from that of St. Bonaventure. In a sense this is true, since neither of them admitted an explicit innate idea of God; but St. Bonaventure thought that there is a kind of initial implicit awareness of God, or at least that the idea of God can be rendered explicit by interior reflection alone, whereas the proofs actually given by St. Thomas all proceed by way of the external world. Even if we press the 'Aristotelian' aspect of Bonaventure's epistemology, it remains true that there is a difference of emphasis and approach in the natural theology of the two philosophers" (Copleston, 2: 337).

85 When I use the word "innate" for this kind of knowledge of God, it must be remembered that no actually explicit knowledge is meant here. Rather, this knowledge ("Deus non potest non esse nec cogitari non esse") is an effect or result of a *resolutio plena* upon the idea of being ("Deus sive summa veritas est ipsum esse, quo nihil melius cogitari potest") *I Sent.* d. 8, p. 1, a. 1, q. 2, concl. (I, 155a).

86 The ten "self-evident postulates" are given by St. Bonaventure in *Myst. Trin.* q. 1., a. 1, 11–20 (V, 46b–47a). Their headings are: (1) Si est ens posterius, est ens prius; (2) Si est ens ab alio, est ens non ab alio; (3) Si est ens possibile, est ens necessarium; (4) Si est ens respectivum, est ens absolutum; (5) Si est ens diminutum sive secundum quid, est ens simpliciter; (6) Si est ens propter aliud, est ens propter seipsum; (7) Si est ens per participationem, est ens per essentiam; (8) Si est ens in potentia, est ens in

the senses sometimes may impede our spiritual access to God,[87] but because a higher and surer way of knowing God is, in itself, at the basis of finding God in creatures. What the three ways have in common, then, might be considered their causal relationship to one another.[88]

The third, or highest approach, therefore occupies a special place in Bonaventure's ways to God through reason. What he attempts to do, in brief, is raise to the level of awareness a knowledge of which we, albeit unconsciously, are already in possession. Bonaventure affirms that this knowledge is found implanted in the human mind in virtue of God's intimate presence in the soul: "God is most present to the soul and is knowable in Himself. Therefore some knowledge of God Himself is implanted in the very soul."[89]

Evidently, knowledge of God's existence does not form a part of our conscious, objective intellectual data. That is, when it comes to God, we are not in the position of a subject beholding an object as we are in regard to other objects of our knowledge. The objective data which make up our fund of knowledge either are part of our present awareness, or can be called into present awareness from the memory. In the case of God, as an *object* of our knowledge, we are unable to see him due to an inherent limitation in our nature. For the same reason, we are unable to *know* him in the same way we know any other object because he cannot fall beneath our gaze in a way comprehensible to human nature.[90]

---

actu; (9) Si est ens compositum, est ens simplex; (10) Si est ens mutabile, est ens immutabile.

87 "Ratio est in promptu, quia mens humana, sollicitudinibus distracta, non intrat ad se per memoriam; phantasmatibus obnubilata, non redit ad se per intelligentiam; concupiscentiis illecta, ad se ipsam nequaquam revertitur per desiderium suavitatis internae et laetitiae spiritualis. Ideo in his sensibilibus iacens, non potest ad se tanquam ad Dei imaginem reintrare" *Itin.* 4, 1 (V, 306a).

88 T. Mathias states that the common denominator of each of the three Ways is "in the fact of causality in its various aspects. . . In the aggregate then, the prime cause is the origin, sustenance and consummation of all finite being; it is the Alpha and Omega to which every other being ultimately owes its all." At the same time, Mathias recognizes that this conviction can only be the fruit of "metaphysical reflection" and "human insight peculiarly its own" ("Bonaventurian Ways to God through Reason," *FS* 37 [1977]: 187–88).

89 "Deus praesentissimus est ipsi animae et se ipso cognoscibilis: ergo inserta est ipsi animae notitia Dei sui" *Myst. Trin.* q. 1, a. 1, 10 (V, 46a).

90 B. Lonergan observes that the existence of affirmative theology depends on the answer to the delicate question of whether God can be studied as an object: "If there is to be an affirmative or kataphatic, as well as a negative or apophatic, theology, there must be confronted the question whether God is an object. Now certainly God is not an object in the naive realist sense of what is already out there now, or already up there now, or already in here now. Further he is not an object if one retreats from naive realism to an empiricism, a naturalism, a positivism, or an idealism. But if by an object one means anything that is intended in questions and known through correct answers, anything within the world mediated by meaning, then a distinction has to be drawn. "On what I have called the

In what sense, then, can St. Bonaventure believe that we are already in possession of this knowledge of God's existence? This knowledge is implicit. Since it forms the context within which we are able to know anything else, it is the necessary basis for us to begin to pose the question about God's existence. B. Lonergan puts it thus: "Could the world be mediated by questions for intelligence if it did not have an intelligent ground? Could the world's facticity be reconciled with its intelligibility, if it did not have a necessary ground?" The whole approach of Bonaventure is to make us perceive what we, in some mysterious way, already know, but of which knowledge we hitherto have remained insensible.[91]

Bonaventure manifests himself here again as the mystagogue. He leads us to an awareness of a knowledge which already forms a part of our interior experience. Since this implicit knowledge through personal experience never *begins* at a precise moment in our rational life, we are not made conscious of it unless we reflect upon our inner world against the widest possible horizons—those of infinity itself.[92] Until now, this infinite interior landscape has been taken for granted to the point of virtual imperception.[93] We might compare this case to our habitual forgetfulness of the context in which our daily lives unfold, until someone or something reminds us of it. The same is true of our thought processes which all too easily become detached from the wider context in which they originate and to which they must be referred in order for truth to be appreciated.

The context of our existence and of our thought processes is what remits us to the third way of knowing God's existence (the Anselmian or so-called ontological argument).[94] He who attempts to reach the conclusion

---

primary and fundamental meaning of the name, God, God is not an object. For that meaning is the term of an orientation to transcendent mystery. Such an orientation, while it is the climax of the self-transcending process of raising questions, none the less is not properly a matter of raising and answering questions. So far from lying within the world mediated by meaning, it is the principle that can draw people out of that world and into the cloud of unknowing" (Lonergan, *Method in Theology*, 341–42).

91 "Buenaventura no postula una idea clara y explícita de Dios en el hombre, y mucho menos una visión o experiencia inmediata de Dios, sino una vaga noticia y un conocimiento implícito, que no se puede negar, y que puede transformarse en claro y explícito a través de la reflexión interior. Se trata de un conocimiento virtual de Dios que puede y debe desembocar en un conocimiento claro y reflexivo" (Merino, 78).

92 "Oculus mentis nostrae, intentus in entia particularia et universalia, ipsum esse extra omne genus, licet primo occurrat menti, et per ipsum alia, tamen non advertit" *Itin.* 5, 4 (V, 309a).

93 "Assuefactus ad tenebras entium et phantasmata sensibilium, cum ipsam lucem summi esse intuetur, videtur sibi nihil videre; non intelligens, quod ipsa caligo summa est mentis nostrae illuminatio, sicut, quando videt oculus puram lucen, videtur sibi nihil videre" (Ibid.).

94 The term itself, "ontological argument," finds its origin in Kant, who attacked this argument..

that God exists, in some way began this attempt with an implicit knowledge of God, because any concern about God's existence presumes some knowledge about him that precedes such an inquiry: "Praedicatur clauditur in subiecto."[95]   This is what brings Bonaventure to conclude: "If God is God, God exists."[96]   Then, after giving Anselm's argument, Bonaventure remarks: "If you see this in the pure simplicity of your mind, you somehow will be bathed in the brilliance of eternal light."[97]

Some awareness of God's existence, although vague, is necessarily prior to our understanding of other beings created by him: "Oh the blindness of an understanding that does not consider this, since it is the first thing the understanding sees, and without which nothing else can be understood."[98] Being (*ens primum cognitum*) forms the necessary context for understanding beings, because the latter depend on Being for their very truth (i.e., their knowableness).[99]

It is not my purpose here to discuss Bonaventure's possible traces of ontologism.   Suspicions of that nature appear to have been refuted abundantly.[100]   Our attention, preferably, is given to the procedure Bonaventure followed in manifesting God's existence. The question may be reduced to one: What does Bonaventure see happening to us in the process of our recognizing God's existence?

Once I am made aware of the infinite backdrop surrounding my finite existence, and that of all other created beings, my implicit knowledge becomes explicit. The conviction of God's existence is born from the personal interior experience of man, whose awareness of this experience brings him to affirm as true what he has taken unconsciously for granted until this point.

95   *I Sent.* d. 8, p. 1, a. 1, q. 2, concl. (I, 155a).

96   "Si Deus est Deus, Deus est; sed antecedens est adeo verum, quod non potest cogitari non esse; ergo Deum esse est verum indubitablile" *Myst. Trin.* q. 1, a. 1, 29 (V, 48a).

97   "Si hoc vides in pura mentis simplicitate, aliqualiter perfunderis aeternae lucis illustratione" *Itin.* 5, 6 (V, 309b).

98   "Mira igitur est caecitas intellectus, qui non considerat illud quod prius videt et sine quo nihil potest cognoscere" *Itin.* 5, 4 (V, 309a).

99   *Myst. Trin.* 1, 1, 25+26 (V, 47b). "Nisi igitur cognoscatur, quid est ens per se, non potest plene sciri definitio alicuius specialis substantiae" *Itin.* 3, 3 (V, 304a).

100   As Mathias explains, "It was not until the time of Malebranche (1638–1715) that isolated passages, particularly from the *Itinerarium*, were wrenched from their context and offered as support for the claim that Bonaventure indeed espoused such a view. The reason of course is obvious: by employing the illustrious name of Bonaventure, the Ontologists sought to screen their doctrine from the charge of iconoclastic invention. . . It should be adequate to state that Bonaventure. . . consistently held that the human soul has no direct or immediate knowledge of God" ("Bonaventurian Ways to God through Reason," *FS* 37: 195–96). See: D. Connell, "St. Bonaventure and the Ontologist Tradition" Vol. 2 of *SB*, 289–308.

This is why the conviction of God's existence based on such an approach is far stronger than the evidence afforded by the senses. The metaphysical proofs derived from sense data simply come to confirm a truth already possessed within the soul in a vague manner.[101] But such a truth remains imperceptible to those who would not descend to a level of experience much deeper than the senses and reason alone. The inner experience, since it is by nature incommunicable, merely is evoked by Bonaventure who is confident in the power of the idea of God to communicate itself to us. This idea, unlike any other concept, involves an active and creative life of its own: "Ratio fecunditatis ad concipiendum, producendum et pariendum."[102]

In the words of Bernard Lonergan, it is man's "intending" alone that enters the region of the divine:

> The question of God, then, lies within man's horizon. Man's transcendental subjectivity is mutilated or abolished, unless he is stretching forth towards the intelligible, the unconditioned, the good of value. The reach, not of his attainment, but of his intending is unrestricted. There lies within his horizon a region for the divine, a shrine for ultimate holiness. It cannot be ignored. The atheist may pronounce it empty. The agnostic may urge that he finds his investigation has been inconclusive. The contemporary humanist will refuse to allow the question to arise. But their negations presuppose the spark in our clod, our native orientation to the divine.[103]

Since it has been my purpose to illustrate Bonaventure's method by choosing one of his theological applications as an example, the proof of God's existence at first might be considered too exceptional among other possible topics. However, I find this choice opportune. As we have seen, the question of God's existence somehow pervades all other topics in Bonaventure's theology for two reasons: (1) All theology is essentially the study of God; and (2) the Bonaventurian approach to God's existence virtually establishes the same *itinerarium* followed in all theological research, no matter what topics are under scrutiny. What Bonaventure pretends to do in theology is lead us by the hand to an awareness of truth as already possessed and loved, and to which the explicit knowledge of God's

---

101 "Hoc verum [the existence of God] non indiget probatione propter defectum evidentiae ex parte sua, sed propter defectum considerationis ex parte nostra. Unde huiusmodi ratiocinationes [the arguments taken from the exterior world] potius sunt quaedam exercitationes intellectus, quam rationes dantes evidentiam et manifestantes ipsum verum probatum" *Myst. Trin.* q. 1, a. 1, concl. ad 12 (V, 51a).

102 *Hex.* 20, 5 (V, 426a).

103 Lonergan, *Method in Theology*, 103.

existence and nature can be considered secondary.[104] Since the theological journey is essentially faith seeking understanding, the latter simply raises the former to the level of explicit knowledge. Faith, in some mysterious way, is already a kind of knowledge. This knowledge, however, is not conceptual but primordial.[105] Faith, as an experience of God's existence, remains irreflexive in the heart until it becomes explicit through the acquisition of another kind of knowledge that affords understanding to the mind through reason.[106] But this understanding "simply increases our consolation."[107] On the other hand, if an understanding of the faith is divorced from the experience of faith, Bonaventure warns us that "arguments of this sort are exercises of the intellect rather than proofs that provide evidence and make the truth manifest as proven."[108] Since all knowledge about God ultimately is consequent upon his existence, the path toward such knowledge is the same. The same God who personally reveals himself to us is found addressing us from within any other article of belief. Every article of belief leads us to this existence-presence of God.

Conclusion

Faced with unleashed rationalism, would Bonaventure have us return to monastic theology? Or, faced with a spiritualist anti-intellectualism, does Bonaventure simply equate rational theological study with spirituality? In many ways, Bonaventure represents the delicate balance that should be

104 "Will I love him in return, or will I refuse? Will I live out the gift of his love, or will I hold back, turn away, withdraw? Only secondarily do there arise the questions of God's existence and nature, and they are the questions either of the lover seeking to know him or of the believer seeking to escape him. Such is the basic option of the existential subject once called by God" (Ibid., 116).

105 "Before it enters the world mediated by meaning, religion is the prior word God speaks to us by flooding our hearts with his love. That prior word pertains, not to the world mediated by meaning, but to the world of immediacy, to the unmediated experience of the mystery of love and awe" (Lonergan, *Method in Theology*, 112).

106 If an example may be taken from world literature, we observe such a process of discovering God, already implicitly known, in Tolstoy's character of Levine who, at final success in a long, but unconscious, search for God, says: "I have discovered nothing. I have merely found out what I knew. . . I looked for an answer to my question. But reason could not give me the answer, for it is incommensurable with the answer. Life itself has given me the answer, in my knowledge of what is good and what is evil. This knowledge, though, I did not acquire in any way; it was given to me as it is given to everyone, *given* because I could not have got it from anywhere" *Anna Karenina*, trans. D. Magarshack (New York: New American Library of World Literature; Signet Classics, 1964³), 787–88.

107 *I Sent.* prooem., q. 2, ad 6 (I, 11b).

108 "Unde huiusmodi ratiocinationes potius sunt quaedam exercitationes intellectus, quam rationes dantes evidentiam et manifestatntes ipsum verum probatum" *Myst. Trin.* q. 1, a. 1, concl. ad 12 (V, 51a).

maintained between the two tendencies in theology prevalent in his century and recurrent thereafter.[109]

We have spoken of the eventual victory of the speculative approach. Fr. Chenu points out how "the use of the *quaestio* expanded to gain a greater understanding of its divine object: . . . In the very fabric of theological science in the thirteenth century, it served as the instrument of a new metaphysics, of a new psychology, of a new ethics."[110] But such a victory did not imply the demise of monastic theology: "Rather than speak of continuity in this development, we ought better to say coexistence, and always a fruitful coexistence at that. Monastic theology was not an outmoded, downgraded item. It expressed, as did the *ordo monasticus* itself, permanent values for the church and for all of humanity."[111] Chenu visualizes this "delicately balanced coexistence" in the historical figures of Anselm and Abelard who, although representing opposing camps, both were responsible for the creation of scholasticism.[112]

Through personal experience of the conflicts erupting at the University of Paris during his pastoral years, Bonaventure was forced to distinguish carefully between two extremes: exaggerated confidence in human reason and an almost narrow-minded distrust of scholarly pursuits. These distinctions form the membrane of his later works, making of them

---

109 Although Bernard Lonergan sees the necessity of the separateness between theology and religion, he does recognize that theology must return to religion as to its source: "So religion and theology become distinct and separate in the very measure that religion itself develops and adherents to religion move easily from one pattern of consciousness to another. Still this withdrawal must not be without a compensating return. Development is through specialization but it must end in integration. Nor is integration to be achieved by mere regression. To identify theology with religion, with liturgy, with prayer, with preaching, no doubt is to revert to the earliest period of Christianity. But it is also to overlook the fact that the conditions of the earliest period have long since ceased to exist... So it is that we have been led to the conclusion of acknowledging a distinction between the Christian religion and Christian theology... Religion and theology become distinct and separate. But the separateness of theology is a withdrawal that always intends and in its ultimate stage effects a return" (*Method in Theology*, 139–40). This statement would appear to be the greatest contrast between Lonergan and Bonaventure, except for Lonergan's insistence on the mutual dependence between theology and religion.

110 Chenu, *Twelfth Century*, 297.

111 Ibid., 308–9.

112 "Anselm and Abelard were the creators of scholasticism. This all-too-simple cliché voiced by historians has the merit at least of pointing out, in these protagonists, the two opposed but vital and delicately balanced components of the school" (Ibid., 309). Commenting on Chenu's work, T. Camelot arrives at a similar conclusion, while underlining the historical suitability of each theology: "Théologie monastique et théologie scolastique, cela ne fait pas deux théologies disparates. L'une et l'autre représentent deux états successifs, deux 'moments' de la pensée chrétienne en appétit de l'intelligence de sa foi, mais dans des conditions spirituelles, institutionelles, ecclésiales différentes. De la *lectio divina* à la *doctrina sacra* le passage ne s'est pas fait sans 'traumatisme', dit le P. Chenu. . . Au demeurant l'immense bénéfice que représente pour la pensée chrétienne la naissance d'une

an indispensable guidebook (*viz.*, itinerary) for persevering in theology as a spiritual life. They show how reason, if it is "to ascend to God must . . . bring the natural powers of the soul . . . under the way of knowledge which enlightens."[113]

The more the theologian approaches the light, the more assistance he receives from this light. Although the light, in its lower form, always has been present in virtue of man's being an *imago Dei*, our dependence on this light, through willing collaboration with God, is meant to increase continually.[114] Just as man becomes freer through the potentiating activity of grace, and grace thereby becomes a key to true humanism, so the light coming from above brings our mind to its fullest competence.[115] The superior light neither hinders nor diminishes reason's activity. Although the role of God predominates and man's role becomes more passive, this progressive passivity of reason is not to be understood as progressive inactivity, but rather, as a more vigorous receptivity. Reason, instead of becoming inert, becomes more actively receptive by cooperating with God's help. It is precisely this active receptivity to light which constitutes the spiritual life of the theologian. Again, the activity on the part of God does not annihilate the theologian's powers of reasoning, but rather brings them to their fullest natural potential. *Gratia supponit perficitque naturam.*[116] When man's submission to the light coming from above becomes ever greater, his mastery over reason increases proportionately.

---

théologie 'scientifique' ne doit faire méconnaître les 'valeurs permanentes' de la théologie monastique. . . Elle pourra aussi leur rappeler que si le théologien 'parle de Dieu' avec toute l'audace de sa confiance dans la raison, il ne peut le faire que dans le respect du mystère. Ces deux théologies sont complémentaires: l'unique théologie garde cette double fidélité à S. Bernard comme à S. Thomas" ("Théologie monastique et scolastique," *RevSciPhilThéol* 42 [1958]: 251–53).

113 *Itin.* 1, 8 (V, 298a).

114 "Iustum enim est, ut intellectus noster ita captivetur et subiaceat summae Veritati. . . Nemo enim plus credit Deo quam sibi, nisi per hoc, quod *vult* intellectum suum captivare *in obsequium Christi* (II Cor 10:5)" *III Sent.* d. 23, a. 1, q. 1, concl. (III, 471a).

115 "La libertà nell'uomo concreto, che è in continuo divenire verso la forma-perfezione, è come una *ratio-seminalis* che si autorealizza incessantemente mediante la progressiva integrazione, nell'autopossesso e nell'autodominio dell'io, delle forze e dei contenuti psichici. Forze e contenuti che vengono via via interiorizzati e compenetrati e fusi dall'agire libero, a livelli sempre più profondi dell'io stesso" (V. C. Bigi, "La libertà in San Bonaventura," *SB*, 3: 618). For a concise treatment on Bonaventure's teaching of free will in its relation to reason, see W.G. Thompson, "The doctrine of Free Choice in St. Bonaventure," *FS* 18 (1958): 1–8.

116 "Gratia est perfectio naturae. Est enim gratia perfectio naturae non tantum habilitans, verum etiam reformans et elevans. Reformando autem et elevando non destruit ipsam naturam, nec aliquid, quod sit de ipsa natura, sed defectum circa naturam" *Myst. Trin.* q. 1, a. 2, concl. ad 5.6 (V, 57b; Hayes, *Mystery of the Trinity*, 134).

The gradual influence of this uplifting power of the light upon man's reason explains why St. Bonaventure conceives the spiritual life of the theologian as an upward journey. This is *sursumactio*, or an upraising, that comprises the entire cognitive process until union with God.[117] We are on our way toward ever greater participation in the light. One day this light will dazzle our mind's eye through excessive proximity. Reasoning, in the conceptual, discursive way to which we are accustomed, no longer will stand the radiance of this light and will give way to the experience of the unknowable. Such an experience already has been incipient, guiding our steps into this fullness of light, through the gift of wisdom. We eventually must dare to turn toward this source of light that blinds us, so that all becomes "a darkness that is resplendent above all splendor, and in which everything shines forth."[118] Is this step taken against our reason? When speaking of what is, for reason alone, beyond the credible (e.g., the Trinity), Bonaventure firmly asserts: ". . . yet it is credible for reason aided by grace and by the light poured in from above. What is credible in this way is not believed irrationally since the grace and light infused from above do not pervert reason but rather direct it."[119] It remains for us now to examine concretely how this superior influence on man's cognitive faculties, i.e., wisdom and the other gifts of the Holy Spirit, operate to constitute theology.

---

117 *Sursumactio* is an expression that is peculiar to Bonaventure's mysticism, and refers to a special action of grace by which the soul is raised toward, and eventually united to, God. For example, Bonaventure twice speaks of a *'sursumactio mentis in Deum'* in *Apol. paup.* 3, 6 (VIII, 246a); and of a *'sursumactio in Deum'* in: Ibid.. 3, 10 (VIII, 247a). Cf. Ibid., 3, 8 (VIII, 246b); Ibid., 8, 22 (VIII, 294a); *Hex.* 22, 22 (V, 440b–441a).

118 *Itin.* 7, 5 (V, 313a; Boehner, 99) cited from Dionysius, *De mystica theologia*, c. 1, §1, (*PG* 997B).

119 ". . . est tamen credibile ex ratione adiuta per gratiam et lucem desuper infusam. Et quod sic est credibile non irrationabiliter creditur, quia gratia et lux desuper infusa potius rationem dirigit, quam pervertat" *Myst. Trin.* q. 1, a. 2, concl., ad 3 (V, 57a; Hayes, *Mystery of the Trinity*, 134).

You do not need anyone to teach you,
since the anointing he gave you
teaches you everything.

1 Jn. 2:27

VI.

THEOLOGY UNDER THE GIFTS OF THE HOLY SPIRIT

Supernatural illumination, and its role in the theologian's task, becomes most evident when we consider the mission of the Holy Spirit as teacher of the truth.[1] Since the purpose of this mission is to bring us to a comprehension of the truth about God, the seven gifts of the Holy Spirit are dispensed as the means to that end. Consequently, Saint Bonaventure's teaching on the spiritual life is seen precisely to intertwine most intimately with his concept of theology where the teaching on the gifts is concerned.[2] The gifts, placed between the virtues (faith without understanding) and the beatitudes (the vision of what is understood), bring us to a comprehension of what we have accepted on faith.[3] Evidently, Bonaventure has assigned to the gifts the same purpose as theology—to understand what is believed.[4] Thus, Etienne Gilson was to remark about the gifts that "their intermediate *rôle*—which is to assure the passage from faith alone to mystical vision—bears an exact analogy to the transient and intermediate nature assigned by St. Bonaventure to theology."[5] In this manner, by not only locating the gifts within this intermediate stage, but by assigning to the gifts of the Holy

---

1 St. Bonaventure assigns to the Holy Spirit the mission of sanctifying the Church, communicating to it the grace of Christ and teaching it the divine truth. J.F. Quinn makes the following comment on the Holy Spirit's mission of teaching the divine truth: "It is in virtue of his office as teacher of truth that the appropriation is made to him by Bonaventure of a distinctive rôle in the formation of theology" ("The Rôle of the Holy Spirit in St. Bonaventure's Theology," *FS* 33 [1973]: 275).

2 J.F. Quinn points out the decisive role attributed by Bonaventure to the gifts of the Holy Spirit in the constitution of theological knowledge: "Bonaventure's intention is to establish a theology drawing together, for the good of the Christian, faith and philosophy within a total order of wisdom perfecting his knowledge and love of God as He is known and loved in a natural and in an infused manner. In establishing such a theology, Bonaventure depends largely on the gifts of the Holy Spirit. . . [The gifts] function in the constitution of his theological knowledge" (J.F. Quinn, *Historical Constitution*, 685).

3 "Et quoniam quaedam sunt opera moralia primaria, sicut credere; quaedam media, sicut intelligere credita; quaedam vero postrema, sicut videre intellecta . . . ideo gratia gratum faciens ramificatur in habitus virtutum, quorum est animam rectificare; in habitus donorum, quorum est animam expedire; et in habitus beatitudinum, quorum est animam perficere" *Brev.* 5, 4, 3 (V, 256a–b).

4 *I Sent.* prooem., q. 1, concl. (I, 7b).

5 Gilson, *Philosophy of Bonaventure*, 100.

Spirit the same purpose as theology, Bonaventure has made of theology a paradigm of the illuminative way.[6]

In our introductory chapter we spoke of the similarities and differences between theology and the spiritual life. We could summarize our conclusions by stating that all theologians, by the activity itself of theological study, are following the spiritual life in its second phase, the illuminative way. This at least is presumed to be true for all theologians, whether or not it is verified in each case. In other words, it is not proposed as an ideal but as a norm, in virtue of the very nature of revelation as an invitation to relationship with God. The theologian who approaches the data of revelation presumably respects the form of appeal in which this message of the Crucified is communicated.[7] To do otherwise, immediately prevents the theologian from understanding revelation on its own terms and produces a theology that inevitably distorts the very revelation it attempts to render intelligible.

On the other hand, even though the theologian's life is found within the illuminative way, we have not affirmed that only theologians are to be found along this way. The specific action of the gifts in this second way is to «urge on» —*expedire*[8]— by removing obstacles and empowering the soul to continue progressing. There are three different manners in which this progress may be brought about: through the 'magnitude of devotion', the 'magnitude of admiration', and the 'magnitude of exultation'.[9] Saint Bonaventure teaches that theology, through the work of the gift of understanding, brings us to the 'magnitude of admiration', which is the same as imperfect contemplation. Imperfect contemplation is a prelude for infused (or perfect) contemplation, because it properly disposes the soul for this supreme gift.[10] There are two other causes by which the soul may

---

6 The use of the three 'ways' is also referred to as the triple hierarchization: "Hic autem triplex intellectus respondet triplici actui hierarchico, scilicet purgationi, illuminationi et perfectioni" *Trip. via*, prol. 1 (VIII, 3a–b).

7 "Nam haec cognitio, quod Christus pro nobis mortuus est, et consimiles, nisi sit homo peccator et durus, movet ad amorem" *I Sent.* prooem., q. 3, concl. (I, 13b).

8 E. Gilson explains this word as a technical expression in Bonaventure that "is difficult to translate, implying both that the soul is liberated from the bonds that would hold it back and fortified with the resources necessary for actual advance" (*Philosophy of St. Bonaventure*, 100).

9 "Tribus de causis in mentis alienationem deducimur: aliquando prae magnitudine devotionis, aliquando prae magnitudine admirationis, aliquando prae magnitudine exultationis" *Perf. vitae* c. 5, n. 6 (VIII, 119a–b). We find St. Bonaventure often making use of this exposition; see: *Itin.* 4, 3 (V, 306b–307a); *Sermo 2 pro Dom. 3*, p. 3 (IX, 229b); *Sermo 8 in Ascensione*, p. 3 (IX, 325b); *Decem praec.* 4, 12 (V, 521b). St. Bonaventure employs here the teaching of Richard of St.-Victor (see *Benjamin Major* 5, 5).

10 "Quando volumus videre simplici intuitu quomodo illa ars est una et tamen multiplex, quia immiscet se phantasia, cogitare non possumus quomodo infinita sit nisi per distensionem; et ideo

be rendered disposed for perfect contemplation: the 'magnitude of devotion' (spiritual fervor) and the 'magnitude of exultation' (spiritual happiness). All three causes are available to any soul that may travel the illuminative way.[11] At the same time, any of the three causes is sufficient in itself to produce this effect. Thus, even the illiterate, by persevering either in devotion, or in admiration, or in spiritual happiness, can arrive at the unitive way. The goal is the same—through infused contemplation we are brought to permanent union with Christ. Although imperfect contemplation (the 'magnitude of admiration') certainly is not reserved to theologians, this form of prayer, coming as a result of beholding the truth in awe, is typical of theologians because their study brings them into living contact with the light of divine truth.[12]

For Bonaventure, knowledge and love are the means by which we become like God.[13] Thus, even though theology is not the exclusive context in which the gifts of the Holy Spirit operate, Saint Bonaventure could esteem theology as the most excellent way in which to live under the illumination of these gifts, particularly the gifts of piety, knowledge, understanding and wisdom. He affirms the supremacy of theology as the summit of human sciences, to which all other human sciences must return for their ultimate meaning.[14] In an analogous way, all human sciences are to theology what

---

videre non possumus simplici intuitu nisi ratiocinando" *Hex.* 12, 11 (V, 386a); "Haec autem ars et est una et multiplex. Quomodo autem hoc esse possit, videri non potest nisi veniat illuminatio a montibus aeternis..." (Ibid., 9 [V, 385b]); see also: *Christus mag.* 15 (V, 571b). This is the interpretation given to Bonaventure's teaching by J.F. Bonnefoy (*Le Saint-Esprit et ses dons selon St. Bonaventure,* 196–99). See: E. Longpré, "St. Bonaventure. C.— La Contemplation intellectuelle," *DS*, 1819–1824.

11 Bonnefoy, 199–202.

12 Bonnefoy expresses it thus: "Le second moyen de se disposer immédiatement à la suppression de l'activité intellectuelle, premier degré de l'extase, consiste à porter cette activité à son maximum par l'exercice de la contemplation imparfaite. La simple contuition de la Vérité éternelle 'suspend' l'âme dans l'admiration, impose le silence aux sens et à l'imagination" (Ibid., 201).

13 "Per hunc modum intellige, quod a summo Opifice nulla creatura processit nisi per Verbum aeternum, 'in quo omnia disposuit', et per quod produxit non solum creaturas habentes rationem vestigii, sed etiam imaginis, ut eidem assimilari possint per cognitionem et amorem" *Red. art.* 12 (V, 323a).

14 "Et sicut omnes illae ab una luce habebant originem, sic omnes istae cognitiones ad cognitionem sacrae Scripturae ordinantur, in ea clauduntur et in illa perficiuntur, et mediante illa ad aeternam illuminationem ordinantur. Unde omnis nostra cognitio in cognitione sacrae Scripturae debet haberse statum, et maxime quantum ad intellectum anagogiae, per quem illuminatio refertur in Deum, unde habuit ortum" *Red. art.* 7 (V, 322a). In the concluding remarks of her commentary of this work, E. Healy summarizes Bonaventure's thought: "Theology is the queen of the sciences—the rule, the measure, the ultimate interpretation, and harmony of them all. With a light far more distinct and beautiful than the natural light, the light of Sacred Scripture illumines the attributes of God" (Healy, *Bonaventure's «De reductione artium ad theologiam»,* 157).

creatures are to the divine exemplar. The inferior human sciences are arranged in hierachized fashion according to their relative power to represent the ultimate truth.[15]

In order for us to appreciate the role of theology in the illuminative way of the spiritual life, it would help at this point to view Bonaventure's doctrine on the gifts within the larger framework of his teaching on the supernatural habits.

1. The supernatural habits

Saint Bonaventure, as we saw at the very beginning of our study, assigns to each of the three stages of the spiritual life the preponderance of supernatural habits according to the nature of the stages in question. He does this without compartmentalizing the spiritual life into three watertight stages.[16] Even though "all holy souls possess the Holy Spirit as an infused gift,"[17] the first stage, or purgative way, is characterized by seven infused

---

15 "The purpose of the *De Reductione* is not so much to show that the material world which emanated from God was patterned after the ideas of God and must therefore return to Him, but rather that the secular sciences under the *lumen exterius, inferius and interius* must borrow the *lumen superius* of revelation in order fully to understand and appreciate the material universe and to refer it to the *Principium*. It is, therefore, primarily a *reductio* of all *lumina* to the *lumen superius* and then to the *Pater luminum* or to the *lux fontalis, faciens lumen*" (Ibid., 117). Healy likewise characterizes Bonaventure's purpose in life as contained in the very title of this treatise: "His entire life was the title of this little book, a constant adaptation of all knowledge to the knowledge and love of God" (Ibid., 158).

16 For the sake of simplification, we always risk distorting important nuances found in St. Bonaventure's mystical teaching. In describing the experience of life as lived in the stages of spiritual progress, the specific risk is that of isolating each stage from the one preceding or following it. While perceiving the differences between these three 'ways', it is important to recall, as we pointed out in our introductory chapter, how Bonaventure sees these ways as somehow parallel. Thus, even though Bonaventure can sometimes be found to suppose their graded structure (e.g., "Secundo loco post viam purgativam sequitur illuminativa" *Trip. via* 1, 2, 10 [VIII, 6a]), we find him elsewhere respecting the influences of all three ways as they are exercised upon the soul at any point in the soul's progress (*Trip. via*, prol. + n. 1 [VIII, 3a–b]; *Itin.* 4, 6 + 7 [V, 307b–308a]). J.F. Bonnefoy, while admitting that Bonaventure sometimes refers to the three ways as graded, warns us to pay due attention to their parallel dynamism since it is essential for a correct understanding of Bonaventure's teaching. Perhaps the key word here for Bonnefoy is 'prépondérance': "Il va de soi que tout autre est la purification du commençant, tout autre celle du parfait; de même pour la voie illuminative et la voie unitive. Et c'est pourquoi notre Docteur les distingue suivant les trois degrés de la vie spirituelle. Leur prépondérance respective aux divers moments de la vie surnaturelle explique l'appropriation des trois voies aux trois degrés. Cette appropriation, on l'a vu, est devenue identification dans la terminologie de la spiritualité moderne. S'il y a parfois appropriation chez saint Bonaventure (cf. V, 305a), il n'y a certainement pas identification" (Bonnefoy, *Saint-Esprit et ses dons*, 219).

17 "Omnis autem spiritus iustus et sanctus habet donum Spiritus sancti sibi infusum" *Brev.* 2, 12, 2 (V, 230a).

virtues: the three theological virtues and the four cardinal virtues.[18] These habits of the virtues are received at baptism along with sanctifying grace, which is "their origin, their end, and their form,"[19] and constitute the way of beginners in a Christian life aimed at salvation. The effect brought about in the soul by this first supernatural influence is called its "first rectification."[20] Works of precept, concretely the commandments, are made possible by the help of these supernatural habits. No further habits are needed to attain salvation than these virtues.[21]

Bonaventure gives a succinct exposition on the gifts of the Holy Spirit in the *Breviloquium* (Part V, chap. 5), reviewing what already he had taught in the *Commentary on the Sentences* (*III Sent*. dd. 34 + 35).[22] He teaches that the gifts are needed, *as further habits*, in order to integrate the spiritual organism and perfect the work of sanctification. In the *Breviloquium*, Bonaventure clings to the number seven in ascribing the proper function of the gifts:

> (1) To diminish the difficulties from the after-effects of the seven capital sins; (2) Assist the natural faculties toward a greater docility to supernatural motions; (3) Help in perfecting the theological and moral virtues (seven in number); (4) Help us to suffer in the same spirit as Christ; (5) To help us act effectively; (6) To help us contemplate; (7) To faciltate action and contemplation.[23]

---

18 *Brev*. 5, 4, 2–3 (V, 256a–b).

19 *Brev*. 5, 4, 2 (V, 256a).

20 "Habitus rectificantes recte dicuntur virtutes, pro eo quod virtus de ratione sui nominis dicit, quod ad agendum erigit et vigorat" *III Sent*. d. 34, p. 1, a. 1, q. 1, concl. (III, 738a); *Brev*. 5, 4 , 3–6 (V, 256a–257a). By comparing the virtues with the gifts, Bonaventure is able to clarify the special roles of each kind of habit: *III Sent*. d. 34, p. 1, a. 1, qq. 1–3 (III, 735a–743b).

21 "[Virtutes ordinant] quantum ad ea quae sunt rectitudinis et necessitatis, utpote quantum ad illos actus primos, in quibus primaria rectitudo consistit" *III Sent*. d. 34, p. 1, a. 1, q. 1, ad 5 (III, 738b).

22 Surprisingly, Bonaventure's conferences *De donis* and the *Hexaëmeron* are not the best sources for a general teaching on the gifts of the Holy Spirit. J.F. Bonnefoy explains why: "Les conférences *De donis* et celles dites *in Hexaëmeron*, qui en sont la suite, sont, pour notre étude, moins riches de renseignements qu'on ne pourrait le croire à juger par leur titre. Le double but d'édification et d'apologie qu'elles poursuivent ouvertement, les préoccupations doctrinales d'ordre très général qui retenaient l'attention universelle au moment où elles furent prononcées (1268 et 1273), en font des documents très précieux pour connaître la position de l'école augustinienne en ces années troublées et la pensée du Docteur Séraphique. Ces diverses circonstances expliquent en même temps que l'orateur, tout absorbé par la défense des principes fondamentaux de l'augustinisme franciscain, se soit assez peu arrêté aux menus détails de doctrine que nous serions tentés d'y chercher, la doctrine des dons, par example" (Bonnefoy, 7–8).

23 These seven points are set forth in *Brev*. 5, 5, 2–9 (V, 257a–258a).

In brief, Bonaventure defines the gifts as *habitus* (dispositions) whose purpose, in the expression of J.F. Bonnefoy, is to dispose us "to accomplish with ease not only those actions which are imposed by precept, and are therefore necessary for salvation, but also the works of counsel and of supererogation."[24] From the list given above, the more important help, for my purpose, would seem to be the second—the aid given to the faculties of the soul:

> The concupiscible power needs help . . . in loving God, and finds it in wisdom. The rational power needs help in considering, choosing and following the truth: understanding is a help in the consideration of the truth, counsel in its election, and knowledge in its fulfillment.[25]

What specifically is this aid when it comes to studying theology? Before answering this question, it helps at this point to observe an important difference between Bonaventure's teaching and that of St. Thomas Aquinas. By making this comparison, we may better visualize the function which the gifts perform in the Franciscan Doctor's system.[26]

For Saint Thomas, the gifts of the Holy Spirit, even though superior to and distinct from the virtues, are supposed as necessary for salvation.[27] The Thomistic teaching thus fittingly is characterized by a more organic development of grace into virtues, which in turn are like roots from which

---

24 "Nous savons qu'ils sont *des habitus nous disposant à accomplir avec facilité non seulement les actes qui sont de précepte, et par suite, nécessaires au salut, mais encore les oeuvres de conseil et de surérogation*" (Bonnefoy, 99). This statement is based on Bonaventure's explanation: "Licet [virtutes] ordinent sufficienter quantum ad ea quae sunt rectitudinis et necessitatis, utpote quantum ad illos actus primos, in quibus primaria rectitudo consistit, tamen ultra hoc liberalitas benignitatis divinae providit homini et contulit habitus per quos expediretur non solum ad opera necessaria rectitudinis sed etiam perfectionis et supererogationis" *III Sent.* d. 34, p. 1, a. 1, q. 1, ad 5 (III, 738b). Cf. *III Sent.* d. 36, au., q. 2, concl. (III, 795b).

25 "Concupiscibilis indiget expediri quantum ad . . . affectum respectu Dei, et hoc fit per gustum sapientiae. Rationalis vero indiget expediri in veritatis speculatione, electione et exsecutione; per donum intellectus expeditur ad verum speculandum, per donum consilii ad verum eligendum, per donum scientiae ad electum exsequendum" (*Brev.* 5, 5, 4 [V, 257b; de Vinck, *The Breviloquium*, 199]).

26 "Qui hodie de Bonaventura disserit, saltem implicite etiam de Thoma loqui debet: non est melior via ad nostrum Doctorem intelligendum, quam via comparationis cum 'altero candelabro in domo Dei lucente'" (Z. Alszeghy, "Studia Bonaventuriana," *GR* 29 [1948]: 148).

27 The superiority of the gifts to the virtues is affirmed in *Summa Theologiae* I–II, q. 68, a. 8. St. Thomas believes in the necessity of the gifts for salvation on scriptural evidence: "Neminem diligit Deus nisi eum qui cum sapientia inhabitat" (Wisdom 7:28); and "Qui sine timore est, non poterit iustificari" (Ecclesiasticus 1:28). Since wisdom is the highest gift and fear of the Lord the lowest, the other five gifts necessarily must be included (*Summa Theologiae* I–II, q. 68, a. 2).

the gifts are derived.[28]

In the case of the gifts of the Holy Spirit in Bonaventurian teaching, even though these gifts are received inherently from the first moment of grace, they are more like seeds that have not yet blossomed.[29] They remain, for the most part, inactive until the soul desires to cooperate with the action of grace ordered toward sanctity, that is, when works of supererogation are attempted.[30] Now, since advancement in the spiritual life supposes our going beyond what is strictly necessary for salvation, the purpose of the gifts is to potentiate a more generous response.[31] They are needed, then, not for salvation but for sanctity.[32] Their very nature as *gifts* thus is underlined. A gift is not something we are entitled to receive on account of a natural development of grace, but something that God, from his own liberality, chooses to lavish upon us.[33] He lavishes us with these gifts in order to make us saints.

The gifts therefore predominate in the illuminative way since their purpose is to raise the soul from the state of beginners (the first

---

28 "Sicut ab essentia animae effluunt eius potentiae, quae sunt operum principia; ita etiam ab ipsa gratia effluunt virtutes in potentias animae, per quas potentiae moventur ad actus" *Summa Theologiae* I–II, q. 110, a. 4, ad 1; "Est enim gratia principium meritorii operis mediantibus virtutibus: sicut essentia animae est principium operum vitae mediantibus potentiis" (Ibid., ad 2). "Prima autem unio hominis est per fidem, spem et caritatem. Unde istae virtutes praesupponuntur ad dona, sicut radices quaedam donorum. Unde omnia dona pertinent ad has tres virtutes, sicut quaedam derivationes praedictarum virtutum" (Ibid., q. 68, a. 4, ad 3).

29 Although the expression is mine only as applied to the gifts, it responds to a Bonaventurian way of conceiving the action of God in creation, both on the natural and supernatural levels. This is, of course, based on the Augustinian 'ratio seminalis'. Bonaventure explains this teaching in *II Sent.* d. 18, a. 1, q. 3, concl. (II, 440a–b): "Ad praedictorum intelligentiam est notandum, quod cum satis constet, rationem seminalem esse potentiam activam, inditam materiae; et illam potentiam activam constet esse essentiam formae, cum ex ea fiat forma mediante operatione naturae, quae non producit aliquid ex nihilo: satis rationabiliter ponitur, quod ratio seminalis est essentia formae producendae, differens ab illa secundum esse completum et incompletum, sive secundum esse in potentia et in actu." Elsewhere he compares this to a rosebud that becomes the rose: *II Sent.* d. 7, p. 2, a. 2, q. 1, concl. (II, 198b).

30 "Quando Spiritus sancti gratia infunditur, ita sufficienter datur, quod omnes habitus gratuiti ex ipsa possunt oriri, si nos velimus susceptae gratiae cooperari, non solum habitus virtutum, sed etiam habitus donorum et beatitudinum" *III Sent.* d. 36, au., q. 2, concl. (III, 795a–b); cf. *Brev.* 5, 4, 3 (V, 256a).

31 "Homo . . . ineptus est ad opera maioris excellentiae, nisi ad haec iuvaretur per habitus donorum" *III Sent.* 34, p. 1, a. 1, q. 1, ad 5 (III, 739b).

32 The question asked in our first chapter, about wisdom being necessary for sanctity, might be answered in two ways that are not incompatible with each other: St. Bonaventure is making an exhortation to holiness; the wisdom he is speaking about is not the gift of the Holy Spirit. I would prefer to interpret his statement in the first sense, to protect the universal call to sanctity in Bonaventure.

33 "Habitus vero expedientes recte dicuntur *dona*, pro eo quod dicunt quandam ulteriorem abundantiam bonitatis ad agendum, ac per hoc magis attestantur divinae liberalitati; et propter hoc recte censentur nomine *doni*" *III Sent.* d. 34, p. 1, a. 1, q. 1, concl. (III, 738a); "Donum vero omne quod divinitus gratis datur" (Ibid., ad 1 [III, 738b]).

'hierarchization')[34] and operate in it a transformation ('second hierarchization')[35] by which the soul eventually may attain the state of the perfect ('third hierarchization').[36] This process of the mind's transformation constitutes the intermediate stage of the spiritual life, the stage of those souls advancing toward perfection, striving toward it with hopes of eventually arriving at the characteristic peace and repose of the perfect.[37]

In order for us to appreciate the illuminative way as paradigmatic of the way of sanctity, it is enough for us to observe that St. Bonaventure dedicated his spiritual treatises primarily to this intermediate stage.[38]

In contrast, we find no special treatise dedicated to the habits characteristic of the perfect.[39] These succeeding habits are the beatitudes,

---

34 *Hex.* 22, 24 (V, 441a); cf. 22, 39 (V, 443a). This is also called a 'rectification': *Brev.* 5, 4 (V, 256b).

35 The illumination in the contemplative soul brings about a transformation of the mind in God: "In illo [radio] anima absorbetur per mentis transformationem in Deum" *Hex.* 20, 8 (V, 426b; de Vinck, *Six Days*, 304); "Secunda hierarchizatio mentis est quantum ad potentias interiores; quod est magis difficile quam primum" *Hex.* 22, 36 (V, 442b).

36 "Tertia hierarchizatio est gratia super naturam et industriam, quando scilicet anima supra se elevata est" *Hex.* 22, 27 (V, 441b).

37 With the triple hierarchization, the soul might be imagined as a building that arises, clearly delineated by structural laws. It is no surprise that Bonaventure should use the imposing temple in Jerusalem as a symbol for the soul's desires and efforts to ascend to God. Such a symbol is precisely the object of Lillian Turney's thesis, "The Symbolism of the Temple in St. Bonaventure's Itinerarium mentis in Deum," Fordham University, 1968. What Bonaventure ultimately is attempting to do is have us visualize the soul as the *imago Dei*, regaining the *similitudo Dei* through the process of deification or *deiformitas*. A more general study, which sees medieval architecture as an expression of scholastic thought, is Erwin Panofsky's *Architecture gothique et pensée scolastique*, trad. P. Bourdieu (Paris: Minuit, 1967).

38 As we have seen earlier, the *Itinerarium mentis in Deum* is a description of the illuminative way. Even though this work is addressed chiefly to intellectuals, it shares in the author's customary preoccupation with souls in the intermediate stage. The *Itinerarium*, in fact, has been judged as the perfect résumé of Bonaventure's spiritual doctrine and even of all his work: "The *Itinerarium* is the most typical example of the Bonaventurian spirit and synthesis" (G. Melani, "Ispirazione e aspetti filosofici nell'*Itinerarium mentis in Deum*," *DtS* 15 [1968]: 21–69); it is the work in which is found "the dominant motif of the entire Bonaventurian production," (P. Brezzi, "La storia nel pensiero di san Bonaventura," *SB*, 2:390); it is the writing in which, just as in his other works, all of Bonaventure is contained (A. Gerken, "Identität und Freiheit-Ansatz und Methode im Denken des heiligen Bonaventura," *W W* 39 [1976]: 102); it is the most explicit and formal of the different itinerariums that are found throughout his works (F. Chauvet, "Los diversos 'Itinerarios' espirituales compuestos por San Buenaventura," *SBM*, 2:407–18). Speaking of his spiritual theology as such, J.G. Bougerol has stated that "Bonaventure's spiritual theology is but his general theology directed toward wisdom" (Bougerol, *Introduction to Bonaventure*, 156).

39 See: *Brev.* 5, 6 (V, 258b–260a); *III Sent.* d. 34, p. 1, a. 1, q. 1, concl. (III, 737a–738a); *I V Sent.* d. 1, p. 1, au., q. 6, concl. (IV, 28b); *De donis* 1, 17–18 (V, 461b). Even where he does speak of the beatitudes, it seems to be more a function of completing his teaching on the gifts, or of preparing for his teaching on the fruits and spiritual senses.

which confirm souls in perfection, a state which consists of spiritual enjoyment of their union with God, bringing about perfect unity of the active and contemplative life.[40]

Thus, the illuminative way, the way of those actively striving toward holiness, aptly becomes the object of Bonaventure's principal interest in his spiritual works. He wants to help the soul recognize and overcome difficulties and thereby grow in holiness by responding generously to the activity of the gifts. To respond to this supernatural illumination demands that the soul know what God expects of him at this juncture. Therefore it only is natural that St. Bonaventure, as a teacher of holiness, should focus his attention here, since these souls not only stand in need of instruction but also truly desire to learn the means to holiness. Furthermore, precisely because it is along this path that advancement toward holiness is expected to take place, this stage more properly may be designated a 'way' than the other two stages.

While the illuminative way remains Bonaventure's chief object of interest, by simply contrasting it with the state of the beginner and the state of the perfect, he pretends to provide a clearer concept of its nature. He organizes his thought around the comparison of the three classes of supernatural habits with each other.[41] The soul in the illuminative way already has knowledge of the purgative way, supposedly through personal experience, and now aims at entering the unitive way. Now, knowledge of the end pretended inevitably must throw light on the path leading upward to these heights. And although what lies ahead shall occupy the soul's attention less than the dynamics of the illuminative way itself, the third stage evidently holds more importance for him than the purgative way, since it is a source of judgment about his present spiritual condition. He admires the perfect who, although not counted among the blessed in heaven, have attained in a stable way the object of his own striving (union with God without vision).[42] By emphasizing the illuminative way, it certainly is

---

40 *Brev.* 5, 6, 7 (V, 259b).

41 This is his procedure in treating the habits. Comparing the gifts with the virtues (*III Sent.* d. 34, a. 1 [III, 734a–743b]), he investigates: whether these two classes of habits differ from each other (Ibid., q. 1); which set of habits are prior (Ibid., q. 2); which are more excellent (Ibid., q. 3). In the same work, when mentioning the beatitudes, they are simply compared or contrasted with the other two classes of habits (*III Sent.*, d. 34, p. 1, a. 1, q. 1, concl. (III, 737a); ibid. (III, 738a); ibid., q. 3, ad 2 (III, 742b–743a); ibid., a. 2, q. 1, concl. (III, 746a). This is also done in the *Breviloquium: Brev.* 5, 4, 3 (V, 256b). Even when the beatitudes are expressly approached in the *Breviloquium* we find the tendency to justify their existence by way of completing the virtues and the gifts (*Brev.* 5, 6 [V, 258b–260a]).

42 This is a state of joy and repose in the union attained with Christ who is now known through purity of heart (a quasi-direct experience of the invisible).

not Bonaventure's intention to reduce the other two ways to *termini a quo et ad quem*. Between these two ways, the advancing soul is in a state of continual transition and movement toward the goal. This is an *itinerarium*, a journey, a way, in the truest sense of the word. If the beginner is content to fulfill the minimum by keeping the commandments, he pretends no more than is strictly necessary for salvation.[43] By not striving for more than salvation, no further graces will be given to him.[44] This is not a spiritual life, unless it is taken up as a preparation (purgative way), that is, as a transitional stage for what lies ahead.[45] However the first stage is lived, our author sees it as relatively easy to enter into the illuminative way,[46] but counting on the desire of the soul to do so.[47] As we saw at the outset, he sees it as everyone's duty to seek for holiness, in virtue of baptism.

It is otherwise with knowledge about the state of the perfect. Although this end of the spectrum likewise does not receive special treatment from Bonaventure, he recognizes that knowledge of it is already a source of orientation and encouragement, for a holy life must be so directed as to point a soul toward that perfect state. Thus he speaks of the beatitudes, but contrasts them with the gifts, evidently to clarify his teaching on the gifts.

To clarify this teaching on the gifts, we then ask ourselves: Where does the spiritual journey culminate? The end is an experiential knowledge of God. Such knowledge is so superior to that knowledge attained through the senses and through abstraction, that many have preferred to call such knowledge an 'unknowing'.[48] How can it be that the way leading to it should be called an illumination? Paradoxically, the light, because of its ever greater intensity, gradually blinds the soul. But this blindness only is

---

43 As we have seen, even though all souls are called to holiness, the desire to follow this way is only rarely found.

44 "Nemini datur, nisi ei qui se exercet ad illam" *Brev.* 5, 6, 8 (V, 260a).

45 Unfortunately, as we have seen, this is usually not the case. Desires for sanctity rarely may be found among those who occupy, at least theoretically, the purgative way. This merely sociological fact does not, however, invalidate the role Bonaventure assigns to the purgative way.

46 "Patet etiam, quam ampla sit via illuminativa, et quomodo in omni re, quae sentitur sive quae cognoscitur, interius lateat ipse Deus" *Red. art.* 26 (V, 325b).

47 "Hanc autem rectitudinem non habet quis nolens, sed volens" *III Sent.* d. 23, a. 1, q. 1, concl. (III, 471a). On the desire of contemplation, he states: "Hunc modum cognoscendi arbitror cuilibet viro iusto in via ista esse quaerendum" *II Sent.* d. 23, a. 2, q. 3, ad 6 (II, 546a).

48 Lonergan prefers to see this experience as the result of God's 'prior' word progressively drawing us away from a world mediated by meaning: "The prior word in its immediacy, though it differs in intensity, though it resonates differently in different temperaments and in different stages of religious development, withdraws man from the diversity of history by moving out of the world mediated by meaning and towards a world of immediacy in which image and symbol, thought and word, lose their

worthy of such a name when it is considered by those who still are approaching it. Because this light strips the soul of former ways of knowing, it is a blindness for the operation of the natural powers. Bernard Lonergan explains that without *knowing* mystery, we still can be conscious of it.[49] For the theologian this means that former rational supports are rendered so inadequate as to appear to be removed altogether.[50] Thus, even though this way traditionally is called 'illuminative', its second function is to wean the soul of any security found in this light.[51] This accounts for the progressive stripping of the soul which is at the basis of Bonaventure's concept of intellectual poverty, or *nuditas cordis*.[52]

When the soul finally reaches the threshold of the unitive way, the beatitudes then begin to operate by endowing the soul with a fruition of its union with Christ. The effect of the beatitudes, then, is to capacitate the soul for this fruition, or delectation, whose perception is effected through the fruits of the Holy Spirit and the spiritual senses, neither of which are new habits.[53] St. Bonaventure speaks of the "sufficiency, number, and order" of the beatitudes as "derived from the integrity, the modes, and the preliminary dispositions of perfection [the gifts]."[54] In a sense, then, Bonaventure treats

---

relevance and even disappear" (Lonergan, *Method in Theology*, 112).

49 "To say that this dynamic state is conscious is not to say that it is known. For consciousness is just experience, but knowledge is a compound of experience, understanding, and judging. Because the dynamic state is conscious without being known, it is an experience of mystery" (Lonergan, *Method in Theology*, 106).

50 Reason is not renounced, but its limits are recognized as insufficient before a more powerful source of knowledge. As Tina Manferdini points out: "Ciò che Bonaventura respinge è la pretesa del sapere scientifico e della corrispettiva ragione di porsi come unico o come superiore modo o livello di attuazione della razionalità, e in quanto tale come norma criteriante di ogni altro modo e livello. In definitiva ciò che Bonaventura non è disposto ad accettare è l'indebita estrapolazione della ragione scientifica fuori dal proprio limitato ambito de competenza e la sua applicazione ad oggetti che richiedono un tipo di razionalità e un livello de intelligibilità essenzialmene diverso da quello scientifico. In altri termini Bonaventura è un consapevole critico dello scientismo" ("La problematica della ragione nel pensiero di S. Bonvantura," *DtS* 27 [1980]: 35).

51 This is why, as we have seen, Bonaventure warns the soul against believing it knows through revelation (*Hex.* 22, 42 [V, 444b]).

52 Since our mind seeks to contemplate "those things whose likenesses can in no way be found in creatures and which surpass all penetration by the human intellect". . . . "all intellectual activities must be left behind" *Itin.* 7, 1+4 (V, 312b; E. Cousins, *The Soul's Journey to God*, pp. 111+113). That Bonaventure is the author of the *Expositio super regulam FF. Minorum* is held in doubt, but the expression 'nuditas cordis' found in this work (VIII, 399a) seems to reflect his thought.

53 "Ad has beatitudines propter sui perfectionem et plenitudinem duodecim fructus Spiritus et quinque sensus spirituales consequuntur; qui non dicunt novos habitus, sed status delectationum et usus spiritualium speculationum, quibus replentur et consolantur spiritus virorum iustorum" *Brev.* 5, 6, 1 (V, 258b).

54 ". . . quarum sufficientia, numerus et ordo colligitur ex integritate perfectionis, ex modis perfectionum et ex dispositionibus ad perfectionem" *Brev.* 5, 6, 2 (V, 258b; de Vinck, *The Breviloquium*, 203).

the beatitudes more like rewards bestowed upon the soul subsequent to the efficient use of the gifts, whose purpose was to "urge it on."[55]

The perfect, therefore, no longer stand in need of special instructions on their 'way' of union, which in fact no longer appears as a road to be traveled. They have reached union and are living a life that docilely follows the mysterious, supernatural laws of God's motions within them.[56] Out of respect for mystery, Bonaventure, the mystagogue, seems to have desisted lest his role become a usurpation inasmuch as God himself henceforth becomes the soul's unique teacher.[57]

The perfect no longer need to occupy themselves with means to attaining sanctity, but only of preserving it.[58] Having reached its fulfillment, it more truly can be affirmed that the spiritual life is now being lived *through* these souls by God as the protagonist of divine life within them. And because they have attained the perfect unity of the active and contemplative lives, now they principally are occupied, unhindered by methods, in irradiating the goods they acquired in contemplation (*bonum diffusivum sui*).[59] The

---

55 ". . . in habitus donorum, quorum est animam expedire" *Brev.* 5, 4, 3 (V, 256b; de Vinck, *The Breviloquium*, 194); cf. *III Sent.* d. 34, p. 1, a. 1, q. 1, concl. (III, 737a). That the beatitudes are more like rewards than stimulants to virtuous behavior is evident from the attention St. Bonaventure dedicates to the role of the beatitudes in bringing about the fruition of the union attained between the soul and God. Likewise, to end the chapter on the beatitudes, seemingly to justify the teaching he has just expounded, his last utterance points to the question of merit: ". . . ideo deinceps consideranda sunt exercitia meritorum" *Brev.* 5, 6, 8 (V, 260a), and this forms the subject of the following chapter.

56 In the last paragraph of his short treatment on the beatitudes, Bonaventure describes the soul endowed with them as follows: "In its burning desire, the soul becomes not only an agile flame swift to rise: it even transcends itself, entering mystical darkness and ecstasy through a certain wise unknowing. . . Experience alone can tell the wonder of this obscure, delightful light" *Brev.* 5, 6, 8 (V, 260a; de Vinck, *The Breviloquium*, 206); cf. *Trip. via* 1, 15–17 (VIII, 7a–b).

57 "Christus est doctor interius" *Hex.* 12, 5 (V, 385a); cf. *Hex.* 1, 13 (V, 331b). One of Bonaventure's deepest convictions concerns this unique magisterium of Christ. See: *Christus mag.*, passim (V, 567a–574b; Russo, *La metodologia del sapere*, 100–133). Likewise, if he had been convinced of the utility of speaking about the beatitudes, he may not have found it too arduous a task, as the following statement seems to betray: "Dicere etiam de septem beatitudinibus . . . ad praesens esset nimis arduum" *De donis* 1, 18 (V, 461b). On the other hand, out of respect for this mysterious grace, he may have preferred silence to speech, since silence is certainly a condition for experiencing such a grace: "Ad cuius experientiam plus valet internum silentium quam exterius verbum. Et ideo hic finis verbi habendus est, et orandus Dominus, ut experiri donet quod loquimur" *Scien. Chr.* q. 7, concl. (V, 43b).

58 Only in this sense are perfect souls in some manner never dissociated from the purgative way. In fact, when treating of the beatitudes, we find Bonaventure still speaking of "a perfect withdrawal from evil, a perfect progress in good, and a perfect repose in what is the best" *Brev.* 5, 6, 3 (V, 258b; de Vinck, *The Breviloquium*, 203). Nevertheless, he views this more as a crowning effect of grace than as an invitation by God to further effort.

59 That good inherently tends to communicate itself is an important Bonaventurian concept: "Nam «bonum dicitur diffusivum sui»; summum igitur bonum summe diffusivum est sui" *Itin.* 6, 2 (V, 310b).

spiritual life has become a spontaneous living out of God's charity. A certain *docta ignorantia* in which they now are immersed has overtaken their daily lives.[60] The way of the perfect is "so closely related to the final end," as to justify the name of the habits (beatitudes) characterizing this stage of spiritual life which resembles the state of the blessed.[61] Since the soul now shares overwhelmingly in the mysterious life of God, man's activity has been rendered almost entirely receptive, as well as incomprehensible.[62] At the same time, the preponderance of God's activity in this stage explains the limitations set on our comprehension of the soul's experience.[63]

2. A gift is freely given

Even though the call to holiness is universal, and even though it is relatively easy to begin the illuminative way, the gifts of the Holy Spirit are still *gifts* that God freely gives to those who need them. This idea of liberality on the part of God is important to Bonaventure's teaching on the Holy Spirit, a teaching which in turn derives from his trinitarian theology.[64] The Holy Spirit is the Gift, par excellence: "The Holy Spirit is the first Gift. Whatever comes afterwards must be referred to what is prior. Consequently every gift is reduced to the gift that is the Holy Spirit. Hence in every gift the reason of its donation is the Holy Spirit."[65]

This concept is the object of Joseph Walsh's study: "The Principle 'Bonum diffusivum sui' in St. Bonaventure: Its Meaning and Importance" (Thesis, Fordam University, 1958). The ultimate purpose of the beatitudes is to fit the soul for the perfection of both the active and the contemplative life. See: *Brev.* 5, 6, 7 (V, 259b; de Vinck, *The Breviloquium*, 205). Thus, personal perfection—characterized by the experience of fruition of the union with Christ—is ordered in its turn to apostolic irradiation.

60 *Brev.* 5, 6, 8 (V, 260); *II Sent.* d.23, a. 2, q. 3, concl., ad 6 (II, 546a).

61 "Ideo gratiae donum ab ipso manans liberaliter et abunde ramificari debet usque ad habitus perfectionum, qui, cum fini approximant, recto vocabulo nuncupantur ex nomine beatitudinum" *Brev.* 5, 6, 2 (V, 258b; de Vinck, *The Breviloquium*, 202–03).

62 "Gratia unionis excedit quantamcumque gratiam comprehensionis improportionaliter" *Scien. Chr.* q. 6, fund. 8 (V, 32b).

63 The experience itself is the only key to an understanding of what is experienced: "Quam nocturnam et deliciosam illuminationem nemo novit nisi qui probat" *Brev.* 5, 6, 8 (V, 260a); "Quia istum cognoscendi modum vix aut nunquam intelligit nisi expertus" *Scien. Chr.* q. 7, concl. (V, 43a).

64 J.F. Bonnefoy points out the varied expressions used by Bonaventure to indicate the modus procedendi of the Holy Spirit. The one most often used is *per modum liberalitatis*. Other expressions are similar: *per modum amoris; per modum liberalis voluntatis; per modum liberalitatis et amoris; per modum voluntatis; per liberalitatem.* (Bonnefoy, 13–57). See: *I Sent.* d. 10, a. 1, q. 1 (I, 194a–196b).

65 "Spiritus sanctus est primum donum; sed omne posterius ad prius reducitur: ergo omne donum reducitur ad donum, quod est Spiritus sanctus: ergo in omnibus donis ratio donationis est per

As we pointed out above, here we touch upon one of the chief differences between Bonaventure's teaching on the gifts when compared with that of Saint Thomas. At bottom there is a difference in the way of conceiving the procession of the Holy Spirit. But again, although it is only a nuance, a difference is perceived in their spiritual theology on account of it. St. Bonaventure, depending principally on St. Augustine's *De Trinitate*, gives more emphasis to the procession by way of the will, highlighting the name "Gift" as applied to the Holy Spirit.[66]

The consequence of this difference in theological vision, although such a difference can be judged as slight, is a theology of the gifts with diverse elements. Thus, even though St. Thomas teaches the distinction between the virtues and the gifts,[67] Bonaventure, faithful to the idea of gratuity, gives greater stress to this distinction. Bonaventure does this in two ways: (1) by classifying, as we have seen, each of the three ways of the spiritual life according to the activity of the supernatural habits he considers to be preponderant in each way: [a] for the purgative way, the virtues, [b] for the illuminative way, the gifts of the Holy Spirit, [c] for the unitive way, the beatitudes; (2) and by insisting that the object of the gifts is the *faculties* rather than the virtues.[68]

The overall purpose St. Bonaventure has in this particular arrangement is to underline the free character of the spiritual life as a gift, and to highlight

Spiritum sanctum" *I Sent.* d. 18, au., q. 1, f. 3 (I, 323a).

66   J.F. Bonnefoy explains the difference in the teaching of the two Doctors, based on the use of the names given to the Holy Spirit by each of them: "Tout autre est la genèse des noms propres de la troisième Personne dans la théorie psychologique de saint Thomas. Il affirme aussi qu'elle procède par voie de volonté, mais dans un sens différent de celui de saint Bonaventure. Tandis que ce dernier, et l'école franciscaine avec lui, oppose la procession par voie de volonté à celle qui se fait par voie de nature, saint Thomas l'ajoute à celle qui se fait par voie d'intelligence. Considerée sous ce jour, la deuxième Procession se termine à un Amour subsistant [*S. Th.*, I, q. 27], personnel, et c'est en partant de cette notion qu'il justifie et intègre dans sa théorie les appellations traditionnelles d'Esprit-Saint et de Don" (Bonnefoy, 34). In this regard Bonnefoy singles out a use of the name 'Gift' for the Holy Spirit: "Tandis que l'appellation de Don est postérieure à celle d'Amour dans l'exposition thomiste [*S. Th.*, I, q. 38, a. 2: 'Cum Spiritus sanctus procedat ut amor (sicut jam dictum est), procedit in ratione doni primi'], elle lui est antérieure dans le système bonaventurien, mais ici et là, c'est l'écho de saint Augustin que nous entendons" (Bonnefoy, *loc. cit.*). Bonnefoy also adds that St. Augustine, in using the name of 'Gift', remains within earlier tradition: "Respectueux de la Tradition, il expose longuement ce que signifie ce terme et comment il convient à la troisième personne de la Trinité" (Ibid.).

67   *Summa Theologiae* I–II, q. 68, a. 1.

68   Even though St. Thomas states that the gifts predispose the potencies (or faculties) in order to second the divine motion ("Dona autem Spiritus Sancti sunt quibus omnes vires animae disponuntur ad hoc quod subdantur motioni divinae... Quia dona perficiunt vires animae in comparatione ad Spiritum Sanctum moventem" [*Summa theologiae* I–II, q. 68, a. 8]), the aim of the gifts is to help the virtues against defects ("Dona dantur in adiutorium virtutum contra defectus" [Ibid.]). In Bonaventure we find great similarities of doctrine, but the differences between the two doctors can be considered on

its special nature as something superadded to the life of a Christian.[69] Each of these characteristics implies the other.

The spiritual life, he is stressing, is a free gift of God. Moreover, since the gifts of the Holy Spirit always have been called 'gifts', St. Bonaventure considers another motive for them to contain some benefit over and above the virtues. Since the purpose of the virtues is to develop the purely moral life, that of the gifts is to develop the spiritual life as such, or to "urge it onward" (*expedire*). Although he does mention that the spiritual structure "branches out" (*ramificari*), we have pointed out above that to insist on this image of growth may incur a misunderstanding of Bonaventure's teaching on the gifts and confuse it with that of St. Thomas. In the doctrine of St. Thomas, the almost natural development of the gifts from the virtues takes place as the spiritual life advances, and this normal progress, as we have seen, even is considered necessary to attain salvation.[70]

When it comes to becoming a saint, Bonaventure prefers to see something more dramatic taking place in the soul.[71] By closely associating the gifts with works of supererogation, St. Bonaventure's teaching would widen the distance between beginners and proficients. This could lead his readers to conclude that such a life is only for a select few.[72] However, we have seen the Seraphic Doctor insisting on the universal character of the call to holiness.[73] Such an insistence itself may be compensatory, that is, it

---

various levels. The teaching of Bonaventure manifests a sharper distinction between virtues and gifts as well as a greater insistence on the action of the gifts being directly exercised upon the faculties. J.F. Bonnefoy deals with these differences between the two doctors (see: Bonnefoy, 72–78; 99–100; 118–19), while accepting their agreement on main points: "En somme, saint Thomas est d'accord avec saint Bonaventure sur les points principaux, mais il conçoit autrement le sujet immédiat de la grâce, ses rapports avec les habitus gratuits, et . . . la manière de distinguer ces habitus" (Ibid., 78).

69 "Dona Spiritus Sancti caritatem praesupponunt et ultra habitum caritatis aliquid addunt, sicut habitus sapientia addit aptitudinem et promptitudinem ad faciliter degustandum quam suavis est Dominus" *III Sent.* d. 34, p. 1, a. 1, q. 3, ad 1 (III, 742b).

70 The interpretation of Aquinas' teaching on the gifts as being "distinct but derived from the infused virtues" is generally accepted (*NDCS*, s.v. «Gifts of the Holy Spirit,» by George P. Evans, p. 437).

71 "Si autem loquamur quantum ad status consequentes, cum usus virtutum habeantur in statu imperfectionis, usus vero donorum promoveant hominem ad statum perfectionis; sic dona sunt excellentiora virtutibus, sicut status proficientium est perfectior statu incipientium" *III Sent.* d. 34, p. 1, a. 1, q. 3, concl. (III, 742b).

72 A. Moreno, for example, concludes that for St. Bonaventure Christian perfection consists in doing difficult things, because of their nature as supererogatory and of counsel: "San Buenaventura hace consistir la perfección cristiana en las obras difíciles, por lo que tienen de supererogatorio y aconsejado" ("Espiritualidad -Perfección Sacerdotal y Religiosa, en la controversia medieval de la Universidad de París, 1252–1272," *V V* 23 [1965]: 112).

73 See Chapter I, subdivision 2. "The spiritual life for Saint Bonaventure." Pope Paul VI points out this aspect in Bonaventure's doctrine: "Egli, infatti, ritiene che ogni uomo giusto debba cercare la

may be an offsetting necessity, consequent on his assigning the dominant activity of the gifts uniquely to the illuminative way. A similar compensation may be seen in his need to point out the parallel nature of the three ways.

What can we conclude from these two apparently contradictory attitudes in St. Bonaventure? First, that the spiritual life is indeed something special; it should be esteemed and desired as such by everyone, since it is a gift from God that is not given indiscriminately. But, at the same time, everyone is eligible for such a life of sanctity. I believe any contradiction can be resolved by perceiving that sanctity for Saint Bonaventure, in spite of the relatively secure status of the perfect, is essentially progressive and dynamic, a way to be walked, not a *terminus ad quem*.[74] Everyone can attain holiness, understood as a *way of life*, if his desire is applied to working for it.[75] God will give these "gifts" to those whose dispositions are prepared for them. This preparation does not condition God's freedom, rather it conditions our capacity to receive a gift, making us more open and generous in the suffering that accompanies growth in the spirit.

The aspect of "liberality" in Bonaventure's teaching, as we have pointed out above, serves to emphasize the special nature of the spiritual life as 'gift', calling for a free response from the soul. Just as the Holy Spirit proceeds from the Father and the Son as a free gift, the response elicited by the reception of any gift, in this case the gifts of the Holy Spirit, appropriately is offered in utter freedom, which is a condition for merit.[76]

Some of our author's stronger statements seem to limit the range of the activity of the gifts to the faculties (instead of upon the virtues

---

contemplazione e tendere al bene infinito, nel quale l'anima, benché abbia una capacità finita, possa trovare il suo pieno compimento" (Paul VI, Apostolic Letter "Scientia et Virtute", *Insegnamenti*, vol. 12 [1974], p 706.

74 This fits within Bonaventure's vision of the three ways as running parallel to each other, resulting in ascetic efforts never being cast aside. Likewise, the theme of seeking God (*quaerere Deum*) is so much a part of Bonaventurian spirituality, as witnessed in the structure itself of the *Itinerarium mentis in Deum*.

75 Thus, in this light, statements by St. Bonaventure concerning: holiness as a condition or means to obtaining wisdom ("Sine sanctitate non est homo sapiens" *Hex*. 2, 6 [V, 337a]; "Sanctitas immediata dispositio est ad sapientiam" *Hex*. 2, 6 [V, 337a]; "Non est ergo securus transitus a scientia ad sapientiam; oportet ergo medium ponere, scilicet sanctitatem" *Hex*. 19, 3 [V, 420b]); while wisdom is necessary for salvation ("Salus enim non est nisi per sapientiam" *Hex*. 14, 7 [V, 394b]); and perfection is operated by wisdom ("Perfici autem habemus per accessum ad summum, quod consistit in uno, et hoc per donum sapientiae" *Brev*. 5, 5, 8 [V, 258a]), which we saw in our first chapter, only seem complementary to his teaching on the universal call to holiness.

76 "Nullum obsequium est meritorium apud Deum, nisi quod fit liberaliter; sed nihil fit liberaliter, nisi quod fit ex amore, quoniam amor est donum, in quo omnia alia dona donantur: si ero efficacia merendi consistit in liberalitate, et liberalitas primo et principaliter reperitur in motu caritatis et amoris; videtur

themselves).[77] St. Thomas teaches that the role of the gifts is specifically to help and perfect the virtues.[78] This became the traditional teaching of the Church, as has been restated in the *Catechism of the Catholic Church*.[79] Nevertheless, aligning myself within the opinion expressed by E. Gilson, that the teaching of the two most eminent scholastics, although different, is not contrary but complementary,[80] it seems to me that the Catechism's statement does not preclude the Bonaventurian teaching, but remains open to ulterior, noncontradictory, explanations of how the gifts "complete and perfect the virtues."[81] In conclusion, it would seem that Bonaventure's insistence on the special dignity of the gifts is more innate to his theology, and the balancing, but paradoxical, teaching on the universal call to holiness, is rather to be judged as a complementary, or even corrective, consequence of this teaching, than a cause of it.[82]

idem quod prius, videlicet quod motus caritatis primo et principaliter sit meritorius" *III Sent*. d. 27, a. 2, q. 1, f. 5 (III, 602b).

77 "Propria ratio sumendi sufficientiam donorum non est penes expeditionem virtutum, sed magis penes expeditionem ipsarum potentiarum in suis actibus" *III Sent*. d. 34, p. 1, a. 2, q. 1, ad. 4 (III, 746b).

78 The Thomistic doctrine becomes even clearer in the individual treatment of each virtue with its corresponding gift. For example, the gift of counsel connects with the virtue of prudence, to help and perfect the latter: "Unde donum consilii respondet prudentiae, sicut ipsam adiuvans et perficiens" *Summa Theologiae* II–II, q. 52, a. 2, resp.

79 "The seven gifts of the Holy Spirit. . . complete and perfect the virtues of those who receive them" (*Catechism of the Catholic Church*, ¶ 1831 [London: Geoffrey Chapman, 1994], 406).

80 "It must be clear that [St. Bonaventure's doctrine] can never be properly comparable in any point with the doctrine of St. Thomas Aquinas. Obviously it would be absurd to deny their fundamental agreement. . . The attempts sometimes made by their interpreters to transform their fundamental agreement into an identity of content are, from the start, futile and doomed to fail. For it is clear that since the two doctrines are ordered from different starting points, they will never envisage the same problems in the same aspect, and therefore one will never answer the precise question that the other asks. The philosophy of St. Thomas and the philosophy of St. Bonaventure are complementary, as the two most comprehensive interpretations of the universe as seen by Christians, and it is because they are complementary that they never either conflict or coincide" (Gilson, *Philosophy of Bonaventure*, 448–49).

81 It is likewise notable that the new Catechism locates the gifts within "those who receive them," instead of using a more restrictive phrase (such as 'in the baptized'), whereby it might have approximated more closely the Thomistic view that sees the virtues as the roots of the gifts (*S. Th*., I–II, q. 68, a. 4, ad 3). As it stands, the Catechism seems to allow for an interpretation of their special, or more independent, character. In any case Bonaventure, although he emphasized that the gifts perfect, not the virtues themselves but the faculties, also can be found to say that the gifts help (*expedire*) the operation (*officium*) of the virtues (e.g. *Brev*. 5, 5, 5 [V, 253b]). When such freedom of expression is observed both in Aquinas and in Bonaventure it seems exaggerated to insist too much on their differences. In any case, Pope John Paul II enthusiastically uses Bonaventure's teaching on the seven gifts of the Holy Spirit (see: *Dominum et vivificantem*, 42).

82 In fact, I find the teaching on the universal call to holiness to be given less emphasis in his works. And even when it is spoken of, it only is to be found in his pastoral works. On the other hand, the

3. The cognitive gifts in the illuminative way

What we have observed so far concerning the gifts of the Holy Spirit has special importance when we turn to Bonaventure's teaching on theology and the spiritual life. We have seen that Bonaventure assigns to theology certain gifts of the Holy Spirit, particularly knowledge and piety, understanding and wisdom. Although the other gifts—fear, fortitude, and counsel—undoubtedly have an indirect influence on the theologian insofar as he is Christian, St. Bonaventure finds more gifts concerned with the intellect because the light they give to the cognitive operations is a powerful help 'to direct our feet' on the path to God.[83] We may wonder why he does not restrict himself to one gift for theology, wisdom for example, as that is precisely the name he assigns to theology in the beginning of his *Commentary on the Sentences*, thereby recognizing the primary importance of this gift for theology. That he should assign more than one gift to theology is permitted, in any case, by his doctrine on the plurality of forms, a doctrine that is considered so characteristic of Bonaventure. According to this doctrine, a superior form does not suppress an inferior form, but brings it to greater perfection.[84] Thus, just as the gifts do not suppress the virtues, but suppose their existence as a foundation for further spiritual advancement, so

theological teaching on the gifts of the Holy Spirit seems to be more essentially a part of his position. Even so, the two elements are not disconnected, but harmonized by the necessity of desire on the part of the soul. But again, this desire implies a willingness for exertion and struggle.

83 "Plura sunt dona ad intellectum spectantia, quia lux cognitionis vehementer expedit ad dirigendos pedes in viam rectam" *Brev.* 5, 5, 9 (V, 258a).

84 Throughout his works, Bonaventure expresses his recognition of the plurality of forms, without offering arguments to justify this philosophical premise. We see applications of this frequently, for example: "Observatio iustitiae disponit ad eam [sapientiam] habendam, sicut appetitus materiae inclinat ad formam et facit eam habilem, ut coniungatur formae mediantibus dispositionibus; non quod illae dispositiones perimentur, immo magis complentur" *Hex.* 2, 2 (V, 336b). Etienne Gilson, in order to clarify Bonaventure's use of "this doctrine of the plurality of forms that so greatly embarrasses his interpreters," believes it is the terminology that has encouraged such misunderstanding: "The term 'form' in St. Bonaventure has an Aristotelian origin, but the idea of form has not. For him the form has indeed the bestowing of a perfection as its chief function, but it does this by preparing the substance which it informs for other substantial perfections which it cannot itself confer upon it. . . It becomes easier to understand why St. Bonaventure always speaks as if he allowed the plurality of forms without ever feeling the need to justify his attitude by any special theory. The plurality of forms is proved by the presence, at the heart of being or things, of perfections which are substantial to them, for without them they would not be what they are, and which yet require as their causes forms superior to those which define their particular being. We now understand that the contradiction found by the Thomists in the very idea of a plurality of forms proved no obstacle to St. Bonaventure, since, from his point of view, it does not exist. The substantial being of a body, animate or inanimate, with all the properties that define it, is one of the perfections or even the fundamental perfection that the form must explain; but it is not the only one, and the same reasoning that makes us point to the form as the explanation of the essence makes us point to other forms to explain other perfections" (*Philosophy of Bonaventure*, 252–53).

also a gift that is more sublime does not suppress a less sublime gift, but brings it to fuller perfection.[85] In this way we may have different gifts cooperating together in a hierarchized fashion—for example, starting with knowledge and advancing to understanding and then reaching a culmination in the gift of wisdom—without overpowering or curbing the preceding operations of any gift or of any virtue.[86]

Later on in this chapter we will focus on each of these gifts to determine their particular role in the theologian's activity. But first, it is worth pointing out that since theology belongs to the illuminative way, it shares in the basic characteristics of the way of advanced souls. Advanced souls act under the preponderant influence of the gifts of the Holy Spirit, it is true. But these souls, it also must be remembered, are the ones who have decided, from a conscious desire for sanctity, to undertake the ascent to perfection. Because they have undertaken the demands of the spiritual life in its most characteristic form, as is found in the illuminative way, they stand in need of special helps from God. These helps are the gifts of the Holy Spirit. The gifts pertain to God's role in this stage, while man's role consists in his desire and effort to do more than simply attain salvation.

In the illuminative way, what first is needed on the part of man is the intention to become a saint.[87] This decision has immediate consequences for the theologian. Theology has no other alternative than to be undertaken as a means to holiness. It is not an end in itself. The end is union with God.

---

85 "Status ille secundus praesupponit statum praecedentem. Unde sicut bene esse melius est quam esse, quia bene esse dicit esse et adhuc amplius; sic habitus reddentes potentias expeditas ad actus medios, excellentiores sunt habitus reddentibus eas expeditas ad actus primos, non ratione eius quod addunt solum sed ratione eius quod addunt et praesupponunt" *III Sent.* d. 34, p. 1, a. 1, q. 3, concl. (III, 742b).

86 Bonnefoy summarizes Bonaventure's procedure as follows: "En somme, l'habitus qui, dans chaque série inférieure, occupe le premier rang, la charité parmi les vertus, la sagesse parmi les dons, ne mérite le titre de don le plus excellent, que si l'on le considère lui-même comme renfermant les habitus inférieurs et si l'on envisage dans les habitus supérieurs uniquement la perfection qu'ils lui ajoutent" (Bonnefoy, 92). When it comes to several gifts operating together, Bonaventure with ease can fit them into the active and contemplative life, while assigning each gift to a purpose fulfilled by one of the three ways of the spiritual life: "Aliter sumitur distinctio donorum secundum distinctionem duplicis vitae, videlicet activae et contemplativae. Si quantum ad vitam contemplativam, sic est triplex actus correspondens actui hierarchico, videlicet illuminare, purgare et perficere, et secundum hoc, triplex donum: unum quod disponit ad purgationem et hoc est timor, aliud quod attenditur secundum actum illuminandi et hoc est intellectus, tertium quod attenditur secundum actum perficiendi et hoc est sapientia" *III Sent.* d. 34, p. 1, a. 2, q. 1, resp. (III, 746a).

87 For Bernard Lonergan, sanctity might be expressed as "the experienced fulfillment of our unrestricted thrust to self-transcendence" (*Method in Theology*, 115). Man's thrust toward authenticity is God's purpose in creating us in his image: "He made us in his image, for our authenticity consists in being like him, in self-transcending, in being origins of value, in true love" (Ibid., 117).

Theology as a means is simply a spiritual life to be lived and carried out with the primary or overriding desire to become a saint. Apparently this was so obvious for St. Bonaventure that he never needed to expressly formulate that theology *is* a spiritual life. The remark often is made today that St. Thomas did his theology at the prie-dieu, and it is a commonplace for us to imagine theologians in the Middle Ages 'doing theology on their knees'.[88] But in our times, at most we have classified such a concept of theology as an alternative *style* of theology.[89]

4. *Curiositas:* enemy of the gifts

If theology is undertaken with the purpose of attaining holiness, its nature as a spiritual way to holiness even becomes clearer when contrasted with curiosity which Bonaventure sees as the principle vice threatening the theologian.

In effect, if the life of theological study means following obediently the lights and motions coming from above, nothing can be more contrary to this form of the illuminative way than yielding to the temptation to know something for other reasons, no matter how noble these reasons may be. To know for the sake of knowing, that is, to search for truth simply to satisfy a craving for knowledge apart from the larger context of charity usually is not called *vain* curiosity, but simply curiosity.[90] Curiosity alone, even if it is not vain, constitutes a turning away from the light coming from above to

---

88 Romano Guardini believed Bonaventure's theology was born in prayer and even reached perfect fulfillment in it: "Er ist kein unpersönlicher Denker. Seine Werke, selbst der auf den ersten Blick so streng sachliche Sentenzenkommentar, tragen alle den Stempel seiner milden, innigen Art. Die Theologie hat für ihn ihren Ursprung im Gebet. . . Und das Ende der Theologie ist wiederum das Gebet" (*Die Lehre des hl. Bonaventura von der Erlösung*, [Düsseldorf: L. Schwann, 1921], 188).

89 Gerald O'Collins discusses three "styles" of present-day theology: [1] the cultivated use of reason; [2] the desire to promote justice and the common good; [3] prayer and worship forming the context of theology. The three are symbolized by one that "knows how to walk" (social justice theology), another that "knows how to sit" (speculative theology), and one that "knows how to kneel" (prayerful theology). In Medieval times, all three types of theology mentioned by Dionysius (as cited in our first chapter) were done in a spirit of prayer. O'Collins recognizes the dangers implicit in the present-day split in styles of theology: "Experience suggests a word of warning. Developed by itself, each style can fail to be fully faithful and Christian. . . Christianity needs an inclusive approach that allows these three styles to complement and mutually enrich each other" (G. O'Collins, "Catholic Theology [1965–90]," *America* 162 [1990]: 104–5). Evidently for Bonaventure, any theology done outside the scope of a prayer life would be doomed to failure.

90 "Sunt qui scire volunt tantum, ut sciant, et turpis curiositas est" *De donis* 4, 23 (V, 478b). In this case, Bonaventure is quoting St. Bernard who uses a qualifying adjective (*turpis*). Normally, however, Bonaventure speaks of curiosity without feeling any need to accentuate its all too evident [to him] malice.

follow self-directed instincts. We immediately are reminded of man's tendency to bend over downward (*homo recurvatus*).[91] His hierarchized stature restored by grace allows him to look upward to higher things. Since curiosity would pull him downward again, it constitutes the form of egoism at the root of all other manifestations of self-will. This is why Bonaventure considered curiosity to be at the root of original sin.[92]

The relational dependence of man on God, to which Bonaventure grants so much importance, is translated in theology to the realization that research is a personal response to God's revelation of his own intimacy out of charity.[93] This response takes place both on the intellectual and on the affective level, as mind and heart together respond to an initiative coming from above.[94] God extends the invitation to receive a gift that will attract us precisely away from ourselves, through gradual loss of self-love, into union

---

91 "Humana natura non solum corrupta est corruptione poenalitatis, verum etiam corruptione curvitatis, quia videmus, homines ex corruptione sibi indita inclinari ad malum" *II Sent.* d. 30, a. 1, q. 1, fund. 2 (II, 714a).

92 "Adam cum uxore sua contraxit vitium curiositatis, quando diabolus dixit eis: *Eritis sicut dii, scientes bonum et malum"* (*De donis* 4, 21 [V, 478a]); "Sed quando homo horum obliviscitur et delectatur in studio curiositatis, vult scire tantum; et ex hoc nascitur supercilium vanitatis... Et per hoc aufertur homini vera vita; sicut Adam, vel potius mulier, quae curiosa fuit et voluit esse sicut Deus" *Hex.* 18, 3 (V, 415a); "Beatus Bernardus dicit de gradibus superbiae, quod primum vitium est curiositas, per quod lucifer cecidit; per hoc etiam Adam cecidit" *Hex.* 19, 4 (V, 420b). In Umberto Eco's gothic novel, *The Name of the Rose,* this kind of curiosity is censured. Brother William finally unravels the story's mystery for the novice Adso: "[Brother] Benno is the victim of a great lust, which is not that of Berengar or that of the cellarer. Like many scholars, he has a lust for knowledge. Knowledge for its own sake" (trans. William Weaver [New York: Warner Books, 1986²], 478).

93 "Ab aeterno novit Deus creaturam et amat eam, quia praeparavit eam gloriae et gratiae" *Hex.* 12, 7 (V, 385b). In speaking of this openness to God as love in which our being participates, Corrado Gneo explains Bonaventure's thinking as follows: "L'Essere rivelando, nella creazione e nella ricreazione, la sua essenza come amore, pone la realtà sul piano storico e si pone come apertura alla realtà, perchè possa rapportarsi ad esso in una sintesi che è giudizio o 'dire sì' al Amore. L'essere è partecipazione dell'Essere-Amore e perciò è amato dall'eterno essendo fatto per una vita di amore" ("La essenza dell'essere come amore in San Bonaventura," *SB* 3:106).

94 "Oportet iungere cum scientia caritatem, ut homo habeat simul scientiam et caritatem... Ista est scientia, quae est domum Spiritus sancti" *De donis* 4, 24 (V, 478b–479a). In regard to the participation of the mind and heart, J.F. Quinn carefully points out the differences between Bonaventure and Aquinas when the topic is theology as a science: "With regard to theology as a practical science, they concur in saying that theology is essentially practical and speculative, but they differ in saying whether the science is principally practical or speculative. Bonaventure says that it is principally practical, because its end or final cause is to make men good. In his view, the ultimate end of theology is the good of eternal life, which consists in a contemplative love, or a loving contemplation, of God in beatitude... In the view of Aquinas, the ultimate end of theology is the contemplation of truth in beatitude, or the eternal contemplation of God as He is in Himself. Because a science is considered by Aquinas to be determined principally by its end, he maintains that theology is principally speculative. Although theology studies the good of the Christian life as it is presented in Scripture, nevertheless, theology seeks to know the truth of that life more than to direct the believer in his moral actions" (J.F. Quinn, *Historical Constitution*, 709–10).

with him. By contrast, the movement of curiosity comes from within ourselves, and pretends to launch its own search for knowledge, where the vital center is the self.[95] The self in this case avariciously would attract and accumulate into its self-planned center what does not belong to it.[96] This also is a form of ignorance about God as giver, the one who provides everything through creation and then supplies for our self-inflicted deficiencies through redemption. Upon such considerations is based the Franciscan ideal of poverty as extended into the ambit of studies.[97] Eventually, poverty becomes a condition for study.[98]

Now, since nothing created can satisfy man's infinite desire for what is good, he easily confuses multiplicity with the object of all his craving. By not respecting the nature of the truth to be known, curiosity leads to dispersion of the cognitive faculties, that is, to intellectual disorder.[99] Truth, as we have seen, is discovered to exist in hierarchized order. To find this orderly truth, which God has pre-established according to stratified laws, first the soul itself must be hierarchized by grace in order to recognize the

---

95 The self, which is created out of nothing, sins by loving itself in the place of God as the end of its actions. *Regn. Dei* 43 (V, 552a).

96 St. Bonaventure explains there are four types of desire that can never be filled: "Quis est enim qui in praesenti habeat sua desideria? Nullus." The second type of vain desire is to know, which is the root of curiosity. *Regn. Dei* 7 (V, 541a).

97 "The thirst to possess is one in essence with curiosity—and we arrive at the deepest point of the root of evil. Curiosity consists in the desire to know what is hidden simply because we do not know it, to see what is beautiful for its beauty merely, and to seize what we like simply to have it for ourselves. Curiosity thus necessarily implies avarice, and this it was that ruined the first man—the passion to know simply for the sake of knowing, to see for the sake of seeing, to take what he coveted. Hence it is by this that the evil power of the demon holds man's soul, which can become once more its own master only by uprooting concupiscence; and this it can do only by acquiring the three virtues opposed to it—humility, chastity, poverty. Thus the whole monastic discipline, and even the whole Franciscan discipline, is required for the mystical ascent. There is one short formula for all this: only a life entirely made of sacrifice can conquer concupiscence" (Gilson, *Philosophy of Bonaventure*, 407–8). Gilson is here commenting *Hex.* 22, 36 (V, 443a); *Trip. via* 1, 1, 5 (VIII, 4b); *Perf. vitae* 1, 3 (VIII, 108b); *Perf. ev.* (V, 117–198)

98 "Absolute poverty, assuring complete liberty of heart and excluding temporal cares, is the most favourable condition for study, and in those who embrace it, is a great aid to prayer, reading, meditation and contemplation" (Gilson, *Philosophy of Bonaventure*, 58). The value of this comment is weakened since Gilson refers here to the (now considered) spurious *Determinationes Quaestionum* (VIII, 337–374). Ignatius Brady treats the question of the authenticity of this work in: "The Writings of St. Bonaventure regarding the Franciscan Order," *MF* 75 (1975): 89–112. Nevertheless the statement accords well with the Franciscan charism in general.

99 "Et quia nihil creatum recompensare potest bonum amissum, cum sit infinitum, ideo appetit, quaerit et nunquam quiescit; et ideo declinando a rectitudine infinitis quaestionibus se immiscuit. Unde intelligentia, avertendo se a summa veritate ignara effecta, infinitis quaestionibus se immiscuit per curiositatem" *II Sent.* prooem. (II, 5b).

truth within that framework into which man himself fits as an integral part.[100] The tendency of curiosity toward disorder in the use of the faculties impedes the apprehension of truth on its own terms. And since curiosity is the starting point from which concupiscence begins to manifest itself, we need divine help to control this impulse.

The help granted through the gifts of the Holy Spirit therefore necessarily is communicated to the cognitive faculties. This accounts for Bonaventure's stressing that the gifts perfect the faculties and not the virtues, unless in an indirect way. The help given to the faculties comes precisely in the form of directive powers exerted upon the mind.[101] As we stated above, the gifts of the Holy Spirit have as their mission to enable us to comprehend what first we have accepted on faith in an obscure manner.[102]

5. Intentionality

By contrasting curiosity with intellectual activity under the gifts of the Holy Spirit, immediately we are made aware of the inherent struggle involved in the acquisition of knowledge if truth is to be attained. Since curiosity sprouts as concupiscence's firstfruits, the theologian is constrained at the outset of his study to dispose within himself the aim of his activity. After affirming with St. Bernard that curiosity is the principal vice deriving from pride, St. Bonaventure devotes the remainder of Chapter 19 of his *Hexaëmeron*, which can be considered the key chapter of this work, to

---

100 "Necesse est enim, ut anima, quae est hierarchizata, habeat gradus correspondentes supernae Ierusalem. Grandis res est anima: in anima potest describi totus orbis. Pulchra dicitur sicut Ierusalem, quia assimilatur Ierusalem per dispositionem graduum hierarchicorum. Disponuntur autem in anima tripliciter: secundum ascensum, secundum descensum et secundum regressum in divina; et tunc anima videt *Angelos Dei ascendentes et descendentes per scalam*, ut vidit Iacob in mente sua" *Hex.* 22, 24 (V, 441a).

101 Commenting on *Hex.* 22, 24 (V, 441a) which we have cited in our immediately preceding note, Gilson describes the hierarchizing help given to the faculties by grace: "Thus it [grace] falls upon the free will and the faculties dependent thereon. Once it has taken possession of these, grace sets them in order by situating each in the place it must occupy and regulating its activity as it should be if the soul is to be brought to God. Three principal operations constitute the life of the soul considered in its highest form—to seek God outside itself, within itself and above itself. The hierarchization of our interior life will begin then with the reorganization of the first of these modes by which we know God, and will first regulate the steps by which our mind explores the exterior world" (Gilson, *Philosophy of Bonaventure*, 404).

102 "Et quoniam quaedam sunt opera moralia primaria, sicut credere; quaedam media, sicut intelligere credita; quaedam vero postrema, sicut videre intellecta" *Brev.* 5, 4, 3 (V, 256a–b). The first are the virtues, the second the gifts and the third are the beatitudes.

teaching us how to study.[103] The way to study, he affirms, must incorporate four conditions: order, assiduity, taste, and measure.[104] At the end of this little treatise on study, St. Bonaventure summarizes these four conditions into the will to direct everything to God: "Hoc est sapientis studium, ut non declinet studium nostrum nisi ad Deum, qui est totus desiderabilis."[105] It is precisely here, in the context of intentionality, that theology most clearly is discovered to operate as a spiritual life.[106] Thus, the intention of theology (that is, its formal and final objects), must be translated into concrete psychological choices.[107] In some way, then, we can distinguish between the intention of theology and the intention of the theologian, but only with the purpose of eventually conceding their necessary harmony because of theology's nature as a revealed 'invitation' from God.[108] The attitude of the theologian, faced with disordering influences from curiosity that weakens his mental processes, cannot remain merely theoretical. His collaboration with grace is an active encounter, as in combat, against negative forces exerted upon his cognitive powers. "There is no knowledge without precedent discipline, nor discipline without precedent goodness. Hence it is through

---

103 *Hex.* 19, 4–27 (V, 420a–424b). In Latin, the word *studium* can be translated as: zeal, eagerness, application, as well as 'application to study' (*Cassell's Latin Dictionary* [New York: Macmillan, 1968], 573). In medieval Latin, the latter meaning becomes more common (*Lexicon Latinitatis Medii Aevi* [Turnhout: Brepols, 1975], 871). In St. Bonaventure, the context of Chapter 19 of the *Hexaëmeron* shows study as the acquisition of learning: "Qualiter ergo studendum est scientiae et sanctitati et sapientiae?" *Hex.* 19, 5 (V, 421a); "Qui ergo vult discere quaerat scientiam. . . " *Hex.* 19, 7 (V, 421a).

104 "Modus studendi debet habere quatuor conditiones: ordinem, assiduitatem, complacentiam, commensurationem" *Hex.* 19, 6 (V, 421a).

105 *Hex.* 19, 27 (V, 424b).

106 In his *Collationes de septem donis Spiritus sancti*, Bonaventure quotes St. Bernard as saying: "Vides, quod non approbat Apostolus multa scientem, sed modum sciendi; vide quod omnem fructum et utilitatem scientiae in modo sciendi constituit. Quid dicit modum sciendi? Scire, quo ordine, quo studio, quo fine quisque addiscat: quo ordine, ut id prius addiscat, quod maturius est ad salutem; quo studio, ut id ardentius, quod vehementius trahit ad amorem Dei; quo fine, ut non propter inanem gloriam, aut curiositatem, sed propter aedificationem suam et proximi addiscat" *De donis* 4, 23 (V, 478b). For Bonaventure, any approach to study must be preceded by rectitude of the will. J. Reilly's article, "Rectitude of Will and the Examined Life" (*SB* 4:655–71), is dedicated to this aspect of the Bonaventurian way of studying.

107 The role of intentionality is so important for Lonergan, that he does not hesitate to affirm: "Self-transcendence is the achievement of conscious intentionality, and as the latter has many parts and a long development, so too has the former" (Lonergan, *Method in Theology*, 35). Let us recall that Lonergan sees self-transcendence as the key to achieving authenticity (Ibid., 104). Although authenticity alone is not sanctity, certainly to become a saint man must become to God authentically the image God has of him.

108 I have refrained from exposing Bonaventure's theological perspective from the topics around which it is organized, for example that his theology is specifically trinitarian, or christocentric, or as theology of history, etc. My purpose is to underline the fact that his view of theology as a spiritual life

goodness and discipline that knowledge dwells in us."[109] It is not enough to receive the gifts of the Holy Spirit with baptism. The theologian's life is similar to that of a sick man struggling to regain health and, as such, must be undertaken with a positive cooperation with the remedies: "A man becomes wise not merely by listening: he must also conform. . . A sick man is not healed by listening to a physician: he must also follow his prescription."[110]

In our second chapter, we recognized our nature as sick, as a consequence of the Fall. In this realization, the approach to study always is accompanied by a discipline of the faculties that accompanies the process of hierarchization:

> There follows a disciplined calling. For when the mind is well ordered . . . when it has power over itself . . . when there is domination and command over all the powers, then it is hierarchized. . . Now, in order to achieve this, it is necessary to have dominion over appetites, imaginations, and occupations, so that there be discipline in all three. Then is the soul its own master, when the threefold concupiscence is removed from the affective power, the threefold weakness from the aggressive power, and the threefold error from the rational power. Then the soul has command over its own empire. Then it is not thrown out of its own house as these passions are cut off. And in such a soul, God is dwelling—which He could not have done in case of concupiscence gone wild, and so forth. The devil gladly imprints what he has in himself, that is 'unreasoning anger, mindless desire, headlong fancy'.[111]

In corresponding with grace, the human mind pretending to acquire knowledge must discipline its powers in regard to the three levels of knowledge that are possible to attain: of what is outside it, what is inside it, and what is above it. The powers concerned here are not three new faculties

---

can be applied to divers theological approaches and should be independent of each of them, because their common denominator is revealed truth. On the other hand, to separate the intention of theology from that of the theologian, which can be done on the theoretical level, is dangerous on the practical level. Too much "objectivity" may account for the fact that we even find theologians without faith. As we have seen above, R. Moretti points out the temptation of the theologian to depend excessively on the power of the intellect ("Natura e compito della teologia spirituale," 15–36). C. Bernard also warns about the possibility of doing theology without faith: "Per i grandi autori scolastici, invece, la *teologia veniva considerata un esercizio personale dell'intellectus fidei* e non si discostava dalla vita spirituale. . . Si capisce subito quanto questa teologia differisca dal nostro studio scolastico, per il quale alcuni non richiedono neppure la fede!" (*Teologia spirituale* [Roma: Edizioni Paoline, 1987], 57).

109 "Scientia enim non habetur, nisi praecedat disciplina; nec disciplina, nisi praecedat bonitas; et sic per bonitatem et disciplinam inest nobis scientia" *Hex.* 2, 3 (V, 337a; de Vinck, *Six Days*, 23).

110 "Non audiendo solum, sed observando fit homo sapiens. . . Aegrotus enim audiendo medicum nunquam sanatur, nisi praecepta eius observet" *Hex.* 2, 3 (V, 337a; de Vinck, *Six Days*, 23).

111 "Sequitur districta convocatio. Quando enim mens est ordinata . . . quando habet potestatem supra se. . . quando dominatur et imperat omnibus viribus, tunc est hierarchizata. . . Ad hoc autem faciendum necesse est, ut dominetur appetitibus, phantasmatibus, occupationibus, ut sit districtio in

but actually three operations of the same human faculties when they are directed toward the exterior, the interior or the superior realities.[112] Bonaventure states that "it is fitting that the soul be hierarchized in relation to these powers."[113] For the first kind of knowing of the exterior kind, he assigns a first kind of hierarchization which involves "a discerning investigation, a discerning selection, and a discerning execution."[114] In other words, the mind does not proceed indiscriminately, but with a purpose in view: "There must be a discerning investigation, so that the world be considered discriminately by the soul."[115] For the second kind of "hierarchizing of the mind, related to the interior powers," which he says is "more difficult than the first" he assigns another triple discipline: "a disciplined chastising, a disciplined strengthening, and a disciplined calling."[116] In the case of the third kind of hierarchization "as regards the superior powers," he states that "when the soul does what it can, grace lifts it up easily and God works in it, so that there be a worthy admission, a worthy inspection, and a worthy induction."[117]

In each of the three forms of acquiring knowledge the soul is not idle. Even though it is more active in the lowest forms of knowledge, and gradually becomes more receptive to God's action as it advances to higher knowledge, nevertheless, some activity still is expected of it in the superior form: "When the soul is lifted up, it must not be idle, but should look around. . . Then, indeed, the soul must be fixed, and standing, and expecting."[118] This posture of expectancy would indicate a large degree of active receptivity, in an incipient form, as the peak of the superior form of knowledge is attained, the divine induction: "Then the soul is rapt in God, that is, in the beloved. . . for [the soul] already feels the union and is made one spirit with God. And

---

appetitibus, phantasmatibus, occupationibus. Et tunc est anima domina sui, quando concupiscibili aufertur concupiscentia triplex, irascibili aufertur infirmitas triplex, rationali aufertur error triplex. Tunc anima habet imperium in regno suo; et tunc non expellitur extra domum suam, quando illae passiones sunt amputatae; et in tali anima Deus habitat, non in furiosa concupiscentia etc. Diabolus libenter imprimit quod in se habet; haec sunt 'furor irrationalis, amens concupiscentia, phantasia proterva'" *Hex.* 22, 38 (V, 443a; de Vinck, *Six Days*, 359–60).

112 *Hex.* 22, 34 (V, 442b; de Vinck, *Six Days*, 357). Cf. Philip Reynolds, "Threefold Existence and Illumination in Saint Bonaventure," *FS* 42 (1982): 190–215.

113 "Oportet ergo, ut anima habeat hierarchizationem secundum has potentias" *Hex.* 22, 34 (V, 442b; de Vinck, *Six Days*, 357)

114 Ibid.

115 *Hex.* 22, 35 (V, 442b; de Vinck, *Six Days*, 358).

116 *Hex.* 22, 36 (V, 442b; de Vinck, *Six Days*, 358–59).

117 *Hex.* 22, 39 (V, 443a–b; de Vinck, *Six Days*, 360)

118 *Hex.* 22, 39 (V, 443b; de Vinck, *Six Days*, 360).

this is the highest thing in the soul: it makes it abide in heaven."[119]   During the entire process of knowing, which Bonaventure considers a form of contemplation, the soul manifests some degree of activity which diminishes but never disappears entirely. This is stressed in such a way that Bonaventure warns against considering any of this knowledge, no matter how elevated it may be, as a form of revelation: "Many are deceived who believe they possess everything through revelation."[120]   This is caused by presumption and Bonaventure exhorts the contemplative man to be just as careful about avoiding presumption as he is about avoiding error. Both of these falls from grace must be held at a distance through humility and circumspection, respectively.[121]

The procedure of the mind in the acquisition of knowledge, although a humble and poor search for truth, is nonetheless vigilant and circumspect. The soul's powers are looked upon as a castle that must be guarded against thieves. That is, knowledge must be investigated, selected and judged with cautious discernment.

> It is fitting, then, that there be great discernment in the guarding of the house, lest all have access to these powers. May nothing useless be announced to the king and the queen. For a robber should not be introduced before the king, except perhaps to be condemned. Eve, wretched and imprudent as she was, introduced the serpent's eloquence, and doubted; and many today are corrupted by this eloquence. Wherefore nothing filthy should come in through those doors. *Outside are the dogs, and the sorcerers, and the fornicators.* — Second, there must be a discerning selection. From the fact that what is perceived becomes manifest, it follows that it must be chosen insofar as it is good: for in relation to good things, there is well-ordered selection. . . — Then, there follows judgment which is found in execution. . . From the fact that good is perceived and selected as worthy of action, there must follow a judgment towards its execution.[122]

---

119 "Tunc rapitur in Deum sive in dilectum. . . quia iam sensit unionem et factus est unus spiritus cum Deo; unde: *Qui adhaeret Deo unus spiritus est*; et hoc est supremum in anima, quod animam facit esse in caelo" *Hex.* 22, 39 (V, 443b; de Vinck, *Six Days*, 360–61; Eng. omits Pauline citation).

120 "Multi decipiuntur, quod credunt, se habere omnia per revelationem" *Hex.* 22, 42 (V, 444a; de Vinck, *Six Days*, 362).

121 "Similiter vir contemplativus eclipsatur dupliciter et cadit turpiter et multum periculose, eo quod vix resurgit; nec mirum, quia de alto cadit. Cadit enim per errorem et per praesumptionem. Videt enim se illuminatum et praesumit, et fit luciferianus et cadit a luce in tenebras horribiles. Cadit similiter per errorem aestimationis, quae oritur ex praesumptione, cuando credit, se omnia habere per revelationem. Semper tamen debet esse regula. . . Debet ergo contemplativus esse humilis et circumspectus, ut non ad caput draconis veniat per praesumptionem, vel in cauda involvatur per errorem" *Hex.* 22, 42 (V, 444a–b; de Vinck, *Six Days*, 362–63).

122 "Oportet ergo, quod sit magna discretio ad custodiendam domum, ne omnes intrent ad has vires; nihil nuntietur regi et reginae, quod sit inutile. Latro enim introduci non debet coram rege, nisi forte, ut

The discipline exercised over the cognitive powers is actually the response of the soul alerted by the disordering sway of curiosity that leads to "unreasoning anger, mindless desire, headlong fancy."[123] If it is not to yield before such an unreasoning impulse, the soul has no alternative than to seek holiness. This alternative concretely is formulated by rectifying the intention, or accommodating its response to the nature of revelation as an invitation to union with God. What other aim could be equal to the challenge presented by the study of theology, involving, as it does, a rigorous self-conquest?

Intentionality thus becomes a determining principle in theology.[124] Any other reason except holiness, no matter how elevated at first it may appear, eventually falls victim to the impulsive character of curiosity, because it makes us like Solomon who "forgot about the most important, and thus turned to the vain."[125] Again, the only means to bridge the gap between knowledge and wisdom, between knowing *multa* and *multum*, is holiness.[126]

6. Theology at the service of piety

The gifts of the Holy Spirit, as they are found enumerated in Isaias 11:2, appear for St. Bonaventure to be presented in meaningful pairs, each

---

condemnetur. Eva enim misera et incauta introduxit eloquium serpentis et dubitavit; et isto eloquio hodie multi corrumpuntur. Nihil ergo debet intrare per portas istas inmundum; in Apocalypsi: *Foras canes et venefici et impudici*. Secundum est discreta praeelectio; ex quo apparet, quid percipitur, sequitur, ut praeeligatur, ex quo percipitur bonum; quia in bonis est electio ordinata. . . Post sequitur iudicium . . . quod est in prosecutione. Ex quo bonum percipitur et bonum praeelegitur faciendum, sequi debet iudicium ad prosequendum" *Hex*. 22, 35 (V, 442b; de Vinck, *Six Days*, 358).

123 "Furor irrationalis, amens concupiscentia, phantasia proterva" *Hex*. 22, 38 (V, 443a). Bonaventure is here quoting Dionysius, *Divine Names*, c. 4, § 23 (*PG* 3, 725B; Luibheid, 91).

124 Intentionality, in Bernard Lonergan's view, brings forth two fruits—self-transcendence and love of God: "Self-transcendence is the achievement of conscious intentionality" (*Method in Theology*, 35); "Being in love with God is the basic fulfilment of our conscious intentionality" (Ibid., 105). Practically speaking, then, conscious intentionality is a way of holiness.

125 "Oblitus est principalis, et ideo est factus vanus" *Hex*. 19, 3 (V, 420b).

126 "Non est ergo securus transitus a scientia ad sapientiam; oportet ergo medium ponere, scilicet sanctitatem" *Hex*. 19, 3 (V, 420b). Bernard Lonergan recognizes the importance of holiness when it comes to the meaning given to our knowledge through intentional response: "Besides potential, formal, and full acts of meaning, there are also constitutive and effective acts of meaning. Now the apprehension of values and disvalues is the task not of understanding but of intentional response. Such response is all the fuller, all the more discriminating, the better a man one is, the more refined one's sensibility, the more delicate one's feelings" (Lonergan, *Method in Theology*, 245).

of which is preceded by the repetition of the word *spirit*: spirit of wisdom and understanding, spirit of counsel and fortitude, spirit of knowledge and piety. The final gift, according to the Vulgate, is fear of the Lord, and it is found unpaired. In the biblical account, the seven gifts are given in descending, hierarchized order of importance, starting from the most excellent (wisdom) to the least (fear).[127] Because the gifts are coupled, Bonaventure considers them to work together, as do the intellect and the will, each gift being appropriated to assist one of these faculties.

For his own purposes, Bonaventure inverts the list of gifts to an ascending order. The first pair, then, is the gift of knowledge and the gift of piety, which assists the intellect and the will respectively. The second pair, the gift of counsel and the gift of fortitude, stands in the same relationship to these two faculties, with the cognitive order again taking precedence over the affective order.[128] The last pair, wisdom and understanding, likewise assist these faculties. But in the last case, wisdom, a gift of the affective order, is mentioned first, while understanding, obviously of the cognitive order, is mentioned second; their relation to the faculties is reversed. In all of this, St. Bonaventure only finds the greatest suitability.[129] In each pair, the second gift is subordinated to, and at the service of, the first gift mentioned. Thus, for two out of three pairs, the affective order is subordinated to the cognitive order. Or, stated differently, the will is commanded by the intellect according to the truth the latter faculty discovers.[130] Just as we cannot love unless we first know, love is usually governed by the knowledge furnished to the heart by the intellect.[131] It is only in the case of wisdom that the affective order must precede the cognitive and, as Pascal assured us, the

---

127 "Potest ergo in ordine praeponi donum, quod magis approximat perfectioni Spiritus sancti; et sic praemittitur donum sapientiae, quod est perfectissimum. Potest etiam nihilominus praemitti donum, quod magis approximat imperfectioni liberi arbitrii, et hoc quidem est donum timoris" *III Sent.* d. 34, p. 1, a. 2, q. 2, concl. (III, 748b).

128 "Habitus spectans ad cognitionem praecedit habitum, qui spectat ad affectionem" *III Sent.* p. 1, a. 2, q. 2, concl., ad 2 (III, 748b).

129 "Cum ergo in eis sit ordo secundum gradus excellentiae et dignitatis; non casu et fortuna, sed valde rationabiliter quaedam dona quibusdam aliis praemittuntur" *III Sent.* p. 1, a. 2, q. 2, concl. (III, 748a).

130 "Qui vult expedite procedere, necesse est, ut praecognoscat et praevideat viam: hinc est, quod dona habent sua directiva sibi per appropriationem deputata, et quod quaedam in donis sunt regentia, quaedam recta, sive quaedam regulantia, quaedam exsequentia" (Ibid. [III, 748b]).

131 This is generally the case for most kinds of knowledge. But, as Bernard Lonergan, whose thinking is akin to St. Bonaventure, wisely explains: "The major exception to the Latin tag [*Nihil amatum nisi praecognitum*] is God's gift of his love flooding our hearts. Then we are in the dynamic state of being in love. But who it is we love, is neither given nor as yet understood. Our capacity for moral self-transcendence has found a fulfillment that brings deep joy and profound peace. Our love

heart now will have reasons that are beyond comprehension.[132]

As for the gift of piety in the spiritual life of the theologian, it will be subordinated to the gift of knowledge. Knowledge (*scientia*) will be the rule which piety follows.[133] If it were otherwise, piety, which is so intimately tied to fervor, could blind the reason through overweening sentimentalism. On the other hand, knowledge without piety, "speculation without devotion," precisely is to be avoided because "we have been cleansed from the filth of vice through the blood of Christ crucified."[134] From the context, the vice to which he refers might be the study of theology, of which Christ crucified is the exemplar from whom all meaning derives; theology only is a vice when it is approached as a science without piety, that is, with hardness of heart.[135] A balance is maintained between these two gifts, but knowledge is a directive principle to piety, guiding the latter toward the Truth, which in turn inflames piety to further conquests of the good that is being furnished to it by knowledge. Only in this sense does theology then become the servant of piety.[136]

The very fact that Bonaventure insists on seeing this form of piety as a gift of the Holy Spirit, places the activity of this gift within the dynamics of the spiritual life, because of what we have said above about the predominance of the gifts in the illuminative way. Bonaventure, referring to the teaching of St. Augustine, recognizes that piety has three meanings.[137] One meaning is the cult or respect rendered by man to God. But this, he points out, belongs to the virtue of latria.[138] The second meaning is the respect of children to

---

reveals to us values we had not appreciated, values of prayer and worship, or repentance and belief. But if we would know what is going on within us, if we would learn to integrate it with the rest of our living, we have to inquire, investigate, seek counsel. So it is that in religious matters love precedes knowledge and, as that love is God's gift, the very beginning of faith is due to God's grace" (Lonergan, *Method in Theology*, 122–23: cf. pp. 278, 283, and 340). Lonergan summarizes this idea with a candid proof: "People in love have not reasoned themselves into being in love" (Ibid., 123).

132 B. Lonergan explains Pascal's saying: "The meaning, then, of Pascal's remark would be that, besides the factual knowledge reached by experiencing, understanding, and verifying, there is another kind of knowledge reached through the discernment of value and the judgments of value of a person in love" (Ibid., 115).

133 "Usus doni pietatis attenditur . . . secundum quod et usus doni scientiae, quod est eius directivum" *III Sent.* d. 35, au., q. 6, concl. (III, 786a).

134 *Itin.* prol. 4 (V, 296a).

135 "Pietas est contra indurationem" *III Sent.* d. 35, au., q. 6, concl., ad 1. 2. 3. 4. (III, 786b); "O cor humanum omni lapidum duritia durius, si ad tanti rememorationem piaculi nec terrore concuteris nec compassione afficeris nec compunctione scinderis nec pietate molliris!" *Lig. vit.* 8, 29 (VIII, 79b).

136 See P. Fehlner, "Theology at the Service of Piety," *Inter-Province Conference of the Friars Minor Conventual*, Vol. XII (1961), 69–84.

137 *III Sent.* d. 35, au., q. 6, concl. (III, 785b); cf. ibid., ad 1. 2. 3. 4 (III, 786a); *De civitate Dei*, Book X, chap. 1, n. 3 (*PL* 41, 279).

138 "Secundum quod ordinat erga Deum, non est nomen doni, sed potius est idem quod latria et theosebia sive eusebia" *III Sent.* d. 35, au., q. 6, concl. (III, 785b); cf. *III Sent.* d. 9, a. 2, q. 1, con. 3

parents, and this belongs to the virtue of justice.[139] It is only the third definition given by St. Augustine that Bonaventure recognizes as being proper to the gift of the Holy Spirit: mercy that must be shown to one's neighbor.[140] While the first two meanings are virtues, and consequently are obligatory and not facultative, only the third meaning is of counsel, and thus belongs to the gifts, since they are supererogatory.

By granting the third meaning to piety, Bonaventure is forced to explain in what way this gift differs from the virtue of mercy. He points out that the motives for such an attitude must be different. In the case of mercy, we are moved by the misery we find in our neighbor. On the other hand, what moves us in the case of piety is primarily the image of God in our neighbor who suffers.[141] Again, given this distinction, mercy is an obligation imposed upon us by natural law, while piety is of counsel since it presumes the Christian knowledge that our neighbor is made in the image of God.[142] Since this knowledge is revealed, piety reveres the Holy Scripture and particularly the examples of Christ, both of which make up the sources of that specific kind of *scientia* to which piety is subordinated. This is the root of the relationship of piety to theology. We will be able to say more about this relationship after entering into the gift of knowledge, which immediately follows. Suffice it to say that our understanding of piety is enhanced by Bonaventure's doctrine of exemplarism which, as we explained earlier, underlies his entire system. The image of God, which is what primarily moves us to benevolent acts toward our neighbor, is found in its perfect archetype in Christ. Thus, what we learn about Christ through Scripture activates our feelings of benevolence toward his doctrine, not as a dead letter, but as theology of the Cross.[143]

(III, 213b); ibid., concl., ad 3 (III, 214b).

139 Ibid.

140 Ibid. (III, 786a).

141 "Aliter tamen attenditur erga proximum pietas-donum et misericordia-virtus: quia misericordia-virtus respicit conformitatem in natura et necessitatem in indigentia sive miseria; pietas vero attendit in proximo imaginem divinam" (Ibid.); "A misericordia differt: quia misericordia in proximo considerat conformitatem in natura et similitudinem speciei; pietas vero attendit in homine imaginem Dei. Unde aliqui dixerunt, quod misericordia considerat miserium in imagine, pietas vero considerat imaginem in misero" (Ibid., ad 1. 2. 3. 4. [III, 786b]).

142 "Differt etiam, quia misericordia conformatur dictamini iuris naturalis et secundum regulam prudentiae; pietas vero conformatur suasioni iuris divini, et hoc secundum regulam doni scientiae" (Ibid.).

143 "Et sic patet, quis sit actus et obiectum pietatis-doni, quoniam ipsius est facere hominem benevolum respectu cuiuslibet proximi, in quantum gerit imaginem Dei. Et quoniam ad hoc habet dirigi per donum scientiae, quod quidem fundatur super principia fidei et dirigit in conversatione secundum exemplar

To 'feel benevolence toward doctrine' brings us to the delicate question about the *argumentum ex pietate*.[144] In order to understand this much-debated subject, it helps us to see how Bonaventure, when giving the threefold definition of piety (as a cult rendered to God, as filial respect for parents, and as benevolence toward one's neighbor), does not lose sight of any of these meanings, but sees the second and third as derived from the first. And although he selects the last definition as proper to the gift of piety, he does not divorce its significance from the first two definitions. To understand the activity of the gift, he considers it in an analogous way to the first two definitions. In fact, our benevolence to our neighbor ultimately is based on the image within him reflecting the same God to whom we owe our adoration. Likewise, benevolence to our neighbor is in some ways assimilated to the respect we owe to our parents because their authority reflects the authority of God to whom we owe pious adoration. Thus, when approaching the study of theology, that *pietas* which demands our cult to God, by the analogy Bonaventure follows, would have us respect the authority of God by thinking of his truths in the highest and most devout possible way.[145] Following the same logic, since piety stands in some relationship to our respect for parental authority, we are bound to respect the human authorities through which theological doctrine reaches us (the Fathers and Doctors of the Church).[146] Then, according to the third definition of piety, when it comes to our contemporaries, we show benevolence to those whom we teach, and also are willing to interpret in the best possible light the teachings of other theologians.[147]

Christi; hinc est, quod actus pietatis, etsi principaliter consistat erga proximum, nihilominus consistit respectu sacrae Scripturae, ut eam cum benevolentia audiat, et etiam respectu passionis Christi, ut eam cum benevolentia ad memoriam reducat" (Ibid., concl. [III, 786a]).

144 R. Guardini's article gives a complete treatment of this topic: "Das argumentum ex pietate beim hl. Bonaventura und Anselm Dezensbeweis," *Theologie und Glaube* 14 (1922): 156–65. Cf. J. Garrido, "El «argumentum ex pietate» en la Escuela Franciscana del siglo XIII," *V V* 26 (1968): 291–353.

145 "De primo principio sentiendum est altissime et piissime: altissime, quia a nullo; piissime quia cetera ab ipso" *Myst. Trin.* q. 1, a. 2, concl. (V, 55b–56a); *Brev.* 1, 2, 3–5 (V, 211a–b); *Hex.* 9, 23 (V, 375b–376a).

146 "Moventia autem sicut adminiculantia et quodam modo inducentia plurima sunt: quia movent Scripturae testimonia authentica, movent Sanctorum exempla et martyria, movent Doctorum argumenta et ipsius universalis Ecclesiae sententia, movent et ipsa miracula irrefragabilia" (Ibid., concl. [V, 56b]). He continues by quoting Richard of St. Victor who adduces that the articles of faith were revealed by heaven to the Fathers.

147 This is how we see Bonaventure treating Aristotle: "... dicendum quod illud verbum pium debet habere intellectum" *II Sent.* d. 19, a. 1, q. 1, concl., ad 3 (II, 460b).

The gift of piety, then, is a sense of God in us, and together with the gift of science produces a knowledge unlike any other of the sciences and fittingly is called a 'knowledge according to piety'. We are again in the presence of the argument from authority of faith, but approached from another angle which evidently is motivated by a respectful love of authority, with maximum authority given to the Sacred Scripture, secondly to the saints, then the doctors and finally the philosophers.[148] The purpose is to help us believe what is otherwise difficult for human reason in its dryness.[149] Bonaventure is so convinced of its utility that he does not doubt in affirming that without piety one cannot attain knowledge of salvific truth.[150] Since salvific truth is the object of theology, what theologian can attain such truth without living under the gift of piety, which first manifests itself as reverence for the divine veneration?[151] Again, it is not a question of sentiment outstripping reason. Rather, the more rational the approach by the mind, the more pious must be the adoration by the heart which follows. An intellectual life without a spiritual life motivating it, Bonaventure has explained, will not attain the truth.

7. The gift of knowledge

For St. Bonaventure there are four definitions of knowledge (*scientia*). The first is completely speculative, and includes all branches of human erudition, among which philosophy is the highest example. The second definition is theological science, which is the same as knowledge of the Holy Scripture. The third is the virtue of prudence, since it has to do with knowledge directed to action, but not beyond the ethics of natural law. The

---

148 The respect for authority is hierarchized. See *Hex.* 19, 6–7 (V, 421a–b); ibid., 10 (V, 421b–422a).

149 "Cognitio secundum fidem est cognitio secundum pietatem. . . Et licet intellectui procedenti secundum ariditatem speculationis videatur illud difficillimum credere, quod est, Deum esse trinum et unum; intellectui tamen pietate pleno facillimum est illud sentire de summo Patre, quod Unigenitum habeat, quem sicut se ipsum diligat, quem etiam pro salute hominum tradat" *Mys. Trin.* q. 1, a. 2, ad 8 (V, 57b). J.G. Bougerol, in an article dedicated to the expression 'sentire de Deo' in five Bonaventurian texts, refers to the gift of piety as what empowers knowledge to become wisdom ("Sur le sens de Dieu," *EF* 14 [1964]: 23–30).

150 "Valet pietas ad vera cognoscenda, scilicet salutaria. . . Dat Deus dona sua super quamlibet creaturam; sed notitiam veritatis non dat nisi pie agentibus. . . Oportet, quod homo assentiat doctrinae, quae est secundum pietatem . . . claudetur revelatio impiis. Si vultis esse veri scholares, oportet, vos habere pietatem" *De donis* 3, 17 (V, 472b–473a).

151 "Prima igitur exercitatio doni pietatis consistit in reverentia venerationis divinae" *De donis* 3, 5 (V, 469a).

fourth is the science of the saints, or *scientia gratuita*.[152]   When speaking of these four meanings of knowledge, Bonaventure points out that only two of them conform with the gift of the Holy Spirit, and they are the second and the fourth (i.e., theology and the science of the saints).   After that, it is only a question of determining which of these two must be considered the principle act of the gift.   In this regard, he opts for the fourth definition as having precedence over, but without excluding, the second, for two reasons: a) the fourth kind of knowledge is directed more toward action than to speculation;[153]   b) it presupposes the knowledge of theology and Sacred Scripture, and is ordered entirely to the exalted aim of sanctity.[154]   Let us look at these two meanings of the gift of knowledge to discover in what way the theologian receives their influence.

1) In theological science, the gift of knowledge is necessary over and above the virtue of faith, the latter serving as a foundation upon which theology is to be built.[155]   The virtue of faith teaches us simply what we need to accept as true in order to be saved. The gift of knowledge, however, brings us to a fuller comprehension of Sacred Scripture, in which deeper levels of meaning are opened to us.[156]   This kind of knowledge is supererogatory and thus not of precept but of counsel.[157]   Even though this knowledge shares many of the characteristics of speculative sciences, it adds some degree of influence from the will as we have seen to stem from the ancillary gift of piety.[158]   For this reason, theology never remains on the

---

152   This listing is found in Bonaventure's treatise on the gift of knowledge in *III Sent.* d. 35, au., q. 2, concl. (III, 776b).   A slightly different listing is found in *De donis* 4, 3 (V, 474a).   Nevertheless, the definitions embraced by the gift of knowledge are given in both lists, making it unnecessary for our purposes to clarify these differences.   In brief, it has to do with whether one considers knowledge in its origin and end (first list), or in its object (second list).   The virtue of prudence is found only in the first list, while *scientia gloriosa* only in the second.   Neither of these two kinds of knowledge flows from the gift of the Holy Spirit.

153   *III Sent.* d. 35, au., q. 2, concl., ad 3 (III, 777a).   Here again we witness Bonaventure's greater appreciation for the will and for charity.

154   Ibid. (III, 777a).

155   "Haec [scientia] est fundata super princ̦ipia fidei, quae quidem sunt articuli, et nihilominus acquisita; et haec est scientia Scripturae, quam nullus habere potest, nisi saltem habeat fidem informem" (Ibid., concl. [III, 776b]); cf. Ibid., concl. ad 1 (III, 776b).

156   "Comparatur sacra Scriptura aquae maris propter profunditatem mysteriorum, propter multiformitatem sensuum... In mari sunt diversae scaturitiones; ita in sacra Scriptura in una littera est multiplex sententia" *De donis* 4, 13–14 (V, 476b).

157   *III Sent.* d. 35, au., q. 2, concl. ad 3 (III, 777a–b); *De donis* 4, 13–19 (V, 476a–477b).

158   Cf. *III Sent.* d. 23, a. 1, q. 2 (III, 474a–477b): *Utrum fides sit in parte animae cognitivia, an affectiva.*

purely speculative level, but it belongs to its essence to direct us to action.[159]

Theological science, even acting under the gift of the Holy Spirit, must share the rigorous requirements of any scientific discipline.[160] Accordingly, theology supposes a fair degree of culture as well as competence in the philosophical method.[161] Notwithstanding this secure holding that theology must anchor in rational procedure, as a science it cannot proceed without the help of the gift of knowledge.[162] Theology is directed toward revealed truth, but under the optic of created reasons. This is precisely where it differs from the gifts of understanding and wisdom.[163] Science, whether it be natural science, philosophy unassisted by faith, or theological science which supposes the virtue of faith, is always a way of knowing created truth on the level of the created reasons.[164] Thus any science requires both our sense perception and abstraction process as a means of acquiring knowledge. The only difference in the case of the gift of knowledge is the assistance given to these processes in order to more securely attain truth. The object ultimately reached, considered on the epistemological level, is the same: all our knowing here is *sub ratione creata*. When it comes to theology, what can be known on this level is the humanity of Jesus Christ, or the mysteries of his life and his passion and death, as stimulating models to action.[165]

Thus, if theology were attempted without this gift, which is the same as saying outside the illuminative way in which the gifts predominate, theological science would operate like any other human science, on the level of a purely speculative activity, and certain allowances could not surprise us: excessive rationalism, which always involves the rejection of unverifiable information, such as the possibility of miracles or the value of symbols based on exemplarism.

---

159 "Praecipuus actus doni scientiae est dirigere circa actionem" *III Sent.* d. 35, au., q. 2, concl. (III, 776b).

160 "Et sciendum, quod scientia repellitur, quando homo non curat eam addiscere" *De donis* 4, 18 (V, 477a).

161 "Si illiteratus velit intrare [santuarium Dei], stultus esset. Oportet igitur, quod habeat litteraturam et spiritum" *De donis* 4, 14 (V, 476b); cf. *Hex.* 2, 3 (V, 337a); 19, 16 (V, 422a–b); 19, 20 (V, 423b);

162 "Nec sciens nec non sciens poterit legere. Quis ergo leget ipsum? Dico, quod qui cum superbia vult intrare santuarium Dei non poterit, licet sit litteratus... Oportet igitur... *et spiritum*" (Ibid. [V, 476b; italics mine]).

163 *III Sent.* d. 35, au., q. 1, concl. (III, 774a); *III Sent.* d. 35, au., q. 3, concl. ad 1 (III, 778b); *III Sent.* d. 35, au., q. 3, concl. ad 2 (III, 779a). We treat of the distinction between these objects when dealing with the gifts of understanding and wisdom.

164 "Scientia negotiatur circa creaturas secundum rationes creatas; unde negotiari habet non solum circa creaturas spirituales, quae habent rationem imaginis, sed etiam circa sensibiles et corporales, quae habent rationem vestigii" *III Sent.* d. 35, au., q. 3, ad 1 (III, 778b).

165 *III Sent.* d. 35, au., q. 2, concl. (III, 776b).

2) The second way of defining the gift of knowledge is the Science of the Saints (*scientia sanctorum*), which is above prudence as a directive for action. This capacity St. Bonaventure treasures more than the help the gift of knowledge can lend to theology when considered as a speculative science. The reason for his esteem is evidently that the gift of knowledge, under either of the two definitions, is directed more to action than to speculation.[166] Apparently it is more important to know how to live a holy life than to know theology.[167] Such spiritual activity as witnessed in the lives of the saints, comes from above and is a free knowledge, *scientia gratuita*.[168] Needless to say, Bonaventure does not eliminate the need to study speculative theology. Rather, the deeper knowledge of Scripture comes as a foundation for the principle act of knowledge which pursues holiness as the higher end. This superior knowledge is "a holy knowledge of the truth as lovable."[169] Theological knowledge of a more speculative sort is joined intimately to the principle act of the gift of knowledge, so as to maintain the unity of act proceeding from and presupposed by each gift, following the rule: for each habit there is only one corresponding act.[170] The principle act is to direct the soul toward holy works, and this ordering of action presupposes knowledge of Christ's humanity as model.[171] Thus, speculative theology, even when considered as an act of the gift of knowledge, is impoverished if separated from the science of the saints. If separated, it can bring harm: "This knowledge, if not accompanied by action, is not useful but harmful... This is why another clarity is needed, that is, *scientia gratuita*, which is the form of the two preceding clarities. You fail in the

---

166 The overall aim of Bonaventure's article on the gift of knowledge in his *Commentary of the Sentences* is to prove that the principle act of the gift of knowledge consists in action: "Secundo quaeritur de actu et obiecto doni scientiae, et est quaestio, utrum actus praecipuus doni scientiae consistat in actione, vel in consideratione. Et quod consistat in actione, videtur..." *III Sent.* d. 35, au., q. 2 (III, 775a).

167 "Item, secundum Philosophum, 'scire quod non est coniunctum operationi, parum aut nihil prodest ad virtutem': si ergo scientia, quae est Spiritus sancti donum, multum prodest ad meritum, videtur, quod actus eius circa agenda praecipue sit constitutus" *III Sent.* d. 35, au., q. 2, fund. 2 (III, 775a–b); cf. Ibid., fª 3–5 (III, 775b–776a).

168 *De donis* 4, 19 (V, 477b).

169 "Ista scientia est veritatis ut credibilis et diligibilis notitia sancta" *De donis* 4, 19 (V, 477b).

170 "Ad illud quod obiicitur, quod intelligentia Scripturarum spectat ad donum scientiae; dicendum, quod sicut prius tactum fuit de cognitione eorum quae sunt fidei, quod non principaliter spectant ad donum ipsius scientiae, sed quodam modo antecedenter et quasi praesuppositive; sic etiam intelligendum est de intelligentia sacrae Scripturae... Quoniam unus est eius actus principalis, duo vero annexi" *III Sent.* d. 35, au., q. 2, concl., ad 4 (III, 777b).

171 "Ad illud quod obiicitur, quod ipsius doni scientiae est humanitatem et gratiam Christi nosse; iam patet responsio: quia nec hic est actus ipsius scientiae principalis, sed qui ad principalem habet ordinari;

third sign if you do not have this knowledge."[172]

8. The gift of understanding

As we move from the gift of knowledge to the gifts of understanding and wisdom, we take a quantitative leap. Where the gift of knowledge had enabled us to know all things, both spiritual and material, in their created reasons, the last pair of gifts make it possible to go much further—to know the Creator himself as well as his spiritual creatures, but by a different way of knowing—through the eternal reasons.[173]   We here cross the threshold between the first two chapters of the *Itinerarium mentis in Deum* which treat of knowledge of created truth outside ourselves, corresponding to the object of the gift of knowledge, and the remaining chapters which deal with the spiritual world: the soul inside us (chapters 3+4) and God above us (chapters 5+6).

Because their knowing is achieved through the eternal reasons, the gifts of understanding and wisdom belong in the context of bonaventurian contemplation.[174]   Where the gift of knowledge, we have seen, is a practical science, in the sense that it is directed toward action, the gifts of understanding and wisdom pertain to the quiet of contemplation of the highest truth. The role of the gift of understanding can best be grasped when we consider that St. Bonaventure posits two kinds of contemplation of the eternal truth, each corresponding to one of these two highest gifts. The first is intellectual and is made possible through the gift of understanding. The second is affective and is made possible through the gift of wisdom.[175]

---

sicut cognitio exempli utilis est ad evidentiorem cognitionem rei, quae secundum exemplar illud debet fieri" *III Sent.* d. 35, au., q. 2, concl., ad 2 (III, 777a).

172   "Ista scientia, si non adsit operis impletio, non est utilis, sed damnosa. . . Ideo aliam claritatem oportet habere, scilicet scientiae gratuitae, quae est forma claritatum duarum praecedentium. Deficis in tertio signo, si non habes istam scientiam" *De donis* 4, 18–19 (V, 477b).   The same idea is expressed: "Repellitur scientia, quando homo scit scientiam et non vult secundum scientiam vivere nec eam implere" *De donis* 4, 18 (V, 477b).

173   "Per hunc etiam modum est differentias invenire inter intellectum et scientiam: quia scientia negotiatur circa creaturas secundum rationes creatas; unde negotiari habet non solum circa creaturas spirituales, quae habent rationem imaginis, sed etiam circa sensibiles et corporales, quae habent rationem vestigii. Donum vero intellectus, etsi negotiatur circa creaturas, hoc tamen est secundum rationes aeternas" *III Sent.* d. 35, au., q. 3, concl. ad 1 (III, 778b).   If the eternal reasons are analogous to the 'transcendental notions' of Bernard Lonergan, it is illuminating to note what Lonergan states about these notions in their relation to intentionality: "The transcendental notions are the dynamism of conscious intentionality.   They promote the subject from lower to higher levels of consciousness, from the experiential to the intellectual, from the intellectual to the rational, from the rational to the existential" (Lonergan, *Method in Theology*, 35).

174   *Dictionnaire de Spiritualité*, s.v. «St. Bonaventure,» by E. Longpré.

175   "Necesse etiam habemus quiescere in optimo, et hoc quantum ad intellectum veri et quantum ad affectum boni; primum fit per donum intellectus, secundum per donum sapientiae, in quo est quies"

In his *Commentary on the Sentences*, where he most clearly treats of the gift of understanding, St. Bonaventure takes pains to demarcate the area corresponding to this gift from the gifts of knowledge and wisdom. He does this by comparing and by contrasting. Understanding is above knowledge and below wisdom.[176] In common with the gift of knowledge, whose object is created reality, the gift of understanding extends to created reality, but only to that part of it which images the Eternal Truth, which is its principle object. Material reality, as we have seen, remains on the level of vestiges or traces. In its quest that aims exclusively at comprehending Eternal Truth, the gift of understanding reaches out to spiritual beings for assistance, because in the latter "the eternal reasons shine more greatly expressed."[177] In contrast with the gift of knowledge, it is the *manner* of knowing spiritual beings— through the eternal reasons—which chiefly exalts the gift of understanding over that of knowledge.[178]

When comparing understanding with the gift of wisdom, much is found in common between these two partner gifts. Each of these gifts has spiritual being alone as its object, and both of them know this reality through the eternal reasons. But by contrast, wisdom is confined to knowledge of God and the eternal reasons, and is not extended to other created spiritual beings.[179] Even though both gifts know their object through the eternal reasons, the gift of understanding is directed toward comprehending the highest truth with congruent reasoning, whereas wisdom is directed toward the same eternal truth, but not now through rational activity, but by tasting the truth, that is, through an experiential knowing of the divine sweetness.[180]

For the theologian, what does the gift of understanding add to the light of faith in his search for truth? When stratifying the three sets of habits (virtues, gifts, and beatitudes), St. Bonaventure aligns the gift of intelligence

---

Brev. 5, 5, 7 (V, 258a).

176 "Donum intellectus est infra sapientiam et supra scientiam" *III Sent.* d. 35, au., q. 3, concl., ad 2 (III, 779a).

177 "Donum vero intellectus, etsi negotiatur circa creaturas, hoc tamen est secundum rationes aeternas; et ideo solum est circa creaturas spirituales, in quibus rationes aeternae relucent magis expresse" *III Sent.* d. 35, au., q. 3, concl., ad 1 (III, 778b). These secondary objects are the soul and its faculties, and the hierarchized created spirits between God and ourselves (*Hex.* 5, 33 [V, 359b]).

178 "Donum vero intellectus, etsi negotiatur circa creaturas, hoc tamen est secundum rationes aeternas; et ideo solum est circa creaturas spirituales" *III Sent.* d. 35, au., q. 3, concl., ad 1 (III, 778b).

179 "Donum sapientiae in actu suo versatur solum circa aeterna, donum vero intellectus non solum circa aetaerna, sed etiam circa creata" *III Sent.* d. 35, au., q. 3, concl., ad 5 (III, 779b).

180 "Donum sapientiae est ad cognitionem aeternorum secundum aeternas rationes, secundum tamen quod illae aeternae rationes sunt via ad gustum et experimentalem cognitionem divinae suavitatis" *III Sent.* d. 35, au., q. 3, concl., ad 1 (III, 778b). J. Quinn summarizes the role of the gift of understanding as follows: "The virtue of faith rectifies the human intellect by a simple assent to divine truth. Expediting

to perfect the virtue of faith and to lead eventually to the beatitude of purity of heart.[181]   To the gift of understanding, the Seraphic Doctor ascribes "a contemplation that is clearer and more excellent than the knowledge of faith."[182]   After the gift of understanding, it is the beatitude of purity of heart which allows the soul to see God.[183]   The gift of understanding, on the intermediate level between the virtues and the beatitudes, comes as a spiritual power to raise the theologian from a necessary and basic scientific appreciation of his faith to a contemplation of Eternal Truth: "The act of this gift is to contemplate the truth of faith itself, so that it is devoutly believed and ardently loved."[184]   Because it more directly influences the rational operations than does the gift of wisdom, for which it immediately prepares the way,[185] some have considered it the theological gift par excellence.[186]

---

the act of faith in the speculative order, the gift of understanding brings about a reasoned assent to the same divine truth. Formed by the gift, the speculative knowledge of theology is directed toward a contemplation of God by adding to faith appropriate reasons taken from the Creator and his creatures, especially the rational creature which is an image of God. Regulated by divine revelation, this theological contemplation is ordered to a more devout faith in God and to a more ardent love of God, thus disposing the theologian for the loftier contemplation of God through wisdom" (J.F. Quinn, "The Rôle of the Holy Spirit in St. Bonaventure's Theology," *FS* 33 [1973]: 278).

181 "Cognitio de Deo sub ratione veri potest haberi secundum triplicem modum: uno modo habetur cognitio de Deo per simplicem assensum; alio modo per rationis adminiculum; tertio modo per simplicem contuitum. Primum est virtutis fidei cuius est assentire; secundum est doni intellectus cuius est credita per rationem intelligere; tertium est beatitudinis munditiae cordis, cuius est Deum videre" *III Sent.* d. 35, au., q. 3, concl. (III, 778a). The same tripartite scheme can be found in: *III Sent.* d.34, p. 1, a. 1, q. 1, concl. (III, 737a); ibid., a. 2, q. 1, concl. ad 6 (III, 743b); *Brev.* 5, 4, 3 (V, 256a–b); *Christus mag.* 1 (V, 567b).

182 "Ad donum intellectus spectat contemplatio clarior et excellentior quam sit cognitio fidei" *III Sent.* d. 35, au., q. 3, concl., ad 4 (III, 779a); cf. *III Sent.*, d. 24, dub. 4 (III, 531b).

183 As stated in the previous chapter, when speaking of ontologism, this is not a direct vision of God. See *II Sent.* d. 23, a. 2, q. 3, concl.: "Secundum autem modus. . . " (II, 544a).

184 "Actus vero eius est contemplari ipsum verum creditum, ut devotius credatur et ardentius diligatur" *III Sent.* d. 35, au., q. 3, concl. (III, 778b).

185 ". . . et intellectus, qui est praeambulum respectu sapientiae" *III Sent.* d. 34, p. 1, a. 2, q. 1, concl. (III, 745b). J. Quinn summarizes the role of the gift of understanding for the formation of theology as follows: "Expediting the act of faith in the speculative order, the gift of understanding brings about a reasoned assent to the same divine truth. Formed by the gift, the speculative knowledge of theology is directed toward a contemplation of God by adding to faith appropriate reasons taken from the Creator and his creatures, especially the rational creature which is an image of God. Regulated by divine revelation, this theological contemplation is ordered to a more devout faith in God and to a more ardent love of God, thus disposing the theologian for the loftier contemplation of God through wisdom" ("The Rôle of the Holy Spirit in St. Bonaventure's Theology," *FS* 33 [1973]: 278).

186 This is how Jørgen Pedersen sees it: "C'est le don d'*intelligence* qui est le don théologique par excellence, il est au coeur de l'inspiration centrale de la théologie. . . Le don d'intelligence correspond

Essentially this gift transforms the theologian into a contemplative.[187]

9. The gift of wisdom

The gift of wisdom presupposes the gift of understanding which is the last step before entering the realm of wisdom's activity.[188] The movement from understanding to wisdom obeys the principle that knowledge leads to desire.[189] The study of theology should effect such a desire for God as to lead one to the contemplative experience of love.[190] Such a consequence is assigned, *a fortiori*, to the two highest gifts, since it is the aim of the gifts in general.[191]

The two highest gifts, as we have seen, dispose the soul for two kinds of contemplation: intellectual and sapiential. Intellectual contemplation is considered imperfect in comparison with sapiential contemplation which is perfect.[192] This means that the contemplation prepared by the gift of understanding, although more adapted to our human capacity to comprehend, is considered, for that very reason, inferior to the contemplation prepared by wisdom. Nothing is actually "seen" of this wisdom, which becomes a love transcending all understanding and

---

à la pénétration intellectuelle parfaite à laquelle aspire le vrai théologien" ("L'Intellectus fidei et la notion de théologie chez saint Bonaventure," *Studia Theologica* 5 [1951]: 33–34).

187 "Donum intellectus—cuius actus est in contemplationem summi Veri elevare per lumen, quod non solum facit assentire, sed etiam per congruas rationes credita intelligere . . ." (*III Sent*. d. 35, au., q. 3, concl. (III, 778a).

188 "Et iste intellectus proprie est donum. Ab intellectu inchoandum est, et perveniendum ad sapientiam" *Hex*. 3, 1 (V, 343a).

189 "Cognitio enim praeambula est et dirigit affectum ad exspectandum et ad desiderandum" *III Sent*. d. 23, a. 1, q. 1, concl. (III, 471b).

190 Following Hugh of St. Victor, Bonaventure affirms that contemplation is the eye that makes it possible to see what is above us: "Oculo carnis videret homo ea quae sunt extra se, oculo rationis ea quae sunt intra se, et oculo contemplationis ea quae sunt supra se" *Brev*. 2, 12, 5 (V, 230b). J. Quinn explains this contemplative aspect of theology in the following terms: "The rôle of the Holy Spirit in constituting the wisdom of theology is, therefore, to unite by the bond of charity the science of Scripture and the science of faith while directing them through Christian piety to a loving contemplation or an experiential knowledge of God" (J. Quinn, "The Rôle of the Holy Spirit in St. Bonaventure's Theology," *FS* 33 [1973]: 283).

191 "Ex dictis igitur manifeste colligitur, quod habitus virtutum principaliter disponunt [vitae] activae, habitus vero donorum ad otium contemplativae" *Brev*. 5, 6, 7 (259b).

192 *Hex*. 20, 9 (V, 427a). To illustrate the difference between imperfect and perfect contemplation, St. Bonaventure uses the allegory of the sun and the seasons it produces. The seasons of greater darkness and cold (winter and spring) represent imperfect contemplation. The seasons of greater light and heat (summer and fall) represent perfect contemplation. The sun at its zenith (noonday) is the contemplation reserved for heaven, of which perfect contemplation is a foretaste.

knowledge.[193]

In the *Commentary on the Sentences*, Bonaventure's chief concern in his short *quaestio* dedicated to the gift of wisdom is whether the act of this gift consists in the knowledge of truth or in the experience of good.[194] He resolves the question by affirming that "the principal act of the gift of wisdom is from the affective part."[195] Nevertheless, in the process leading up to this assertion, he takes great care to explain that the act of this same gift involves some knowledge, particularly at its point of departure, but never really disappearing completely, making the gift "partly cognitive and partly affective."[196]

We are to understand, then, that over and above whatever knowledge the gift of understanding affords to the operation of the gift of wisdom, some kind of cognitive aspect can be discovered at all times in the act of wisdom itself.[197] Without such knowledge, we might imagine that wisdom would be wholly unconscious of the divine sweetness it enjoys. In fact, in defining the gift of wisdom, St. Bonaventure, in opposition to three other definitions he examines and rejects, finds a fourth acceptation of the word wisdom (*sapientia*) entirely appropriate (*propriissime*), because of its basis on the word 'savor' (*sapor*).[198] Besides comparing it with the sense of taste, he employs the sense of touch to characterize the gift of wisdom in its

---

193 "Iste amor transcendit omnem intellectum et scientiam. — Sed si scientiam transcendit, quomodo videri potest sapientia ista?" *Hex.* 2, 30 (V, 341a).

194 The title to this section on wisdom is: *«Utrum actus doni sapientiae attendatur penes cognitionem veri, an penes affectionem boni»III Sent.* d. 35, au., q. 1 (III, 772). The whole of this short treatise on the gift of wisdom is given in: *III Sent.* d. 35, au., q. 1 (III, 772a–775b). Likewise, special attention is given to wisdom in many other places in St. Bonaventure, but particularly in: *Collationes in Hexaëmeron; Itinerarium mentis in Deum; Breviloquium;* and *Collationes de septem donis Spiritus sancti.*

195 "Actus doni sapientiae praecipuus est ex parte affectionis" *III Sent.* d. 35, au., q. 1, concl. (III, 774b).

196 "Actus doni sapientiae partim est cognitivus, et partim est affectivus: ita quod in cognitione inchoatur et in affectione consummatur" *III Sent.* d. 35, au., q. 1, concl. (III, 774b).

197 Bonaventure speaks of both aspects of wisdom, the cognitive and the affective, as two ways of knowing: "Sapientia est cognitio . . . non tantum per modum cognitionis speculativae et intellectualis, verum etiam saporativae et experimentalis" *Perf. ev.* q. 1, concl. (V, 120b). When presenting this aspect of Bonaventure's teaching on wisdom, Aloysius Benigar concludes: "Videtur ergo, quod actus doni sapientiae omnino se teneat ex parte affectionis et nullatenus ex parte cognitionis" (*Compendium theologiae spiritualis* [Roma, 1959], 182–83).

198 "Et ideo actus praecipuus doni sapientiae propriissime dictae est ex parte affectivae, ratione cuius dicit Ecclesiasticus, quod *sapientia secundum nomen suum est*"(*III Sent.* d. 35, au., q. 1, concl. [III, 774b]). Typically, a biblical quotation is the most important argument for St. Bonaventure. In this case he uses the same text from Ecclesiasticus 6:23 (Vg) which he used when discussing theology's final cause in the Prologue to the *Sentences*, which we studied in our introductory chapter. Note also: "'Sapientia doctrinae secundum nomen suum est, et non in multis est manifesta', si ergo sapientia

distinctive capacity to both know and feel at the same time.[199]

As we have seen when treating of the gift of knowledge, so also with the gift of wisdom, nothing prohibits ascribing two acts to the same habit, as long as one act is subordinated to the other, or "one is disposing, the other is completing."[200] This subordinative interaction between thought and affection brings the Seraphic Doctor to call the act of this gift "a taste or savoring of an experimental good and a sweet knowledge."[201] Although the affective part remains paramount for St. Bonaventure, he is deliberately cautious in not eliminating the cognitive aspect nor of minimizing too much its preparatory role. Thus, when he says "It cannot be held that knowing is the principal act of wisdom," he is quick to add that knowing "in some way concurs with its [wisdom's] principal act."[202] Against the argument that love increases in the measure that knowledge of the loved object increases, he replies: "This is true; however, in the love of God, knowledge is conjoined to the taste itself. The best way of knowing God is through the experience of sweetness; it is much more excellent and nobler and more delectable than that obtained through rational arguments."[203]

When we recall that St. Bonaventure, at the outset of the *Commentary on the Sentences*, identified theology with wisdom, we now realize that particular kind of wisdom only can be equated with the fourth definition of wisdom, that is, with the gift of the Holy Spirit. This is so principally because the Seraphic Doctor uses the same etymology and Biblical references in both places, and then, when defining the gift of wisdom, he distinguishes

---

a *sapore* dicitur, et *sapor* respicit affectionem interiorem; videtur, quod proprius actus doni sapientiae sit affectivus" (*III Sent*. d. 35, au., q. 1, con. 1 [III, 773a]).

199 "Sicut tactus est, sapientia in se claudit utrumque actum; unde quodam modo respicit intellectum, quodam modo respicit affectum" *III Sent*. d. 35, au., q. 1, concl. ad 5 (III, 775b).

200 "Nihil tamen impedit, duos esse, ita quod unus sit primus, alter vero praecipuus; unus sicut disponens, alter vero complens" *III Sent*. d. 35, au., q. 1 concl. ad 5 (III, 775b). Cf. *III Sent*. d. 35, au., q. 2, concl. ad 4 (III, 777b). Bonaventure takes a similar approach in his treatise on faith, in which a cognitive and an affective element are conjoined. See: *III Sent*. d. 23, a. 1, q. 2, concl. (III, 477b)

201 "Ipse gustus vel saporatio est experimentalis boni et dulcis cognitio" *III Sent*. d. 35, au., q. 1, concl. (III, 774b).

202 "Ex hoc non habetur, quod cognoscere sit actus ipsius doni sapientiae praecipuus, sed quod quodam modo concurrit ad eius actum praecipuum" *III Sent*. d. 35, au., q. 1, concl. ad 5 (III, 775a–b).

203 "Illud est verum; attamen in amore Dei ipsi gustui coniuncta est cognitio. Optimus enim modus cognoscendi Deum est per experimentum dulcedinis; multo etiam excellentior et nobilior et delectabilior est quam per argumentum inquisitionis" *III Sent*. d. 35, au., q.1, concl. ad 5 (III, 775a). William of St.-Thierry says it in capsule form: "[God is] more loved than known, more tasted than understood" *In Cant.* (*PL* 180, 507C).

it from three other definitions of wisdom, none of which refer to theology. On the other hand, it may seem disconcerting to observe that Bonaventure has assigned theology to the domain of three other gifts, namely the ones we have studied just prior to wisdom. Perplexed, we might ask to which of these gifts theology chiefly belongs, as if St. Bonaventure himself were vague on this score. Nevertheless, any confusion disappears when we remember Bonaventure's doctrine on the plurality of forms, which we examined above. According to this doctrine, higher or subsequent habits raise the habits already received to greater perfection.[204] Thus, theology can operate under four gifts at the same time. If theology also reaches the level of wisdom, it is operating at its best.

To answer the question how the gift of wisdom precisely helps the study of theology, we must keep in mind that the higher the gift, the more mysterious its action. The less conditioned by our intellectual operations, the more difficult it is to scrutinize with the human eye. For this reason, as we ascend the ladder of the gifts, we find ourselves more and more at a loss to be concrete about the exact nature of their influences. Bonaventure points out this difficulty and concludes that the limit of Christian wisdom is found at this juncture: "This wisdom is veiled in mystery, but how? If it has not entered into the heart of a man, how can it be understood, since it is without form? Note that this is the highest state of achievement of Christian wisdom."[205] Because of this difficulty, Bonaventure depends heavily on Dionysius the Areopagite.[206] If this fourth "face" of wisdom is "nulliform," it might seem destructive of the previous forms. Bonaventure assures us this is not the case.[207] He admits there are two ways to ascend to this wisdom, one positive, the other negative, but that the best way is the latter, or Dionysian

---

204 See footnote 84. There it was explained that subsequent forms bring to perfection previous forms without eliminating any form. This doctrine is characteristic of Bonaventure's philosophy. In the case of faith being perfected by knowledge, and knowledge by wisdom, Bonaventure adopts the Gospel cure of the man born blind (Jn. 9:6) to illustrate how these three habits work together as the three elements (mud, saliva, and dust) did miraculously to produce perfect vision: "Oportet prius linire oculos luto ex sputo et pulvere facto; saliva est sapientia; pulvis, caro Christi; lutum, fides de mysterio incarnationis" *Hex.* 17, 27 (V, 413b–414a).

205 "Haec sapientia abscondita est in mysterio. Sed quomodo? Si in cor hominis non ascendit, quomodo comprehendetur, cum sit nulliformis? —Nota, quod hic est status sapientiae christianae" *Hex.* 2, 29 (V, 341a; de Vinck, *Six Days*, 35).

206 "Unde cum Dionysius multos libros fecisset hic consummavit, scilicet in *Mystica Theologia*" *Hex.* 2, 29 (V, 341a).

207 "Quarta facies sapientiae est difficillima, quia est nulliformis, quod videtur destructivum praecedentium, non tamen est" *Hex.* 2, 28 (V, 340b).

negative theology.[208] Let us permit Bonaventure himself to defend this method.

This kind of wisdom is without form, Bonaventure explains, because it is produced "in the suspensions of the divine excesses."[209] We are talking about love more than about knowledge, and "love always follows negation."[210] By a negative approach, he continues, "I do not deprive God of what is His or within Him, but I attribute it in a higher and better manner than I am able to understand."[211] Such a procedure in theology "leaves in us a most noble disposition."[212] Even though "the understanding does not comprehend, the soul is highly illuminated."[213] Here again, between the positive and the negative approach to theology, it appears the former is still present, but subordinated to the latter, making it possible for Saint Bonaventure to declare that "knowledge which passes to the affective faculty is wisdom."[214] The very word 'negative theology' implies that there is something to be negated or superseded.[215] What is understood is surpassed by what is mysterious, or secret, but without altogether abandoning the data of intelligence.[216] Saint Bonaventure calls this a 'double operation' composed of contuition and tasting: "The divine operation or potency is double: one turns toward contuiting the divine spectacles, the other turns toward tasting the divine consolations. The first is done through the intelligence, the second, through the unitive or loving potency, which is secret, and of which the philosophers knew little or nothing."[217]

---

208 "Iste autem ascensus fit per affirmationem et ablationem: per affirmationem, a summo usque ad infimum; per ablationem, ab infimo usque ad summum; et iste modus est conveniens magis" *Hex.* 2, 33 (V, 342b).

209 "Nulliformis in suspendiis divinorum excessuum" *Hex.* 2, 8 (V, 337b); "Forma autem sapientiae est mirabilis, et nullus eam aspicit sine admiratione et ecstasi" *Hex.* 2, 7 (V, 337b).

210 "Ablationem sequitur amor semper" *Hex.* 2, 33 (V, 342b).

211 "Nec privo ego a Deo quod suum est, vel in ipso est, sed attribuo meliori modo et altiori, quam ego intelligo" *Hex.* 2, 33 (V, 342b; de Vinck, *Six Days*, 40).

212 "Notitia divinitatis per ablationem relinquit in nobis nobilissimam dispositionem" *Hex.* 2, 33 (V, 342b).

213 "Intellectus non capit; et tamen anima summe illustratur" *Hex.* 2, 32 (V, 342a).

214 "Notitia igitur transiens in affectum est sapientia" *Hex.* 5, 13 (V, 356a).

215 The same idea is expressed through Bonaventure's insistence on knowledge as a prerequisite for attaining wisdom: "Oportet scire, ut de fructibus sapientiae habeatur, et per portas civitatis possimus introire" *Hex.* 19, 5 (V, 421a).

216 Rather than abandoning the understanding, a man must humbly bring it under control: "Secundum quod homo magis intellectum captivat, secundum hoc sapienter efficitur, et fides habetur per humilitatem" *Hex.* 2, 19 (V, 339b).

217 "Operatio vel potentia divina duplex est: una, quae se convertit ad contuenda divina spectacula; alia quae se convertit ad degustanda divina solatia. Primum fit per intelligentiam, secundum per vim

The double operation of wisdom is found to work both ways. When speaking expressly of the gift of wisdom, Bonaventure sometimes asserts that it first influences the intellect, and from the intellect it descends to the affective potency and finally to the operative potency: "What is the wisdom that is from above? . . . This light descends to illuminate our cognitive potency, to gladden our affective potency and to fortify our operative potency. From the highest God it descends to the understanding; from the understanding, to the *affectus* and until the lowest, that is, to the operative."[218] Nevertheless, only the secret experience of wisdom can explain that a desire for this gift might be enkindled in the soul, so that the desire itself might become the "gateway to wisdom."[219] Wisdom's influence simply does not terminate on the affective level in *docta ignorantia*, but produces an "elevation of our mental considerations."[220] In this sense, even though in wisdom "the mind cannot contemplate with the intellectual eyes,"[221] and it is "not the understanding but the heart which enters here,"[222] nevertheless wisdom is called a light that illuminates our intellective potency.[223]

It is not the path followed by the gift of wisdom—from the intellect to the *affectus* —that decides which potency plays the more important role

---

unitivam sive amativam, quae secreta est, et de qua parum vel nihil noverunt" *Hex.* 5, 24 (V, 358a). As we stated earlier, *contuitio* is a Bonaventurian term used in contrast to *intuitio*. The latter is knowledge by immediate or direct vision; the former is indirect or mediate knowledge, as expressed by Bonaventure in the following statement: "Mens nostra contuita est Deum extra se per vestigia et in vestigiis, intra se per imaginem super nos relucentem et in ipsa luce, secundum quod possibile est secundum statum viae et exercitium mentis nostrae" *Itin.* 7, 1 (V, 312a). For further study on this manner of knowing, see: R. Sciamannini, *La Contuizione Bonaventuriana* (Firenze: Città di Vita, 1957).

218 "Quae est sapientia, quae est desursum?. . . Lux ista descendit ad nostram potentiam cognitivam illuminandam, ad nostram affectivam laetificandam et ad nostram operativam corroborandam. Descendit a summo Deo in intellectum, ab intellectu in affectum et usque ad infimum, scilicet operationem" *De donis* 9, 5 (V, 500a).

219 "Porta sapientiae est concupiscentia eius et vehemens desiderium" *Hex.* 2, 2 (336a).

220 Bonaventure compares the gift of wisdom with the single glance of the beloved in the *Song of Songs* 4:9, which ravished the heart of the lover. This, he explains, is the "affectus" which "goes right to the very depth of Christ." It is the beloved's braid which "signifies the elevation of the mental considerations" *Hex.* 2, 32 (V, 342a).

221 "Mens oculis intellectualibus aspicere non potest" *Hex.* 2, 32 (V, 342a). B. Lonergan prefers to give eyes to love: "That fulfillment [of the capacity to transcend oneself] is not the product of our knowledge and choice. On the contrary, it dismantles and abolishes the horizon in which our knowing and choosing went on and it sets up a new horizon in which the love of God will transvalue our values and the eyes of that love will transform our knowing" (*Method in Theology*, 106).

222 "Ibi non intrat intellectus, sed affectus" *Hex.* 2, 32 (V, 342a).

223 "Quod sit lux descendens ad nostram potentiam intellectivam illuminandam, patet" *De donis* 9, 5 (V, 500a).

here.[224] St. Bonaventure, faithful to his preference for loving God more than knowing him, is clear in reserving to the *affectus*, or the heart, the principal role.[225] What really matters here is that the experience of wisdom engenders such a desire in the soul that all other desires are thereby extinguished, and man is raised above the world.[226] This explains why curiosity has no place in the search for wisdom, since nothing else can be desired. "If [wisdom] is the highest good, it must be loved in the highest way; if it is all good, it must be loved universally and above all things."[227] Such love for other things is opposed to wisdom and charity and is nothing but vanity, which must be

---

224 Karl Rahner observes that for Bonaventure the *apex affectus* is on a deeper level than both the intellect and the will. Even though the will still plays a more important role, Rahner's observations may help at this point to appreciate the depth of God's communication: "Nun kommt in unserem Fall hinzu, daß der *apex affectus*, in dem Gott gegenwärtig ist, nicht einfach eine Fähigkeit neben dem Intellekt, auf gleicher Ebene mit ihm ist. Er ist ja das *summum et intimum* der Seele, liegt also auf einer tieferen Seinsschicht als die Seele—echt franziskanisch gedacht—eine größere Verwandtschaft mit dem Willen als mit dem Intellekt, sie ist ja ein *apex affectus*, ist das Innerste, in das der *affectus*, nicht aber der Intellekt 'eintreten' kann. Trotzdem bleibt wahr, daß dieser *apex* tiefer liegt als der Intellekt und der Wille, daß er der Seelengrund ist, der die beiden Fähigkeiten Verstand und Willen trägt. Wenn nun aus diesem Innersten und tiefstem Seelengrund die Fähigkeiten Intellekt und Wille gewissermaßen erst herauswachsen und herausfließen (eine allgemeine scholastiche Idee der Metaphysik der Seele), so kann diese tiefste Seinsschicht der Seele Eigenschaften in sich vereinigt besitzen, die sich erst auf einer weiter nach 'außen' liegenden Seinsschicht der Seele in zwei verschiedene Fakultäten entfalten. Wenn nun Gott von innen heraus diesen tiefsten Punkt der Seele gleichsam 'informierend' berührt, so wird der *apex affectus* dieser unmittelbaren Liebeseinigung inne werden können, ohne daß der Intellekt dabei in Tätigkeit tritt. Freilich erfährt dann auch dieser Seelengrund Gott nur unmittelbar als die bewegende Kraft ihrer alles Erkennen hinter sich lassenden, ekstatischen Liebe, und so bleibt diese Erfahrung dunkel, bis einmal in der *visio beatifica* auch der Intellekt von innen her vom Lichte Gottes überflutet wird, ohne geblendet zu werden. Hier ist Gott noch das dunkel Feuer der Liebe, *non lux sed ignis; caligo non claritas* (*Itin. 7, 6*); *caligo inaccessibilis quae tamen illuminat mentes* (*Hex. 20, 11*)" (K. Rahner, "Der Begriff der ecstasis bei Bonaventura," *ZAM* 9 [1934]: 16–17).

225 "Si magnum est illustrari sapientia, plus est laetificari, in quantum diligit principium suum" *De donis* 9, 6 (V, 500b). The same order is expressed by Lonergan as love's longing for knowledge and bliss already being a kind of knowledge: "From an experience of love focused on mystery there wells forth a longing for knowledge, while love itself is a longing for union; so for the lover of the unknown beloved the concept of bliss is a knowledge of him and union with him, however they may be achieved" (*Method in Theology*, 109).

226 "Huiusmodi autem concupiscentia extinguit omnes concupiscentias et hominem sublevatum facit a mundo" *Hex.* 2, 6 (V, 337b). For Bernard Lonergan, it is love that causes the world of interiority to precede the worlds of theory and common sense: "To speak of the dynamic state of being in love with God pertains to the stage of meaning when the world of interiority has been made the explicit ground of the worlds of theory and common sense. It follows that in this stage of meaning the gift of God's love first is described as an experience and only consequently is objectified in theoretical categories" (*Method in Theology*, 107).

227 "Si enim summum bonum est, summe amanda est; si autem omne bonum est, universaliter appetenda est et super omnia" *Hex.* 2, 6 (V, 337b).

overcome.[228] This vehement desire for wisdom then generates a desire for discipline.[229] In the same place, where St. Bonaventure is speaking of the knowledge that is characteristic of wisdom, he stresses that the condition for such knowledge is discipline, but a discipline preceded and accompanied by goodness.[230] Even though discipline is needed, it remains true "that this ascension takes place through a force and a most powerful movement of the Holy Spirit."[231] But this grace always supposes a man's efforts.[232] As we have seen, these efforts presuppose diligent study of a scientific nature. But these efforts are conceived as harmoniously joined to a proper ascetical life, which Bonaventure summarizes in four practices: recognition of one's own interior defects, mortification of the passions, ordering of the thoughts, and the raising up of the desire.[233] But the dynamism beneath this way of life is the ardent desire of wisdom that necessarily springs from an experience of it.[234] Once wisdom is experienced, not only is desire inflamed, but the soul becomes God-like and the faculties are enriched admirably for further pursuing wisdom.[235] This is a continuous circular movement from science to wisdom through the discipline of study and holiness: "The passage [from science to wisdom] is exercise; exercise from the study of science to the study of holiness, and from the study of holiness to the study of wisdom."[236]

---

228 "Sapientia ergo et caritas sunt principales fructus; quibus principaliter est contraria vanitas" *Hex.* 19, 2 (V, 420a); "Illi autem transeunt, qui totum suum studium ponunt, qualiter a vanitatibus transeant in regionem veritatis" *Hex.* 19, 1 (V, 420a).

229 "Concupiscentia ergo sapientiae generat concupiscentiam disciplinae" *Hex.* 2, 3 (V, 337a).

230 "Scientia enim non habetur, nisi praecedat disciplina; nec disciplina, nisi praecedat bonitas; et sic per bonitatem et disciplinam inest nobis scientia" *Hex.* 2, 3 (V, 337a). The immediate context is wisdom, thus I have interpreted this 'scientia' to mean the kind of knowledge specific to 'sapientia'.

231 "Et innuit, quod iste ascensus fit per vigorem et commotionem fortissimam Spiritus sancti" *Hex.* 2, 32 (V, 342b).

232 "Haec autem contemplatio fit per gratiam, et tamen iuvat industria, scilicet ut separet se ab omni eo, quod Deus non est" *Hex.* 2, 30 (V, 341a).

233 These are found in chapter 19 of the *Hexaëmeron* (V, 424a–b): recognition of one's own interior defects (*Hex.* 19, 24); mortification of the passions (*Hex.* 19, 25); ordering of the thoughts (*Hex.* 19, 26); raising up of the desire (Hex. 19, 27).

234 "Et ibi est operatio transcendens omnem intellectum, secretissima; quod nemo scit, nisi qui experitur" *Hex.* 2, 29 (V, 341a).

235 "Sapientia est *lux descendens a Patre luminum* in animam et radians in eam facit animam deiformem et domum Dei. Ista lux descendens facit intellectivam speciosam, affectivam amoenam, operativam robustam" *Hex.* 2, 1 (V, 336a).

236 "Transitus autem est exercitium; exercitatio a studio scientiae ad studium sanctitatis, et a studio sanctitatis ad studium sapientia" *Hex.* 19, 3 (V, 420b).

Conclusion: In praise of sapiential theology

That wisdom for Saint Bonaventure ultimately can be a source of speculative knowledge seems to be clear.[237] To attempt to explain concretely how this occurs leads us to the same conclusion, that is, experience alone provides the kind of knowledge that must remain for the most part incommunicable, as the mysteries of revelation remain more hidden than revealed.[238] Or, we may compare wisdom to the breathtaking beauty of a painting. Such an experience moved Bonaventure to exclaim: "True beauty is in the beauty of wisdom."[239] Who can put this beauty into words? Even the Church's Magisterium eventually must point our minds in this direction, simply inviting us to "taste the sweetness of consenting and believing the truth."[240]

In his major work on St. Bonaventure, J.F. Quinn specifically points out that Aquinas and Bonaventure differ most in regard to the role of the gift of wisdom in the constitution of theological knowledge.[241] Bonaventure's

---

237 Gilson, among others, sees it this way: "St. Bonaventure was expressly to accept this idea and make it an integral part of his mysticism. The gift of Wisdom which is superior to the gift of understanding, and on which depends mystical ecstasy, is source of speculative knowledge" (*Philosophy of Bonaventure*, p. 454, n. 72). Charles Bernard arrives at a similar conviction but clarifies that "spiritual experience does not lead to new objective knowledge" ("La spiritualità come fonte dottrinale," in: *La Spiritualità come Teologia*, ed. *Idem*, [Cinisello Balsamo: Edizioni Paoline, 1993], 346). Bernard, however, judges that "since the sapiential understanding of the Mystery cannot be the immediate fruit of dialectical sagacity, but rests on the experiential sense of God, we must conclude that theological research requires optimal spiritual conditions in order to arrive at a purer, richer, and more elevated sense of God" (Ibid., 348; *my translation*).

238 The first Vatican council declares: "The divine mysteries so exceed created intellect that, even when given in revelation and received by faith, they remain covered over by the very veil of faith itself" (*DS* 3019).

239 "Vera autem pulchritudo est in illa pulchritudine sapientiae" *Hex*. 20, 24 (V, 429b).

240 Council of Orange, II, can. 7 (DZ 180), quoted by Vatican II: "If this faith is to be shown, the grace of God and the interior help of the Holy Spirit must precede and assist, moving the heart and turning it to God, opening the eyes of the mind, and giving 'joy and ease to everyone in assenting to the truth and believing it'. To bring about an ever deeper understanding of revelation, the same Holy Spirit constantly brings faith to completion by His gifts" (*Dei Verbum*, 5).

241 "It is in regard to the unity of theology as a wisdom ordering all things to God that Aquinas and Bonaventure manifest their greatest differences. In this respect, Bonaventure speaks of theology as having the perfection of a speculative habitus and the perfection of a practical habitus; the two perfections are made one in a habitus of wisdom uniting the intellect and the will while ordering the whole of theology through love to the good of eternal contemplation. The unity of theological knowledge, therefore, and its order to the end of Christian life, are established by the gift of wisdom coming from the Holy Spirit, to whom Bonaventure attributes a most important rôle in the constitution of theological knowledge. Aquinas does not concur with Bonaventure in attributing the unity of theology to the work of the Holy Spirit, or to His gift of wisdom. According to Aquinas, the gift of wisdom belongs to the practical order of Christian virtue, and so the knowledge obtained by the gift of wisdom does not pertain to the constitution of theological wisdom" (J.F. Quinn, *Historical Constitution*, 710–11).

particular contribution is to make of theological study a spiritual life, by considering theology as that particular operation of the gift of wisdom which raises man's study to the level of contemplation.[242] For Bonaventure, we actually ignore the things of God unless wisdom produces this contemplation of the highest good, and this is only possible if the Spirit of God enters into us.[243] Far from excusing us from diligent study and from the ardors of ascesis, it presupposes these activities as united intimately in the operation of wisdom: "He, therefore, who wishes to ascend to God must . . . bring the natural powers of the soul under the influence of grace . . . under the power of wisdom which perfects, and this in contemplation."[244]

---

242 Wisdom's predominant role in theology made it possible for Bougerol to affirm: "Bonaventure's spiritual theology is but his general theology directed toward wisdom" (*Introduction to Bonaventure*, 156).

243 "Tertius fructus sapientiae est contemplari summum bonum . . . ita et quae Dei sunt nescimus, nisi Spiritus Dei intret in nos" *Hex.* 18, 24 (V, 418a).

244 "Qui igitur vult in Deum ascendere necesse est, ut . . naturales potentias supradictas exerceat . . . ad sapientiam perficientem et hoc in contemplatione" *Itin.* 1, 8 (V, 298a).

Non dimittam te, nisi benedixeris mihi.

Gen. 32:27

GENERAL CONCLUSION

To reach the end of our journey we must heed the words of our guide: "In this passing over, if it is to be perfect, all intellectual activities must be left behind and the height of our affection must be totally transformed into God" (*Itin.* 7, 4). At this point, when the experience of wisdom attains its highest intensity, we can safely conjecture why Bonaventure imposed a procedural reverse upon all his theology. That is, he posited wisdom as our point of departure after he himself had attained the point of arrival, which he experienced as wisdom beyond the power of human reason to comprehend.

Although human reason is barred from this experience until passing beyond to the transformation into God, Bonaventure presumes that for theology to be undertaken wisdom in some manner must accompany us from the very beginning. Man's gradual mastery over reason only comes through his progressive growth in experiential knowledge of God. Paradoxically, this mastery is more of an unknowing than a knowing: "There new, absolute and unchangeable mysteries of theology are hidden in the superluminous darkness of a silence teaching secretly in the utmost obscurity which is supermanifest—a darkness which is super-resplendent and in which everything shines forth and which fills to overflowing" (*Itin.* 7,5; quoting Dionysius, *De mystica theologia*, I, 1). Since the end of the spiritual life, as well as of theology, is this same experiential knowledge of God—this 'unknowing' which paradoxically forms the highest knowledge of God in this life—the theologian finds himself progressively enveloped in the mysterious wisdom of God, once spoken of by Saint Paul (Rm. 16:25.27; I Cor. 1:25; 2:5; 2:7; Ep. 3:9; Col. 2:2–3) as foolishness to human beings. But, "God's folly is wiser than human wisdom" (I Cor. 1:25).[1]

The mysterious wisdom of God is the Crucified Christ, which ultimately is what motivated Saint Bonaventure to love theology, and why he invited his disciples to consider holiness as the unique incentive for studying theology: *Nam haec cognitio: quod Christus pro nobis mortuus est . . . nisi sit homo peccator et durus, movet ad amorem. . . Concedendum*

---

[1] Here we may understand why St. Thomas Aquinas, when he reached this point, could no longer write.

ergo, quod est, ut boni fiamus.[2]

Because reason properly is equipped for theological study by the gift of wisdom, Bonaventure would have us somehow taste the final fruit of theology prior to approaching study, and thereafter never labor in theology without this experience as our guiding source of intellectual pursuit. This position stems from what is original in the teaching of Saint Bonaventure, that is, the direct influence of the gifts of the Holy Spirit on the faculties. The sapiential experience of God unhesitatingly is imposed at the outset as the very definition of theology because without the gift of wisdom no sensibility of the aim pursued, transformation into God, would be possible. Even if such an experience as the taste of God unconsciously is pursued, this gift, so distinct from conceptual knowledge, progressively develops in the cognitive faculties until the perception by taste predominates over reason.

The consequences of this experience upon St. Bonaventure are observable in all his works first by the particular theological-spiritual stance he displays in the method employed in his earlier works and later in the explicit assertions of his pastoral exhortations during the final period, of which the conferences at the University of Paris are the best example. Theology and spiritual life virtually are equated because the experience of wisdom, at the heart of both, is their ultimate cause. The wisdom experience is the essential trait of theology, so much so that it is considered to inhere in the theologian — an affective disposition — empowering theology to accomplish its end through transformation by love.

For our times, I believe that any consideration of the distinctly Bonaventurian approach to theology will be rewarded amply. The originality of the Seraphic Doctor's contribution is a fitting perspective from which to evaluate a personal approach to theological studies as a way of holiness. But beyond assuming his perspective, I am convinced it is impossible to obtain or to control the experience of theology by applying a strict method since wisdom will never be subject to our authority. The conclusion to the *Itinerarium mentis in Deum* forewarns us about trying to understand anything. Nevertheless, along the path leading to this unknowing we have been guided by a master who simply points out a way of looking upon reality around us, within us, and above us. After studying Bonaventure's approach I can only conjecture what this may imply in a contemporary setting, but would suggest that others, through their own experiences, make up for the deficiencies I meet with in speaking of something so enveloped in mystery.

---

2 *I Sent.* prooem., q. 3, resp. (I, 13b).

Bonaventure's approach seems to suggest three broad areas that make up the theologian's journey — study, prayer, and leisure — which need to be analyzed in our own circumstances if we are to permit theology to develop in the Bonaventurian spirit of wisdom. The quality of our own theological-spiritual life can be enriched powerfully if we are willing to welcome wisdom in the role of guide on our journey toward knowledge of God. Once this gift of the Holy Spirit is engaged, new attitudes should inevitably follow. These attitudes lead to practical applications which necessarily are conditioned by individual capacities and preferences. The task of the student himself is to seek solutions to his own difficulties. Although analogies can be drawn in order for one to make personal changes in study habits, I feel Bonaventure's original intuition is of vital importance as a starting point for all theologians who undertake to reflect upon their own spiritual life. What matters above all, as anyone can discover through contact with Bonaventure himself, is the approach. To this end, I would like to focus on the three areas (study, prayer, and leisure) in which some personal revision may be attempted in our times for a fruitful application of Bonaventure's insight.

1. Theological study as experience of Scripture

Saint Bonaventure conceived the process of learning theology as an experience of growth in wisdom through a knowledge and a love that are inseparable and which bring about personal transformation. He saw the study of theology as one of the principle ways of sanctification and as somehow paradigmatic of all spiritual paths, in virtue of the healthy interplay between intellect and will in cooperating with illuminating grace to reach union with God. The theology student, therefore, was in a privileged position since he dedicated his life expressly to this same sanctifying activity.

Our Master defined theology as a subjective attitude (*habitus*) with which the object studied is to be approached. This at first may appear to weaken, or at least condition in some way, the objective or scientific nature of theology. Nevertheless, on deeper reflection, we realize that since all theology is based on revelation by a God who invites us into interpersonal relationship with him, a God unknowable in his person by the philosophers, no other element is more important than the very approach with which we undertake theology. The approach is personal contact, for revelation by the Person God calls for personal response, without which revelation remains ineffectual. Such a response necessarily is subjective, but this subjectivity never arises first, since it is consequent to the objective revealed data that call it forth. Bernard Lonergan's expression becomes unambiguous: "Genuine objectivity is the fruit of authentic subjectivity."[3] What authenticates our subjectivity is the truthful and sincere response to the God who reveals Himself. This response always involves conversion, because revelation never is given to us simply as information, but as growth in transformation.

The disposition of the student of theology, then, subordinated to what is studied (God), becomes the necessary condition for learning theology. We approach theology with the same attitude with which we approach God. In St. John's First Letter we find the statement: "We are declaring to you what we have seen and heard, so that you too may share our life" (I Jn. 1:3). The specific way in which God shares His life with the theologian is the communication of knowledge about Himself. This knowledge evidently is the vehicle of a deeper and more mysterious reality — His very life. "Will I love him in return, or will I refuse? Will I live out the gift of his love, or will I hold back, turn away, withdraw?"[4] Theology as personal relationship is the first obvious consequence of equating theology to Sacred Scripture. In many ways St. Bonaventure, by taking this equation as his point of departure, not only supplies the firmest basis for defining theology as wisdom, but likewise provides a strong medieval vote in favor of the biblical insistence so particular to our own theology. The Dogmatic Constitution on Divine Revelation not only affirmed that "sacred theology rests on the written word of God," but that "the study of the sacred page is, as it were, the soul of sacred theology" (*DV* 24). Although at present no one doubts this subordination, the Council in firmly situating theology upon the Scriptural foundation also recognized the same consequences regarding personal openness to revelation, an openness that is nothing less than "the entrusting of one's whole self freely to God, offering the full submission of intellect and will to God who reveals" (*DV* 5). But, similar to what we found in St. Bonaventure's works, the Council, by emphasizing personal openness, calls attention in the same place to the need of grace upon the

---

3 "The elimination of the unauthentic . . . is effected in the measure that theologians attain authenticity through religious, moral, and intellectual conversion. Nor may one expect the discovery of some «objective» criterion or test or control. For that meaning of the «objective» is mere delusion. Genuine objectivity is the fruit of authentic subjectivity. It is to be attained only by attaining authentic subjectivity. To seek and employ some alternative prop or crutch invariably leads to some measure of reductionism. As Hans-Georg Gadamer has contended at length in his *Wahrheit und Methode*, there are no satisfactory methodological criteria that prescind from the criteria of truth" (Lonergan, *Method in Theology*, 292).

4 Ibid., 116.

faculties, and concretely, of the gifts of the Holy Spirit, for understanding Scripture: "The grace of God and the interior help of the Holy Spirit must precede and assist, moving the heart and turning it to God, opening the eyes of the mind, and giving 'joy and ease to everyone in assenting to the truth and believing it'. To bring about an ever deeper understanding of revelation, the same Holy Spirit constantly brings faith to completion by His gifts" (*DV* 5). Such assistance by divine grace and the gifts of the Holy Spirit is necessary for learning the divine truths because these include "divine treasures which totally transcend the understanding of the human mind" (*DV* 6).

These statements, besides reminding us of theology's aim of transforming us into God, recall Bonaventure's insistence on fallen nature and the conditions placed upon theology due to our wounded intellectual capacity. Thus, on account of the sublimity of both the origin and the aim of theology, which is divine life, we are moving primarily in the realm of mystery. Our minds *in via* (in need of the healing process through continual hierarchization), are called to understand divine life in the only way possible to us, which is quite limited. In Holy Scripture, this mysterious life only is hinted at, for the very reason that it is humanized. The analogy of the Incarnation often is applied here to depict God's Word assuming human words. Entirely adapted to our weakness as fallen creatures, this 'hinting at' by the inspired words might be viewed as exemplaristic creativity in God's hands. While we cannot fully understand what is signified, we are invited to experience this knowledge, though symbols. Christ, key Exemplar of all exemplarism, is the source and the end of all theological knowledge. Christ, through his humanity, is the ultimate reason why the Council compares our understanding of Sacred Scripture with Mary's interior experience of living in continual contact with her Son: "There is a growth in the understanding of the realities and the words which have been handed down. This happens through the contemplation and study made by believers, who treasure these things in their hearts (Lk. 2:19, 51), through the intimate understanding of spiritual things they experience" (*DV* 8).

Since authentic sanctity usually is typified as charity, theology can be a road to holiness only when knowing God is a loving union with Him through wisdom. How this loving union is developed in each case is a mystery, a unique interaction of theological truths and personal reactions to them. This often may involve inner struggles; which accounts for Bonaventure's specifying for theologians the energetic practice of mortification and the virtues. The struggle may be like that of Jacob with his mysterious visitor.[5] If so — and this appears to be true for Bonaventure and could be for us — our only motive must be to obtain the blessing (*ut boni fiamus*).

Recently we have become more appreciative of the experience of the theologian as a source of doctrine. However, this was something Bonaventure apparently presumed as necessary for knowledge: *Nunquam intelligit nisi expertus*,[6] and *Nemo novit nisi qui probat*.[7] Such an attitude certainly is not exclusive to Bonaventure, but was part of the theological environment of his day. When we question the Middle Ages about their doctrine on the Gifts of the Holy Spirit, to take one example, we at first may be surprised by the plethora of details afforded us, ultimately only backed by one Scriptural reference (Is. 11:2). Bonaventure's access to certain traditional doctrines, as in the case of the Gifts of the Holy Spirit, cannot suffice for the richness of his own teaching. His treatise is not simply a compendium of prior literature on the subject. I suspect his ardent convictions principally spring from his own spiritual life upon which he confidently bases the minute nuances concerning life in the Holy Spirit.

This supposition seems more plausible when we consider that theologians of the Middle Ages worked together as 'schools of thought', unconcerned about being singled out as authors. The fact accounts for the eventual discovery of works of lesser known masters intermingled in those of leaders of schools, for example, the works of William of St.-Thierry which recently were extricated carefully from St. Bernard's output. Close personal interaction lends itself to sharing confidences, many of which originate in spiritual experiences, in an age when theology and spirituality were not separate disciplines. Apparently, then, theologians not only shared their experience with confreres, but traditional teaching itself went beyond doctrinal transmission and constituted a shared *Erlebnis* confided by the forefathers to their spiritual sons (e.g. Alexander of Hales to Bonaventure).[8]

Now, over against personal experience one might take a different standpoint, or even hesitate for serious reasons. The objective standards set for theology by revealed data and official Church teaching appear to restrict the interior freedom necessary for spiritual life. The existence of authorized norms might seem to warn against too tight a bond between

---

5 Bonaventure uses Jacob's wrestling with the angel to encourage us to perseverance in prayer (*De annun B.V.M.*, 6 [IX, 686a–b]).

6 *Scien. Chr.* q. 7, concl. (V, 43a).

7 *Brev.* 5, 6, 8 (V, 260a).

8 This was entirely the mind of Saint Augustine, whose supreme love for wisdom found its fullness in sharing this gift with others: "Now I at least love Wisdom for herself alone. . . But what measure can the

theology and spiritual life. Respect for the objective criteria of belief, which situates the student in a role subservient to the subject matter, could interfere, if not collide, with personal convictions. Such personal convictions should stem from the different subjective experiences upon contact with the mysteries of faith through contemplation. Should not the spiritual life remain a secret place in which one freely experiments with personal concepts about God, some of which concepts may, at least initially, be entertained unwittingly in distorted forms? And, perhaps if they settle into and impress the affective part of our fallen nature, might not a reaction to such inner experience ultimately be at the root of some theological dissent? Such reasoning would urge us to establish and safeguard definite boundaries between theologizing and the more personal, interior life.

In Bonaventure's teaching on exemplarism we may anchor a solution to the question, both about interior spiritual freedom and theological dissent. As I suggested in my introduction, "to know God on our own terms, that is, outside an interpersonal relationship with Him, inherently distorts the object of theological study, to say nothing of the harm it may cause to the human spirit."[9] It may not so much be a problem of experiencing distorted personal reactions as of lacking true intimacy with God. Clearer perception of the Divine Exemplar is an ideal to which we constantly must aspire, as we pass from the weaker exemplars (our theological ideas *in via*) in a purifying and healing upward and honest search toward theological truth. But, how far can exemplars take us?

What St. Bonaventure chiefly rejected in Aristotle is the latter's failure to accept Plato's exemplarism. As a consequence, in this matter we meet one of the more characteristic differences between our Seraphic Doctor and Saint Thomas Aquinas. As we have seen, through exemplarism we are placed in direct contact with the reality represented symbolically. In theology, ideas about God are the very means of our interrelationship with Him. Fidelity to truth demands uprightness on our part. Now, no student of theology, be his intentions ever so exalted, personally can feel equal to the demands of the subject matter; surely not at the beginning, but neither at the end of his studies, when the mysteries studied loom ever larger before him.[10] Thus, before the mystery of revealed truth (which always remains

---

love of that beauty have in which I not only do not envy others, but even long for as many as possible to seek it, gaze upon it, grasp it and enjoy it with me; knowing that our friendship will be the closer, the more thoroughly we are in the object of our love?" (*Soliloquies,* I, 22).

9 p. 11

10 St. John of the Cross encourages us to honor God greatly by conceiving of Him as far above our capacity to understand Him (*Cántico Espiritual* 1, 12).

far more mysterious than comprehended), our attitude only can be of respect and awe. Such an attitude both permits the widest margin of freedom for interior activity and prohibits an attitude of defiance when our own ideas do not appear to agree with objective norms. In the latter case, even though the Church sometimes imposes silence, she respects the secrets of conscience, as another inviolable mystery.[11] On beholding the limitless reach of any single theological truth beyond its conceptual representation, we become more ready to doubt our own theological findings than to resent opposition to our statements.[12] In this regard, Bonaventure's statements about the role of piety in learning are particularly relevant. As we saw, he urges us to think of God's truths in the highest and most devout possible way.[13] J. G. Bougerol, commenting on this teaching, sees the gift of piety as that which empowers knowledge to become wisdom.[14]

Touching the truth through exemplarism also directs us to the demands of the intellectual life in St. Bonaventure. The hearty practice of the virtues, implying mortification of the senses and the faculties, effects the purification needed to behold the truth, not as we prefer it to be, but as God communicates it to us. This results in *sursumactio*, a rising above ourselves, which involves the action of grace and of our own effort until we reach union with God. In Bernard Lonergan's system, this undertaking could be compared to the process of 'transcendence by conscious intentionality'. By becoming more and more conscious of our rational procedure, of the necessary and universal steps in learning (experiencing, understanding, judging, and deciding), we rise above our personal limitations, and subjectivity then coincides with objectivity.

Such attitudes toward theology can be grouped within the consideration of theological study as an experience of Sacred Scripture. Saint Bonaventure often called theology simply by the name of 'Sacred Scripture' because of the close similarity between the object of theology and Scripture. The inner experience of the theologian during his hours of study are parallel to that of anyone scrutinizing the Word of God. This Word challenges the student to

---

11 Not all difference of opinion takes on the force of dissent. Many theologians whose viewpoints were at first silenced, later were vindicated (e.g., St. Thomas of Aquinas, and in our times, Père Lagrange, Henri de Lubac, Hans Urs von Balthasar, Yves Congar, etc.).

12 St. Teresa of Avila, far from pressing others to accept her convictions, manifested a healthy skepticism, expecting her mentors to rescue her from error. See: *Libro de la Vida,* letter-epilogue, 2–4; *Camino de Perfección,* prologue, 1; *Las Moradas del Castillo Interior,* epilogue, 24; *Cuentas de conciencia,* 53ª, 9.

13 *Myst. Trin.* q. 1, a. 2, concl. (V, 55b–56a); *Brev.* 1, 2, 3–5 (V, 211a–b); *Hex.* 9, 23 (V, 375b–376a).

14 "Sur le sens de Dieu," *EF* 14 (1964), 23–30.

submit to the transforming life flowing from it.

2. Theology and prayer

In an age that champions academic freedom, what can be gained by Bonaventure's approach to theology as spiritual life? When theorizing descends to practical applications, the two extremes must be avoided. In our case, it may be best to invoke personal experience in order to outline the twofold difficulty: on one hand, of divorcing prayer from intellectual life and, on the other hand, of confusing the two.

Let us consider the following circumstances many of us may have felt as students of theology. Soon after beginning studies, a dilemma arises. Prayer life, which has been the driving force behind the vocation and has led one to enroll in theological studies, now calls for serious modifications. Invariably, a way of adapting prayer life to studies is sought, so as to fit prayer into a new context of intellectual demands. Certainly, a life of study, with its multiple demands on time, warrants a change in the organization of one's prayer life. Much more time must be consumed in study than in prayer. We observe from the life of Saint Ignatius of Loyola, and from his dispositions for scholastics in the Society of Jesus, that time allotted for prayer was reduced drastically for those who, after finishing their initial years of spiritual formation, had embarked upon a life of study.[15] We admire his judiciousness in governing others, as well as his humility and fortitude concerning himself when, in order to persevere in studies, he rejected the recurring temptations to indulge in mystical consolations.[16] Such a sacrifice evidently proceeded from a sense of submission to the divine will even at the risk of losing what first appeared to be an extraordinary grace.

Evidently, then, we cannot question such drastic modifications made at the outset of any theology career. A phase of one's life has passed. The all-absorbing dedication to prayer we find in young persons who recently have undergone a personal conversion eventually gives birth to a mission in life. So, such exclusive dedication to prayer usually constitutes the necessary prelude to the apostolate and to the election of a state of life. We see this reflected in the lives of most of the saints whose 'desert experience'

---

15 "Considering the end of study," St. Ignatius wrote, "the scholastics can hardly give themselves to prolonged meditations" *Epist. Ignat.*, III, 510. See the excellent article "Finding God in All Things" by Maurice Giuliani, in *Finding God in All Things,* trans. W.J. Young (Chicago: Henry Regnery Company, 1958), 3–24. This article originally appeared in *Christus* (Paris), No. 6, April 1955.

16 See *Autobiography* of St. Ignatius of Loyola, #19 and #31.

was a normal prerequisite for their self-denying gift of integral service to the Church. One's psychological readjustment justifies a period, more or less prolonged, of solitude and silence dedicated to the mystery of Christ who personally calls each of us to transcend our old ways of thinking and feeling before reassuming activity.

An eventual position to be feared is that theological study becomes a lofty pinnacle from which all other personal decisions are faced, including those vital questions which could compromise the spiritual life. Now, prayer usually is considered to play, if not the most essential part, at least a key role in the interior life. But, if prayer is not cherished as the freest and most human kind of activity, transcending all theological considerations, and within which form and content merely are means to an end, what eventually will become of our interior freedom?

What appears unacceptable is not our limiting time for prayer, but that our psychological and spiritual focus in prayer should shift to a new center of gravity. Often this change is so subtle that we do not recognize it, particularly because theology professedly has God as its object. If theology, at least implicitly, deals with God, it would seem that no danger could arise here. Even the change that theology has undergone on account of field specialization does not appear to touch this question.

The change which is referred to as 'subtle' is not the change in lifestyle, as that is what remains most external to the problem. The subtle change is the interior one. We may suspect at this juncture a questionable change of heart from *homo orans* to *homo doctrinae studiosus*. No one who has spent a few years dedicated to prayer, whether in a novitiate or in the privacy of one's home, is insensitive enough consciously to abandon the Person with whom he has been in dialogue for so long. Rather, what happens inside at first even may seem a praiseworthy act of renunciation. We most willingly assume the lifestyle and the duties of the student, realizing that God's ways often are mysterious, preferring not to inquire deeper into the validity of our intentions, because they are included in our abandonment to God.

The indefinable change that often takes place, whether immediately or gradually, substitutes the life of personal sanctification for the scholarly life. The scholarly life, together with the discipline implied in regular schedules, hours of tedious application which often render less fruit than the effort invested, the suffocatingly competitive atmosphere we frequently find in university libraries—cannot all this exertion still constitute the offering rendered to God? What other opportunities for virtue can be expected for the student who, in any case, has no time to indulge in apostolic labors or external works of charity?

The real danger lies in subordinating the spiritual life to theology, and considering the latter primarily on the level of truths or facts to be learned, but rarely as a way inherently suitable of approaching God.

For the theologian's intention to remain vigorous and entirely sustain his intellectual efforts, prayer must be practiced as one's principle source of inspiration. After all, prayer is where faith is nurtured, and theology simply is the quest to understand our faith. For this reason, St. Augustine sees prayer as the indispensable condition for understanding: *«Orent ut intellegant!»*

Prayer, as described by Fr. Charles A. Bernard, opens an infinite horizon before which we place each of our thoughts and, more so, all our being. Bernard explains that "there is a dialectical relation between prayer and reflection."[17] The theologian, therefore, must be willing to sacrifice some part of his daily schedule in chapel. We must be willing to approach the hour of prayer as the painful experience of 'time lost'. Gradually, as the mind becomes accustomed, it takes a more passive role before the infinite void, in a milieu of rest. Eventually too, the theologian becomes aware that more is done in his hour of prayer than in all the hours spent at his desk. *In oratione datur homini intelligentia Scripturarum.*[18] There is no explanation for this. It is simply the conclusion a theologian invariably reaches from personal verification over a significant period. There is some congruence to be found in this experience, which I will try to justify as follows.

Living faith is a living source of theology. An oscillating movement exists between faith and study. A good habit is formed by letting God take over and 'capture the mind', as Bonaventure expresses it. Our thoughts, principally our theological reasoning, must be placed under the light God alone gives. This prepares the interaction of which the Seraphic Doctor speaks between taste and *contuitio*, which is characteristic of the gift of wisdom. We taste the sweetness of divine truth, a tasting that when raised to the conscious level, is perceived as a kind of knowledge. However, the principle effect of this tasting experience is to make what we have been studying understandable in a new way, by means of *contuitio* which accompanies it. The special kind of knowledge that results in us simply is experienced through what usually we call 'realizing'. Another way to say this in English is "it dawned on me," meaning that something became apparent, not *primarily* because we reasoned it out, even though such rational

---

17 From class notes transcribed by author, Rome, 17 January 1994.

18 *Comm. Lc.* 9, 55 (VII, 234b).

work must be necessary.[19]   Rather, something independent of our thinking processes overcomes us, much as the sun at dawn after we have walked through the night which first bewilders our sense of time because its radiance arrives too gradually to be verified. Because of the disproportion between the higher synthetic insight attained and the various conceptual elements which have led up to this experience, God's intervention is suspected to be near, subtly at work. If this is one of the meanings expressed by illumination, an increasing dependence on God is deemed to be in order, both to rise above the limitations of human reasoning and to receive what no human curiosity could ever claim to merit.

Attempts have been made to ascertain the illuminating influence of God upon study. Sometimes, a 'motivating and ordering influence' of grace upon the soul is judged necessary. Although grace does not substitute for the effort put forth by the theologian at his desk, a complementarity is inferred between effort and grace, no matter how superior the latter principle may be. Seeking grace, we bring to the chapel ourselves and our study, that is, all our thoughts and feelings, which are the sum of our interior life at any given moment. The reward for submitting everything on our mind to God is the satisfaction eventually experienced of being admitted into God's way of seeing these same things. This is the perspective prayer, in due time, brings back to study. And it is received by those who are willing to "lose time" until it comes, even though that is not their intention. This new perspective, arising not from ourselves, often can be surprising. Yet always it involves our entire selves in an intimate way through our growing union with God, a union which is the chief result of prayer. The two subjectivities, God's and our own, become closer partners in theology. Divine intimacy through theology will grow as long as prayer remains the lifespring of theology.

3. Theology and leisure

The rigors of Bonaventure's rational method are evidenced in his theological works, and yet the preferred definition of theology remains the *habitus*, or affective disposition alone, with which the theologian is invested. Evidently theology, by virtue of this habit, becomes an entire way of life, so deep as to permeate other human activities, all of which are integrated under the guidance of wisdom, the chief gift of the Holy Spirit.

---

19 In Spanish, this expression is usually translated as *caer en la cuenta.*

Bonaventure made very clear from the beginning that theology purely and simply is the gift of wisdom. And because "all wisdom comes from the Lord" (Si. 1:1), our role is primarily receptive. The nature of this particular gift demands from us not the passivity of quietism, but an openness that is peacefully attentive to the spiritual movements coming from God, in order to second these movements. Interferences from our own thought processes, if not controlled, may give way to intellectual activism and gradually ignore *Christus, unus omnium magister*. A life of study, then, challenges us to harmonize our own labor and God's assistance. As this assistance grows, our dependence upon it increases without, however, our ever renouncing the strenuous effort needed to respond faithfully to God's activity. This effort has nothing to do with curiosity. We begin to experience how more is done on God's time than on our own. After restful moments in prayer, we may realize more has been accomplished inside us, producing a new perspective for comprehending, or reordering, our previous rational labor.

To explain this disproportion between effort and results, we could begin by contextualizing our study. As we have seen in Chapter Five,[20] all theological activity is affected for better or for worse by the culture in which it thrives. Today's context would seem to be at the origin of our exaggerated emphasis on acquiring knowledge (*scientia*) and then imposing intricate analytical structures upon our findings. Meanwhile we neglect contemplative insight and wisdom which are parents to a transcendent synthesis. Greedily, we concern ourselves with knowing many things (*multa*), but our hearts are too glutted to know well or in depth (*multum*). The more we gain in extension the more we lose in intensity. We might qualify the backdrop of contemporary academic culture as "intellectual consumerism."

A comparison can be found in Martha's attitude (Lk. 10:38–42). The activity of Martha, who personifies busy research and analysis, certainly is necessary. This activity however is only a preliminary aspect of learning. The final aspect crowns our efforts: contemplation of the transcendent synthesis. Without this result, our efforts do not achieve the *unum necessarium,* the better part, which Mary enjoyed, and which Our Lord promised would not be taken away from her. A main objection, similar to Martha's, may be raised: we seem to have no time to sit down and savor the fruits of our labor. From this standpoint, modern ears may be surprised by the ancient biblical advice: "Leisure gives the scribe the chance to acquire wisdom; a man with few commitments can grow wise" (Si. 38:24 *NJB*).

---

20 Particularly M.D. Chenu's comments on monastic theology.

Leisure is not the end result of this work, but rather a necessary condition for it.

The famous, penetrating essay by Josef Pieper, "Leisure the Basis of Culture," is a prophetic denunciation of a culture that virtually excludes the possibility for wisdom.[21]   What threatens culture itself, Mr. Pieper contends, is our incapacity of understanding or even tolerating leisure, as it was understood and enjoyed from classical times into the Middle Ages.[22] Today intellectual activity is seen as one more form of work and is subject to the "total work" mentality.[23]   This attitude automatically excludes the conditions necessary for contemplation,[24] because knowledge involves some amount of nonactivity, the receptive-contemplative element.[25]   Unless we respect this vital element, which Bonaventure's age took for granted, wisdom becomes unattainable.   As a consequence, knowledge without leisure cannot escape the fate of all reasoning without contemplation —rationalism, utilitarianism, and even skepticism— traits that enervate intellectual development.

Due to intellectual consumerism, a university career today often amounts to an insatiable acquisition of data, whether scientific or historical.[26] Because there is nothing specifically utilitarian about contemplation and the leisure necessary for it to thrive, the humanities likewise are threatened in

---

21   Josef Pieper, *Leisure the Basis of Culture,* trans. Alexander Dru (New York: Pantheon Books, 1952; reprint, New American Library, 1963).

22   "The value we set on work and on leisure is very far from being the same as that of the Greek and Roman world, or of the Middle Ages, for that matter—so very different that the men of the past would have been incapable of understanding the modern conception of work, just as we are unable to understand their notion of leisure simply and directly, without an effort of thought" (Ibid., 22).

23   "Nowadays the whole field of intellectual activity, not excepting the province of philosophical culture, has been overwhelmed by the modern ideal of work and is at the mercy of its totalitarian claims" (Ibid., 24).

24   "Is there such a thing as pure 'intellectual contemplation'—to adopt the terminology of the schools? In antiquity the answer given was always yes; in modern philosophy, for the most part, the answer given is no" (Ibid., 25).

25   "Our knowledge in fact includes an element of nonactivity, of purely receptive vision—though it is certainly not essentially human; it is, rather, the fulfillment of the highest promise in man, and thus, again, truly human (just as Aquinas calls the *vita contemplativa* 'non proprie humana sed superhumana', not really human but superhuman, although it is the noblest mode of human life)" (Ibid., 27).

26   The acquisition of knowledge for its own sake, leaving no time for relaxed savoring, reminds me of the young disciple who was reputed far and wide as a genius. When his master was questioned about his disciple's reputation, the master replied: "Truth to tell, the fellow reads so much I don't see how he could ever find the time to know anything" (Anthony de Mello, "Ignorance," in *One Minute Wisdom* [New York: Doubleday Image, 1985], 22).

their very existence.[27] Since contemplative intuition provides our knowledge with a foothold, or an ulterior vantage point, from which to judge itself, the absence of contemplation has another unfortunate effect. To remain on the purely scientific level ends in intellectual relativism: one can know any number of things, while proudly admitting that nothing can be affirmed as objectively true.[28]

Certainly it is not my intent to advocate intellectual idleness. Leisure is not idleness, and the Middle Ages understood that *acedia,* paradoxically, manifests itself in an incapacity for leisure, bringing forth its first fruits in restlessness.[29] Seen through the medieval lens, our workaholic ethic would be reproached as an unconscious repugnance for work. Excessive busyness was seen to spring from a refusal to be at one with oneself and with reality; possibly from a unsettled, or bad, conscience. In modern times, mental activism seems to come as natural to us as our unintentional materialism.[30]

For work to be truly human, we need space for receiving the superhuman influences upon us, by which God himself participates in the work process. The sense behind resting on Sunday is the same. Sunday rest is for receiving and celebrating the source of all activity, God as Creator, and enough free time in which to recognize ourselves as created. When we permit God to act in us, even (and especially) by restfully opening our hearts to him, he fills us with His energy, which then operates through us as his instruments, while restoring and rectifying our defective creatureliness.[31]

---

27   See Robert E. Proctor's *Education's Great Amnesia: Reconsidering the Humanities from Petrarch to Freud* (Bloomington: Indiana University Press, 1988), winner of the Ness Book Award. The author, after reviewing the history of the humanities in education, today finds us bereft of them and of a true understanding of what they are.

28   After thirty years as professor at Cornell University, University of Chicago, and Hebrew University, the conclusion of Allan Bloom is a sharp condemnation of relativism (*The Closing of the American Mind* [New York: Simon & Schuster, 1987]).

29   St. Thomas sees acedia as a sin against the third commandment, because acedia does not permit the "rest of the spirit in God" (*Summa Theologica,* II, II, 35, 3 ad 1; *Quaest. disp. de malo,* 11, 3 ad 2).

30   In the 1830s, Alexis de Tocqueville wrote of a "restlessness in the midst of prosperity" which he observed in the Americans, and that their "minds are more anxious and on edge." He attributed this restlessness to a spirit of greed: "they clutch everything and hold nothing fast"; "they never stop thinking of the good things they have not got." At the same time, he detected that this restlessness was accompanied by sadness, even in very educated persons: "In America I have seen the freest and best educated of men in circumstances the happiest to be found in the world; yet it seemed to me that a cloud habitually hung on their brow, and they seemed serious and almost sad even in their pleasure" (Alexis de Tocqueville, *Democracy in America,* trans. George Lawrence, ed. J.P. Mayer [New York: Doubleday, Anchor Books, 1969] pp. 565, 536, 538).

31   Two poems by Charles Péguy illustrate this better than any prose analysis. The poems are called "Abandon" and "Sommeil." In the latter poem, God says about the insomniacs: "Ils ont le courage de

When speaking of prayer, I mentioned that the lifestyle is what remains most external to the problem of harmonizing prayer and study. We might clarify that theology is a way of life, although not a lifestyle, because it involves both internal and external aspects. In today's terminology, we could call it a 'mindset'. Or better, a 'heartset', because it involves important elements that are untraceable to the mind alone. The production of theological works calls for a way of life that favors it, which in turn supposes a cultural environment that makes such a way of life possible. As the environment of the thirteenth century recedes further and further from our own, it becomes more difficult for us to appreciate why Bonaventure could equate theology with wisdom, even judging by the atmosphere we often find in our seminaries and other institutions of higher learning.

Priests sometimes state how, in their youth, seminaries were, unfortunately (in their opinion) more like monasteries. This refers to the rule of silence, the absence of apostolates, and the normal protections against outside distractions.[32] An enforced regime of solitude and prayer no longer appears to be possible.[33] Where are we to find an adequate answer to the challenge of providing an atmosphere conducive to the wisdom-theology ideal? It seems that when an entire culture militates against serenity, the principal countercultural action only can be waged by the individual. The aim, at least directly, is not to change the culture, but to live in fidelity to the truth one studies. Even when a culture may favor leisure, this advantage does not suffice for a person to persevere in his search for peace of soul and the presence of God. Twenty centuries ago, Our Lord used to go off to lonely places to pray.

---

travailler. Ils n'ont pas le courage de ne rien faire. / Ils ont la vertu de travailler. Ils n'ont pas la vertu de ne rien faire. / De se détendre. De se reposer. De dormir. / Les malheureux ils ne savent pas ce qui est bon. / Ils gouvernent très bien leurs affaires pendant le jour. / Mais ils ne veulent pas m'en confier le gouvernement pendant la nuit. / Comme si je n'étais pas capable d'en assurer le gouvernement pendant une nuit" (*Basic Verities* [Chicago: Regnery, 1965] 138).

32   It is still true that the Church recommends an atmosphere of silence: "The whole seminary program, permeated with a cultivation of reverence and silence. . ." (*Optatam totius,* 11). My comments are based on my experience as a teacher in a diocesan seminary.

33   However, the Council seems to favor the leisure necessary for reflection by the comment: "Excessive multiplying of subjects and classes is to be avoided" (*Optatam totius,* 17).

✠   ✠   ✠

What Bonaventure ultimately teaches is how to live. For us, such a message is critical. For Bonaventure, if wisdom is lacking, we do not have theology. Theology's context involves a triple submission: to Sacred Scripture, in assiduous contact with God through prayer, and with an attitude emanating from leisure. This context seems to make up the soil in which the seed of wisdom is planted and flourishes. In an age in which theology often is treated as another commodity to be submitted to our minds, the task may appear impossible. This is where the effort it takes to become holy must be engaged. If theology is to remain faithful to the Revelation it attempts to explain, the theologian must live by the wisdom the God of all theology proclaimed from the cross in his own 'transitus'.[34] Then theology as a spiritual life means to assume the position of the Crucified, by allowing the truth we are studying to transform our entire being.

---

34 The Latin *transitus* is synonymous to *Pascha*.

SELECTED BIBLIOGRAPHY

Primary Sources: The Works of Saint Bonaventure

Critical Editions

Doctoris Seraphici S. Bonaventurae Opera Omnia. Ed. PP. Collegii a S.
  Bonaventura. 10 vols. Quaracchi: Collegium S. Bonaventurae,
  1882–1902.
Collationes in Hexaemeron et Bonaventuriana quaedam selecta. Ed. F.
  M. Delorme. Quaracchi: Collegium S. Bonaventurae, 1934.
Sancti Bonaventurae Sermones Dominicales. Ed. Jacques Guy Bourgerol.
  Grottaferrata: Collegio S. Bonaventura, 1977.
*Metodologia del sapere nel sermone di s. Bonaventura «Unus est magister
  vester Christus.»* Ed. Renato Russo. Grottaferrata: Editiones
  Collegii S. Bonaventurae, 1982.
Sermones de Tempore. Ed. Jacques Guy Bougerol. Paris: Editions
  Franciscaines, 1990.

English Translations

Works of St. Bonaventure. Vol. I: *De reductione artium ad theologiam.*
  Introd., Trans., and Comm. Emma Thérèse Healy. Saint
  Bonaventure, N.Y.: The Franciscan Institute, 1955.
Works of St. Bonaventure. Vol. II: *Itinerarium mentis in Deum.* Introd.,
  Trans., and Comm. Philotheus Boehner. Saint Bonaventure, N.Y.:
  The Franciscan Institute, 1956.
Works of St. Bonaventure. Vol. III: *Disputed Questions on the Mystery of
  the Trinity.* Introd. and Trans. Zachary Hayes. Saint
  Bonaventure, N.Y.: The Franciscan Institute, 1979.
Works of St. Bonaventure. Vol. IV: *Disputed Questions on the Knowledge
  of Christ.* Introd. and Trans. Zachary Hayes. Saint Bonaventure,
  N.Y.: The Franciscan Institute, 1992.

194

Works of St. Bonaventure. Vol. V: *Writings Concerning the Franciscan Order.* Introd. and Trans. Dominic Monti. Saint Bonaventure, N.Y.: The Franciscan Institute, 1994.

The Works of St. Bonaventure. 5 Vols. Trans. José de Vinck. Paterson, N.J.: St. Anthony Guild Press, 1960–1970.

Major and Minor Life of St. Francis, with excerpts from other works by St. Bonaventure. Trans. Benen Fahy. In *St. Francis of Assisi: Writings and Early Biographies, English Omnibus of the Sources for the Life of St. Francis.* Ed. Marion A. Habig. Chicago: Franciscan Herald Press, 1973. 627–851.

What Manner of Man? Sermons on Christ by St. Bonaventure. Trans., Introd., and Comm. Zachary Hayes. Chicago: Franciscan Herald Press: 1974.

Rooted in Faith: Homilies to a Contemporary World by St. Bonaventure. Trans. and Introd. Marigwen Schumacher. Chicago: Franciscan Herald Press, 1974.

Bonaventure. The Soul's Journey into God, The Tree of Life, The Life of St. Francis. Trans. and Introd. Ewert Cousins. Pref. Ignatius Brady. New York: Paulist Press, 1978.

The Disciple and the Master. St. Bonaventure's Sermons on St. Francis of Assisi. Trans., Ed., and Introd. Eric Doyle. Chicago: Franciscan Herald Press, 1983.

Bringing forth Christ, the Son of God. Five Feasts of the Child Jesus. St. Bonaventure. Trans. and Introd. Eric Doyle. Oxford: SLG Press, 1984.

Other Primary Sources

Patristic and Medieval

"Alexander of Hales." *Summa fratris Alexandri.* Vols. I– IV. Ed. Quaracchi, 1924–1948. (For problems of authenticity, see V. Doucet, "The History of the Problem of the Authenticity of the Summa," *FS* 7 [1947]: 26–41; 274–312.)

_____. *Prolegomena.* Ed. V. Doucet. Quaracchi, 1948.

_____. *Glossa in I, II, III, IV Sent.* Quaracchi, 1951–1957.

Alexander of Hales. *Quaestiones antequam esset frater*. Quaracchi, 1960.

Anselm of Canterbury. *Opera omnia*. Vols. I–VI. Ed. F.S. Schmitt. Edinburgh, 1946–1961.

Augustine. *Opera omnia*. *PL* 32–45. 1841–1865.

Bernard of Clairvaux. *Opera omnia*. Eds. Jean Leclercq, Henri Rochais, and Charles Talbot. Rome: Editiones Cistercienses, 1957–1958.

Chronica fratris Salimbene de Adam. Vol. 32 of *Monumenta Germaniae Historica: Scriptorum*. Hannover and Leipzig: O. Holder-Egger, 1912.

Francis of Assisi. *Die Opuscula des hl. Franziskus von Assisi. Neue textkritische Edition*. Ed. Kajetan Eßer. Grottaferrata: Collegium S. Bonaventurae, 1976.

Hugh of St. Victor. *Opera omnia*. *PL* 175–177. 1854.

Pseudo-Dionysius Areopagita. *Opera omnia*. *PG* 3. 1857.

Richard of St. Victor. *Opera omnia*. *PL* 196. 1855.

Robert Grosseteste. *De luce seu de inchoatione formarum*. In: *Die philosophischen Werke des Robert Grosseteste, Bischof von Lincoln*. Münster: Ed. L. Baur, 1912. 51–59.

Speculum perfectionis ou Mémoires de frère Léon sur la seconde partie de la vie de saint François d'Assise I. Ed. Paul Sabatier. Manchester: University Press, 1928.

Thomas of Aquinas. *Summa theologiae*. Biblioteca de Autores Cristianos. Madrid: Editorial la Católica, 1951–1952.

Secondary Sources

Books

Alszeghy, Zoltan. *Grundformen der Liebe: die Theorie der Gottesliebe bei dem hl. Bonaventura*. Roma: Typis Pontificiae Universitatis Gregorianae, 1946.

Balthasar, Hans Urs von. *Fächer der Stile*. Vol. 2 of *Herrlichkeit: eine theologische Ästhetik*. Einsiedeln: Johannes Verlag, 1961–1962.

Baum, Hermann. *Das Licht des Gewissens: Zu Denkstrukturen Bonaventuras*. Frankfurt: Peter Lang, 1990.

Beauchemin, Félix. *Le savoir au service de l'amour*. Montréal: Librairie de St. François, 1933.

Benigar, Aloysius. *Compendium theologiae spiritualis*. Roma: Tip. "Pax et Bonum", 1964².

Bernard, Charles A. *Théologie affective*. Paris: Les Editions du Cerf, 1984.

Bettoni, Efrem. *Il problema della conoscibilità di Dio nella scuola francescana: Alessandro d'Ales, S. Bonaventura, Duns Scoto*. Padova: Cedam, 1950.

_____. *Saint Bonaventure*. Trans. Angelus Gambatese. Notre Dame: University Press, 1964.

Bissen, Jean-Marie. *L'exemplarisme divin selon S. Bonaventure*. Paris: J. Vrin, 1929.

Blasucci, Antonio. *La teologia spirituale di S. Bonaventura*. Firenze: Città di Vita, 1974.

Bonafede, Giulio. *Il pensiero francescano nel secolo XIII*. Palermo: G. Mori, 1952.

Bonnefoy, Jean François. *Le Saint Esprit et ses dons selon S. Bonaventure*. Paris: J. Vrin, 1929.

Bougerol, Jacques-Guy. *St. Bonaventure et la sagesse chrétienne*. Maîtres spirituels. Paris: Editions du Seuil, 1963.

_____. *Introduction to the Works of Bonaventure*. Trans. José de Vinck. Paterson, N.J.: St. Anthony Guild Press, 1964.

_____. *Saint Bonaventure un maître de sagesse*. Paris: Editions Franciscaines, 1966.

_____. *Solo i poveri possono capire: San Bonaventura e l'uomo d'oggi*. Roma: Studium, 1975.

Catazzo, Euthymius. *De Iustitia et peccato originali iuxta S. Bonaventuram*. Vicenza: Terz'Ordine Francescano - Convento S. Lucia, 1942.

Chenu, Marie-Dominique. *La théologie comme science au XIIIe siècle*. Paris: J. Vrin, 1957³.

_____. *La théologie au douzième siècle*. Paris: J. Vrin, 1957.

_____. *Is Theology a Science?* Trans. A.H.N. Green-Armytage. London: Burns & Oates, 1959.

_____. *Nature, Man, and Society in the Twelfth Century*. Selected, Trans. and Ed. Jerome Taylor and Lester K. Little. Pref. Etienne Gilson. Chicago: University Press, 1968.

Copleston, Frederick. *Medieval Philosophy*. Vol. 2 of *A History of Philosophy*. New York: Doubleday, 1993.

Corvino, Francesco. *Bonaventura da Bagnoregio: francescano e pensatore.* Saggi, 53. Bari: Dedalo libri, 1980.

Crivelli, Riccardo. "L'esperienza cristiana: figura, senso e logica secondo S. Bonaventura." Thesis, Pontificia Università Gregoriana, 1983.

Dady, Mary Rachael. *The Theory of Knowledge of Saint Bonaventure.* Catholic University of America Philosophical Studies, 51. Washington: Catholic University of America Press, 1939.

De Ghellinck, Joseph. *Le mouvement théologique du XIIe siècle: Etudes, recherches et documents.* Bruges: Editions "De Tempel," 1948[2].

Del Zotto, Cornelio. *La Teologia dell'immagine in San Bonaventura.* Vicenza: Ed. L.I.E.F., 1977.

De Wachter, Maurits. *Le péché actuel selon Saint Bonaventure.* Paris: Editions Franciscaines, 1967.

De Wulf, Maurice. *History of Mediaeval Philosophy.* Trans. Ernest C. Messenger. 3rd ed. New York: Longmans, Green and Co., 1936–1938.

Gaddi, Alessandro. *Il carattere pedagogico-mistico della filosofia di S. Bonaventura.* Bagnoregio: Centro Studi Bonaventuriani, 1958.

Gerken, Alexander. *Theologie des Wortes: Das Verhältnis von Schöpfung und Inkarnation bei Bonaventura.* Düsseldorf: Patmos Verlag, 1963.

Gilson, Etienne. *The Unity of Philosophical Experience.* London: Sheed & Ward, 1938.

_____. *The Christian Philosophy of Saint Augustine.* Trans. L.E.M. Lynch. New York: Random House, 1960.

_____. *The Philosophy of St. Bonaventure.* Trans. Dom Illtyd Trethowan and Frank J. Sheed. Paterson, N.J.: St. Anthony Guild Press, 1965.

Gneo, Corrado. *Conoscere è amare. Note di ontologia della conoscenza secondo la mente di S. Bonaventura.* Roma: L'Italia Francescana Editrice, 1985.

Gratien de Paris. *Histoire de la fondation et de l'évolution de l'Ordre des Frères Mineurs au XIIIe siècle.* Reprint of 1928 edition with updated bibliography by Mariano d'Alatri and Servus Gieben. Roma: Istituto Storico dei Cappuccini, 1982.

Guardini, Romano. *Die Lehre des hl. Bonaventura von der Erlösung: Ein Beitrag zur Geschichte und zum System der Erlösungslehre.* Düsseldorf: L. Schwann, 1921.

_____. *Systembildende Elemente in der Theologie Bonaventuras.* Ed. W. Dettloff. Leiden: Brill, 1964.

Hayes, Zachary. *The Hidden Center: Spirituality and Speculative Christology in St. Bonaventure.* St. Bonaventure, N.Y.: The Franciscan Institute, 1992².

Hellmann, J. A. Wayne. *Ordo. Untersuchung eines Grundgedankens in der Theologie Bonaventuras.* München: Verlag Ferdinand Schöningh, 1974.

Hemmerle, Klaus. *Theologie als Nachfolge. Bonaventura—ein Weg für heute.* Freiburg: Herder, 1975.

Hülsbusch, Werner. *Elemente einer Kreuzestheologie in den Spätschriften Bonaventuras.* Düsseldorf: Patmos Verlag, 1968.

Iammarrone, Giovanni. *L'antropologia bonaventuriana.* Napoli: Dehoniane, 1979.

Imle, Fanny. *Gott und Geist: das Zusammenwirken des erschaffenen und des ungeschaffen Geistes im höheren Erkenntnisakt nach Bonaventura.* Werl/Westfalen: Franziskus Druckerei, 1934.

_____. *Des geistliche Leben nach der Lehre des hl. Bonaventura.* Werl/Westfalen: Franziskus Druckerei, 1939.

Iriarte, Lazaro. *Historia Franciscana.* Valencia: Editorial Asís, 1979.

Jeauneau, Edouard. *La philosophie médiévale.* Que sais-je?, 1044. Paris: Presses Universitaires de France, 1963.

Johnson, Timothy. *Iste Pauper Clamavit: Saint Bonaventure's Mendicant Theology of Prayer.* Frankfurt: Peter Lang, 1990.

Jörgensen, Johannes. *Saint Francis of Assisi.* Trans. T. O'Connor Sloane. New York: Longmans, Green & Company, 1912.

Knowles, David. *The Evolution of Medieval Thought.* London: Longmans Green and Co., 1962.

Lambertini, Roberto. *Apologia e crescita dell'identità francescana (1255–1279).* Nuovi Studi Storici, 4. Roma: Istituto Storico Italiano per il Medio Evo, 1990.

Landini, Lawrence. *The Causes of the Clericalization of the Order of Friars Minor: 1209–1260.* Chicago: Franciscan Herald Press, 1968.

Lazzarini, Renato. *S. Bonaventura filosofo e mistico del Cristianesimo.* Milano: Fratelli Bocca, 1946.

Léthel, François-Marie. *Connaître l'amour du Christ qui surpasse toute connaissance.* Venasque: Editions du Carmel, 1989.

Lonergan, Bernard. *Insight. A Study of Human Understanding.* London: Longmans, Green and Co., 1958.

_____. *Method in Theology.* New York: Herder and Herder, 1972.

Longpré, Ephrem. *La théologie mystique de saint Bonaventure.* Quaracchi: Collegium S. Bonaventurae, 1921.

Lottin, Odon. *Psychologie et Morale aux XII et XIII siècles.* 6 vols. Gembloux: Duculot, 1942–1960.

Lutz, Eduard. *Die Psychologie Bonaventuras.* Münster: Aschendorff, 1909.

Luyckx, Bonifaz. *Die Erkenntnislehre Bonaventuras.* Münster: Aschendorff, 1923.

Marcellino da Caggio Montano. *Dottrina bonaventuriana sul peccato originale.* Bologna: Tip. S. Giuseppe, 1943.

Marthaler, Berard. *Original Justice and Sanctifying Grace in the Writings of St. Bonaventure.* Roma: Miscellanea Francescana, 1965.

Martini, Cherubino. *San Bonaventura (1274–1974): Presenza e testimonianza.* Vicenza: Edizioni ESCA, 1973.

Mathieu, Luc. *La Trinité créatrice d'après saint Bonaventure.* Paris: Editions Franciscaines, 1992.

Mauro, Letterio. *Bonaventura da Bagnoregio: Dalla «philosophia» alla «contemplatio».* Collana di monografie, 2. Genova: Accademia Ligure di Scienze e Lettere, 1976.

Ménard, André. "Structures de la foi: Contribution à l'étude d'une théologie bonaventurienne de la foi." Thesis, Faculté Catholique de Toulouse, 1971.

Merino, José Antonio. *Historia de la Filosofía Franciscana.* Madrid: B.A.C., 1993.

Mouroux, Jean. *L'expérience chrétienne: Introduction à une théologie.* Paris: Aubier, 1954.

Nguyen Van Si, Ambrogio. *Seguire e imitare Cristo secondo san Bonaventura.* Trans. Simpliciano Olgiati. Milano: Bilbioteca Francescana, 1995.

O'Donnel, Clement. *The Psychology of St. Bonaventure and St. Thomas Aquinas.* Washington: Catholic University Press, 1937.

O'Neill, Reginald. "The Meaning of our World as seen by St. Bonaventure in the Light of Exemplary Causuality." Philosophy Thesis, Fordham University, 1952.

Panofsky, Erwin. *Architecture gothique et pensée scolastique.* Trad. P. Bourdieu. Paris: Editions de Minuit, 1967.

Piazza, Leonardo. *Mediazione simbolica in S. Bonaventura.* "Presenza culturale", 2. Vicenza: L.I.E.F., 1978.

Pieper, Josef. *Scholasticism: Personalities and Problems of Medieval Philosophy*.Trans. Richard and Clara Winston. London: Faber and Faber, 1961.

Prentice, Robert. *The Psychology of Love according to St. Bonaventure.* St. Bonaventure, N.Y.: The Franciscan Institute, 1957.

Prunières, Louis. *S. Bonaventure: Itinéraire de l'âme en elle-même... Commentaire par le P. Louis Prunières.* Blois: Libr. mar. et fr., 1956.

Quinn, John F. *The Historical Constitution of St. Bonaventure's Philosophy.* Toronto: Pontifical Institute of Medieval Studies, 1973.

Quinn, Mary. *To God Alone the Glory: A Life of St. Bonaventure.* Westminster, MD: The Newman Press, 1962.

Ratzinger, Joseph. *The Theology of History in St. Bonaventure.* Trans. Zachary Hayes. Chicago: Franciscan Herald Press, 1971.

Russo, Renato. *La metodologia del sapere nel sermone di S. Bonaventura: «Unus est Magister vester, Christus».* Spicilegium Bonaventurianum, 22. Grottaferrata: Collegio S. Bonaventura, 1982.

Sakaguki, Fumi. *Der Begriff der Weisheit in den Hauptwerken Bonaventuras.* Epimeleia, Beiträge zur Philosophie, Band 12. München: Verlag Anton Pustest, 1968.

Schalück, Hermann. *Armut und Heil: Eine Untersuchung uber den Armutsgedanken in der Theologie Bonaventuras.* München: Verlag Ferdinand Schöningh, 1971.

Schlosser, Marianne. *Cognitio et amor: Zum kognitiven und voluntativen Grund der Gotteserfahrung nach Bonaventura.* München: Verlag Ferdinand Schönigh, 1990.

Sciamannini, Raniero. *La contuizione bonaventuriana.* Firenze: Città di Vita, 1957.

Sepinski, Augustin. *La psychologie du Christ chez saint Bonaventure.* Paris: J. Vrin, 1948.

Simonelli, Nicolaus. *Doctrina christocentrica Seraphici Doctoris S. Bonaventurae.* Iesi: Scuola Tip. Francescana, 1958.

Sirovic, Franz. *Der Begriff «affectus» und die Willenslehre beim hl. Bonaventura: Eine analytisch synthetische Untersuchung.* Mödling bei Wien: Missions-Druckerei St. Gabriel, 1965.

Smalley, Beryl. *The Study of the Bible in the Middle Ages.* Oxford: Blackwell, 1983[a].

Soiron, Thaddeus. *La condition du théologien*. Introduction and French adaptation by Yves Becker and Jean-Robert Hennion. Paris: Plon, 1953.

Speer, Andreas. *Triplex veritas: Wahrheitsverständnis und philosophische Denkform Bonaventuras*. Franziskanische Forschungen, 32. Werl/ Westfalen: Dietrich-Coelde-Verlag, 1987.

Strack, Bonifatius. *Christusleid im Christenleben: Ein Beitrag zur Theologie des christlichen Lebens nach dem heiligen Bonaventura*. Werl/Westfalen: Dietrich-Coelde-Verlag, 1960.

Tavard, George. *Transiency and Permanence: the Nature of Theology according to St. Bonaventure*. Bonaventure, N.Y.: The Franciscan Institute, 1954.

Tekippe, Terry. "An Investigation of the Balance between Conceptual and Primordial Knowing in Major Figures of the Western Philosophical Tradition." Ph.D. Thesis, Tulane University, 1980. Ann Arbor: University Microfilms International, 1980. Printed in 1991 by xerographic process.

Tononi, Renato. *Attesa umana e salvezza di Cristo: Una rilettura dell'opera bonaventuriana*. Brescia: Morcelliana, 1983.

Van der Laan, Hendrik. *De wijsgerige grondslag van Bonaventura's theologie*. Amsterdam: Buijten & Schipperheijn, 1968.

Van Steenberghen, Fernand. *The Philosophical Movement in the Thirteenth Century*. Edinburgh: Nelson, 1955.

Veuthey, Léon. *S. Bonaventurae philosophia christiana*. Roma: Officium Libri Catholici, 1943².

_____. *La filosofia cristiana di S. Bonaventura*. Roma: Agenzia del Libro Cattolico, 1971².

Walsh, Joseph. "The Principle «Bonum diffusivum sui» in St. Bonaventure: Its Meaning and Importance." Thesis, Fordham University, 1958.

Zigrossi, Antonio. *Saggio sul neoplatonismo di S. Bonaventura*. Firenze: Edizioni Studi Francescani, 1954.

Zubiri, Xavier. *Historia, naturaleza y Dios*. 4th edition. Madrid: Alianza, 1959.

Articles

Allard, Guy. "La technique de la «Reductio» chez Bonaventure." Vol. 2 of *SB*, 395–416.

Alszeghy, Zoltan. "Studia Bonaventuriana." *GR* 29 (1948): 142–151.

Arosio, Marco. "«Credibile ut intelligibile»: Sapienza e ruolo del «modus ratiocinativus sive inquisitivus» nell'epistemologia teologica del Commento alle Sentenze di Bonaventura da Bagnoregio." *DtS* 41 (1994): 175–236.

Artuso, Lorenzo. "Bibbia e pietà nel pensiero bonaventuriano." In: *La Sacra Scrittura e i Francescani*, pp. 113–121. Roma: Ed. Antonianum, 1973.

Balthasar, Hans Urs von. "Teologia e santità." In: *Verbum caro*, pp. 200–229. Brescia, 1970².

_____. "L'unità fra teologia e spiritualità." In: *Con occhi semplici*, pp. 11–29. Brescia, 1970.

Berg, L. "Die Analogielehre des hl. Bonaventura." In: *Studium Generale* 8 (1965): 662–670.

Bernard, Charles A. "Vie spirituelle et connaissance théologique." *GR* 51 (1970): 225–244.

_____. "Les formes de la théologie chez Denys l'Areopagite." *GR* 59 (1978): 39–69.

_____. "Conoscenza e amore nella vita mistica." In Vol. 2 of *La Mistica*, pp. 253–293. Eds. E. Ancilli and M. Paparozzi. Roma: Città Nuova, 1984.

_____. "Saint Bonaventure, lecteur de Denys dans l'Itinerarium mentis in Deum." In: *Studies in Spirituality* 1 (1991): 37–56.

_____. "La spiritualità come fonte dottrinale." In: *La spiritualità come teologia*. Simposio organizzato dall'Istituto di Spiritualità dell'Università Gregoriana, Roma 25–28 aprile 1991, pp. 336–351. Ed. Charles A. Bernard. Cinisello Balsano (Milano): Edizioni Paoline, 1993.

_____. "Le dépassement vers Dieu." In idem: *Le Dieu des mystiques: les voies de l'intériorité*, pp. 315–362. Paris: Editions du Cerf, 1994.

Bernardino de Armellada. "San Buenaventura ¿Un San Francisco metido a filósofo? La filosofía de San Buenaventura según Camillo Bérubé." *CF* 60 (1990): 429–457.

Bérubé, Camille. "De la philosophie à la sagesse dans l'itinéraire bonaventurien." *CF* 38 (1968): 258–307.

_____. "De la théologie à l'Ecriture chez saint Bonaventure." *CF* 40 (1970): 5–70.

Bérubé Camille. "Saint Bonaventure philosophe, théologien, mystique." In idem: *De la philosophie à la sagesse chez saint Bonaventure et Roger Bacon.* Bibliotheca Seraphico-Capuccina, no. 26, pp. 258–282. Roma: Istituto Storico dei Cappuccini, 1976.

_____. "Guillaume de Saint-Thierry source de la pensée franciscaine." *CF* 61 (1961): 117–148.

Bettoni, Efrem. "La dottrina bonaventuriana dell'illuminazione intellettuale." *RFN* 36 (1944): 139–158.

_____. "San Bonaventura e il valore del sapere." *SFr* 67 (1970): 129–140.

Beumer, Johannes. "Die Aufgabe der Vernunft in der Theologie des hl. Bonaventura." *FzS* 38 (1956): 129–149.

_____. "Theologische und mystische Erkenntnis in ihrer einheitlichen Zusammenschau bei Bonaventura." *ThPh* 49 (1974): 163–180.

_____. "Franziskus von Assisi und Bonaventura." *FzS* 58 (1976): 78–91.

Bigi, Vincenzo. "La dottrina della luce in San Bonaventura." *DTh.P* 64 (1961): 395–422.

_____. Vincenzo. "Il valore filosofico-mistico dell'Itinerarium mentis in Deum di San Bonaventura." *IncBonav* 6 (1970): 85–110.

Bissen, Jean-Marie. "La contemplation selon saint Bonaventure." *FrFr* 14 (1931): 175–192.

_____. "Les degrés de la contemplation selon saint Bonaventure." *FrFr* 15 (1932): 87–105.

_____. "L'importance de la contemplation selon saint Bonaventure." *FrFr* 15 (1932): 437–454.

_____. "De la contuition." *EF* 46 (1934): 559–569.

_____. "Les conditions de la contemplation selon saint Bonaventure." *FrFr* 17 (1934): 387–404.

_____. "Des effets de la contemplation selon S. Bonaventure." *FrFr* 19 (1936): 20–29.

Blasucci, Antonio. "Teologia e spiritualità." *MF* 59 (1959): 3–29.

_____. "Problematica dei rapporti tra conoscenza naturale e sopranaturale." *MF* 63 (1963): 137–182.

_____. "La conoscibilità di Dio in San Bonaventura." *IncBonav* 5 (1969): 39–58.

_____. "La spiritualità di San Bonaventura." Vol. 4 of *SB,* 567–606.

_____. "Contemplazione e santità in San Bonaventura." Supplement II of *SBM*, 361–386.

Boehner, Philotheus. "The Spirit of Franciscan Philosophy." *FS* 2 (1942): 217–237.

Bonafede, Giulio. "Il problema dell'illuminazione in S. Bonaventura." *Sophia* 4 (1936): 78–82; 5 (1937): 78–85.

Bougerol, Jacques Guy. "Sur le sens de Dieu." *EF* 14 (1964): 23–30.

_____. "Fonction du théologien." *EF* 18 (1968): 5–19.

_____. "La perfection chrétienne et la structuration des trois voies de la vie spirituelle dans la pensée de saint Bonaventure." *EF* 19 (1969): 397–409.

_____. "St. Bonaventure et la hiérarchie dionysienne." *AHDLMA* 44 (1969): 131–167.

_____. "Saint Bonaventure, le savoir et le croire." *Ant* 50 (1975): 124–140.

_____. "L'aspect spirituel de la spéculation bonaventurienne." *Ant* 52 (1977): 695–701.

Camelot, Thomas. "Théologie monastique et scolastique." *RSPT* 42 (1958): 240–253.

Capone, Domenico. "Il Magistero del Cristo in teologia come scienza, secondo San Bonaventura." *SBM*, 581–595.

Châtillon, Jean. "Le primat de la vertu de charité dans la théologie de Saint Bonaventure." Supplement II of *SBM*, 217–238.

_____. "Saint Bonaventure et la philosophie." *SBM*, 429–446.

Chauvet, Fedele. "Il metodo della vita intellettuale secondo San Bonaventura." *VM* 29 (1958): 136–141; 165–169; 30 (1959): 1–30.

_____. "Los diversos «Itinerarios» espirituales compuestos por San Buenaventura." Supplement II of *SBM*, 407–418.

Chavero Blanco, Francisco. "Ser y significar: Aproximación al simbolismo bonaventuriano." *Thémata* (Sevilla) 5 (1988): 51–71.

_____. "Teología y antropología: Sus relaciones en el pensamiento de San Buenaventura." *EsF* 89 (1988): 229–277.

Coccia, Antonio. "S. Bonaventura e il problema critico della conoscenza." Vol. 1 of *Bonav*, 257–276.

Connell, Desmond. "St. Bonaventure and the Ontologist Tradition." Vol. 2 of *SB*, 289–308.

Crowley, Theodore. "Illumination and Certitude." Vol. 3 of *SB*, 431–448.

_____. "St. Bonaventure and Reform." *SBM*, 129–135.

Cruz, Luís. "La participación en la filosofía de San Buenaventura." *Eclesiástica Xaveriana* (Bogotá), 1 (1951): 164–277.

Daniel, E. Randolph. "St. Bonaventure a Faithful Disciple of Saint Francis? A Reexamination of the Question." Vol 2 of *SB*, 170–187.

Del Zotto, Cornelio. "Per una teologia «sapienziale»." *VM* 47 (1976): 155–159; 243–247; 349–351; 475–477; 48 (1977): 143–148.

_____. "La sapienza come amore del Dottore Serafico." *DtS* (1986): 29–58.

_____. "Il Dottore Serafico nel magistero recente della Chiesa." *VM* 38 (1987): 599–617.

_____. "L'*Itinerarium* nel Magistero recente della Chiesa." *SFr* 85 (1988): 365–393.

Dettloff, Werner. "«Christus tenens medium in omnibus»: Sinn und Funktion der Theologie bei Bonaventura." *WW* 20 (1957): 28–42; 120–140.

_____. "Studium cum devotione." *Sein und Sending* 29 (1964): 269–271.

_____. "Die Franziskanische Theologie des Hl. Bonaventura." *SBM*, 495–512.

_____. "Licht und Erleuchtung in der christlichen Theologie, besonders bei Bonaventura." *WW* 50 (1987): 140–149.

_____. "Die Bedeutung des Lichtes für die Interpretation und die Erkenntnis des Seienden bei Bonaventura." *WW* 52 (1989): 179–193.

Di Monda, Antonio. "La S. Scrittura per S. Bonaventura." *SRF* 4 (1975): 97–117.

Dreyer, Elizabeth. "«Affectus» in St. Bonaventure's Theology." *FS* 42 (1982): 5–20.

Epping, Adelhard. "Seraphische Weisheit." *FzS* 56 (1974): 221–248.

Fajdek, Bogdan. "La necessità dello studio nell'Ordine Francescano secondo San Bonaventura." *VM* 5 (1991): 437–447.

_____. "Gli studi nell'Ordine dei Frati Minori secondo le Costituzioni di Narbona di San Bonaventura." *VM* 6 (1991): 527–534.

Farrell, Gary. "Bonaventure's Mystical Approach to Studies: True Wisdom Leads to Union with God." *Round Table of Franciscan Research* 28 (1963): 108–123.

_____. "Studies in Franciscan Formation: Bonaventure Looks into the Mind and Will of Francis." *Round Table of Franciscan Reseacrch* 28 (1963): 62–70.

Fehlner, Peter. "Theology at the Service of Piety." *Inter-Province Conference of the Friars Minor Conventual*, XII (1961): 69–84.

Report of the Fourteenth Annual Meeting, Assumption Seminary, Chaska, Minnesota, Aug. 30 – Sept. 1, 1960.

Felder, Hilarius. "De spiritu studiorum franciscano." *CF* 3 (1933): 161–181.

Fischer, Konrad. "Hinweise sur Gotteslehre Bonaventuras." *SBM*, 513–25.

Foshee, Charles. "St. Bonaventure and the Augustinian Concept of *mens*." *FS* 27 (1967): 163–175.

Gaddi, Alessandro. "Il carattere pedagogico-mistico della filosofia di San Bonaventura." *DtS* 3 (1956): 3–19.

Galeazzi, Umberto. "Conoscibilità di Dio e fattori extrateorici in San Bonaventura." Supplement I of *SBM*, 57–66.

Garrido, Javier. "El «argumentum ex pietate» en la Escuela Franciscana del siglo XIII." *V V* 26 (1968): 291–353.

Gendreau, Bernard. "The Quest for Certainty in Bonaventure." *FS* 21 (1961): 104–227.

Gerken, Alexandre. "Identität und Freiheit: Ansatz und Methode im Denken des hl. Bonaventura." *W W* 37 (1974): 98–110.

Ghinato, Alberto. "San Francesco esemplare concreto della perfezione nell'interpretazione mistica di S. Bonaventura." *IncBonav* 6 (1970): 19–41.

Gneo, Corrado. "La essenza dell'essere come amore in San Bonaventura." Vol. 3 of *SB*, 83–106.

Guillen, Fernando. "Algunos aspectos del Itinerario mentis in Deum." *EsF* 70 (1969): 69–85.

Gumbinger, Cuthbert. "The Primacy of Charity in Franciscan Theology." *FS* 3 (1943): 209–240.

Hayes, Zachary. "Toward a philosophy of education in the spirit of St. Bonaventure." In: *Celebrating the Medieval Heritage*, pp. 9–27. A Colloquy on the thought of Aquinas and Bonaventure, drawn from a colloquy held at the University of Chicago in November 1974. Ed. David Tracy. Chicago: University Press, 1979.

Hellmann, J. A. Wayne. "Scripture: the dawn of contemplation as found in the Collationes in Hexaëmeron." *SBM*, 563–570.

Hemmerle, Klaus. "Bonaventura und der Ansatz theologischen Denkens." *W W* 37 (1974): 89–97.

Hinwood, Bonaventure. "The Principles Underlying Saint Bonaventure's Division of Human Knowledge." Vol. 3 of *SB*, 471–504.

Hülsbusch, Werner. "Christus—Weisheit und Heiligung: Bonaventura in der Auseinandersetzung mit dem lateinishchen Averroismus und mit den Mendikantengegnern in den letzten Lebensjahren." *W W* 37 (1974): 110–122.

_____. "Die Theologie des Transitus bei Bonaventura." Vol. 4 of *SB*, 533–565.

Hurley, Michael. "Illumination according to St. Bonaventure." *GR* 32 (1951): 388–404.

Iammarrone, Giovanni. "La contuizione bonaventuriana." *MF* 58 (1958): 36–42.

_____. "Il progetto teologico di San Bonaventura: presupposti antropologici e problematica della su attualità." *SBM*, 637–705.

Imle, Fanny. "Die Gabe des Intellectes nach dem hl. Bonaventura." *FzS* 20 (1933): 34–50.

_____. "Die Gabe der Weisheit." *FzS* 20 (1933): 286–297.

Iriarte de Puyau, Delia. "La naturaleza de la teología en San Buenaventura." *SBM*, 527–533.

Javelet, Robert. "Réflexions sur l'exemplarisme bonaventurien." Vol. 4 of *SB*, 349–370.

Jean de Dieu. "L'intuition sans concept et la théorie bonaventurienne de la contemplation." *EF* 7 (1956): 63–74 + 133–154.

_____. "Intuition sans concept, expérience religieuse et formation du concept." *EF* 19 (1958): 35–56.

Klauck, Hans Josef. "Theorie der Exegese bei Bonaventura." Vol. 4 of *SB*, 71–128.

Kuntz, Paul. "The Hierarchical Vision of St. Bonaventure." Supplement I of *SBM*, 233–248.

Lazzarini, Renato. "Originalità del messaggio bonaventurale: Lo *Status* trasnaturale." *DtS* 67 (1960): 5–19.

_____. "«Status viae» e filosofia nella speculazione bonaventuriana." Vol. 3 of *Contributi*, 123–138.

Levasti, Arrigo. "Il Misticismo di San Bonaventura." *DtS* 2 (1955): 2–15.

Liberat de Roulers. "Le rôle du mot «habitus» dans la théologie bonaventurienne." *CF* 26 (1956): 225–250; 337–372.

Longpré, Ephrem. "La théologie mystique de Saint Bonaventure." *AFH* 14 (1921): 36–108.

_____. "St. Bonaventure." Vol. 1 of *DS*, 1768–1843.

Lottin, Odon. "Le péché originel chez Albert le Grand, Bonaventure, et Thomas d'Aquin." *RTA M* 12 (1940): 275–328.

Luciani, Albino Card. "San Bonaventura ai cristiani del secolo XX." *SBM*, 39–53.

Madariaga, Bernardo. "La «imagen de Dios» en la metafísica del hombre, según San Buenaventura." *V V* 7 (1949): 145–194; 297–335.

_____. "La filosofía al interior de la teología." *V V* 19 (1961): 193–267.

Magrini, Egidio. "La metodologia teologica di S. Bonaventura." *SFr* 71 (1974): 29–43.

Malaguti, Maurizio. "Umiltà e intelligenza della verità secondo S. Bonaventura." *DtS* 39 (1992): 93–107.

Manferdini, Tina. "L'esemplarismo di San Bonaventura." *IncBonav* 7 (1972): 41–80.

_____. "La ragione teologica in San Bonaventura." *SBM*, 535–552.

_____. "La problematica della ragione nel pensiero di S. Bonaventura." *DtS* 27 (1980): 21–49.

Manno, Ambrogio. "Attualità dell'antropologia teocentrica bonaventuriana." *SFr* (1974): 45–77.

Manselli, Raoul. "San Bonaventura e l'ordine francescano nel secolo XIII." *DtS* 12 (1965): 39–49.

_____. "St. Bonaventure and the Clericalization of the Friars Minor." *Greyfriars Review* 4/2 (1990): 83–98.

Maranasi, Pietro. "«Revelatio» e conoscenza «per lumen inditum»: la posizione media di Bonaventura tra Bacone e Tommaso nel proble ma gnoseologico." *CF* 61 (1991): 491–511.

Marcolino, Venicio. "Elementos do Desenvolvimento dogmatico segundo São Boaventura." Vol. 4 of *SB*, 177–219.

Mariani, Eliodoro. "I doni intellettuali nel pensiero di S. Bonaventura." *V M* 10 (1968):5–19.

_____. "Scienza e sapienza in San Bonaventura." *DtS* 20 (1973): 41–53.

Martini, Cherubino. "Le scienze sacre in S. Bonaventura." *IncBonav* 7 (1972): 7–12.

Mateos de Zamayon, Pelayo. "Teoría del conocimiento según San Buenaventura: la iluminación." Vol. 3 of *SB*, 407–430.

Mathias, Thomas. "Bonaventurian Ways to God through Reason." *FS* 36 (1976): 192–232; *FS* 37 (1977): 153–206.

Mauro, Letterio. "«Meditatio» e cultura come preparazione all'ascesa a Dio in San Bonaventura." Supplement II of *SBM*, 51–62.

McCool, Gerald. "Scientific theology: Bonaventure and Thomas revisited." *Thought* 49 (1974): 374–394.

McEvoy, James. "Microcosm and Macrocosm in the Writings of St. Bonaventure." Vol. 2 of *SB*, 309–343.

McGinn, Bernard. "Ascension and Introversion in the Itinerarium mentis in Deum." Vol. 3 of *SB*, 535–552.

_____. "The Influence of St. Francis on Theology of the High Middle Ages: The Testimony of St. Bonaventure." Vol. 1 of *Bonav*, 97–118.

Melani, Gaudenzio. "Inspirazione ed aspetti filosofici nell'Itinerarium mentis in Deum di San Bonaventura." *DtS* 15 (1968): 51–69.

Ménard, André. "Une leçon inaugurale de Saint Bonaventure: le Proemium du Livre des Sentences." *EF* 21 (1971): 273–298.

_____. "L'esprit de sagesse." *EF* 22 (1972): 111–127.

_____. "L'intelligence exhaussée par la lumière de foi selon les Collationes VIII à XI in Hexaëmeron." *EF* 23 (1973): 227–296.

_____. "Spiritualité du Transitus." Vol. 4 of *SB,* 607–635.

Moreno, Antonio. "Espiritualidad-Perfección Sacerdotal y Religiosa, en la controversia medieval de la Universidad de París (1252–1272)." *V V* 23 (1965): 85–119.

Moretti, Robert. "Natura e compito della teologia spirituale." In: *Spiritualità: fisionomia e compiti*, pp. 15–36. Biblioteca di Scienze Religiose, 45. Eds. B. Calati, B. Secondin, and T.P. Zecca. Roma: Libreria Ateneo Salesiano, 1981.

Moretti-Costanzi, Teodorico. "Attualità di San Bonaventura." *Sophia* 33 (1965): 314–340.

Mulligan, Robert. "Portio Superior and Portio Inferior Rationis in the Writings of St. Bonaventure." *FS* 15 (1955): 332–349.

Nachbahr, Bernard. "Pure Reason and Practical Reason: Some Themes in Transcendental Philosophy and in Saint Bonaventure." Vol. 3 of *SB*, 449–461.

Natoli, Grace. "Bonaventure and Rosmini on Illumination." *SBM*, 711–720.

Nemetz, Anthony. "What Saint Bonaventure has given to Philosophers Today." *FS* 19 (1959): 1–12.

_____. "The Itinerarium Mentis in Deum: The Human Condition." Vol. 2 of *SB*, 345–359.

210

Norbert de Guise. "La recherche de la vérité chez Bonaventure." *EF* 12 (1962): 161–177.

Nyssen, Wilhelm. "Die Contemplatio als Stufe der Erkenntnis nach Bonaventura." In: *Bonaventura: Studien zu seiner Wirkunggeschichte*, pp. 79–93. Ed. I. Vanderhijden. Werl/Westfalen, 1976.

Nyssen, Wilhelm. "Die «contemplatio» als äußerste Aktivität des Menschen nach Bonaventura." *Studia Medievistyczne* 25 (1988): n. 2, 3–16.

Oltra, Miguel. "Teoría del amor en San Buenaventura." *V V* 7 (1949): 233–257.

Omaechevarría, Ignacio. "Teología mística de san Buenaventura." Vol. 4 of *Obras de San Buenaventura*, pp. 36–44. Eds. L. Amorós and others. Madrid: B.A.C., 1963².

Orbetello, Luca. "«Apprehensio» e «comprehensio» nel pensiero di S. Bonaventura da Bagnoregio." *DtS* 34 (1987): 5–18.

Oromí, Miguel. "Filosofía ejemplarista de san Buenaventura." Vol. 3 of *Obras de San Buenaventura*, pp. 3–136. Eds. L. Amorós and others. Madrid: B.A.C., 1972³.

Ozilou, Marc. "«Sapientia et experientia» dans les «Collationes in Hexaëmeron» de saint Bonaventure." *CF* 61 (1991): 513–533.

Paredes, Juan Antonio. "Teología y experiencia." *V V* 155 (1981): 173–189.

Pedersen, Jorgen. "L'intellectus fidei et la notion de théologie chez saint Bonaventure." *Studia Theologica* 5 (1951): 1–36.

Pegis, Anton. "St. Bonaventure, St. Francis and Philosophy." *MS* 15 (1953): 1–13.

_____. "St. Bonaventure revisited." Vol. 2 of *SB*, 21–44.

Petry, Ray. "Verbum Abbreviatum: St. Bonaventure's Interpretation of the Evangelical Preaching of St. Francis." Vol. 2 of *SB*, 209–223.

Philippe, Paul. "Contemplation au XIII siècle. 5. St. Bonaventure." Vol. 2 of *DS*, 1979–1981.

Picard, Novatus. "Gnoseologia bonaventuriana?" *Ant* 18 (1943): 217–244.

Pincherle, Alberto. "S. Bonaventura Agostiniano e Francescano." *DtS* 10 (1963): 5–27.

Plagnieux, Jean. "Aux sources de la doctrine bonaventurienne sur l'état originel de l'homme: Influence de saint Augustin ou de saint Irénée?" Vol. 4 of *SB*, 311–328.

Pompei, Alfonso. "S. Francesco «Maestro» di S. Bonaventura." *DtS* 16 (1969): 16–30.

_____. "Bonaventura da Bagnoregio filosofo e teologo francescano." *Studia Patavina* 21 (1974): 274–297.

_____. "Amore ed esperienza di Dio nella mistica bonaventuriana." *DtS* 33 (1986): 5–27.

_____. "The role of Christ in human knowledge according to St. Bonaventure." *Greyfriars Review* 6 (1992): 211–235.

_____. "Il «De reductione artium ad theologiam» di S. Bonaventura per i teologi d'oggi." In: *Bonaventura da Bagnoregio: Il pensare francescano*. Roma: Miscellanea Francescana, 1993. 169–193.

_____. "Il «De reductione artium ad theologiam»: Espressione di posizioni caratteristiche di Bonaventura da Bagnoregio." In: *Bonaventura da Bagnoregio: Il pensare francescano*. Roma: Miscellanea Francescana, 1993. 155–168.

_____. "L'amore nella mistica bonaventuriana." *DtS* 42 (1995): 31–52.

Poppi, Angelico. "La passione di Gesù nelle opere di S. Bonaventura." In: *Teologia e filosofia nel pensiero di S. Bonaventura: Contributi per una nuova interpretazione*, pp. 67–122. Brescia: Morcelliana, 1974.

Poppi, Antonino. "Se e come è possibile la filosofia in s. Bonaventura." In: *Teologia e filosofia nel pensiero di S. Bonaventura: Contributi per una nuova interpretazione*, 175–198. Brescia: Morcelliana, 1974.

Prini, Pietro. "Il filosofare nella fede secondo san Bonaventura." *SBM,* 399–407.

_____. "«Ars aeterna» e «memoria» nel pensiero di S. Bonaventura." *DtS* 22 (1975): 2–29.

_____. "L'itinerario bonaventuriano e il nostro." *SFr* 85 (1988): 209–223.

_____. "Verbum divinum omnis creatura." *DtS* 32 (1985): 5–10.

Prunières, Louis. "L'Itinéraire de l'esprit en Dieu." *EF* 22 (1972): 11–17; 39–68; 129–174; 23 (1973): 13–77; 127–182.

Quinn, John F. "The Rôle of the Holy Spirit in St. Bonaventure's Theology." *FS* 33 (1973): 273–284.

_____. "St. Bonaventure and the Magisterium of the Church." *SBM,* 597–610.

Rahner, Karl. "Der Begriff der ecstasis bei H. Bonaventura." *ZAM* 9 (1934): 1–19.

Rahner, Karl. "La doctrine des «sens spirituels» au moyen âge, en particulier chez Saint Bonaventura." *RAM* 14 (1933): 263–299.

Ratzinger, Joseph. "La sinfonia della Croce: La conscenza di Dio che rifulge sul volto di Cristo." *Ant* 55 (1980): 280–286.

Reilly, James. "Rectitude of Will and the Examined Life." Vol. 4 of *SB*, 655–671.

Reynolds, Philip. "Threefold Existence and Illumination in Saint Bonaventure." *FS* 42 (1982): 190–215.

Rézette, Jean. "Grâce et similitude de Dieu chez saint Bonaventure." *ETL* 32 (1956): 46–64.

Rigobello, Armando. "Teologia e preghiera in S. Bonaventura: confronto tra due esperienze." Supplement II of *SBM*, 41–50.

Rivera de Ventosa, Enrique. "El voluntarismo psicológico de San Buenaventura." *EsF* 52 (1951): 289–315.

Robert, Patrice. "St. Bonaventure Defender of Christian Wisdom." *FS* 24 (1943): 159–179.

Roch, Robert. "The Philosophy of St Bonaventure: A Contoversy." *FS* 19 (1959): 209–226.

Rodríguez Neira, Teófilo. "Los niveles de la memoria en San Agustín y San Buenaventura." *Augustinus* 19 (1974): 221–229.

Rolandetti, Vittorio. "Esperienza metafisica ed esperienza mistica in San Bonaventura: un sapere que ama e un amore che sa." Supplement II of *SBM*, 387–394.

Roques, René. "La notion de Hiérarchie selon le Pseudo-Denys." *AHLDMA* 17 (1949): 183–222; 18 (1950–1951): 5–54.

Ruello, Francis. "Le dépassement mystique du discours théologique selon saint Bonaventure." *Recherches de science religieuse* 64 (1976): 217–270.

Sala, Gervasio. "Il concetto di sinderesi in S. Bonaventura." *SFr* 54 (1957): 3–11.

Salmon, Pierre. "L'ascèse monastique et la spiritualité." *VieSpirSupplém* 7 (1954): 195–240.

Scala, Albina. "Il passaggio dal credibile all'intelligibile nel Commento alle Sentenze di San Bonaventura." *SBM*, 553–562.

Schaefer, Alexander. "The Position and Function of Man in the Created World According to Saint Bonaventure." *FS* 20 (1960): 261–316; 21 (1961): 233–282.

_____. "Der Mensch in der Mitte der Schöpfung." Vol. 3 of *SB*, 337–392.

Schalück, Hermann. "Was hat Bonaventura der Theologie heute zu sagen?" In: *Bonaventura: Studien zu seiner Wirkunggeschichte*, pp. 9–16. Ed. I. Vanderhijden. Werl/Westfalen, 1976.

_____. "Armut und Heil: Die theologische Implikationen des Armutsgedankens bei Bonaventura." Vol. 4 of *SB*, 673–683.

Scheltens, Gonsalvus. "Kritische Würdigung der Illuminationslehre des hl. Bonaventura." *WW* 24 (1961): 167–181.

Schlosser, Marianne. "Lux Inaccessibilis: Zur negativen Theologie bei Bonaventura." *FzS* 68 (1986): 3–140.

_____. "«Caligo illuminans»: Gotteserkenntnis zwischen Licht und Dunkelheit bei Bonaventura." *WW* 50 (1987): 126–139.

Schorn, Auguste. "Über die Gabe der Weisheit nach Bonaventura." *WW* 9 (1942): 41–54.

Schulte, Heinz. "Gotteserkenntnis und «conversio» bei Bonaventura." *ThPh* 49 (1974): 181–198.

Sequeira, Remigius. "The act of Faith according to St. Bonaventure." *Laurentianum* 12 (1971): 129–168.

Servais, Jacques. "Filosofia e riflessione spirituale." In: *La spiritualità come teologia*. Simposio organizzato dall'Istituto di Spiritualità dell'Università Gregoriana, Roma 5–28 aprile 1991, pp. 169–179. Ed. Charles A. Bernard. Cinisello Balsano (Milano): Edizioni Paoline, 1993.

Soiron, Thaddeus. "Vom Geist der Theologie Bonaventuras. *WW* 1 (1934): 28–38.

_____. "Die Aszese des Erkennens nach St. Bonaventura." *WW* 1 (1934): 310–316.

Solignac, Aimé. "Connaissance de Dieu et relation à Dieu selon saint Bonaventure (*Sc. Chr.*, q.4)." Vol. 3 of *SB*, 393–405.

_____. "«Memoria» chez saint Bonaventure." Vol. 2 of *Bonav*, 477–492.

Spanjol, Nicola. "El concetto dell'istruzione in S. Bonaventura." *RFN* 26 (1934): 341–385.

Speer, Andreas. "Wissenschaft und Erkenntnis: Zur Wissenschaftslehre Bonaventuras." *WW* 49 (1986): 168–198.

Strack, Bonifatius. "Das Leiden Christi im Denken des hl. Bonaventura." *FzS* 41 (1959): 129–162.

Szabó, Titus. "Homo imago Christi, Christus imago Dei: Principia S. Bonaventurae pro anthropologia in Christo instauranda." Vol. 4 of *SB*, 329–347.

Szabó, Titus. "Extase, IV. Chez les théologiens du XIIIe siècle." Vol. 4 of *DS*, 2120–2131.

Tavard, George. "The Light of God in the Theology of St. Bonaventure." *Eastern Churches Quarterly* 8 (1950): 407–417.

_____. "St. Bonaventure as Mystic and Theologian." In: *The Heritage of the Early Church*. Essays in Honor of the V.R. Georges Vasilievich Florovsky. Eds. D. Neiman and M. Schatkin. (Orient. Christ. Analecta, 195), Rome: 1973.

Thompson, William. "The Doctrine of Free Choice in Saint Bonaventure." *FS* 18 (1958): 1–8.

Todisco, Orlando. "Introduzione." In: *Bonaventura. Itinerario della mente in Dio*. Padova: Ed. Messaggero, 1993². 5–76.

Torgal Mendes Ferreira, Januario. "O Problema do mal a luz da concepção antropologica de São Boaventura." Vol. 4 of *SB*, 523–532.

Uribe Escobar, Diego. "La iluminación según San Buenaventura." *Franciscanum* (Bogotá), 5 (1963): 24–57.

Valderrama Andrade, Carlos. "San Buenaventura y la filosofía del amor." *Franciscanum* (Bogotá), 8 (1966): 147–166.

Vandenbroucke, François. "Le divorce entre théologie et mystique: Ses origines." *NRT* 82 (1950): 372–389.

Van Der Laan, Hendrikus. "The Idea of Christian Philosophy in Bonaventure's Collationes in Hexaëmeron." Vol. 3 of *SB*, 39–56.

Van Steenberghen, Fernand. "Saint Bonaventure et la philosophie." In: *La philosophie au XIIIe siècle*, pp. 190–271. Paris: Béatrice Nauwelaerts, 1966.

Veuthey, Léon. "Scientia et sapientia in doctrina S. Bonaventurae." *MF* 43 (1943): 1–13.

_____. "Esistenzialismo in S. Bonaventura." In: *L'Esistenzialismo*. Essays and studies edited by Luigi Pelloux, pp. 135–158. Roma: Studium, 1943.

_____. "La connaissance mystique." *MF* 45 (1954): 29–48.

_____. "Filosofia e teologia nell'insegnamento di S. Bonaventura." *MF* 67 (1967): 237–245.

_____. "Le potenze dell'anima secondo S. Bonaventura." *MF* 69 (1969): 134–139.

_____. "Orazione e contemplazione in S. Bonaventura." *IncBonav* 6 (1970): 111–130.

_____. "Il Volontarismo di San Bonaventura." *IncBonav* 7 (1972): 81–92.

_____. "La filosofia di un teologo." *IncBonav* 8 (1973): 67–75.

Vignaux, Paul. "Condition historique de la pensée de saint Bonaventure: christocentrisme, eschatologie et situation de la culture philosophique." *SBM*, 409–427.

Villalmonte, Alejandro. "Orientación cristocéntrica en la teología de san Buenaventura." *EsF* 59 (1958): 321–372.

Webster, Richard. "St. Bonaventure and the problem of the concrete existential man." *SBM*, 809–819.

Zafarana, Zelina. "Pietà e devozione in san Bonaventura." In: *S. Bonaventura francescano. 14–17 ottobre 1973*, pp. 127–157. Convegni del Centro di Studi sulla spiritualità medievale, 14. Todi: L'Accademia Tudertina, 1974.

Zappitello, Giorgio. "La «Vanità» in San Bonaventura. Un esempio di ciò che ha significato il messaggio de S. Francesco per il Medio evo." Vol. 4 of *SB*, 637–654.

Zavalloni, Roberto. "Il problema del «filosofare nella fede»: Linee emergenti nel dibattito." *Ant* 64 (1989): 431–469.

_____. "L'antropologia dell' «Itinerarium mentis»." In: *L'antropologia dei maestri spirituali*. Simposio organizzato dall'Istituto di Spiritualità dell'Università Gregoriana 28 aprile – 1 maggio 1989, pp. 178–194. Ed. Charles A. Bernard. Cinisello Balsamo (Milano): Edizioni Paoline, 1991.

Index of Proper Names